STEPHEN LAWRENCE

THE STEPHEN LAWRENCE INQUIRY

REPORT OF AN INQUIRY
BY SIR WILLIAM MACPHERSON OF CLUNY

ADVISED BY
TOM COOK, THE RIGHT REVEREND DR JOHN SENTAMU, DR RICHARD STONE

*Presented to Parliament by the Secretary of State for the Home Department
by Command of Her Majesty.
February 1999*

CM 4262-I

£26.00

THE INQUIRY INTO THE MATTERS ARISING FROM THE DEATH OF STEPHEN LAWRENCE

Chairman: Sir William Macpherson of Cluny
Secretary: Stephen Wells
Room 313
Hannibal House
Elephant & Castle
London SE1 6TE

Telephone No: 0171 277 4326
Fax No: 0171 708 4665

15 February 1999

The Rt Hon Jack Straw MP
The Home Secretary
Home Office
50 Queen Anne's Gate
London SW1H 9AT

Dear Home Secretary —

On 31 July 1997 you asked me to inquire into the matters arising from the death of Stephen Lawrence, in order particularly to identify the lessons to be learned for the investigation and prosecution of racially motivated crimes.

The three people appointed to support me in my task were Mr Tom Cook, the Rt Revd Dr John Sentamu and Dr Richard Stone. They have acted as full members of a team in all respects. I am pleased to tell you that the Inquiry Report, which I deliver to you today, is accepted by all three "Advisers" in its entirety. The Report therefore sets out our unanimous views, based upon the evidence and material put before us during both parts of the Inquiry.

I take personal responsibility for all that is set out in the Report.

Yours sincerely,

SIR WILLIAM MACPHERSON OF CLUNY
CHAIRMAN

MR TOM COOK

THE RT REVD DR JOHN SENTAMU
BISHOP FOR STEPNEY

DR RICHARD STONE

CONTENTS

	Paragraph	Page

CHAPTER FOURTEEN   106
The Second Senior Investigating Officer
Detective Superintendent Brian Weeden

CHAPTER ONE

THE MURDER OF STEPHEN LAWRENCE

1.1   Descriptions of the murder of Stephen Lawrence have been given in thousands of newspapers and television programmes since his horrific death on 22 April 1993. The whole incident which led to his murder probably lasted no more than 15-20 seconds. A map and aerial photographs of the area are reproduced at the end of this Report.

1.2   Stephen Lawrence had been with his friend Duwayne Brooks during the afternoon of 22 April. They were on their way home when they came at around 22:30 to the bus stop in Well Hall Road with which we are all now so familiar. Stephen went to see if a bus was coming, and reached a position almost in the centre of the mouth of Dickson Road. Mr Brooks was part of the way between Dickson Road and the roundabout when he saw the group of five or six white youths who were responsible for Stephen's death on the opposite side of the road.

1.3   Mr Brooks called out to ask if Stephen saw the bus coming. One of the youths must have heard something said, since he called out *"what, what nigger?"* With that the group came quickly across the road and literally engulfed Stephen. During this time one or more of the group stabbed Stephen twice. One witness thought that Mr Brooks was also attacked in the actual physical assault, but it appears from his own evidence that he was a little distance away from the group when the killing actually took place. He then turned and ran and called out to Stephen to run and to follow him.

1.4   Three eye witnesses were at the bus stop. Joseph Shepherd knew Stephen. He boarded a bus which came to the stop probably as Stephen fell. He went straight to Mr & Mrs Lawrence's house and told them of the attack. Alexandra Marie also boarded the bus. She was seen later, and gave all the help she could. Royston Westbrook also boarded the bus. It was he who believed that Mr Brooks had also been physically attacked. None of these witnesses was able later to identify any of the suspects. All of them said that the attack was sudden and short.

1.5   The group of white murderers then disappeared down Dickson Road. We refer to them as a group of murderers because that is exactly what they were; young men bent on violence of this sort rarely act on their own. They are cowards and need the support of at least a small group in order to bolster their actions. There is little doubt that all of them would have been held to be responsible for the murder had they been in court together with viable evidence against them. This murder has the hallmarks of a joint enterprise.

1.6   Mr Brooks ran across the road in the direction of Shooters Hill, and he was followed by his friend Stephen Lawrence, who managed somehow to get to his feet and to run over 100 yards to the point where he fell. That place is now marked with a granite memorial stone set into the pavement.

1.7   Stephen had been stabbed to a depth of about five inches on both sides of the front of his body to the chest and arm. Both stab wounds severed axillary arteries, and blood must literally have been pumping out of and into his body as he ran up the road to join his friend. In the words of Dr Shepherd, the pathologist, *"It is surprising that he managed to get 130 yards with all the injuries he had, but also the fact that the deep penetrating wound of the right side caused the upper lobe to partially collapse his lung. It is therefore a testimony to Stephen's physical fitness that he was able to run the distance he did before collapsing".*

1.8   No great quantities of blood marked the scene of the attack or the track taken by Stephen, because he wore five layers of clothing. But when he fell he was bleeding freely, and nearly all of the witnesses who saw him lying there speak of a substantial quantity of blood. There are variations in their description of the amount and location of the blood. The probability is that the blood came out in front of his body as he lay by chance in the position described, which appeared to many witnesses to be the *"recovery"* position. His head looked to the left into the roadway and his left arm was up.

1.9   The medical evidence indicates that Stephen was dead before he was removed by the ambulance men some time later. The amount of blood which had been lost would have made it probable that Stephen died where he fell on the pavement, and probably within a short time of his fall.

1.10   What followed has ultimately led to this public Inquiry. Little did those around Stephen, or the police officers, or indeed the public, expect that five years on this Inquiry would deal with every detail of what occurred from the moment of Stephen's death until the hearings at Hannibal House, where this Inquiry has taken place.

1.11   Stephen Lawrence's murder was simply and solely and unequivocally motivated by racism. It was the deepest tragedy for his family. It was an affront to society, and especially to the local black community in Greenwich.

1.12   Nobody has been convicted of this awful crime. That also is an affront both to the Lawrence family and the community at large.

CHAPTER TWO

SINCE THE MURDER

2.1   Those violent seconds in 1993 have been followed by extraordinary activity, without satisfactory result. From the Lawrence family's point of view there has been a sequence of disasters and disappointments.

2.2   Prolonged police investigations, in two distinct phases, produced no witnesses other than Mr Brooks who could properly purport to identify any of the attackers. Other sound evidence against the prime suspects, or against anybody else, is conspicuous by its absence. Even now after the unprecedented publicity of this Inquiry nobody has come forward to advance the case.

2.3   **Three of the prime suspects were taken to trial in 1996 in a private prosecution which failed because of the absence of any firm and sustainable evidence. The trial resulted in the acquittal of all three accused. They can never be tried again in any circumstances in the present state of the law.**

2.4   Two other suspects were discharged at the committal stage of the prosecution in 1995. Upon the existing evidence there is no prospect of them being prosecuted again. General publicity and comment over the last five years which assumed their guilt would in the absence of most compelling fresh evidence mean that no Court would countenance such a trial.

2.5   **The Inquest jury returned a unanimous verdict after a full hearing in 1997, that *"Stephen Lawrence was unlawfully killed in a completely unprovoked racist attack by five white youths"*.**

2.6   The Police Complaints Authority (PCA) engaged the Kent Police (Kent) to investigate Mr & Mrs Lawrence's complaint that the first Metropolitan Police Service (MPS) investigation had been bungled. The Kent Investigating Officer's report runs to 459 pages. 19 officers spent a year investigating the complaint. The PCA Report roundly criticised many aspects of the MPS investigation.

2.7   At the request of Mr & Mrs Lawrence this Inquiry was established by the Rt Hon Jack Straw MP, the Home Secretary, in July 1997.

2.8   We sat for 59 days in Hannibal House hearing the evidence and submissions on Part 1 of our Inquiry, the investigation into *"the matters arising from the death of Stephen Lawrence"*. We sat for 10 days to hear and to consider recommendations suggested to us by about 100 people and organisations in connection with Part 2 of our Inquiry, *"to identify the lessons to be learned for the investigation and prosecution of racially motivated crimes"*. More than 12,000 pages of transcript were produced. The submissions of Counsel for represented parties alone ran to around 1,000 pages. Our aim has been to inquire into each and every issue raised by all represented parties. 88 witnesses gave evidence.

2.9   The attendant documentation is literally vast. It is estimated that there are more than 100,000 pages of reports, statements, and other written or printed documents which have been surveyed and checked. Many have been used during our Inquiry. We express our gratitude to those who worked so efficiently to produce daily transcripts, and to display documents used during our hearings.

2.10 There is no doubt whatsoever but that the first MPS investigation was palpably flawed and deserves severe criticism. Nobody listening to the evidence could reach any other conclusion. This is now plainly accepted by the MPS. Otherwise the abject apologies offered to Mr & Mrs Lawrence would be meaningless.

2.11 The underlying causes of that failure are more troublesome and potentially more sinister. The impact of incompetence and racism, and the aura of corruption or collusion have been the subject of much evidence and debate.

2.12 We refer to these facts and figures not in order to gain sympathy as to the task which confronted us, but to indicate that this Report is an attempt to distil all that raw material rather than tediously to rehearse or repeat all that is contained in the transcripts and the volumes of documents. They are available should anybody wish to survey them. Anything other than a distillation would result in an unreadable Report of inordinate length.

2.13 The Report is in any event inevitably long and detailed. Those who are daunted by the full Report can turn at once to Chapter 46 which sets out a summary of our conclusions. The Chapters and narrative which make up the rest of our Report are written in order to follow approximately the order in which witnesses were called and issues were covered during our hearings. It is necessary that those most closely concerned should be able to see that our conclusions have been reasonably deduced from the evidence considered. There will be some overlap of issues and evidence, but we hope that this will not result in confusion.

2.14 It is to the credit of the MPS and its officers, many of whom are retired, that all those involved have co-operated fully with this Inquiry. It has been a chastening and unpleasant experience for those who have been subjected to rigorous cross-examination. But this has been necessary in order that the case could be thoroughly and perhaps sometimes brutally laid bare. We have had full assistance from all involved in the production of relevant documents and in the conduct of our Inquiry. We do not believe that in the end anything relevant has been held back. No party can justifiably complain that it has been denied full access to relevant material or representation in order to make its views known.

2.15 We believe that the immediate impact of the Inquiry, as it developed, has brought forcibly before the public the justifiable complaints of Mr & Mrs Lawrence, and the hitherto underplayed dissatisfaction and unhappiness of minority ethnic communities, both locally and all over the country, in connection with this and other cases, as to their treatment by police.

2.16 The Inquiry was not of course an inquiry into the general relationship between police and minority ethnic communities, and detailed examination of other individual cases would have been misplaced. Inevitably the Inquiry has heard many sounds and echoes concerning, for example, stop and search and the wide perceptions of minority ethnic communities that their cases are improperly investigated and that racist crime and harassment are inadequately regarded and pursued.

2.17 We believe that the Stephen Lawrence Inquiry has provided such publicity and such awareness of the problems directly and indirectly revealed that there is now a signal opportunity to deal with specific matters arising from the murder and all that followed. We believe that there should be a clarion call to seize the chance to tackle and to deal with the general problems and differing perceptions that plainly exist between the minority ethnic communities and the police. If these opportunities are not appreciated and used the Inquiry will have achieved little or nothing for the future. We do not

pretend that our conclusions or recommendations will themselves solve these problems or ease these adverse and negative perceptions. We do believe that the debate about policing and racism has been transformed by this Inquiry, and that the debate thus ignited must be carried forward constructively and with imagination into action.

2.18 We stress one aspect of the case which has perhaps received less attention than it should. The very existence of a sub-culture of obsessive violence, fuelled by racist prejudice and hatred against black people, such as is exemplified in the 1994 video films of the five prime suspects is a condemnation of them and also of our society. These men are not proved to have been the murderers of Stephen Lawrence. We are unable to reach any such conclusion upon the evidence, and no fresh evidence is likely to emerge against them now. They remain however prime suspects. And the nature of them in 1994, and indeed during their limited testimony in 1998, must surely make us all determined that by education, family and community influence, proper policing, and all available means society does all that it can to ensure that the minds of present and future generations are not allowed to become violent and maliciously prejudiced. If these suspects were not involved there must have been five or six almost identical young thugs at large on the night of 22 April 1993 to commit this terrible racist crime. We must all see to it that such crimes do not and can not happen again. A high priority must be for society to purge itself of such racist prejudice and violence which infected those who committed this crime for no other reason than that Stephen Lawrence was black.

2.19 **In his evidence during Part 2 of our Inquiry, Chief Constable Burden (South Wales Police) rightly impressed upon us that racism exists within all organisations and institutions, and that it infiltrates the community and starts amongst the very young. Recent research in Cardiff showed that 50% of the racist incidents considered by the Race Equality Council involved young people under 16 years old, and 25% of these incidents involved children between the ages of six and 10 years. The problem is thus deeply ingrained. Radical thinking and sustained action are needed in order to tackle it head on, not just in the Police Services of our country, but in all organisations and in particular in the fields of education and family life.**

2.20 Lord Scarman, at page 135 of his Report relating to the Brixton disorders of 1981 said this:-

> *"The evidence which I have received, the effect of which I have outlined ...., leaves no doubt in my mind that racial disadvantage is a fact of current British life ..... . Urgent action is needed if it is not to become an endemic, ineradicable disease threatening the very survival of our society .... racial disadvantage and its nasty associate racial discrimination, have not yet been eliminated. They poison minds and attitudes; they are, as long as they remain, and will continue to be a potent factor of unrest".*

It is a sad reflection upon the intervening years that in 1998-99 those extracted words have remained relevant throughout both parts of our Inquiry.

CHAPTER THREE

THE INQUIRY

3.1   On 31 July 1997 the Home Secretary announced in Parliament that the terms of reference of this Inquiry would be:-

> *"To inquire into the matters arising from the death of Stephen Lawrence on 22 April 1993 to date, in order particularly to identify the lessons to be learned for the investigation and prosecution of racially motivated crimes."*

Soon afterwards HM Attorney General authorised the Inquiry:

> *"to undertake in respect of any person who provides evidence to the Inquiry that no evidence he or she may give before the Inquiry, whether orally or by written statement, nor any written statement made preparatory to giving evidence nor any document produced by that person to the Inquiry will be used in evidence against him or her in any criminal proceedings, except in proceedings where he or she is charged with having given false evidence in the course of this Inquiry or with having conspired with or procured others to do so".*

3.2   The first preliminary hearing of the Inquiry took place at Woolwich on 8 October 1997. Then and thereafter full legal representation was allowed to those involved who merited representation and who applied for it. The names of Counsel and Solicitors are set out in the Appendices to this Report. We are grateful to all the teams of lawyers who took part in the Inquiry.

3.3   It had become obvious that all those parties required and deserved representation because the Inquiry would need to address specific issues, and criticism of the actions of many police officers would be expected. This became even more plain when the PCA Report was published in December 1997. That Report, in its short statutory form, and in the full text of the Kent inquiry, roundly and severely criticised many aspects of the MPS investigation, and specifically blamed individual officers.

3.4   **Accordingly a detailed and comprehensive list of Issues was prepared by the Inquiry's legal team, in close consultation with other represented parties. Those officers who might be called to address each Issue were named in the comprehensive document. There can have been no possible doubt in the minds of any witness that his or her own actions and part in the investigation would be closely and critically examined. Furthermore the possible impact of racism and collusion was foreshadowed in those Issues.**

3.5   All parties and witnesses were given every opportunity to see all potentially relevant documents which were disclosed to the Inquiry. It should be stressed that the Inquiry itself had few documents. All the vast documentation came from others. In particular the MPS, the PCA, Mr & Mrs Lawrence, the CPS and others helpfully provided the Inquiry with documents in their possession. The Inquiry expresses its gratitude for their co-operation. During the Inquiry we were particularly grateful to Detective Chief Inspector Ragna Tulloch and Police Constable Reg Perriss, who assisted not only the Inquiry but all parties who sought further documents or information from the MPS.

3.6   The Inquiry was alert to the principles which govern the conduct of inquiries generally. In particular we heeded the recommendations of the Royal Commission on Tribunals of Inquiry 1966 (the Salmon Report), and the six principles laid down by Lord Salmon. As Lord Bingham said in <u>Crampton and others v Secretary of State for Health (9 July 1993)</u> *"...the rationale of the six cardinal principles is undoubtedly sound and anyone conducting an inquiry of this kind is well advised to have regard to them, (although) the Royal Commission Report itself has not been embodied in legislation and numerous inquiries have been conducted, and satisfactorily conducted, since 1966 without observing the letter of those principles"*.

3.7   In this case the Inquiry did send "Salmon" letters to virtually all witnesses before they came to give evidence. So that the gist of possible criticism was again transmitted to those involved. To their credit all the witnesses came to give evidence.

3.8   During the hearings complaint was made that the attack upon witnesses aimed particularly by Mr & Mrs Lawrence's legal team was wider and harder than had been foreshadowed. This matter was raised fully and formally and in public. The Inquiry required further notices to be given in this regard, before witnesses were called. In one instance a witness' evidence was interrupted, so that notice of additional allegations could be given. The witness was then recalled and agreed to further questioning.

3.9   Every witness was represented by leading and/or junior Counsel, and by his own or his professional body's solicitors. So that any suggestion of unfair treatment or surprise could have been and should have been raised during the hearings which lasted for 59 days, including the final submissions.

3.10   **The criticisms and allegations against the police and individual officers were certainly hard-hitting. In the circumstances, and bearing in mind the abject apologies offered by Assistant Commissioner Johnston and later by the Commissioner himself, this can have been no surprise to anybody, let alone the witnesses themselves.**

3.11   In considering the Inquiry's procedures we stress the concluding words of Sir Richard Scott, in his lecture to the Chancery Bar Association on 2 May 1995:- *"The golden rule is that there should be procedural flexibility, with procedures to achieve fairness tailored to suit the circumstances of each inquiry"*. We believe that our procedures did ensure fairness. It should be noted that the procedures were expressly or tacitly accepted by all the legal teams involved, throughout the preparatory months and the 59 days of our hearings.

3.12   Inquiries have many purposes. Some are concerned with establishing simply what happened and why. For example, the King's Cross Fire Inquiry and other railway accident inquiries have focused upon this purpose, the process of learning, and of establishing the facts. Some, such as the PCA inquiry in this case, focus upon discipline. Many inquiries, including this Inquiry, involve catharsis and close analysis of what may have gone wrong.

3.13   Our terms of reference required us to consider *"the matters arising from the death of Stephen Lawrence"*. The Inquiry came into existence because of explicit complaints and serious unease about the conduct by individual officers and the MPS itself of the investigation of Stephen Lawrence's murder.

3.14   It was obvious and publicly known that we would therefore have to decide whether criticisms of the investigation were made out, and whether individual officers and the team involved, or the MPS itself, should be blamed for the alleged failures of the investigation. It has also always been known that Mr & Mrs Lawrence's allegations included suggestions that the investigation had been flawed by racism and collusion. Hence full representation, and a procedure which was in the result adversarial rather than inquisitorial.

3.15 **This has led to complaints, publicly made, that the Inquiry has allowed unfair cross-examination, and that the Inquiry has been "stage managed". The latter complaint was never particularised and can be dismissed as unworthy. The former complaint came from the Commissioner, in a statement read publicly on 20 April 1998 which included the following passages. The full text is in the transcript for Day 13.**

> *"The Commissioner appreciates the need for thorough and fearless investigation, which may well include criticism of police officers, but he is concerned that the confrontational nature of cross-examination of some of the police officers has not assisted the search for truth.... such cross-examination may be appropriate in adversarial procedures but not to an inquisitorial hearing, where it may lead to witnesses failing to do themselves justice by adopting an unduly defensive attitude..... .*

> *More seriously the Commissioner is concerned about the damage which is being done to the relationship between the police and the black community. If police witnesses are constantly pilloried by a barrage of confrontational cross-examination the attempts by the MPS to rebuild that relationship, which was seriously harmed in the aftermath of Stephen's murder, could be set back significantly".*

3.16 **Cross-examination of many officers was undoubtedly robust and searching. But the harm to the relationship between the police and the black community was the result of police failures, and the answers to the questions rather than the nature of the questioning. It is of central importance that the Commissioner and his officers should recognise and accept this fact. Failure to do so can only reflect a lack of understanding of the essential problem and its depth, which would make progress difficult if not impossible.**

3.17 We hope and believe that the first part of the Inquiry has achieved catharsis. Our Report does focus upon errors and criticisms. This was inevitable, given the origins of the Inquiry. Neither catharsis nor identification of those errors might have been achieved without searching cross-examination. We do not believe that the Commissioner's complaint was justified.

3.18 The Chairman, his Advisers and his legal team were throughout ready and willing to entertain any application for further information, or for time to consider any allegation made. Nobody listening to the whole of the case could with justification allege any unfairness in the procedures and conduct of the Inquiry. Ultimately in final submissions the only complaint made was voiced on behalf of Detective Chief Superintendent John Barker, the author of the flawed Review. We do not accept that the strong submission made on his behalf was justified.

3.19 At the end of the evidence the Inquiry adjourned for some six weeks. This gave all parties the chance to prepare written submissions. When the Inquiry reconvened every legal team was given a full opportunity to make oral submissions. These extended over three days. The written submissions were detailed and indeed voluminous. The MPS written submission alone ran to 230 pages, plus appendices.

3.20 It was probably not necessary to give further notice of possible conclusions which the Inquiry might reach. Suggestions that critical passages of the Report should be shown to those involved before publication were certainly inappropriate in this case, bearing in mind the procedure set out above. Even less appropriate was a suggestion made, and quickly dropped, that the Commissioner should see the full Report before it was handed to the Home Secretary. Since the conduct of the Inquiry was largely adversarial the Report is in this case in the nature of a judgement. It is thus markedly different from other inquiries which are wholly inquisitorial in nature and in conduct.

3.21 **In order to ensure that no complaint of unfairness could possibly be made or sustained, letters were written before the Report was concluded to those persons against whom adverse findings might be made, so that any fresh comment might be made by them or on their behalf.**

3.22 Only then and after further consideration of all the submissions made did the Inquiry reach its final conclusions, which are set out in this Report.

3.23 **Three Advisers were appointed by the Home Secretary to advise and support the Chairman. These Advisers were Mr Tom Cook, retired Deputy Chief Constable for West Yorkshire; The Right Reverend Dr John Sentamu, the Bishop for Stepney; and Dr Richard Stone, Chair of the Jewish Council for Racial Equality.**

3.24 **The Inquiry's Advisers have been fully involved in every step and action taken since July 1997. They have all attended virtually every day of the hearings in Part 1 and Part 2 of the Inquiry. Their advice has been invaluable to the Chairman. Their contributions to the Report and to the conclusions and recommendations made have been imaginative, radical and of incalculable worth. Without their advice and support the Inquiry would have been infinitely less effective. This Report sets out the unanimous views of the Chairman and his three Advisers.**

3.25 Counsel to the Inquiry were Mr Edmund Lawson QC, Miss Anesta Weekes and Mr John Gibson. Mr David Penry-Davey QC was appointed as leading Counsel initially, but upon his appointment to the High Court Bench Mr Edmund Lawson QC took over that onerous task.

3.26 The Solicitors to the Inquiry were Mr Peter Whitehurst and Miss Linda Dann.

3.27 The legal team prepared and conducted the case with skill and dedication. The Inquiry's debt to all those concerned is great. Mastery of the voluminous documents, preparation of the issues involved, organisation of the witnesses, and ultimately the calling and questioning of 88 witnesses involved much hard work and preparation, and the exercise of tact and discretion. Anybody listening to the evidence must have realised that the Inquiry's legal team presented the case fairly and fearlessly. Where criticism was necessary it came both from the Inquiry's legal team and from the represented parties.

3.28 **Mr Stephen Wells has throughout been Secretary to the Inquiry and his Deputy is Miss Alison Foulds. Both of them have organised and conducted the administration of the Inquiry with matchless ability and energy. Setting up the Inquiry's headquarters at Hannibal House by 1 December 1997 was in itself a mammoth task. Dealing with every aspect of the Inquiry's work and activity here and elsewhere during exacting visits to other places during Part 2 of the Inquiry, was no lesser burden. Mr Wells and Miss Foulds have contributed immensely to the Inquiry's smooth running, sometimes in**

difficult and indeed challenging situations. Their dealings and relationship with the public have throughout been friendly and ever helpful.

3.29   Mr Michael Booker, the Inquiry's Press Officer, complemented the part played by our Secretary and his Deputy. He returned to New Zealand before our business was completed. His helpful and cheerful relationship with press and media representatives has been of great value during the highly publicised year during which he worked for the Inquiry.

3.30   Mrs Janet Crowl, Mr Gerry Ranson, and Miss Jayne Wiltshire completed the Inquiry's team. Mrs Crowl and Miss Wiltshire's secretarial and management skills have been invaluable. Mr Ranson's work with documentation, and in other fields, has been much appreciated. All three have helped to maintain the cohesion and the spirits of everybody involved throughout the Inquiry's life. We are grateful also for the secretarial skills of Miss Maureen Puttnam who joined our team for the final weeks of preparation of our Report.

3.31   We thank also the security officers and staff at Hannibal House. Their task has been much increased by our presence here. We also thank Superintendent John Godsave and his officers from Walworth Police Station, who have in difficult and sometimes dangerous circumstances helped to keep order when emotions ran high during some of our hearings.

3.32   We express our thanks to the staff of Legal Technologies Limited for the scanning of the documentation and to Sellers Imago who produced our running transcripts with great efficiency and cheerfulness. We also thank Miss Grace Vaughan for her skill in exhibiting documents on our screens on the instant throughout our hearings.

3.33   A detailed history of the Inquiry is included in the Appendices.

CHAPTER FOUR

MR & MRS LAWRENCE AND STEPHEN

4.1   Neville and Doreen Lawrence have together been the mainspring of this Inquiry. Their persistence and courage in the face of tragedy and bitter disillusionment and disappointment have been outstanding. They attended virtually all the hearings of the Inquiry including those held in Part 2 out of London. Their dignity and courtesy have been an example to all throughout.

4.2   Neville Lawrence came to England in 1960 from Jamaica. Doreen Lawrence came to England from Jamaica in 1962. They met in South London in 1970, and they were married at Lewisham in 1972. Stephen was born on 13 September 1974. At that time the family lived in Plumstead.

4.3   Both Neville and Doreen Lawrence told their own story in their own words at the Inquiry. It would be impudent to try to summarise all that they said. Both their statements are set out in full in the Appendices to our Report. The transcript of Day 42 will show that Neville and Doreen Lawrence answered questions put by Miss Weekes on behalf of the Inquiry. Mr Gompertz asked some questions of Doreen Lawrence. The nature and content of the questions made Mrs Lawrence protest that her perception was that she was being put on trial. Wisely Mr Gompertz desisted. Neville Lawrence was not questioned except by Miss Weekes.

4.4   It does seem right simply to quote a small number of passages from their evidence which highlight some of their deep-seated feelings about the case.

> Day 42. Page 8072. Doreen Lawrence.

> *"Basically, we were seen as gullible simpletons. This is best shown by Detective Chief Superintendent Ilsley's comment that I had obviously been primed to ask questions. Presumably, there is no possibility of me being an intelligent, black woman with thoughts of her own who is able to ask questions for herself. We were patronised and were fobbed off...*

> *I thought that the purpose of the meetings was to give us progress reports, but what actually happened was that they would effectively say: "Stop questioning us. We are doing everything"...*

> *...we hoped to get some feedback from the Barker review...*

> *...he promised that we would meet again so that he could tell us what he had found out. That was the first and last time we ever saw him."*

> Day 42. Page 8089. Doreen Lawrence.

> *"No black person can ever trust the police. This idea is not preconceived. It is based on experience and people that I know who have had bad experiences with the police."*

> *"DCS Ilsley believed that we were primed beforehand, that we were told what sort of questions to ask and how to ask them. There was one incident that stuck out in my mind when I was asking about the boys in*

prison. I was asking: "Why couldn't they put a bug in with them in the room to listen to what was being said", because if they wouldn't talk to the police they would talk to individuals. Ilsley said: "We don't do things like this. No way." I could remember he was very angry because he assumed that I was told to ask the question.

.... There were many incidents like this where they patronised me as if I can't think for myself."

Day 42. Page 8108. Doreen Lawrence.

<u>Question -</u> *"Those you had connections with, those that you dealt with, is it your case that their attitude towards you was racist?"*

<u>Answer -</u> *"It was a patronising way in which they dealt with me and that came across as being racist."*

Day 42. Page 8131. Neville Lawrence.

"It is clear to me that the police come in with the idea that the family of black victims are violent criminals who are not to be trusted."

Day 42. Page 8133. Neville Lawrence.

"When the committal took place it was the first time I heard the details of what happened on the night; this was three years later."

4.5   **Neville Lawrence ended his statement with these words:-**

"One of the things that I hope will come out of the Inquiry is for everyone to see that the things we have been saying for the past 5 years are true. I hope that this can be a step towards ensuring that when another tragedy is suffered by the black community the police act responsibly and investigate the crime properly. When a policeman puts his uniform on, he should forget all his prejudices. If he cannot do that, then he should not be doing the job because that means that one part of the population is not protected from the likes of those who murdered Stephen."

4.6   Perhaps Neville Lawrence will feel that the long trauma of the Inquiry may have been worthwhile. Overall he is shown to have been right as to his misgivings and criticism of the conduct of the investigation into Stephen's murder.

4.7   **Doreen Lawrence ended her statement with these words:-**

"I would like Stephen to be remembered as a young man who had a future. He was well loved, and had he been given the chance to survive maybe he would have been the one to bridge the gap between black and white because he didn't distinguish between black or white. He saw people as people."

4.8   Perhaps as time passes Doreen Lawrence will be able to see and to believe that the start of the building of that bridge has sprung from all that has followed her son's death. At least this Inquiry has explored and exposed the flaws in the investigation of the murder.

4.9   **These extracts, and indeed their full statements show that Neville and Doreen Lawrence feel deeply that they were patronised and side-lined. Together with many others they have an inherent distrust which the police must move fundamentally to overcome. Any protestation that Mr & Mrs Lawrence's attitude stems from perception and not reality must be abandoned. Only when the police show movement can they expect response from minority ethnic communities. That shift must be fundamental and may take time. But it must be achieved.**

4.10   No doubt Neville Lawrence and Doreen Lawrence will still hope that justice may be done, and that the murderers, or some of them, will eventually be convicted. The case will never be closed until then.

4.11   Stephen Lawrence was only 18 years old when he was murdered. He was happy and, as Doreen Lawrence told us, very bright. He wanted to be an architect. He was healthy and athletic, and he was much loved. Neville and Doreen Lawrence's accounts of his life and his character should not be summarised. They too appear in full in their moving evidence. Nothing can compensate for the loss the family suffered in Stephen's death at the hands of violent racists on 22 April 1993. His legacy must be the root and branch change that has to take place in society.

4.12   At the final meeting of the Inquiry at Birmingham on 13 November 1998 Neville Lawrence said this, at the end of the day's hearing:-

> *"We know at this point we need to accept the inevitable that things are wrong. I have just had quite a few interviews and one of the things which I have said is before people can go ahead and make changes, we have to admit what is wrong. It is no use people blaming each other for what has gone wrong in the past. We have to look forward; and we keep talking about the millennium, we have been here for a very long time and lot of us are not going anywhere, we have brought a lot of diversity, we have brought change, cultural, music, food everything. This is a very small place, this world of ours, we have to live together and we now have to say; let us put the past behind us, join hands and go forward."*

4.13   **That should be the spirit in which the future is approached. Acceptance of the reality of the problem is first and foremost. Our hope is that the impact of the case and of the Inquiry is such that everybody's conscience will ensure that the fundamental problems which have been exposed are radically treated, so that there can be real change. Mr & Mrs Lawrence won the confidence of the Home Secretary, the Rt Hon Jack Straw MP, who in July 1997 set up this Inquiry, which does seem to us to have provided a springboard for the future. We believe that the present Government and society as a whole do have the will to achieve that change. Let us all hope that the opportunity will not be missed. Joint action to achieve it can and must then follow.**

CHAPTER FIVE

DUWAYNE BROOKS

5.1   Duwayne Brooks was born on 27 September 1974. He was thus a fortnight younger than Stephen Lawrence. The two boys met in 1985, on their first day at Blackheath Bluecoats Church of England School. They became friends, and saw each other regularly even after Mr Brooks left school to study electrical engineering at college.

5.2   On 22 April 1993 the two friends, who were then 18 years old, had been together, and after visiting Stephen Lawrence's uncle they set off home by bus, reaching Well Hall Road roundabout at approximately 22:30.

5.3   **The murder of Stephen Lawrence has already been described. Mr Brooks was plainly fortunate to have escaped unharmed physically. The trauma of the attack and the terrible murder of his friend, and all that has followed, has left him seriously affected and stressed. So much so that his doctors strongly advised that he should not be called as a witness or questioned at this Inquiry, except under some proposed special arrangements which we found to be impracticable. We were ourselves concerned about his well being should he have given evidence and been subject to cross-examination.**

5.4   Mr Brooks did in the course of the murder investigation make nine statements of varying length. The longest was made on the night of the murder to Detective Constable David Cooper at Plumstead Police Station. We have seen all those statements. Two further statements were written for this Inquiry on 6 April and 5 May 1998. Both were read to the Inquiry by Counsel in Mr Brooks' presence. He was present on that day, 15 May 1998, and on one other day. Otherwise understandably he did not attend the Inquiry.

5.5   **Mr Brooks personally verified both statements, together with material from his earlier witness statements. The transcript of all that was read to us appears in the Appendices to our report. It has to be said that evidence in this form cannot carry the full weight of evidence which has been tested by cross-examination. This is no criticism of or reflection upon Mr Brooks. It is simply a statement of the obvious. He must rest assured that we give to his evidence all the weight that it should be given, when looked at in the light of all that has been said and written about Stephen Lawrence's murder and the years that have followed.**

5.6   Medical evidence about Mr Brooks has been seen by the Chairman and his Advisers, with his consent. Everything that he has suffered since the murder is part and parcel of psychological injury which stems from the murder and all its consequences to Mr Brooks. Other than that we say nothing about the details of his suffering since they are confidential and private. We are heartened to know that in May 1998 he had been employed for six or seven weeks, after help from the Prince's Trust, and that he had continued his college education until 1997, earning valuable qualifications. All this is to his credit. We simply hope that he will continue to live a fulfilling life. And we add that we are wholly convinced that he bears no responsibility for anything that has happened. The fact that the prosecution of three of the suspects failed is certainly not something for which he can in any way be blamed. The circumstances are such that his evidence was not, when tested, of such strength that it could be used to prove the case against the suspects. That is in no way the fault of Mr Brooks. "Fleeting glimpse" evidence is always difficult to use. The problems of the evidence in this case were great, and the trial decision established that this was so, quite apart from the complication of the evidence of Detective Sergeant Christopher Crowley. That issue is fully discussed in Chapter 22. We do not rehearse it here, although it must be stressed that it looms large in our consideration of the identification evidence given by Mr Brooks and the case as a whole.

5.7   **The greatest trauma suffered by Mr Brooks was that he saw his friend murdered, dying on the pavement, and dead as he was carried into the hospital. And he has had to endure that night, and the whole course of the failed investigation. He was a primary victim of the racist attack. He is also the victim of all that has followed, including the conduct of the case and the treatment of himself as a witness and not as a victim.**

5.8   Lengthy submissions set out the nature of his complaints. To a considerable extent, to the credit of the MPS, they are accepted. The MPS accept that he should have received better initial treatment, and that except when Detective Sergeant John Bevan was helping him he did not receive the level of support to which he was entitled. Assistant Commissioner Ian Johnston accepted in evidence that the MPS were to be criticised. He said:-

> *"There is a real lesson for us to learn in how we handled Duwayne Brooks at the scene".*

> *"I don't think we dealt with Duwayne Brooks very well at all. I think we let him down. I think we did some things to try and help him ..... my assessment of how Mr Brooks was dealt with at the early stages, and this is one of the major lessons from this Inquiry, he should have been dealt with better".*

These are understatements, but they do at least demonstrate acceptance of fault.

5.9   We do not propose here to set out in detail all the evidence which goes to these issues. We should and will deal with conclusions which follow and which are proved beyond reasonable doubt.

5.10   We have to conclude that no officer dealt properly at the scene with Mr Brooks. His first contact was probably with Police Constable Linda Bethel. She described Mr Brooks as being *"very agitated"*. Police Constable Joanne Smith said that he was *"jumping up and down and being very aggressive"*. Police Constable Anthony Gleason said that Mr Brooks was *"Highly excitable. Virtually uncontrollable"*. Considering what Mr Brooks had seen and been involved in none of that should have been surprising. Furthermore Mr Brooks was justifiably frustrated and angry, because he saw the arrival of the police as no substitute for the non-arrival of the ambulance, and to his mind the police seemed more interested in questioning him than in tending Stephen.

5.11   **Yet there is no evidence that any officer tried properly to understand that this was so, and that Mr Brooks needed close, careful and sensitive treatment. Furthermore even if it was difficult at first to gain a coherent story from him the officers failed to concentrate upon Mr Brooks and to follow up energetically the information which he gave them. Nobody suggested that he should be used in searches of the area, although he knew where the assailants had last been seen. Nobody appears properly to have tried to calm him, or to accept that what he said was true. To that must be added the failure of Inspector Steven Groves, the only senior officer present before the ambulance came, to try to find out from Mr Brooks what had happened. He, and others, appear to have assumed that there had been a fight. Only later did they take some steps to follow up the sparse information which they had gleaned. Who can tell whether proper concern and respect for Mr Brooks' condition and status as a victim might not have** helped to lead to evidence should he have been used in a property co-ordinated search of the estate?

5.12 We are driven to the conclusion that Mr Brooks was stereotyped as a young black man exhibiting unpleasant hostility and agitation, who could not be expected to help, and whose condition and status simply did not need further examination or understanding. We believe that Mr Brooks' colour and such stereotyping played their part in the collective failure of those involved to treat him properly and according to his needs.

5.13 The ambulance men understandably would not allow Mr Brooks into the ambulance. PC Smith took him by car to the hospital, where she dropped him off at the entrance. At about 23:30 he was seen by PC Gleason, who recorded in his notebook a statement which was of great importance, since it was the first account recorded, and it contained at least one reasonable description of one of the attackers, including the information that the attacker had light brown hair. PC Smith found Mr Brooks to have been *"irate and aggressive"*. She said that he used strong language saying *"Who called you fucking cunts anyway, pigs ...... I only called the fucking ambulance"*. These things may well have been said. Perhaps they account for the fact that Mr Brooks was left to go into the hospital unaccompanied. **Thereafter apart from the contact with PC Gleason, which lasted until 23:57, when Mr Brooks signed his name in PC Gleason's notebook, nobody, and in particular no police officer, at any time treated him properly as a victim. He was left on his own, and eventually was told that he could not leave. Acting Inspector Ian Little told him to wait either in the hospital or in the police car. Mr Brooks did not want to be in the hospital, so he sat in the car. This treatment of Mr Brooks at the hospital is plainly subject to severe criticism. The support of a victim in such circumstances is essential. Mr Brooks was simply treated as a potential witness, and inadequately treated at that. We are convinced that the conclusion set out in Paragraph 5.12 must also apply to the treatment of Mr Brooks at the hospital.**

5.14 At Plumstead Police Station the treatment of Mr Brooks was mixed. At first he was left alone in the CID office for a considerable time. At some stage he was seen and spoken to by Detective Superintendent Ian Crampton, who described Mr Brooks as *"very calm"*, and *"truthful and helpful"*, and *"a bit shocked"*. Mr Brooks' mother was asked by the police to attend, and she did attend in the early hours, and the taking of a long statement by DC Cooper was broken off so that Mr Brooks could see his mother. That statement taking started at about 01:30, and the statement was not completed until about 05:30. Mr Brooks accepts that he was given the chance to go home before making his statement, but he chose to stay. DC Cooper was an impressive witness, and he described Mr Brooks as being *"remarkably together"* and perceptive and intelligent. The statement is commendably clear and comprehensive in many respects. Mr Brooks was a vital witness as well as a victim. DC Cooper and other police officers treated Mr Brooks at the Police Station appropriately and professionally. Mr Brooks responded calmly and appropriately and gave all the information that he had. Later he was to say that he believed that officers at the Police Station did not want to believe him, particularly when he said that the attack had been motivated by racism, because of the words used. We believe that he may not have recalled the incident accurately, since at the time and thereafter Mr Brooks made no complaint about his treatment, nor did the police officers involved say that Mr Brooks had been anything other than co-operative during those hours at the Police Station.

5.15 An inexcusable mis-identification led to suspicion that Mr Brooks had purposely broken a window at the Police Station. This emerged in 1997, but fortunately the officer involved discovered that this conclusion was wholly mistaken, and the suggestion was withdrawn. Another black youth had broken a window, and Police Constable David Pennington's wrong conclusion is accepted to have been baseless.

5.16 Another example of bad and insensitive practice in connection with Mr Brooks was the request made through DS Bevan for a photograph of Mr Brooks, said (according to Detective Inspector Benjamin Bullock) to have been wanted *"to show it to other witnesses that may have seen him in the area on the night for example or the bus stop"*. We see no reason whatsoever for this request. No wonder Mr Brooks was upset and worried. He thought that this might imply that he was himself in some way a suspect. In May Detective Superintendent Brian Weeden correctly cancelled the request, which should never have been made in the first place. No other witness was asked to provide a photograph.

5.17 Mr Brooks lived in April 1993 in a hostel, and he told us that after 23 April he spent his time alone there, playing computer games. Within a few days DS Bevan and Detective Constable Linda Holden were detailed to be his liaison officers. They were at the time engaged in many other activities. It is fair to say that this liaison, particularly with DS Bevan, was reasonably successful. Mr Brooks himself agrees that DS Bevan was a "straight talker", and that he questioned why DS Bevan was taken off this task, probably towards the end of May 1993. Mr Brooks also accepts that DS Bevan offered witness protection which Mr Brooks declined.

5.18 That liaison was in our view inadequate. Mr Brooks was never fully and properly looked after in accordance with the Victim's Charter which provides that *"It is essential that every possible step is taken to minimise the upset and even the hardship which may be caused."* There is no evidence that positive steps were taken to arrange for full victim support or proper care. Mr Noel Penstone did see Mr Brooks in August 1993 and with others gave helpful support. At the time Mr Penstone was an Education Officer for the London Borough of Greenwich and, at the time of the murder, was Acting Deputy Chair of the Greenwich Race Equality Council. But this does not remove the responsibility of the MPS senior officers to ensure that this young man was regularly monitored and was very carefully and sensitively treated.

5.19 When DS Bevan was away, or perhaps after he was taken off this task, Detective Constable Michael Tomlin did see Mr Brooks when he was instructed to do so. DC Tomlin was an unsatisfactory witness. Mr Brooks says that DC Tomlin treated him *"in a funny way. He was awkward with me. He had an attitude problem which came over when he spoke to me"*. DC Tomlin denied that the term *"liaison officer"* was appropriate, although he had himself used the term in a questionnaire sent to those officers who had contact with Mr Brooks in 1993. DC Tomlin's memory was poor and selective. For example he denied that Mr Brooks had given his girlfriend's address to him. Mr Brooks says that he did give DC Tomlin that address, and that this is confirmed by the fact that Mr Brooks was found and arrested at that address in October 1993, in connection with the allegation that he had damaged a car during the disturbance which took place at Welling on 8 May 1993.

5.20 There was plainly some contact maintained between the police and Mr Brooks from time to time. It is not easy to establish how much contact there was, because we have seen no detailed records as to liaison with Mr Brooks. Further statements were taken by DS Bevan late in 1993, and later still Mr Brooks gave evidence both at committal and trial, when the case was in the hands of Mr Imran Khan as the solicitor for Mr & Mrs Lawrence.

5.21   There is positive evidence in Computer Assisted Despatch (CAD) messages that DS Bevan and others were keeping in touch with Mr Brooks during the summer and early autumn of 1993. Furthermore there was contact early on and later with Mr Brooks' parents. On 26 July 1993, for example, Mr Bullock, DS Bevan and DC Tomlin all went to Mr Brooks' former address to warn him to attend Court for the committal proceedings of two of the suspects in August. Mr Brooks was offered transport, but he declined the offer, saying that he would travel with his mother. He refused to give his present address, but said that he would ring through his new telephone number when he was connected. Mr Brooks' mother had already told the police that her son had moved his address, and that he would not disclose the new address.

5.22   On 29 July Mr Bullock was telephoned by Mr Brooks, who had heard from Mr Khan about the discontinuance of the prosecution of Neil Acourt and Luke Knight. Again he refused to give his address, and said that he could be contacted through his mother. He was asked to keep in touch by telephone. We see no strength in the suggestion made that contact with or through Mr Brooks' parents was to be criticised, either at this stage or at the start when Mr Weeden sought to reassure the parents by letter that accusations being made about their son were indeed false.

5.23   These contacts were not "victim support" contacts. They were necessary contacts in order to maintain arrangements for the use of Mr Brooks as a witness.

5.24   We stress again that Mr Brooks made nine statements to the police. He attended all the identification parades which he was required to attend. It is plain that there was improper control of the witnesses attending those parades, and comment is made elsewhere about Mr Brooks' behaviour during the time spent at the identification suite. On one occasion he was, as we know, in contact by telephone with Mr Khan, the solicitor for Mr & Mrs Lawrence who was by then acting as his solicitor. Mr Khan had seen Mr Brooks on 2 May and had taken a draft statement from Mr Brooks. The nature and extent of the relationship between Mr Brooks and Mr Khan is somewhat mysterious. Mr Brooks said on 3 June to officers who came to interview him after his identification of Luke Knight that he would not see them unless his solicitor was present. On 4 June two statements were taken, but Mr Khan was not present.

5.25   Mr Khan never complained to the police on Mr Brooks' behalf about lack of liaison or lack of care or support being given to Mr Brooks. Nor was there specific complaint made by Mr Brooks himself in that respect until after the event. It is however clear that the liaison and support given to him was patchy, and there is little indication of any regular monitoring or supervision of the steps taken to protect and to supervise this victim who was the vital witness in the case.

5.26   The sad truth is that there were in any event great problems about Mr Brooks' evidence, as the events at committal and trial show. We stress that this was no fault of Mr Brooks. There simply was no other satisfactory evidence against those who were tried, and Mr Brooks' evidence could not be put before the jury. It is understandable that Mr Brooks should resent this rejection of his evidence. In all the circumstances that rejection was inevitable and correct.

5.27   By about October 1993 Miss Jane Deighton, of Deighton Guedella, was acting for Mr Brooks, particularly in connection with the prosecution against him for criminal damage done to a car during the 8 May demonstration. That matter is dealt with in Chapter 39, para 49 et seq. It should here be said that there was clear evidence of the actual conduct which founded that prosecution. The defence depended upon medical evidence which indicated that Mr Brooks was already and understandably affected and disturbed by 8 May as a result of his terrible experiences. It was proposed that the difficult defence of automatism should be raised. That resulted in the obtaining of the opinions of all officers who had been in contact with Mr Brooks since the murder by means of questionnaires.

5.28   There is no doubt but that in their answers to questionnaires some police officers gave opinions about Mr Brooks' conduct and behaviour which appeared to cast him in a worse light than was justified. Several officers used similar expressions about Mr Brooks, suggesting that there had been some unfair consultation.

5.29   Whether the prosecution of Mr Brooks should or should not have been brought or persisted in is a vexed question. As we have indicated in Chapter 39 the decision of the CPS is open to some criticism, although decisions of this kind are by no means open and shut.

5.30   Overall we accept that Mr Brooks was undoubtedly not treated as he should have been. We have to conclude that in particular both at the scene and at the hospital he was doubted and wrongly assessed. Thereafter he was given scant and inadequate support. He himself in spite of this did all that could be expected of him. He never refused to make a statement or to comply with police demands to act as a witness. Witness protection was given to Mr Brooks during the Central Criminal Court Trial in 1996. Officers were recruited and allocated to this task through Detective Superintendent William Mellish. At the Inquiry, much was made of the use of Sgt XX (see Chapter 13) on one night (after Mr Brooks' evidence had been given) to perform this duty. But there is no evidence whatsoever of complaint as to the conduct of the protecting officers. The only complaint made by Mr Brooks is that on one night a hotel in Eltham was used. Mr Brooks says that, *"The next day, weak and tired, I had to give my evidence in Court"*. This is mistaken, since his evidence was complete when he stayed in Eltham. The experience of the trial must have been daunting, but in our view the protection of Mr Brooks during it cannot be fairly criticised.

5.31   **Sometimes, both during the Inquiry and in submissions made on his behalf, his case has been put too high. Allegations of "criminalisation" and "demonisation" are inappropriate. Yet at the end of the day we are satisfied that the lack of respect and sensitivity in handling him must reflect unwitting and collective racism particularly in those who dealt with him both at the scene of the murder and at the hospital. Mr Brooks was the victim of racist stereotyping. By way of example, in her written statement made at the scene PC Bethel described Mr Brooks as *"very distressed"* and *"very excitable and upset"*. In her answer to a 1994 questionnaire she said that he was *"aggressive, anti-police, distressed and unhelpful"*. To the Kent police she said that Mr Brooks was *"powerful and physically intimidating"*, and that his behaviour was *"horrendous"*. We do not believe that PC Bethel consciously sought to attack Mr Brooks by this crescendo of criticism, but the evidence does show how racist stereotyping can develop. We do not believe that a young white man in a similar position would have been dealt with in the same way. He simply was not treated professionally and appropriately and according to his needs.**

5.32   Further examination here of each and every aspect of Mr Brooks' statements and of the course of his evidence at committal and trial would in our view be unhelpful. We have given all that he has said in his statements the weight that it deserves. Our hope is that once this part of Mr Brooks' life is over he will be able to cope with his memories and lead a normal life again. He has suffered greatly as a result of the events of 1993, and also because he too is obviously affected by the failure of the investigation into his friend's death. Perhaps acceptance of his case to the extent here set out will help him to come to terms with life for the future.

CHAPTER SIX

RACISM

6.1 A central and vital issue which has permeated our Inquiry has been the issue of racism. The chilling condemnation, made by and on behalf of Mr & Mrs Lawrence at and after the Inquest in February 1997 (see Chapter 42, paras 13 & 37), of the police and of the system of English justice, has sounded through all the months of our consideration of the evidence. Mr & Mrs Lawrence allege and fervently believe that their colour, culture and ethnic origin, and that of their murdered son, have throughout affected the way in which the case has been dealt with and pursued. Similarly strong allegations are made on behalf of Duwayne Brooks. These allegations are plainly supported by many people, both black and white, in our Public Gallery and in the community at large.

6.2 **The Kent Report *"found no evidence to support the allegation of racist conduct by any Metropolitan Police Officer involved in the investigation of the murder of Stephen Lawrence"*, (Kent Report, para 14.28). The Kent investigation was however (as is set out at paragraph 14.25) *"an investigation into complaints against specific officers and as such could not cover the broader issues of racism and whether or not it existed within the MPS"*. Each of 17 officers interviewed by Kent was baldly asked whether his or her *"judgment and subsequent actions were based on the fact that Stephen was black"*. In some cases Mrs Lawrence's condemnatory words about the lack of first aid were quoted to the officers. Each officer roundly denied racism or racist conduct. Each officer plainly and genuinely believed that he or she had acted without overt racist bias or discrimination. The answers given were thus predictable.**

6.3 **In this Inquiry we have not heard evidence of overt racism or discrimination, unless it can be said that the use of inappropriate expressions such as "coloured" or "negro" fall into that category. The use of such words, which are now well known to be offensive, displays at least insensitivity and lack of training. A number of officers used such terms, and some did not even during their evidence seem to understand that the terms were offensive and should not be used.**

6.4 **Racism in general terms consists of conduct or words or practices which disadvantage or advantage people because of their colour, culture, or ethnic origin. In its more subtle form it is as damaging as in its overt form.**

6.5 We have been concerned with the more subtle and much discussed concept of racism referred to as institutional racism which (in the words of Dr Robin Oakley) can influence police service delivery *"not solely through the deliberate actions of a small number of bigoted individuals, but through a more systematic tendency that could unconsciously influence police performance generally"*.

6.6 **The phrase "institutional racism" has been the subject of much debate. We accept that there are dangers in allowing the phrase to be used in order to try to express some overall criticism of the police, or any other organisation, without addressing its meaning. Books and articles on the subject proliferate. We must do our best to express what we mean by those words, although we stress that we will not produce a definition cast in stone, or a final answer to the question. What we hope to do is to set out our standpoint, so that at least our application of the term to the present case can be understood by those who are criticised.**

6.7   In 1981 Lord Scarman's Report into The Brixton Disorders was presented to Parliament. In that seminal report Lord Scarman responded to the suggestion that *"Britain is an institutionally racist society,"* in this way:-

> *"If, by* [institutionally racist] *it is meant that it* [Britain] *is a society which knowingly, as a matter of policy, discriminates against black people, I reject the allegation. If, however, the suggestion being made is that practices may be adopted by public bodies as well as private individuals which are unwittingly discriminatory against black people, then this is an allegation which deserves serious consideration, and, where proved, swift remedy"*. (Para 2.22, p 11 - Scarman Report).

6.8   In policing terms Lord Scarman also rejected the allegation that the MPS was a racist force. He said:-

> *"The direction and policies of the Metropolitan Police are not racist. I totally and unequivocally reject the attack made upon the integrity and impartiality of the senior direction of the force. The criticisms lie elsewhere - in errors of judgment, in a lack of imagination and flexibility, but not in deliberate bias or prejudice"*. (Para 4.62, p 64).

6.9   Lord Scarman accepted that some police officers, particularly those below the level of the senior direction of the force were guilty of *"ill considered immature and racially prejudiced actions .... in their dealings on the streets with young black people"*. (Para 4.63, p 64). He stressed that "racist" prejudice and behaviour *"does occur and every instance of it has an immense impact on community attitudes and beliefs. The damage done by even the occasional display of racial prejudice is incalculable. It is therefore essential that every possible step be taken to prevent and to root out racially prejudiced attitudes in the police service. The police cannot rest on the argument that since they are a cross-section of society some officers are bound to be racially prejudiced. In this respect, as in others, the standards we apply to the police must be higher than the norms of behaviour prevalent in society as a whole"*. (Para 4.64, p 64).

6.10   Lord Scarman (Para 4.63) moreover referred specifically to the dangers of "racist" stereotyping when he said:

> *"Racial prejudice does manifest itself occasionally in the behaviour of a few officers on the street. It may be only too easy for some officers, faced with what they must see as the inexorably rising tide of street crime, to lapse into an unthinking assumption that all young black people are potential criminals"*.

6.11   **Such assumptions are still made today. In answer to a question posed to a member of the MPS Black Police Association, Inspector Leroy Logan, he referred to "what is said in the canteen", citing simply as an example his memory that "** *... as a Sergeant I was in the back of a car and a female white officer on seeing a black person driving a very nice car just said "I wonder who he robbed to get that?", and she then realised she was actually voicing an unconscious assumption"*. **(Part 2, Day 2, p 215). This is a mere example of similar experiences repeatedly given to us during our public meetings.**

6.12   Lord Scarman further said:-

> "*All the evidence I have received, both on the subject of racial disadvantage and more generally, suggests that racialism and discrimination against black people - often hidden, sometimes unconscious - remain a major source of social tension and conflict*".
> (Para 6.35, p 110).

6.13   **Thus Lord Scarman accepted the existence of what he termed *"unwitting"* or *"unconscious"* racism.   To those adjectives can be added a third, namely *"unintentional"*. All three words are familiar in the context of any discussion in this field. The Commissioner used all three in his letter written to the Inquiry on 2 October 1998, after his appearance at Hannibal House during our hearings.**

6.14   Dr Oakley indicates (in his first submission to the Inquiry, Paragraph 2) that in spite of Lord Scarman's use of the words *"hidden and unconscious"* and *"unwitting"* the concept of "racist conduct" that became established following his Report *"was one of overt acts of discrimination or hostility by individuals who were acting out their personal prejudices. Racism was therefore a problem specifically of individual officers, of 'rotten apples' within the service who 'let the side down'. On this diagnosis, the solution to the problem would lie (a) at the selection stage, at which prejudiced individuals should be identified and weeded out, and (b) through the application of disciplinary sanctions against those who display such behaviour on the job. This conception of racism appears still to be the normal understanding in police circles, and appears also to have informed the conclusion by the PCA"*.

6.15   When Lord Scarman asserted in his final conclusion that *"institutional racism does not exist in Britain: but racial disadvantage and its nasty associate racial discrimination have not yet been eliminated"*, (Para 9.1, p 135), many took this statement as the classic defence against all allegations that *"institutional racism"* exists in British society.   His earlier words ***"knowingly,** as a matter of policy, discriminates"* and *"practices may be adopted .... which are **unwittingly** discriminatory,"* were not separated and given equal weight. Whilst we must never lose sight of the importance of explicit racism and direct discrimination, in policing terms if the phrase "institutional racism" had been used to describe not only explicit manifestations of racism at direction and policy level, but also unwitting discrimination at the organisational level, then the reality of indirect racism in its more subtle, hidden and potentially more pervasive nature would have been addressed.

6.16   **The officers questioned by the Kent investigators expressed their indignation at any suggestion of overt racism.   The Kent Report in our view however, never dealt satisfactorily with the other evil of unwitting racism, in both talk and action, played out in a variety of ways. The evidence we heard in this Inquiry revealed how unwitting racist discriminatory language and behaviour may arise.**

6.17   **Unwitting racism can arise because of lack of understanding, ignorance or mistaken beliefs. It can arise from well intentioned but patronising words or actions. It can arise from unfamiliarity with the behaviour or cultural traditions of people or families from minority ethnic communities. It can arise from racist stereotyping of black people as potential criminals or troublemakers.   Often this arises out of uncritical self-understanding born out of an inflexible police ethos of the "traditional" way of doing things. Furthermore such attitudes can thrive in a tightly knit community, so that there**

can be a collective failure to detect and to outlaw this breed of racism. The police canteen can too easily be its breeding ground.

6.18 As Lord Scarman said (Para 4.97) there can be " .... *failure to adjust policies and methods to meet the needs of policing a multi-racial society"*. Such failures can occur simply because police officers may mistakenly believe that it is legitimate to be **"colour blind"** in both individual and team response to the management and investigation of racist crimes, and in their relationship generally with people from minority ethnic communities. Such an approach is flawed. A colour blind approach fails to take account of the nature and needs of the person or the people involved, and of the special features which such crimes and their investigation possess. As Mr Dan Crompton, Her Majesty's Inspector of Constabulary (HMIC), helpfully said to us it is no longer enough to believe *"all that is necessary is to treat everyone the same. .... it might be said it is about treatment according to need."* (Part 2, Day 2, p 57).

6.19 Professor Simon Holdaway (in his helpful statement to the Inquiry, para 3.3, 12 June 1998) says this:-

> *"By policing normally, in what officers regard as common sense ways, in failing to reflect on the implications of their ideas and notions, negative relationships between the police and ethnic minorities are created and sustained".*

6.20 In the Rotterdam Charter, *"Policing for a multi-ethnic society; Principles, Practices and Partnership (1996)"* (para 2, p 10), the following words appear:-

> *"A multi ethnic society places special demands on the police organisation. As a result the police must accept the need to adapt their professionalism, quality of service and their legal and wider responsibilities to the needs of a continually changing population. The goal is to provide services that are applicable and accessible to all citizens regardless of their ethnic background".*

6.21 **The failure of the first investigating team to recognise and accept racism and race relations as a central feature of their investigation of the murder of Stephen Lawrence played a part in the deficiencies in policing which we identify in this Report. For example, a substantial number of officers of junior rank would not accept that the murder of Stephen Lawrence was simply and solely "racially motivated". The relevance of the ethnicity and cultural status of the victims, including Duwayne Brooks, and Mr & Mrs Lawrence, was not properly recognised. Immediately after the murder Mr Brooks was side-lined, and his vital information was inadequately considered. None of these shortcomings was corrected or overcome.**

6.22 What may be termed collective organisational failure of this kind has come to be labelled by academics and others as institutional racism. This is by no means a new term or concept. In 1967 two black activists, Stokely Carmichael and Charles V Hamilton stated that institutional racism *"originates in the operation of established and respected forces in the society. It relies on the active and pervasive operation of anti-black attitudes and practices. A sense of superior group position prevails: whites are 'better' than blacks and therefore blacks should be subordinated to whites. This is a racist attitude and it permeates society on both the individual and institutional level, covertly or overtly"*. (Black Power: the Politics of Liberation in America, Penguin Books, 1967, pp 20-21).

6.23   Reference to a concept described in a different national and social context over 30 years ago has its dangers; but that concept has been continuously debated and revised since 1968. History shows that "covert" insidious racism is more difficult to detect. Institutions such as Police Services can operate in a racist way without at once recognising their racism.

6.24   **It is vital to stress that neither academic debate nor the evidence presented to us leads us to say or to conclude that an accusation that institutional racism exists in the MPS implies that the policies of the MPS are racist. No such evidence is before us. Indeed the contrary is true. It is in the implementation of policies and in the words and actions of officers acting together that racism may become apparent. Furthermore we say with emphasis that such an accusation does not mean or imply that every police officer is guilty of racism. No such sweeping suggestion can be or should be made. The Commissioner's fears are in this respect wholly unfounded.**

6.25   Sir Paul Condon himself said this in his letter to the Inquiry dated 2 October 1998:-

> *"I recognise that individual officers can be, and are, overtly racist. I acknowledge that officers stereotype, and differential outcomes occur for Londoners. Racism in the police is much more than 'bad apples'. Racism, as you have pointed out, can occur through a lack of care and lack of understanding. The debate about defining this evil, promoted by the Inquiry, is cathartic in leading us to recognise that it can occur almost unknowingly, as a matter of neglect, in an institution. I acknowledge the danger of institutionalisation of racism. However, labels can cause more problems than they solve."*

Sir Paul will go thus far, but he did not accept that there is institutional racism within his force.

6.26   We understand Sir Paul's anxiety about labels. But the fact is that the concept of institutional racism exists and is generally accepted, even if a long trawl through the work of academics and activists produces varied words and phrases in pursuit of a definition. We repeat that we do not pretend to produce a definition which will carry all argument before it. We approach the question by setting out some helpful quotations from evidence put before us, and we then set out our current standpoint. We began our Inquiry without presuppositions in this field. All the evidence and submissions that we have heard have driven us to the conclusions set out in this Report.

6.27   The MPS Black Police Association's spokesmen, in their written submission to the Inquiry, para 3.2, said this:-

> *".... institutional racism .... permeates the Metropolitan Police Service. This issue above all others is central to the attitudes, values and beliefs, which lead officers to act, albeit unconsciously and for the most part unintentionally, and treat others differently solely because of their ethnicity or culture".*

6.28 The oral evidence of the three representatives of the MPS Black Police Association was illuminating. It should be read in full, but we highlight two passages from Inspector Paul Wilson's evidence:-

(Part 2, Day 2, p 209):

> *"The term institutional racism should be understood to refer to the way the institution or the organisation may systematically or repeatedly treat, or tend to treat, people differentially because of their race. So, in effect, we are not talking about the individuals within the service who may be unconscious as to the nature of what they are doing, but it is the net effect of what they do".*

(Part 2, Day 2, p 211):

> *"A second source of institutional racism is our culture, our culture within the police service. Much has been said about our culture, the canteen culture, the occupational culture. How and why does that impact on individuals, black individuals on the street? Well, we would say the occupational culture within the police service, given the fact that the majority of police officers are white, tends to be the white experience, the white beliefs, the white values.*
>
> *Given the fact that these predominantly white officers only meet members of the black community in confrontational situations, they tend to stereotype black people in general. This can lead to all sorts of negative views and assumptions about black people, so we should not underestimate the occupational culture within the police service as being a primary source of institutional racism in the way that we differentially treat black people.*
>
> *Interestingly I say we because there is no marked difference between black and white in the force essentially. We are all consumed by this occupational culture. Some of us may think we rise above it on some occasions, but, generally speaking, we tend to conform to the norms of this occupational culture, which we say is all powerful in shaping our views and perceptions of a particular community".*

We believe that it is essential that the views of these officers should be closely heeded and respected.

6.29 The 1990 Trust in their submission wrote:-

> *".... racism can be systemic and therefore institutional without being apparent in broad policy terms. Racism within the police can be both covert and overt, racism can be detected in how operational policing decisions are carried out and consequently implemented, and indeed how existing policy is ignored or individual officers' discretion results in racist outcomes".*

6.30   The Commission for Racial Equality (CRE) in their submission stated:-

> *"Institutional racism has been defined as those established laws, customs, and practices which systematically reflect and produce racial inequalities in society. If racist consequences accrue to institutional laws, customs or practices, the institution is racist whether or not the individuals maintaining those practices have racial intentions".*
> *(Para 2).*

> **".... organisational structures, policies, processes and practices which result in ethnic minorities being treated unfairly and less equally, often without intention or knowledge".** (Para 3).

6.31   Dr Robin Oakley has submitted two helpful Notes to our Inquiry. It is perhaps impudent to cite short extracts from his work, but these passages have particularly assisted us:-

> *"For the police service, however, there is an additional dimension which arises from the nature of the policing role. Police work, unlike most other professional activities, has the capacity to bring officers into contact with a skewed cross-section of society, with the well-recognised potential for producing negative stereotypes of particular groups. Such stereotypes become the common currency of the police occupational culture. If the predominantly white staff of the police organisation have their experience of visible minorities largely restricted to interactions with such groups, then negative racial stereotypes will tend to develop accordingly."*

In Dr Oakley's view, if the challenges of 'institutional racism' which potentially affect all police officers, are not addressed, this will:-

> *"result in a generalised tendency, particularly where any element of discretion is involved, whereby minorities may receive different and less favourable treatment than the majority. Such differential treatment need be neither conscious nor intentional, and it may be practised routinely by officers whose professionalism is exemplary in all other respects. There is great danger that focusing on overt acts of personal racism by individual officers may deflect attention from the much greater institutional challenge ... of addressing the more subtle and concealed form that organisational-level racism may take. Its most important challenging feature is its predominantly hidden character and its inbuilt pervasiveness within the occupational culture."*

He goes on:-

> **"It could be said that institutional racism in this sense is in fact pervasive throughout the culture and institutions of the whole of British society, and is in no way specific to the police service. However, because of the nature of the police role, its impact on society if not addressed in the police organisation may be particularly severe. In the police service, despite the extensive activity designed**

to address racial and ethnic issues in recent years, the concept of 'institutional racism' has not received the attention it deserves." (Institutional Racism and Police Service Delivery, Dr Robin Oakley's submission to this Inquiry, parts of paras 6, 7, 8, and 11).

6.32 Dr Oakley in his second Note (17 December 1988) echoes the view of Professor Holdaway who has argued rightly that emotively powerful words such as "racism" must not be used simply as rhetorical weapons:-

> *"Such terms need to be given a clear analytic meaning which can demonstrably help illuminate the problem at hand". (Para 1.4).*

> **"The term institutional racism should be understood to refer to the way institutions may systematically treat or tend to treat people differently in respect of race. The addition of the word 'institutional' therefore identifies the source of the differential treatment; this lies in some sense within the organisation rather than simply with the individuals who represent it. The production of differential treatment is 'institutionalised' in the way the organisation operates". (Para 2.2).**

Towards the end of his Note Dr Oakley says this:-

> **"What is required in the police service therefore is an occupational culture that is sensitive not just to the experience of the majority but to minority experience also. In short, an enhanced standard of police professionalism to meet the requirements of a multi-ethnic society"** (Para 5.6).

6.33 We are also grateful for the contribution to our Inquiry made by Dr Benjamin Bowling. Again it must be said that summaries of such work can be unhelpful. But we hope that he will forgive us for quoting here simply one important passage:-

> *"Institutional racism is the **process** by which people from ethnic minorities are systematically discriminated against by a range of public and private bodies. If the result or **outcome** of established laws, customs or practices is racially discriminatory, then institutional racism can be said to have occurred. Although racism is rooted in widely shared attitudes, values and beliefs, discrimination can occur irrespective of the intent of the individuals who carry out the activities of the institution. Thus policing can be discriminatory without this being acknowledged or recognised, and in the face of official policies geared to removal of discrimination. However, some discrimination practices are the product of **uncritical** rather than unconscious racism. That is, practices with a racist outcome are not engaged in without the actor's knowledge; rather, the actor has failed to consider the consequences of his or her actions for people from ethnic minorities. Institutional racism affects the routine ways in which ethnic minorities are treated in their capacity as employees, witnesses, victims, suspects and members of the general public."* Violent Racism: Victimisation, Policing and Social Context, July 1998. (Paras 21-22, pp 3-4).

6.34   Taking all that we have heard and read into account we grapple with the problem. For the purposes of our Inquiry the concept of institutional racism which we apply consists of:

> **The collective failure of an organisation to provide an appropriate and professional service to people because of their colour, culture, or ethnic origin. It can be seen or detected in processes, attitudes and behaviour which amount to discrimination through unwitting prejudice, ignorance, thoughtlessness and racist stereotyping which disadvantage minority ethnic people.**

It persists because of the failure of the organisation openly and adequately to recognise and address its existence and causes by policy, example and leadership. Without recognition and action to eliminate such racism it can prevail as part of the ethos or culture of the organisation. It is a corrosive disease.

6.35   As Dr Oakely points out, the disease cannot be attacked by the organisation involved in isolation. If such racism infests the police its elimination can only be achieved "by means of a fully developed partnership approach in which the police service works jointly with the minority ethnic communities. How else can mutual confidence and trust be reached?" (Para 14, p 6).

6.36   Thus in this Inquiry we have looked to see whether racism of this type lay behind the steps taken, or not taken, or pursued inadequately. Was there an adequate and thoughtful understanding of action to be taken when a racist crime was palpably identified? Did the officers involved behave at each stage as "colour blind", denying the relevance and particular reactions and needs of the victims and their families? Did the officers involved fail fully to accept "racism and race relations" as a central feature of the investigation? Did the officers involved act sluggishly, and in a way which they would not have acted had the victim been white and the attackers black?

6.37   Professor Holdaway ends his statement to the Inquiry with the following perceptive assessment:-

> *"The sustaining of negative relationships with the Lawrence family and Duwayne Brooks; a failure to undertake an adequate investigation; a lack of competent management; and a lack of a particular approach to the investigation of a racial attack were compounded precisely because the officers in charge of the inquiry did not place race at the centre of their understanding of the Lawrence murder and its investigation. Race relations were consistently under-played or ignored".* (Paragraph 11.3).

6.38   Can this indictment be spelt out of the facts or legitimate inferences to be drawn from the facts of this murder investigation? Does the condemnation by Mr & Mrs lawrence of the police and the criminal justice system have validity? Do the submissions of Counsel on behalf of Mr & Mrs Lawrence and Mr Brooks lead to the conclusions which they advocate in connection with the issue of racism? Was the case so clearly foreshadowed on the opening statement of Counsel to the Inquiry made out? These are the questions which must be addressed. We address them upon a fair assessment and judgement of all the facts and circumstances which have been rehearsed before us in both parts of our inquiry.

6.39 **Given the central nature of the issue we feel that it is important at once to state our conclusion that institutional racism, within the terms of its description set out in Paragraph 6.34 above, exists both in the Metropolitan Police Service and in other Police Services and other institutions countrywide.** In this context we stress what Sir Herman Ouseley, Chairman of the CRE, has written to us:-

> *"This Inquiry offers a unique opportunity to make a difference; not only with the MPS and its failings, but for all our institutions .... there should be coherence across all institutions and organisations as part of a national framework for change. Without this any change would be merely piecemeal, limited, and unlikely to be long-lasting".*

6.40 In reaching this conclusion we have considered the primary evidence which has been put before us and the legitimate inferences which can fairly and as a matter of "common-sense and not law" be drawn from that evidence, as May LJ indicated in <u>North West Thames RHA v Noone</u> (1988) IRLR 195 CA. Furthermore we apply the civil standard of proof, namely that we are satisfied upon a balance of probability that any conclusion we reach is justified.

6.41 Mummery J said in <u>Quereshi v Victoria University of Manchester and Brazier</u> (1996) EAT 484, at page 495, an employment case, *"The process of inference is itself a matter of applying common-sense and judgment of facts, and assessing the probabilities on this issue of whether racial grounds were an effective cause of the acts complained of or were not. The assessment of the parties and their witnesses when they give evidence also form an important part of the process of inference. The Tribunal may find that the force of the primary facts is insufficient to justify an inference on racial grounds. It may find that any inference that it might have made is negated by a satisfactory explanation by the Respondent of non racial grounds for the action or decision."*

6.42 The only explanation or excuse offered to us for the failures and mistakes in this case are that they were the result of incompetence or misjudgement. Such explanation or excuse cannot in our view negate the reasonable inferences and conclusions which we make from the evidence that we have heard.

6.43 We note the words of Leggatt LJ, in <u>Quereshi v London Borough of Newham</u> (1991) 10 RLR (p 267), in which the Court of Appeal held that failure on the part of an employer to take steps to counter racial discrimination could be evidence from which unlawful prejudice could be inferred. Leggatt LJ said, *"Incompetence does not, without more, become discrimination merely because the person affected by it is from an ethnic minority".*

6.44 **We heed this warning, but upon all the facts we assert that the conclusion that racism played its part in this case is fully justified. Mere incompetence cannot of itself account for the whole catalogue of failures, mistakes, misjudgements, and lack of direction and control which bedevilled the Stephen Lawrence investigation.**

6.45 **Institutional racism is in our view primarily apparent in what we have seen and heard in the following areas:-**

    (a)   in the actual investigation including the family's treatment at the hospital, the initial reaction to the victim and witness Duwayne Brooks, the family liaison, the failure of many officers to recognise Stephen's murder as a purely *"racially motivated"* crime,

the lack of urgency and commitment in some areas of the investigation.

(b) **countrywide in the disparity in "stop and search figures". Whilst we acknowledge and recognise the complexity of this issue and in particular the other factors which can be prayed in aid to explain the disparities, such as demographic mix, school exclusions, unemployment, and recording procedures, there remains, in our judgment, a clear core conclusion of racist stereotyping;**

(c) **countrywide in the significant under-reporting of "racial incidents" occasioned largely by a lack of confidence in the police and their perceived unwillingness to take such incidents seriously. Again we are conscious of other factors at play, but we find irresistible the conclusion that a core cause of under-reporting is the inadequate response of the Police Service which generates a lack of confidence in victims to report incidents; and**

(d) **in the identified failure of police training; as evidenced by the HMIC Report, *"Winning the Race"* and the Police Training Council Report, and the clear evidence in Part 1 of this Inquiry which demonstrated that not a single officer questioned before us in 1998 had received any training of significance in racism awareness and race relations throughout the course of his or her career.**

6.46　In reaching our conclusions we do not accept the contention of the Commissioner of the Metropolitan Police Service that,

> *"....... if this Inquiry labels my Service as institutionally racist the average police officer, the average member of the public will assume the normal meaning of those words. They will assume a finding of conscious, wilful or deliberate action or inaction to the detriment of ethnic minority Londoners. They will assume the majority of good men and women who come into policing ..... go about their daily lives with racism in their minds and in their endeavour. I actually think that use of those two words in a way that would take on a new meaning to most people in society would actually undermine many of the endeavours to identify and respond to the issues of racism which challenge all institutions and particularly the police because of their privileged and powerful position"* (Part 2, Day 3, pp 290-291).

We hope and believe that the average police officer and average member of the public will accept that we do not suggest that all police officers are racist and will both understand and accept the distinction we draw between overt individual racism and the pernicious and persistent institutional racism which we have described.

6.47　Nor do we say that in its policies the MPS is racist. Nor do we share the fear of those who say that in our finding of institutional racism, in the manner in which we have used that concept, there may be a risk that the moral authority of the MPS may be undermined. Already by the establishment under Deputy Assistant Commissioner John Grieve of the MPS Racial and Violent Crime Task Force the signs are that the problem is being recognised and tackled. Thus the catharsis of this Inquiry will lead to constructive action and not to further divisive views and outcomes. Sir Henry Brooke's perceptive 1993 Kapila lecture should be required reading in the field of race relations. He reminded us that in the 1st Century AD Philo wrote *"When a judge tries a case he must remember that he is himself on trial"*. We ask of the Police Services that in their investigation of racist incidents and crimes and in their work in this field they should remember that they too are being investigated for racism.

6.48 **There must be an unequivocal acceptance of the problem of institutional racism and its nature before it can be addressed, as it needs to be, in full partnership with members of minority ethnic communities. There is no doubt that recognition, acknowledgement and acceptance of the problem by Police Services and their officers is an important first step for minority ethnic communities in moving forward positively to solve the problem which exists. There is an onus upon Police Services to respond to this. Any Chief Officer who feels unable so to respond will find it difficult to work in harmony and co-operation with the community in the way that policing by consent demands.**

6.49 We were heartened by the evidence from the Association of Chief Police Officers (Chief Constable David Blakey, Chief Constable Tony Burden and Assistant Chief Constable Lloyd Clarke, Part 2, Day 1, Page 95) that *"We acknowledge that as in all organisations, there are individuals who have racist attitudes in the police service. And our collective viewpoint can lead to our not understanding, or to our misinterpreting racial incidents and ethnic minority opinions and expectations"*. And by the evidence of Chief Constable David Wilmot (Part 2, Day 2) who plainly accepted that within the Greater Manchester Police *"there was still institutional racism, both in an 'internalised' way (just as in society) and an overt way"* which had to be radically confronted. His views were misinterpreted by many who said that his statements implied that all his officers were racist. This was an unjustified and faulty perception. Mr Wilmot accepted that institutional racism existed within his force, within the terms of the concept described above. Mr Wilmot concluded his opening statement by saying that,

> *"The future is not going to be easy but I would hope, certainly I felt from what I have heard today, that if we took our Manchester Commonwealth Games Symbol and use it as a logo that we are working together in this area. We accept constructive criticism, and try to change as a Service. We accept that we have problems and are working towards them. I also believe that I do have a good work force that tries, in the main, its very best to reduce crime and criminality and racism within the Greater Manchester Police Area and I feel, despite the problems, reasonably confident that working together we can set off on that long road to a future whereby everybody can walk about our community without fear of anything, irrespective of their colour, religion, background, age, sex, whatever, that there is no discrimination in any shape or form"* (p.191).

6.50 We are also encouraged by the letters from the new President of ACPO, Chief Constable John Newing. In his first letter (16 October 1998) he said:-

> **" .... I define institutional racism as the racism which is inherent in wider society which shapes our attitudes and behaviour. Those attitudes and behaviour are then reinforced or reshaped by the culture of the organisation a person works for. In the police service there is a distinct tendency for officers to stereotype people. That creates problems in a number of areas, but particularly in the way**

officers deal with black people. Discrimination and unfairness are the result. I know because as a young police officer I was guilty of such behaviour.

My definition is very similar to the way David Wilmot defined institutional racism in response to you and the press. .....

..... We take the view that the important issue now is to stop arguing about definitions and do something about the racism within the service. Having said that it would be entirely unrealistic to think that the phrase 'institutional racism' will not continue to be used to describe a certain type of racist behaviour. Our hope therefore is that your report will bring greater clarity to its meaning and use."

In his second letter dated 13 November 1998 Mr Newing indicated that he had established a Presidential Task Force to tackle *"the issues concerning racism and those relating to the investigation and prevention of racial and violent crime"*. The aim of that Task Force is *"to increase the confidence in policing among ethnic minority communities by providing better protection from racial and violent crime and demonstrating fairness in every aspect of policing"*.

The terms of reference are:-

"To review and consider all aspects of the work currently being done within the Police Service in respect of relations between the Police Service and ethnic minorities. The aim will be to finalise a comprehensive policy and identify action to ensure that real achievement follows".

Perhaps in this indication, and in the establishment within the MPS of Mr John Grieve's Task Force, the impact of this Inquiry can already be detected.

6.51 **The evidence of the Commissioner of the Metropolitan Police in his opening statement placed too much emphasis upon individual racists and individual malpractice (Part 2, Day 3, page 282), and cautioned against the use of the term institutional racism *"in new and different ways"* (page 292). The Commissioner did not accept that unconscious or covert racism was evident in any area of the Stephen Lawrence investigation. He said, *"I honestly sincerely believe that by any ordinary use of those words those issues did not influence this tragic case"* (pages 307/308). When given examples of the impact of racism; the patronising of Mr & Mrs Lawrence, and the refusal to accept racist motivation by a number of officers, and asked whether such features might amount to institutional racism his response was *"..... I am not challenging the areas of the behaviour you have described. .... but by describing those challenges and those issues as institutional racism I think you then extrapolate to all police officers at all times this notion that they are walking around just waiting to do something that is going to be labelled institutional racism because of some collective failure."* (Part 2, page 311).**

6.52 Later (page 321) the Commissioner summarised his position in these words:-

"I have said today, I thought I had said today, there is racism in the Police Service. There can be unconscious racism, there can be deliberate racism, that racism can be played out in discrimination in disproportionality, the unfair use of arbitrary powers, all of those

issues I acknowledge, I condemn, I seek to reform, I have never ever challenged ....".

However there is a small but significant difference between acknowledging that such features "can" exist and acknowledging that they "do" exist. There is thus a discernible difference between the approach of ACPO and other Chief Officers and the somewhat less positive approach of the Commissioner. We assert again that there must be an unequivocal acceptance that the problem actually exists as a prerequisite to addressing it successfully.

6.53   To his credit the Commissioner was aware of the problem in 1993. In a conference lecture .given on 28 February 1993, shortly after his appointment, in a more general but wholly relevant context, he said:-

> *".... This is an area where we must be totally intolerant; intolerant of racially motivated attacks; intolerant of those who indulge in racial abuse, and intolerant of those who use hatred and violence as the tools of their political expression.*
>
> *But if we are to be intolerant of those outside the police service who fail to treat their fellow human beings with dignity and respect, we must be equally intolerant of our own colleagues who fail to reach the required standards. The argument that there is some excuse for poor behaviour because the culture of the Service can only be expected to mirror that of wider society and its behaviours, since that is from where we draw our personnel, is simply specious. We demand exemplary conduct from those we employ." .....*

6.54   **Racism, institutional or otherwise, is not the prerogative of the Police Service. It is clear that other agencies including for example those dealing with housing and education also suffer from the disease. If racism is to be eradicated there must be specific and co-ordinated action both within the agencies themselves and by society at large, particularly through the educational system, from pre-primary school upwards and onwards.**

6.55   We have already referred in Chapter 2 to the racism observed amongst children of primary and even pre-school age, and to the high proportion of racist incidents attributable to young people. It must be a major concern of Government that our educational system should address these issues.

6.56   There is evidence that there are difficulties in getting some schools individually or locally to acknowledge and tackle racism even where local education authorities have sought to persuade them to do so. The lack of powers available to local education authorities and the fear of negative publicity by schools clearly combine to make anti-racist policies, even where they exist, ineffective. Consequently in order to seek to eradicate racism in the longer term, within society as a whole, the Government should consider how best to empower local education authorities to create, monitor and enforce anti-racist policies through codes of practice and by amendment of the National Curriculum, to provide education which deals with racism awareness and valuing cultural diversity in the multi-cultural and multi-ethnic society in which we live.

6.57 In order to provide the context and climate in which institutional racism can be addressed there is a need, as a matter of basic principle, for Police Services as a whole to be made as open and accountable as possible. To move Police Services forward in this way and to ensure the maximum degree of openness and accountability we will make strong recommendations, which will appear later in this Report.

6.58 As Mr Paul Pugh, the Head of the Operational Policing Policy Unit at the Home Office, said in evidence during Part 2 of this Inquiry:-

> *".... the Department [the Home Office] has a wider role in promoting race equality and combating racial disadvantage, and that is an agenda to which I know Ministers attach great importance .... My personal view is that we are now in a time of tremendous opportunity to make a change .... to make progress and to address some of the central problems. One of those problems is the gap between minority ethnic people's experience of racially motivated crime and the response of the police service to it".*

Fundamental to the closing of the gap is the acceptance and then the elimination of racism within the Police Service.

6.59 We echo Mr Pugh's words, and hope that this opportunity for co-operation between Police Services and minority ethnic communities will not be lost. Both sides have a duty to bridge the gap, since bridges have to be built from both sides. But the first priority is for Police Services to accept the existence of the problem and to address it, since any form of racism associated with power has to be the first target.

6.60 In the context of the need for change we note the helpful evidence of the Reverend David Wise, given to us at Southall. He has been Pastor of Greenford Baptist Church for 11 years and has lived in the area of Southall for 18 years. He said this:-

> *"The police here in West London seem to respond differently to Black and Asian people than the Whites. I used to believe that it was simply that alongside the excellent police officers that there undoubtedly are (we have two who are part of our own church community) there were some police officers who were either inept or were, to put it bluntly, racially prejudiced. I have now been forced to the conclusion, by this and other cases, that the problem is much, much deeper than that. I believe that the procedures and management systems of the police are at fault ... Simply tinkering with the police system and putting in a bit of extra racial awareness training will not address this: a radical transformation is needed"* (Part 2, Day 6, pp.832-834).

6.61 This call for radical cultural transformation has an illuminating echo backwards to words spoken in 1992 by Sir John Woodcock, then HM Chief Inspector of Constabulary in his opening address to the International Conference on Policing (IPEC 1992). The context was very different, but the words used are apt. He said this:

> *"The work place values of the modern police service have not yet fully cut free of the past and the police service faces a massive task, if it is to hold, as the community now demands, integrity and respect for human rights, above all other considerations."*

The main reason Sir John gave for police malpractice in the gathering and presentation of evidence was his belief:-

> *"that most of those who go wrong in this way are misguided rather than evil, and their actions are a result of our collective failures as supervisors ... I don't believe in bad apples.* **I think that the problem is not one of individual predisposition to wrongdoing but of structure, or what I have earlier called cultural failure.** *The culture of the police and some procedures in the criminal justice system actually make it totally improbable that all police officers will behave as the system lays down that they should. However, I believe that the Royal Commission will fail in any attempt fully to guarantee the integrity of police evidence unless the police service itself changes its culture dramatically."*

He concluded with these words, the sense of which are apt in the context of this Inquiry:-

> *"What is happening to the police is that a 19th Century institution is being dragged into the 21st Century. Despite all the later mythology of Dixon, the police never really were the police of the whole people but a mechanism set up to protect the affluent from what the Victorians described as the dangerous classes.* **I believe that the events of the last few years have not only presented British policing with a challenge so formidable that it has come close to disaster: they have also now given the opportunity to the British Police to reinvent themselves. It is now possible to foresee that, through a fundamental shift of culture, the British police service will remain at the worldwide forefront of policing, with a style which draws its legitimacy from an understanding of current public needs and of the nature of the contract between police and a new generation of the public."** (Sir John Woodcock, Her Majesty's Chief Inspector of Constabulary, 'Trust in the Police - the Search for Truth', IPEC '92, Metropolitan Policy Library, 200, 12/12/92, pp. 3, 5, 7, 8, 12).

6.62   Our conclusions and recommendations are designed to guide all police officers towards a transformation of their culture in partnership with others, in the context of policing this present multi-cultural and multi-ethnic Britain. As the Home Secretary, The Rt Hon Jack Straw MP, has emphasised:

> **"It is not enough for a force to pay lip service to the ethos of equal opportunities. It must be shown to be happening, not only in clearly articulated policies, but in clearly defined procedures - including measures to deal with staff whose conduct and behaviour runs contrary to this ethos"** (Speech to the Black Police Association, Monday 19 October 1998, Home Office Press Office, London, para 25).

6.63   **We are confident that the Home Secretary and the Government will perceive the pressures for change which this Inquiry has uncovered, so that the necessary transformation will start to take place. The Inquiry itself cannot mould the future, but Government and society can together go forward.**

CHAPTER SEVEN

THE FIVE SUSPECTS

7.1   Neil and Jamie Acourt lived in 1993 at Bournbrook Road, Eltham. Neil was born on 5 July 1975, Jamie was born on 3 June 1976. They were thus 17 and 16 years old in April 1993.

7.2   David Norris lived with his mother at Berryfield Close, Chislehurst. He was born on 22 August 1976. He was 16 years old in 1993. His father, Clifford Norris, was "on the run" between 1988 and 1994; he was wanted by the Customs and Excise in respect of major drug dealing offences. It is not known where Clifford Norris was until he was arrested in August 1994 by Mr Mellish and his team in Sussex. Clifford Norris was plainly keeping in touch with his family in 1993. It is alleged that he was behind the bribing of Stacey Benefield (see Chapter 9). Clifford Norris must have known about his son's alleged involvement in Stephen Lawrence's murder. It is likely that some of the suspects other than David Norris himself saw Clifford Norris before his arrest in August 1994. It is certain that two or more of them visited Clifford Norris when he was in prison after his arrest.

7.3   **Police officers told us that they believed that the influence or fear of Clifford Norris infected the investigation of the murder, in that potential young witnesses or young people in possession of information held back because they knew of Clifford Norris' existence and close interest in his son's welfare.**

7.4   **Mr Mellish believes that the suspects may have been "schooled" by Clifford Norris, and that this might account for part of their behaviour when they were subjected to sophisticated audio/visual surveillance in 1994. Clifford Norris may also have contributed either personally or through other channels to the decision made by David Norris and both the Acourts that they would keep totally silent during interviews, and at the Inquest.**

7.5   Gary Dobson lived at Phineas Pett Road, Eltham. He was born on 16 June 1975. He was 17 years old in 1993. He lived at home with his parents.

7.6   Luke Knight lived at Well Hall Road, Eltham. He was born on 2 November 1976. He was 16 years old in 1993. He too lived at home with his parents.

7.7   **These five youths have always been the prime suspects in respect of Stephen Lawrence's murder. Many other names have surfaced in the information reaching the investigating team, but these five have always been singled out. In particular, as we have seen, the Acourts and David Norris have featured from the start.**

7.8   Four of these youths lived on or near the Brook Estate. David Norris was plainly well known to the other four, although he lived in apparently luxurious surroundings at Chislehurst. The short surveillance of 102 Bournbrook Road confirmed David Norris' association with the Acourts.

7.9   Those who killed Stephen Lawrence came towards Dickson Road from the Well Hall Road roundabout, and after the murder they ran down Dickson Road which immediately leads towards the estate, and the homes of the Acourts and Dobson.

7.10 When the names of this gang came repeatedly to the investigating team it was apparent that they were known to be potentially violent, and that the Acourts fancied themselves as gang leaders, and apparently referred to themselves as 'the Krays'. It is a feature of the case that people who knew these youths or knew of them had considerable knowledge of their anti-social character, yet little if anything was available or was discovered about them by immediate research or from formal intelligence sources.

7.11 We know that their names were researched when the early messages came in. For example message No 4 from an anonymous source named Neil Acourt and David Norris as members of a *"group of youths on the Kidbrooke Estate who always carry knives and threaten people"*. This was the message received at 13:50 on 23 April. Action to research Mr Acourt and Mr Norris was allocated to Detective Constable Dennis Chase. Eventually much later, on 10 May, after the arrests had in fact been effected, there is a report as to the action taken which indicates that there was no trace of Neil Acourt amongst the collator's cards. The evidence of DC Chase showed that inquiries were made of local intelligence sources, including the collator's cards. **Our impression is that such research and intelligence gathering as did take place was sporadic and delayed. There was no separate research unit in the investigation team. Mr Weeden indicated that he would have liked such a unit, but he did not have enough officers to create and to staff it.**

7.12 It is a feature of the case that although the names of prime suspects repeatedly came in from many directions there was no concerted action taken to discover whether corroborating information could be obtained from other sources. For example DC Chase was asked whether or not he or others thought of checking at the schools or clubs which were attended by these youths for assistance. Apparently nobody did order or suggest that this should be done. We now know that in the case of Neil Acourt an inquiry was made with the help of Mr Penstone at Kidbrooke School in July 1993. This revealed that in September 1991 Neil Acourt pushed a boy called Kalitis down the stairs. In 1993 there was a confrontation between Neil Acourt and Kalitis who was on this occasion supported by some black boys. Neil Acourt was armed with a lump of wood. The incident plainly had racist overtones. Both Acourt and Kalitis were expelled. Further, at the Montague Boys Club in 1992 Neil Acourt brandished a knife and threatened a black boy. Neil Acourt was banned from the club.

7.13 There were some records available both in the collator's index, and to a limited extent in the Racial Incident Unit card index at Plumstead Police Station. Furthermore convictions are recorded at the Criminal Records Office, and central intelligence records could be consulted. But there appears to have been little if any local intelligence available to the investigating team to help immediate research into those whose names were coming forward with such regularity. The Acourts and others associated with them were plainly well known locally, but the local police had clearly not picked up or been made aware of that information. This may have been due to the lack of contact with local people on and around the estate. **Mr William Panton, acting for Greenwich Council, stressed the fact that there appeared to be limited policing on the ground, with the result that valuable information of this kind was lacking.**

7.14 The flow of information from the public about this murder, and the clear information about the Stacey Benefield case, did however in itself give reasonable grounds for suspicion sufficient to found arrests.

7.15   Both Jamie Acourt and David Norris, as well as Luke Knight had allegedly been involved in May 1992 in assaulting two brothers by the name of Witham. It was said that one of the brothers had been stabbed with a butterfly knife. David Norris was charged with wounding, and Jamie Acourt with possession of an offensive weapon. Those charges were subsequently withdrawn by the CPS in January and May 1993 respectively, on the basis that it was not in the public interest to pursue them *"on the grounds of staleness"*. We know that Mr Weeden secured additional evidence of identification later, yet these prosecutions were not restored. The relevant point is that information about these charges, which supported the suggestion that these youths might be violent knife users, was not available to the murder investigating team at once when research was ordered. It would surely have been available from the Chislehurst collator, who should have notified the "home" collator of Jamie Acourt of the arrest and charge, together with details of his association in the Witham case with David Norris.

7.16   In 1991 a youth named Lee Pearson was stabbed outside a kebab shop in Tudor Parade, Well Hall Road, by members of a gang of white youths said by Mr Pearson to have included both Acourts. This assault was referred to specifically by "James Grant" on 23 April 1993. Mr Pearson would not sign a statement implicating the Acourts. This information did not surface until after the murder, and the offences were never proved. This allegation was part of the information available from 23 April about the suspects.

7.17   The stabbing of Stacey Benefield is separately dealt with in Chapter 9. Until after the murder of Stephen Lawrence, Mr Benefield was apparently not prepared to give a signed statement. By Sunday 25 April he had given a full statement to Detective Sergeant John Davidson.

7.18   It should be recorded that racist crime and violence were not new to the district. Both Eltham and Thamesmead had bitter experience of such crime by 1993. In May 1991 a black youth called Orville Blair was killed by a white man called Snell. Eventually Snell was convicted of manslaughter on the grounds of provocation. There is some doubt whether this was in fact a racist crime, but it was so regarded by the community.

7.19   In February 1991 a white man named Thornburrow murdered a young 15 year old black youth named Rolan Adams, in a gross racist attack made at a bus stop after some altercation between rival gangs of white and black youths. Thornburrow did not at his trial contest the fact that he had killed Rolan Adams, but he pleaded various alternative defences which were rejected. He was sentenced to life imprisonment, and other youths, some of whom feature in the evidence about the red Astra car seen in Well Hall Road after Stephen Lawrence's murder, were sentenced for other offences committed during the same violent incident.

7.20   On 11 July 1992 an Asian boy called Rohit Duggal was stabbed to death by a white youth named Peter Thompson outside the kebab shop in Tudor Parade. Thompson was found guilty of the murder in February 1993. Amongst the information received on 23 April was an allegation that Thompson was a member of the Acourts' gang (Message 40, see Chapter 13, para 25).

7.21   Kevin London, a 16 year old black youth, was confronted by a gang of white youths on 16th November 1992. He said that Gary Dobson was one of that gang, and that Gary Dobson threatened him with a large knife. No full report was made to the police at the time. On 28 April 1993, as a result of other information, the matter came to light, and statements were taken from Mr London and his girlfriend. No case followed. Gary Dobson denied involvement during his interviews after he was arrested for Stephen Lawrence's murder.

7.22 Gurdeep Banghal, a 22 year old Asian youth, was stabbed on 11 March 1993 by a white youth while serving in a Wimpy Bar in Eltham High Street. Information indicated that some of the suspects in the Stephen Lawrence murder were implicated. Witnesses failed to identify any of the suspects at later identification parades.

7.23 **We refer to these cases to highlight both the regularity of such offences and the lack in 1993 of co-ordinated information about them. It is vital that there should be full and readily available information about similar attacks or incidents as part of the detectives' armoury in their investigations.**

7.24 **At about 23:45 on 22 April we now know that Gary Dobson left Phineas Pett Road, and called at 102 Bournbrook Road. He told police at interview that he was going to collect a video. Surveillance did later confirm association between suspects.**

7.25 **A witness who has always been known as Witness K, in order to protect his identity, was to say in his only written statement that the Acourts and others were present at No 102 after the murder, and that one of them *"had his T-shirt off"* when Witness K visited the home on the night of the murder. He also said in that statement that one of those present said that they had not committed the murder.**

7.26 Other unsubstantiated reports gave other versions about that visit by Witness K, including the suggestion that some of those at No 102 had washed their hair, or even that they had been washing knives. None of these more vivid rumours or reports led to any further evidence or statements at any stage.

7.27 **Another witness, known as Witness B, in order to protect his identity, eventually gave a statement, alleging that he had seen one or other or both the Acourts and David Norris near the scene of the murder. Witness B was at the time on top of a bus. His evidence is dealt with elsewhere. Eventually no credence could be given to his account.**

7.28 Only Duwayne Brooks identified any of the suspects. The history of his evidence is also dealt with in detail elsewhere.

7.29 As the committal and trial papers show, the case against these youths was weak. Three, Neil Acourt, Luke Knight and Gary Dobson were later tried and acquitted in 1996. Jamie Acourt and David Norris were never committed for trial.

7.30 If these youths were involved in Stephen Lawrence's murder their characteristics would need no elaboration. The crime was a vicious and horrific example of racist violence. If they were not involved, then another group of white youths bore these characteristics.

7.31 **In any event as a result of the intrusive surveillance of late 1994, during the second investigation, we have confirmation that the suspects were then and certainly before that date infected and invaded by gross and revolting racism. Jamie Acourt was not subject to the surveillance, because he was in custody, charged with another offence involving violence in a night club. There is no reason to believe that he was any different from the others so far as overt racism is concerned.**

7.32 A version of part of the protracted record of the surveillance appears in the Appendices to this Report. We and those who attended the Inquiry saw and heard an edited version, lasting over an hour, of part of the many hours recorded. Mr Mellish summed up the tapes when he said that they showed *"appalling racist or raving bigotry"*. Mr Mansfield QC rightly referred to *"racism conjoined with an obsession to extreme violence"*, since on frequent occasions knives were brandished and carried, and stabbing movements and "demonstrations" were practised by the youths.

7.33 **There is no purpose in summarising these long recordings, but since some readers may not have access to our Appendices a flavour of what was repeatedly said should be given. We stress that the sentences used are only part of prolonged and appalling words which sully the paper upon which they have been recorded:-**

<u>Neil Acourt</u>. Sequence 11. *"I reckon that every nigger should be chopped up mate and they should be left with nothing but fucking stumps...."*

<u>David Norris</u>. Sequence 50. *"If I was going to kill myself do you know what I'd do? I'd go and kill every black cunt, every paki, every copper, every mug that I know..*

I'd go down to Catford and places like that I'm telling you now with two sub-machine guns and I'm telling you I'd take one of them, skin the black cunt alive mate, torture him, set him alight .... I'd blow their two legs and arms off and say go on you can swim home now .... (laughs)."

<u>Gary Dobson</u>. Sequence 27. *"He said the fucking black bastard I am going to kill him. I cracked up laughing. I went what black geezer. He went the Wimpy one the fucking black nigger cunt, fucking black bastard. I went what the Paki......"*

<u>Luke Knight</u>. Sequence 11. *".... it was Cameroon, a fucking nigger country... Fucking our presenters saying oh yeah we want Cameroon to win this, why the fuck should he want niggers to win it when they're playing something fucking like Italy....."*

7.34 **The whole sequence showed violent racism at its worst, and while one youth may say more than others they plainly all shared the bigotry and the extremes displayed by each other, both in language and in the brandishing and pretended stabbing with knives.**

7.35 This all showed what kind of people these youths were. But, as Mr Mellish expressly said, it did not add *"one iota"* to the evidence in respect of the murder charges. The Magistrate was persuaded to admit these recordings at the committal hearing, but we very much doubt whether they could have been put before a jury at trial.

7.36 In themselves the recordings showed abundantly that the suspects were the type of people who could or would have committed a crime of this kind. There was never any doubt but that the killers were rabid racists. There was virtually no probative value in these recordings as to the 1993 murder; they were prejudicial to a degree.

7.37 Even if the youths knew or suspected that they were being "bugged", which apparently they did, it is difficult to deduce from that fact any form of admission of involvement in the murder. The argument to that effect put forward at committal appears to us to be flawed. Certainly the tapes in themselves could not have been used to prove the case. Plainly the private prosecution team must have realised that, since no evidence was tendered at the trial after Mr Brooks' evidence had been exploded.

7.38   In 1997 the youths were summoned to appear at the full Inquest. Those proceedings are dealt with elsewhere (Chapter 42). None of them gave any evidence. They all claimed "privilege".

7.39   **Their final appearance was at Hannibal House on 29 and 30 June 1998. All five suspects came into the witness box, and answered questions under oath or affirmation. To say that they gave evidence would be to dignify their appearance. They all relied upon alleged lack of memory. They showed themselves to be arrogant and dismissive. They were forced to accept that numerous weapons had been found, both at 102 Bournbrook Road and elsewhere. A lethal hammer head suspended from a strap was found under some clothing in David Norris' bedroom. Gary Dobson could give nothing but a specious explanation about a large knife recovered from his girlfriend's bedroom. The sword found under the cushions at No 102 was said by the Acourts to be for decorative purposes.**

7.40   **It should be added that before they came to give evidence, as they were bound to do on pain of prosecution should they not have attended or should they have failed to answer questions, they went to the Divisional Court of the High Court in order to try to avoid attendance. Simon Brown LJ refused their application, but he indicated in plain terms that no questions were to be asked seeking to establish the youths' innocence or guilt. To that extent they were protected from full rigorous cross-examination, and indeed from any questions linking them with the murder. This ruling was plainly correct, since as Simon Brown LJ said the youths were not on trial, but the police were, since the Inquiry under the Police Act 1996 is directly an inquiry into every aspect of the policing of the murder.**

7.41   **The only true purpose or reason for calling the youths at all was thus to enquire whether their evidence helped us to any conclusions as to the policing of the murder. In that respect the extreme nature of their racism and violent tendencies suggest to us that they should have been "spotted" for what they were if good intelligence and information had singled them out earlier and detected their evil presence on the estate. Then perhaps they would have been even more obvious targets for early arrest.**

7.42   **Other than that their evidence performed little function in this Inquiry, except to highlight the fact that society allows such people to become or to be as they are. How society rids itself of such attitudes is not something which we can prescribe, except to stress the need for education and example at the youngest age, and an overall attitude of "zero tolerance" of racism within our society.**

7.43   **During the evidence of these five youths they had limited immunity from prosecution, in the sense that their answers could not be used against them in criminal proceedings which might later be brought against them. This did not mean that they could not be prosecuted for perjury, should it be plain that they were lying on oath or affirmation. Our own judgment, supported by legal advice, is that such prosecution should not be proposed by this Inquiry. Their evidence was evasive and vague, but that does not mean that it would be possible to prove that they were lying in the factual answers given. This Inquiry is not in any event a prosecuting authority. If the view of others differs from our's the matter can be reported to the police.**

7.44 **Before the Inquiry began the Chairman indicated that if evidence emerged which made it possible and right to indicate that these suspects were for sure or probably involved in the murder the Inquiry would not hesitate so to indicate. No such evidence has come before us. The situation remains as it was. These youths remain the five suspects, but nothing more than this is proved against them upon the evidence.**

7.45 **If the suspects had positively wished to protest their innocence they twice had the opportunity to do so. Simon Brown LJ pointed this out in his judgement. Neither at the Inquest nor before this Inquiry was the opportunity taken by any of the suspects. They refused to answer any questions, after taking legal advice, at the Inquest. Before this Inquiry they made sure that the questions were limited by taking High Court action in order to try to avoid giving evidence. The press and public cannot be blamed for voicing the suspicions about them which are current and which will remain alive, because nobody has been convicted of the brutal racist murder of Stephen Lawrence.**

7.46 Both we and others during our Part 2 hearings have considered, in the context of this case, whether the law which absolutely protects those who have been acquitted from any further prosecution for the same or a closely allied offence should prevail. If, even at this late stage, fresh and viable evidence should emerge against any of the three suspects who were acquitted, they could not be tried again however strong the evidence might be. We simply indicate that perhaps in modern conditions such absolute protection may sometimes lead to injustice. Full and appropriate safeguards would be essential . Fresh trials after acquittal would be exceptional. But we indicate that at least the issue deserves debate and reconsideration perhaps by the Law Commission, or by Parliament. (See Recommendation 38).

CHAPTER EIGHT

CORRUPTION AND COLLUSION

8.1 During the PCA investigation of the complaint made by Mr & Mrs Lawrence against the MPS the question of corruption and collusion was raised at a fairly late stage. Mr & Mrs Lawrence did not at first feel that they could co-operate with the Kent investigation, but during September 1997 they both gave all the help that they could. On 29 September Mr & Mrs Lawrence expressed the opinion that the quality and conduct of the first investigation could have been deliberately affected by collusion between one or more of the officers involved and one or more of the prime suspects or their families.

8.2 In evidence before this Inquiry Mr Lawrence said this:-

"I would say that both racism and corruption played a part in this investigation .... As to corruption I think that some police officers investigating my son's death were connected to the murderers in some way or other. We keep hearing all sorts of rumours .....".

8.3 In his closing remarks Mr Mansfield put the allegation in this way:-

"We shall be asking the Inquiry to draw such inferences - namely that there must have been collusion between members of the criminal fraternity and some police officers.

There are a number of stages that ultimately must be considered and viewed in a cumulative way. They are:-

(a) the occurrence in terms of quantity and the nature of serious basic errors, made by senior and experienced officers in this investigation, which cannot be explained by accident, oversight or overwork;

(b) clear and obvious examples of senior officers at the centre of this investigation colluding to cover up the truth about vital events; and

(c) the Norris factor."

8.4 **Mr Mansfield did accept that** *"This* [collusion] *is recognised to be a sensitive and controversial area even more difficult to demonstrate than racism".* **He also accepted that it should be** *"recognised that such allegations must be carefully considered and responsibly framed. Like many prosecution cases in relation to criminal allegations the courts trying them are asked to draw inferences from circumstantial evidence which can only be susceptible of one explanation".*

8.5 **These statements must be stressed. Furthermore in this area of the Inquiry it is necessary to indicate that the standard of proof to be applied must be the criminal standard. That is to say we can only reach a conclusion adverse to the MPS or individual officers if we are satisfied beyond reasonable doubt that collusion or corruption is established. In other areas of the case we are entitled to reach conclusions upon a balance of probability; and we are entitled also to voice suspicions should they** be found validly to exist. The standard of proof is not so rigid that we cannot make findings or indicate that a situation may exist otherwise than by applying the well known principles which govern litigation. But where such a serious allegation as collusion with criminals or corruption is made it would be wholly unfair to reach any adverse conclusion without being sure that such a conclusion was justified as a matter of evidence and proper inference.

8.6   We will look therefore at the evidence and the issues with these principles in mind, addressing both the serious basic errors identified in the case, and the specific examples of collusion particularised by Mr Mansfield, namely:-

> *"i.   The handling and non registration of the principal informant James Grant, and consequent events relating to witnesses "B" and "K".*
>
> *ii   All the events surrounding the now discredited Barker Review"* (see Chapter 28*).*

Perhaps more significantly we must take account of the final aspect of these allegations made by Mr Mansfield, namely "The Norris factor". Mr Mansfield warmed to his task in his final remarks in this connection and said that *"There is a matrix of quite exceptional coincidences and connections here which weave such a tight web around this investigation that only an ability to suspend disbelief can provide an innocent explanation".*

8.7   The trouble with such a broad and highly stated case is that it may in the end make proof that much more difficult. But we accept that we must look at all the material available with the greatest care. There was undoubtedly evidence of corruption or attempted corruption of a vital witness in the Stacey Benefield stabbing case, in which the suspect David Norris was accused. The strong inference is that Clifford Norris, David Norris' father, was behind that corruption and that he was closely involved in trying to pervert the course of justice by bribing Stacey Benefield and another witness involved in the case named Matthew Farman (see Chapter 9).

8.8   **In the Stephen Lawrence case there is no evidence of such interference with witnesses. The "Norris factor" is said to have involved the pulling of punches and the deliberate slowing down and "fudging" of the investigation, so that the suspects, and in particular the suspect David Norris, were protected and ineffectively pursued during the whole of the first investigation.**

8.9   No contact during the investigation between Clifford Norris or his agents and any AMIP police officer directly involved in the investigation has been alleged. We are asked to conclude by inference and because of earlier or indirect association that the influence of Clifford Norris must have been at work from the earliest days after Stephen Lawrence's murder and right through to the Barker Review. We are asked to conclude that the influence must in particular have governed or affected the decisions of the more senior officers almost from the start and that such influence must have been widespread.

8.10   Clifford Norris is at present in prison, serving a long sentence for offences involving drug dealing. The Customs & Excise sought to arrest him in 1988, but he avoided arrest and was not in fact caught until Mr Mellish's team, who were running the second investigation into Stephen Lawrence's murder, found him in Kent in August 1994.

8.11 Mr Mellish and his senior officers quickly decided that if possible Clifford Norris should be removed from the scene. It appeared to those officers that his influence while at large was potentially very damaging. Mr Mellish rightly suspected that Clifford Norris was directly in touch with his son and also some of the other suspects. Indeed Mr Mellish believes that Mr Norris could well have "schooled" the suspects both in connection with their arrests and interviews, and in respect of the possibility of intrusive surveillance.

8.12 Quite apart from this direct contact it was also apparent to the first investigating team that young and impressionable witnesses on and around the Brook Estate were holding back because of their fear or apprehension of the Norris family. Mr Bullock and others positively sensed this early on.

8.13 **Even with the knowledge that the evil influence of Clifford Norris was at work the first investigation team failed to seek him out. Positive efforts should have been made to remove Clifford Norris because of his obviously malign influence. It is inexplicable that more was not done until the summer of 1994 to arrest Clifford Norris, particularly after the Benefield bribery was uncovered.**

8.14 **In the body of this Report the other aspects of Clifford Norris' involvement with the police are fully set out. There is without doubt much suspicion about his activities with one officer in particular, namely Sgt XX (see Chapter 13). But that officer was never part of the investigation team. His limited appearance in 1996 during the trial occurred while Mr Mellish was in charge.**

8.15 It must be noted that David Norris was never identified by any witness, and he was not charged with the murder of Stephen Lawrence in 1993. It may seem less likely that Clifford Norris would seek to protect others who were identified and charged during the first investigation. But it must be recalled that David Norris told the Inquiry that Clifford Norris had known both the Acourts since they were five or six years old and that Neil Acourt *"liked"* Clifford Norris because he *"thought he was a nice man"*. Neil Acourt and Gary Dobson visited Clifford Norris in prison. Thus his interest in the other suspects has to be noted. He was in prison when the suspects were arrested in 1995. That would make interference in the second investigation more difficult but certainly not impossible. There is no allegation of corruption or collusion against the second investigating team.

8.17 Furthermore, as we point out later, any conspiracy or attempted corruption of police officers would necessarily have involved action involving members of the team who were making the early and important decisions. There is no evidence of contact by Clifford Norris or any of his agents with any member of the team. His chosen method in the Benefield case was to try to bribe witnesses.

8.18 **The problems in seeking to establish that there was collusion or corruption by inference are obvious. It is right that we should say at once that no collusion or corruption is proved to have infected the investigation of Stephen Lawrence's murder. It would be wrong and unfair to conclude otherwise. It seems to us sensible to record this conclusion at once, so that the text of this Report can be read with this in mind.**

CHAPTER NINE

THE STACEY BENEFIELD CASE

9.1   On 18 March 1993, and thus before Stephen Lawrence's murder, a young white man named Stacey Benefield was stabbed in the chest whilst he was walking in an Eltham street. At the time he was with another young man named Matthew Farman. Later Mr Benefield named and identified David Norris as his assailant. He also said that Neil Acourt was with David Norris at the time. It appears that David Norris accused Mr Farman of calling him names, and produced a miniature sword about nine inches long. Mr Farman ran off, and Mr Norris and Mr Acourt chased him. Mr Benefield followed, asking what the problem was. Mr Norris at once told Mr Benefield to shut up and stabbed him in the chest. Neil Acourt was described as standing by and watching.

9.2   Neither Mr Benefield nor Mr Farman were prepared to give statements or to help the police at first. Thus although the attack was reported no arrest could be made. It is suggested that the reason for the young men's reluctance may be that they knew that David Norris' father was Clifford Norris. Both witnesses may have believed that if they helped the police there would be some form of retribution meted out to them by or on behalf of the Norris family.

9.3   Information reaching the Stephen Lawrence investigation team included the allegation that the Acourts and David Norris were responsible for the attack on Stacey Benefield. In particular this information came from the informant known as "James Grant" who walked into the police station on 23 April. This information was repeated in other messages received.

9.4   DS Davidson saw Stacey Benefield on Sunday 25 April, and Mr Benefield made a statement which named David Norris as his attacker and Neil Acourt as his accomplice.

9.5   **David Norris was identified both by Mr Benefield and Mr Farman as the attacker at an identification parade held at Southwark on 13 May 1993. Neil Acourt was also identified by both witnesses as having been with David Norris at the time of the attack. They were both charged on the same day with attempted murder.**

9.6   David Norris and Neil Acourt faced committal proceedings on 27 May 1993. Only David Norris was sent for trial. After some delay the trial of David Norris started on 15 November 1993 at the Central Criminal Court, before His Honour Judge Richardson, who has since died, and a jury.

9.7   **Meanwhile, shortly after David Norris was charged, both witnesses were approached by a man named Raymond Dewar, who was known to both of them. Mr Dewar wanted the witnesses to meet somebody else who, he said, *"wished to make things right"*, and who would give them money in order that they should not support the charge against David Norris. Both men resisted these approaches, but Mr Benefield eventually gave way, and was taken by Mr Dewar and another man to Eltham Park where he met a man who is believed to have been Clifford Norris.**

9.8   This man made a veiled threat to Mr Benefield, and he then handed £2,000 in cash to Mr Benefield saying that there would be more to follow and intimating that he wanted the case against David Norris dropped. He used the following expression, *"this is how I sort people out not by shooting them"*, or words to that effect. A further meeting was arranged by Mr Dewar at which the same man, presumed to be Clifford Norris, demanded that Mr Benefield should contact a firm of solicitors whose name was given and change his story with a view to the prosecution being abandoned. A further sum of £3,000 was promised to Mr Benefield, which was to be paid when the charges were dropped. Mr Benefield said that he took the first £2,000 because he was too frightened to refuse.

9.9   Mr Benefield's evidence about the money is corroborated because officers including DC Tomlin, checked at various shops where Mr Benefield had told them that he had spent the money, which had been paid largely in £50 notes. Mr Benefield paid £500 to Mr Farman.

9.10   Mr Dewar approached both witnesses thereafter, and a further meeting was held between Mr Benefield and the man presumed to be Clifford Norris at the Black Prince Hotel in Bexley. On this occasion the man was even more insistent that Mr Benefield should follow his instructions.

9.11   After this meeting Mr Benefield decided that he had to bring the events to someone else's attention, and before contacting the police he spoke to a local councillor and to others. Eventually the matter was reported to the police on 12 June 1993. After that both Mr Benefield and Mr Farman were treated as protected witnesses. SO10 (the Special Operations Group of MPS) were informed of the facts, but in the end the protection of the two witnesses was conducted by officers from the Stephen Lawrence murder team, with liaison from SO10.

9.12   **Mr Dewar was arrested on 19 June 1993 and he was charged with perverting the course of justice. On 9 December 1993 that case was heard and he was found not guilty.**

9.13   The trial of David Norris started at the Central Criminal Court on 15 November 1993. The prosecution were represented by Counsel, and David Norris was defended by Mr Stephen Batten QC, who was instructed by Mr Henry Milner.

9.14   The prosecution case was opened and both Mr Benefield and Mr Farman gave evidence, and the remainder of the prosecution evidence was read to the Court. David Norris gave evidence in his own defence but called no witnesses. The trial, excluding the Judge's summing up, was completed by lunch time on Tuesday 16 November 1993.

9.15   **When the Court reconvened at 14:00 Counsel were informed that a juror had approached one of David Norris' escorts, who was employed by a private company, and told the escort that the verdict would be one of not guilty. The escort brought this matter to the attention of the Clerk of the Court who made a note of the events, which was passed to the Judge. Counsel then saw the Judge in his Chambers. Counsel later informed DC Hughes, who was the officer in the case, that the Judge had stated that he would discharge the juror should the defence make an application to do so, but that he would "think hard" about it should the prosecution make such an application.**

9.16   DC Hughes reminded Counsel of the history of the case, particularly stressing the Dewar aspect. Understandably he told Counsel that he suspected impropriety, and asked that the application to discharge the juror should be made. Counsel declined to make the application, but the matter was adjourned until the next day in order that DC Hughes could seek advice. At this point DC Hughes contacted Mr Bullock who then spoke to Mr Medwynter of the CPS. Mr Medwynter's view was that application should be made for the juror to be discharged. It was agreed that a conference should be held on the next day after all parties had received relevant advice.

9.17   Mr Bullock attended the conference and told Counsel that the police view was that an application should be made to the Judge to discharge the juror, or alternatively to arrange for a completely fresh trial. After further consultation it appears that the Judge was told what the police view was, but no application was made to discharge the juror or for a fresh trial. Accordingly the trial continued. The Judge summed up, and David Norris was acquitted.

9.18   The juror involved was in fact the foreman of the jury. Inquiries revealed that that man was arrested in September 1993 and that he was suspected of dishonestly handling a cheque for £23,000 at his place of work. The juror "surfaced" during our Inquiry, in the sense that he gave an interview to a national newspaper. In that interview he indicated that the jury had simply been impressed by David Norris as a witness. He did not respond to a request to provide further information.

9.19   On 18 November 1993 Mr Bullock was again contacted by the escort who told him that at the end of the trial, after David Norris had been released from custody, the same juror had again approached the escort and asked to be furnished with David Norris' home address so that he could offer him employment.

9.20   The whole incident is plainly most disturbing. Unfortunately His Honour Judge Richardson has since died. No further information is available as to the reason why no formal application was made to him.

9.21   **From the point of view of this Inquiry the most sinister aspect of the case concerns the bribery of Mr Benefield. We do not know, and presumably we will never know, what in fact prompted the juror to act as he did. Nor will we know what led the jury to acquit David Norris. The matter of most concern is whether or not the clear evidence of the payment of money by Clifford Norris supports the suggestion that his evil influence must have been brought to bear on the Stephen Lawrence investigation. His presence in the background clearly raises much suspicion.**

9.22   **On the other hand it is apparent from the Benefield case that if Clifford Norris was involved his chosen technique was bribery of witnesses. There is no indication that he approached the police or that he made contact with any police officer directly or indirectly in that case.**

9.23   This is perhaps not surprising, since Clifford Norris was on the run in connection with very serious crimes. Even he might not have been willing to compromise his position by approaching police officers directly or indirectly. Furthermore it is apparent that the police officers involved in this case were keen that the Benefield case should be put right, if possible, either by discharging the juror or by arranging for a new trial. It seems to us that these steps ought to have been taken.

9.24   **It must further be stressed that after David Norris had been arrested both in connection with the Stephen Lawrence murder and the Benefield case no further steps were taken against him in the Stephen Lawrence case until he was arrested in April 1995 in respect of the second investigation leading to the private prosecution. After his arrest in May 1993 he refused to answer any questions about the Stephen Lawrence murder. He was not identified, and he was not in fact charged with murder at that stage. Later the case was discontinued against the two men who had been charged, namely Neil Acourt and Luke Knight.**

9.25   Therefore David Norris was not in direct peril of trial during 1993 or 1994 while Clifford Norris was still at large. Furthermore there is no evidence of any approach being made to the witnesses in respect of the Stephen Lawrence murder. The only witness to identify anybody was Duwayne Brooks, and he has never indicated to us that there was any kind of approach made to him.

9.26   **Nor is there any evidence that any approach was made by Clifford Norris to any of the police officers connected with the Stephen Lawrence murder. It would be most unfair and unjust to draw any conclusion against any of those officers in the absence of any indication or allegation that they have been involved or connected with Clifford Norris except as indicated in the Chapters of this report dealing with the individual officers.**

9.27   **The sinister nature of the Stacey Benefield case and of Clifford Norris' involvement are self evident. But there is in our view no evidence to support the suggestion that the Benefield case should cast a direct adverse shadow upon anybody involved in the Stephen Lawrence investigation, either witnesses or police officers, in order to support allegations of collusion or corruption in connection with the Stephen Lawrence case.**

CHAPTER TEN

FIRST AID

10.1   On the evening of 22 April 1993, Mr & Mrs Conor Taaffe had been to a prayer meeting at their local Catholic church. The church is a short distance north of the point where Stephen fell. They started to walk towards the Well Hall roundabout, and they noticed two young black boys who were running towards them. In his statement Mr Taaffe said that he saw *"a couple of young black boys who were jogging along. They seemed to be running. Also at the time I did sense immediately something wrong, something dangerous, something suspicious ...."*. Mr Taaffe accepted that he did instinctively at first think that an "attack or mugging" might be imminent. Almost instantaneously he overcame that instinctive reaction.

10.2   Mr Taaffe saw that Stephen Lawrence was holding his upper chest with one of his hands, as if he might have been injured in that area. The Taaffes then saw Stephen Lawrence *"crash onto the pavement"*. At once they realised that something very serious had happened, and as soon as they came up to the scene they saw Mr Brooks standing in the middle of the road trying to flag down passing cars. Then they saw him go to the telephone box on the other side of the road, just in front of the church.

10.3   **Mr Taaffe remembered that about a week or two before he had seen a television broadcast talking about St John's Ambulance and giving a description of the recovery position. He was bothered that he could not remember the detail of what had been said sufficiently for him to be confident enough to try to put Stephen into the correct position. But his wife almost at once said *"Oh no, no Conor, he is in the correct position, he is in the recovery position already"*.**

10.4   As Stephen lay on the pavement Mr Taaffe remembers an involuntary movement of the head to the left and a sound as if Stephen was choking and trying to breathe. Mr Taaffe put his hand on Stephen's back and felt some movement.

10.5   Meanwhile, Mr Brooks had made his telephone call to the emergency services and had kicked the telephone, obviously in total frustration after he had tried to flag down cars which drove by. It should be said at once that Mr Brooks was a victim of this terrible onslaught by these young men. Fortunately he escaped physical injury. He was in great distress and obviously confused and very upset. He has been described as *"distraught" and "hysterical"*, and many other descriptions of his condition have been given in evidence. Mr Taaffe described Mr Brooks as *"acting in a desperate and adrenalinated manner"*. PC Geddis said that he was "very upset, understandably upset". Catherine Avery described him as *"distraught and crying"*. He did give a short account of the matter to Mr & Mrs Taaffe, saying to them that some white boys had got Stephen Lawrence and one of them had had an iron bar. Mr Taaffe's reaction was to think *"My God, what did they do with an iron bar to sort of cause these injuries?"*. He saw quite a lot of blood on the pavement and thought that there may have been a severe internal injury.

10.6   Mr Taaffe has no direct memory of the arrival of PC & Mrs Geddis on the scene, but he does remember a man with a beard joining him and his wife near Stephen. After that the first police car arrived, and in that car were PCs Linda Bethel and Anthony Gleason. Mr Taaffe remembered the police woman immediately coming to the area of Stephen's head. He told PC Bethel what Mr Brooks had said. Mr Taaffe believes that within a minute or two of the arrival of the police Stephen had stopped breathing. PC Bethel put a finger to the front of Stephen's mouth and said that she thought that there was some breathing. Mr Taaffe tried the same test and felt nothing. The other police officer, the male police officer, seemed to be in the background, according to Mr Taaffe.

10.7　When the ambulance came it was evident to Mr Taaffe that Stephen was dead. After Stephen's body was taken away, Mr & Mrs Taaffe said to PC Bethel that they were going to go back to the church to pray for Stephen. Mr Taaffe remembered no large police vehicles at the scene before the ambulance came, and indeed before he left.

10.8　When he came back about an hour later there was a PC standing outside a cordon of yellow plastic tape. Mr Taaffe was not conscious of large numbers of officers or indeed of any team of police officers in action at the scene.

10.9　In his evidence Mr Taaffe remembers that PC Bethel stood up and spoke to Mr Brooks or dealt with Mr Brooks, but he confirmed that PC Bethel was indeed crouching down beside the body of Stephen with himself and his wife until the ambulance came. Mr Taaffe did not recall the presence of PC Geddis and his wife, who were plainly at the scene for a substantial time. He does recall PC Gleason leaving the scene to try to find the ambulance.

10.10　It is of course a common experience that memories of an event such as this vary considerably, and any of those present at the scene may be forgiven for not remembering exactly who was where and at what particular moment. Towards the end of his evidence Mr Taaffe said that it was incorrect to say that either his wife or anybody else cradled Stephen's head. This had been reported in the press, and Mr Taaffe said that he supposed that this was indeed *"a loving image, but those are not the facts. She did put her hand on Stephen's head"* said Mr Taaffe, *"and whispered in his ear 'You are loved, you are loved'."*

10.11　A poignant passage in his evidence was that which described his return home when he washed the blood off his hands with some water into a container and poured the water with Stephen's blood in it at the foot of a rose tree.

10.12　**Mr Taaffe's conclusion, as set out in his statement, was that *"looking back on the incident I feel that neither the police nor ambulance staff can be criticised for their actions at the scene"*. He also said that he was of the opinion that further First Aid attempts would have been futile, since Stephen needed a surgeon and not First Aid.**

10.13　The actions of Mr & Mrs Taaffe deserve nothing but praise. They had no training in emergency First Aid, and their actions and attitude are to be applauded.

10.14　**We should say at once that it is the truth that nothing done to Stephen as he lay on the pavement would, in fact, have made any difference, since his loss of blood was extreme. This is confirmed by the doctor who saw Stephen when he was taken to Brook Hospital and by later medical evidence which is available to the Inquiry. That does not mean that steps should not have been taken to follow the rubrics taught to the officers present in their First Aid training. They had no way to know how severe the injuries actually were and they should have performed First Aid in case Stephen's life could have been saved.**

10.15　**The first police officer on the scene was in fact PC James Geddis. He has almost completed thirty years service in the MPS. He was off duty on the night of 22 April, and with his wife he was going home from a prayer meeting. He drove down Well Hall Road, and his attention was drawn to a body lying on the pavement. He actually drove past but turned round and came back to the scene.**

10.16   His immediate reaction was that Stephen Lawrence was in the recovery position. He was lying partly on his right side with one leg up and with one arm extended. One of the reasons why PC Geddis came back was that he had seen Mr Brooks going backwards and forwards across the road and running about waving his arms in the roadway. PC Geddis at once asked Mr Brooks what had happened and in his own words *"all I got was that he had been hit with an iron bar and they had gone, and that was it"*. PC Geddis made a second call at the telephone box where the telephone had been left off the hook by Mr Brooks. PC Geddis told us that he did not know the seriousness of the injury until the ambulance men took Stephen Lawrence onto the stretcher, when he realised how much blood there was underneath.

10.17   There are records in connection with the First Aid courses or refresher training carried out by the police officers involved. PC Geddis' latest certificate expired in June 1993. More will be said about First Aid training later. PC Geddis thought that he could see Stephen's back moving up and down and concluded that he was still breathing, and he also believed that, since Stephen was in the recovery position, he should not be moved. PC Geddis was at the scene when PCs Bethel and Gleason arrived in their panda car. He confirms that Mr Brooks was in a state of *"understandable distress"*.

10.18   PC Geddis was cross-examined on behalf of Mr & Mrs Lawrence by Mr Kamlish. He told the Inquiry that he formed the opinion, when he arrived, that Stephen Lawrence was being looked after and was breathing and was in the recovery position and he felt that it was his duty, if possible, to get information and to ensure that expert help had been summoned to the scene. He felt it best to leave Stephen where he was. The simple fact is that he took no positive step to do anything in connection with Stephen as he lay on the pavement. There was some dispute as to when PC Geddis first saw blood around or near the body. In this connection, Mr Kamlish accused PC Geddis of lying, since the suggestion was that the blood must have been obvious from the start.

10.19   **We formed a favourable impression of PC Geddis and we reject the suggestion that he was not speaking the truth. He was after all the Good Samaritan who stopped when he saw that something had happened on the pavement. Once he came to the scene he was effectively on duty since Police Constables have to take action in accordance with their position, even if they are technically off duty. But we feel that it is hard indeed to accuse PC Geddis of negligence or of thoughtlessness. As with other officers we are sure that any deficiency in the actions taken by PC Geddis was caused by lack of training rather than lack of the will to help. He provided his own rug or blanket to cover Stephen. His failure to provide First Aid or to see that it was provided did not arise from bad motives. He assumed that Stephen was being cared for by others, and after making the second telephone call for the ambulance he, like others, relied upon the imminent arrival of the ambulance.**

10.20   We should finally mention in this context that PC Geddis, when he was seen by the Kent Police force in 1997, said that he felt shocked by what he had seen and felt that *"it was such a waste because I thought he was known to like people in my own family."* His own daughter was in fact in the same class as Stephen Lawrence at school. Six to eight weeks after the murder Police Sergeant Peter Solley told Mrs Lawrence about the part played by PC Geddis and his wife at the scene. Mrs Lawrence asked PSgt Solley to pass on to them her thanks for trying to help Stephen at that time.

10.21 **We have no hesitation in saying that there was no racist motivation or reluctance in PC Geddis' failure to do anything to Stephen Lawrence. He wrongly thought that the best thing was to leave him where he was in order to allow the paramedics to take over, once the ambulance came.**

10.22 Before dealing with the evidence of the other police officers who came to the scene, it should be noted that Mr Brooks' telephone call was made at 22:43. The second telephone call to the emergency services was made at 22:48. The ambulance arrived at the scene at about 22:55. The ambulance arrived at Brook Hospital at 23:05. Dr Patel first saw Stephen Lawrence at 23:07, and he certified that Stephen was dead at 23:17.

10.23 **PCs Bethel and Gleason were alerted probably as a result of the first telephone call. They would have taken only minutes to have come from Plumstead Police Station to the scene. They parked their car by the side of the road near to the body of Stephen Lawrence. The probability is that they were at the scene by about 22:50. So that they were probably with Stephen and the others at the scene for only about five minutes before the ambulance arrived.**

10.24 PC Bethel at once saw a large amount of blood near Stephen's body, and called her control room asking them to hurry up the arrival of the ambulance. At that stage, PC Bethel said that PC Gleason was going to *"head for Stephen Lawrence"*, and she decided to deal with Mr Brooks. She did look to see what might be done in connection with Stephen. She had been told that Stephen had a head injury, and she also concluded that he was in the recovery position when she arrived. There was no obvious wound to see where the blood was coming from, and she believed that the ambulance would be there within minutes. She told the Inquiry that her understanding of head injuries was that they can bleed *"an awful lot more than a normal wound and that doesn't actually suggest that it is incredibly serious"*.

10.25 **Misapprehension as to the nature of the injury is a feature of the evidence of all those who were present. This does not mean that nothing should have been done to try to trace the bleeding. But we believe that PC Bethel's reaction was understandable. Again, as with PC Geddis, the root of the trouble appears to us to have been lack of training rather than any casual approach to what she saw. PC Bethel was trained in First Aid. Her latest certificate was granted on 21 January 1992. If that training had proper content she should have known that it was essential to check at once the source of the bleeding as an elementary first step.**

10.26 For part of the time that she was present at the scene she did deal with Mr Brooks. He was walking or moving about the scene and was in a state of extreme distress. She says that she spent quite a lot of time trying to get details from Mr Brooks, and repeatedly asked him questions. All that she could get from him was that the injuries had been inflicted by a group of six white men. He was using strong language, and was very upset and was indicating roundly that he had not called the police and that he was extremely angry that the ambulance had not come first. As we point out in Chapter 4, PC Bethel's assessment of Mr Brooks at the scene is in marked contrast to her later more critical assessment, particularly as given in evidence to the Kent inquiry.

10.27 We accept that PC Bethel did try to feel a pulse in Stephen Lawrence's neck. Catherine Avery saw this being done, from her home next to the scene. Mr Taaffe confirms that she put her fingers in front of Stephen's mouth to see if there was breathing. PC Bethel believed that she felt a faint pulse and that she felt some degree of breathing. It may well be that this was a mistaken conclusion, but she did at least make that effort to see if there was some life left in Stephen. Afterwards, it is evident that she remained close to the body, but, like Mr & Mrs Taaffe, she did nothing to move Stephen or to adjust his position on the ground so that she could see where the blood was coming from. As the ambulance men picked Stephen Lawrence up she did, of course, see how much blood there was. She still hoped and believed that Stephen would recover.

10.28 **PC Bethel's last refresher course in First Aid took place in 1992. Very little detail could be gleaned from her or from any of the police officers as to what was actually contained in such a refresher course. It is the opinion of the Inquiry that First Aid training and refresher training of police officers as revealed in this case must have been wholly inadequate.**

10.29 Mr Kamlish rigorously cross-examined PC Bethel, and put to her that the first elementary action in First Aid where heavy bleeding is observed is to trace the source of the bleeding and try to staunch the flow. It was her firm brlief that Stephen Lawrence should be left where he was, so she did not obtain a First Aid kit or a torch from the car or turn the lights of the car on to him in order to carry out a closer examination. Towards the end of her cross-examination PC Bethel accepted that she now regrets that she did not look for the injury. But that is said with hindsight, and reveals that PC Bethel was at least prepared to accept now that something else should have been done. That, however, does not mean that her approach to Stephen Lawrence as he lay on the pavement was positively callous or unthinking, even though she took no steps in connection with the bleeding which she had observed. Her inactivity may have been partly caused by her hope that the ambulance woulsd arrive and that professionals would take over.

10.30 There was no indication given to us during her long cross-examination that PC Bethel would have acted differently if the person on the pavement had been white.

10.31 After the ambulance went away, PC Bethel stayed at the scene, and did duties as directed by her seniors. She cannot herself be blamed for any lack of direction or initiative. She saw senior officers present, including Chief Superintendent John Philpott and Chief Inspector Jonathan McIvor. She somewhat graphically described *"quite a lot of senior officers standing around with their hands on their hips"*. She assisted in taping off the area at Dickson Road, , and she took part in what she calls the more serious search in Dickson Road looking for a weapon. She was there when the police dogs arrived and towards the end of her attendance at the scene she made her notes on a bench nearby. There is some criticism of her for doing this, but we do not believe that such criticism is justified. There were other things that she might have done, but she believed that it was important to recall what Mr Brooks had said.

10.32 **When seen by the Kent Police, PC Bethel was asked about the racist aspects of this case, and she said that this had played no part in her conclusions or in what she had done or failed to do. Her failure to administer positive First Aid was primarily the result of the poor level of training. We believe that if she had thought something needed to be done then she would have done it in order to try to help Stephen Lawrence.**

10.33 PC Bethel was further criticised by Mr Macdonald QC on behalf of Mr Brooks. It was suggested that the officer should have asked Mr Brooks if he was injured and that she should have paid more or closer attention to him. There is no doubt that Mr Brooks was in a state of shock and tension and would not have been easy to deal with. There is absolutely no blame to be attributed to him in this regard, because he was a victim and was suffering very considerable stress and distress, both at the scene and thereafter. Mr Macdonald further suggested that PC Bethel was not speaking the truth when she said that Mr Brooks had indicated to her that he had not actually seen the assault on Stephen Lawrence. It is apparent that PC Bethel dealt only briefly with Mr Brooks before turning her attention to Stephen Lawrence.

10.34 PC Gleason also gave evidence. His last refresher course in First Aid appears to have been given in August 1991. He agreed that he arrived at the scene at about 22:50 and in his statement his first description was of "a group of people standing around Stephen Lawrence who was laying on the floor in the recovery position". PC Gleason thought that there was blood around the back, around where the shoulders were. He saw people beside the body, but he did not know who they were. He said that he looked at Stephen Lawrence's head but could find no serious injury to it. He also says that he felt for a pulse and thought that he had found a very weak one. This officer also said that he examined Stephen's body with some care, starting at the head and working downwards. We have to conclude that this was probably not done. He said that there was no evidence to suggest where any wound might have been. Nobody else saw PC Gleason check the body for wounds or injury. Certainly PC Gleason, like the others at the scene, did nothing to administer First Aid by seeking the source of the bleeding and attempting to staunch it. As to the pulse, basic First Aid should teach that the automatic response to failure to detect an adequate pulse at the wrist should be followed by an immediate move upwards to feel for the pulse in the neck.

10.35 **Police must not rely upon the immediate arrival of paramedic help to obviate their responsibility to carry out immediate First Aid. The elementary steps to be taken by anyone who has a minimum of training are to check the airways, to check the breathing, and to check the circulation. This is the *"ABC"* of First Aid. The fact is that PC Gleason, like the others present at the scene, left Stephen where he was, in the mistaken belief that nothing should have been done to move him. Heavy bleeding must be traced as a high priority in a case like this. Police officers ought to have known that.**

10.36 PC Gleason was also firmly cross-examined at length by Mr Kamlish. He stuck to his story, namely that he had examined the body of Stephen Lawrence as it lay on the pavement. As we have already indicated, we doubt very much whether this examination took place. This officer like the others said and indicated that he felt at the time that, because the ambulance was on its way, Stephen was best left in the position that he was in.

10.37 It is of some significance that during his time at the scene PC Gleason went in his car, in the hope of expediting the arrival of the ambulance. This action by him was again subject to firm criticism through Mr Kamlish. Whether he should have left the scene or not is doubtful, since radio contact must have been available, but we do not believe that PC Gleason left otherwise than to do what he said that he was doing. He did not find the ambulance and when he came back he took no further steps in connection with Stephen Lawrence, and shortly after that the ambulance came and he accompanied the ambulance to the hospital.

10.38 **Any deficiency in what PC Gleason did or failed to do in connection with First Aid was in part attributable to lack of satisfactory training. On the other hand the evidence is that such refresher training as these officers received included training as to the essential need to staunch bleeding. It may well be that PC Gleason was also simply hoping for the immediate arrival of the ambulance. We have to conclude that he did to some extent embellish his evidence by indicating that he had done more than we believe that he did by way of examination at the scene. To that extent his evidence was unsatisfactory. He has perhaps persuaded himself that he did more, in the knowledge that he ought to have done more at the time. There is no indication that he was consciously affected by the fact that Stephen Lawrence was black, and that Mr Brooks was also black and was acting in the way which has been described.**

10.39   The last police witness in connection with the First Aid issue, other than professional and expert witnesses was PC Joanne Smith. She was herself called to the scene some time after 22:45. When she got there PCs Bethel and Gleason had already arrived, so that she was there for a shorter time than the other officers. She at once saw that Stephen Lawrence was lying on the pavement covered with a blanket. That blanket had come from the car of PC Geddis, and after the body was covered with the blanket it may be that the blood was less visible to those who came to the scene. PC Smith took no part in the immediate looking after or tending of Stephen Lawrence, but she went to the hospital with Mr Brooks as her passenger. Mr Brooks understandably wanted to go with Stephen in the ambulance, but the paramedics in charge of the ambulance said that that was not possible. All that PC Smith gleaned from Mr Brooks was that he and Stephen had been attacked by some white youths and that Stephen had been hit. She dropped Mr Brooks off at the hospital and collected some scenes of crime tape out of the Area car and took it back to the scene.

10.40   **Later she described Mr Brooks as being highly excitable and particularly unco-operative. She found him to have been aggressive and shouting and swearing whilst she drove him to the hospital. He was all the time in a very agitated condition, but she said that he did calm down somewhat as he sat in the car with her.**

10.41   In common with many other officers PC Smith made no note of what happened on the night in question. She says that she was not asked to make a note, but that she made a statement later in June 1993. Mr Kamlish challenged PC Smith as to her experience or knowledge of racism in the police force.

10.42   It should be noted that when she left to take Mr Brooks to the hospital she confirmed that none of the Territorial Support Group Units had arrived at the scene. She did not recall them being there at any time whilst Stephen was still at the scene. She did suggest that she may have missed seeing them. Upon her return she confirmed that other Units including the TSG had arrived.

10.43   **We do not accept the full thrust of the criticisms of PC Smith advanced by Mr Macdonald in his cross-examination on behalf of Mr Brooks, namely, that she was trying in some way to suggest that he had been *"nothing but a bloody nuisance that night"*. She reported exactly what she had experienced in her short dealings with Mr Brooks at the scene and en route to the hospital. On the other hand it must be said that this officer together with others could and should have shown much more interest in and sympathy for this vital witness both at the scene, where he should have been used to assist in immediate searches for possible perpetrators, and at the hospital where he should have been carefully dealt with as a potential witness and as a victim. Everybody agrees, and the officers themselves agreed, that Mr Brooks was wholly understandably in a state of great distress and agitation. Nobody should blame him for the things that he said at the scene and thereafter. He was a primary victim of the terrible conduct of the young men who killed his friend, and any excitement and stress shown by him is understandable. The virtual abandonment of Mr Brooks at the hospital is to be deplored. Furthermore PC Smith, like PC Bethel, allowed herself to use much more colourful language about Mr Brooks to Kent than she had used in her 1993 statement. We have to say that PC Smith stereotyped Mr Brooks, and failed to treat him as a primary victim.**

10.44   **Two other witnesses most relevant to the issue of First Aid are, of course, the ambulance men who came to the scene. They are Messrs Geoffrey Mann and Michael Salih. Both of them confirm that Stephen Lawrence was lying in what was *"almost the recovery*** *position"* when they arrived. They went to check Stephen Lawrence and found no pulse, and no breathing, and they found that his eyes were fixed and dilated. They immediately put Stephen's body in the ambulance and carried out resuscitation en route to the hospital. Both paramedics confirmed that there was a lot of blood in the area of Stephen's chest, and both of them saw Mr Brooks in a distraught state. He tried to get into the ambulance with his friend, but the paramedics rightly did not allow this to take place.

10.45   Both these men, and the doctors later on, confirmed that First Aid would not, in fact, have made any difference to Stephen's condition. It is confirmed by the post mortem findings that the stab wounds inflicted on Stephen Lawrence were fatal. No medical, surgical or First Aid intervention could in the circumstances have saved his life. He must have been dead a short time after he hit the pavement. **It is of importance from the police officers' point of view, that when Mr Salih was questioned, he said that he would not have advised anyone to move Stephen Lawrence. Knowing that the report had been of a head injury he believed that somebody in that condition should have been left where he was until professional help was available. This does not detract from the necessity when heavy bleeding is observed to examine the patient in order to try to staunch the blood. But Mr Salih's opinion of the situation as he saw it provides some mitigation to the police officers who failed to do anything in respect of Stephen by way of First Aid.**

10.46   Other witnesses who saw Stephen as he lay on the pavement gave evidence to the Inquiry. Miss Catherine Avery and Miss Helen Avery are sisters who lived in the house immediately next to the scene. Miss Helen Avery had been out for the evening with her parents, and her sister was present in the house when the family returned. Both of them confirmed, from their different points of view, that nothing positive had been done in connection with Stephen's body as he lay on the ground. Miss Catherine Avery saw PC Bethel trying to check Stephen's pulse. They saw no other attempts to discover wounds or to take any active step to trace the bleeding. **Miss Helen Avery was only 14 years old at the time, and she was amazed that no-one was attending to the body on the floor or trying to stem the flow of blood. She saw that there was a lot of blood and her knowledge of First Aid told her that something ought to have been done. This evidence is revealing, because a 14 year old girl properly instructed in First Aid knew what ought to have been done where heavy bleeding is observed. Yet police officers who were trained or allegedly trained in First Aid did not appreciate that this was an immediate action which ought to have been taken.**

10.47   In the context of First Aid it is next necessary to refer to the arrival of the first TSG vehicle. There is much confusion as to the number of the first vehicle to arrive, and as to the names of those who were on the vehicle. That will be dealt with in more detail in the section dealing with the initial response to the murder. It does appear from their evidence, however, that those present included Police Sergeant Nigel Clement, Police Sergeant Andrew Hodges, who was a PC in 1993, and in particular, Inspector Steven Groves. There is, as will appear later, also considerable confusion as to who was on which of the TSG carriers. But both PSgt Clement and Mr Groves, who is an important witness in this case, indicated that they got off one of the carriers very close to the place where Stephen Lawrence's body lay.

10.48   Other officers said that they saw the scene, including the body of Stephen Lawrence on the footpath, either from the inside the carrier or from the roadway just outside it. PSgt Clement said in his original statement that upon attending the scene he saw *a male laying on the pavement near number 318*. He said that the man was lying on the pavement close to a large tree, and during his evidence he indicated that the tree must have cast a shadow over the body since he was unable to tell if there was any blood around the body. He says that he saw no blood at that time or indeed at any other time whilst Stephen Lawrence still lay on the pavement. Mr Groves was, of course, the officer in charge of the Unit. PSgt Clement was effectively his second-in-command on immediate arrival at the scene. It is apparent, from cross-examination, that PSgt Clement did not enquire about the state of the casualty on the ground, in particular as to whether he was alive or needed treatment or whether an ambulance was on its way. PSgt Clement played no part in the actions which might have been necessary in respect of First Aid or attention to Stephen Lawrence. Similarly PSgt Hodges, who made a statement on 1 May 1993, told us that there were people attending to Stephen Lawrence. He said that there was nothing that he felt he could do there after he got off the carrier. He agrees that he must have got off the carrier because he went with Mr Groves to the Welcome Inn. He was cross-examined on the basis that he had arrived after the ambulance had left the scene, but he reiterated that he saw a man lying on the floor with others around him. It was apparent, however, that his memory was cloudy, since he had no recollection of seeing PC & Mrs Geddis or Mr & Mrs Taaffe at the scene.

10.49   Mr Groves told the Inquiry that he was on the first carrier to arrive at the scene. He was hideously confused about the other personnel who were with him in that carrier. Simply for example in his statement made on 11 May 1993, he said that the carrier upon which he travelled was driven by PC John Clutterbuck. Further evidence has made it sure that this was not so. Mr Groves did agree that PSgt Clement was with him on arrival. The Inspector was much confused as to the number of the carrier upon which he travelled. The Inspector's evidence will be referred to in more detail in respect of the Initial Response part of this Inquiry (Chapter 11). But the Inspector himself says that when he arrived the ambulance had not yet attended and Stephen Lawrence was lying on the pavement. He told us that he saw Stephen lying near a large plane tree and he also echoed other evidence when he said that he would say that Stephen was in the recovery position. When he got to the scene, Mr Groves said that there were two police officers down on their hands and knees tending to Stephen. He remembered two other people crouched down as well, but he had no idea what any of these people were doing. He says that he asked the officers *"Is he breathing?"* and *"Is he bleeding?"* and he asked if they wanted a hand or needed help. He indicated to the Inquiry that he got no reply at all to these queries posed to the officers. He said that he thought that those around Stephen Lawrence were doing what they should have been doing. He said that he could only assume from the position of Stephen's head and what he saw going on that Stephen was still alive. The officers and those around Stephen appeared to be monitoring his condition and from what he could see it looked, he said, as though they were taking a pulse.

10.50   **The main point, however, is that it was crystal clear that Mr Groves did nothing to find out properly what the situation was or to check properly what was being done, or to ensure that properly qualified First Aid people were dealing with Stephen Lawrence. He said that the ambulance had been called, and that Stephen was being attended to, and he classified what he had seen going on as First Aid. He said that his conclusion was that if Stephen had still not been breathing the officers would have turned him on his back and performed emergency resuscitation. Since they were not doing that he concluded that all that was necessary or correct was being done. Mr Groves says that he saw no blood when he arrived at the scene. It is possible that the blanket was by that time covering the blood, but Mr Groves made no effort to ensure that the steps being taken by the junior officers present were the correct steps. Indeed, it is likely that if Mr Groves himself had been in the position of the other officers he would have done no more than they did. It is palpable from answers given by Mr Groves that his own training in First Aid was minimal, and that he had been on no courses whatsoever for many years. He seemed to think that it was somehow demeaning that it might be suggested that he should go to a refresher course with junior officers, since he had 27**

years service and was capable of acting properly on his own account. Mr Groves had not done any First Aid training since 1985. He can surely be roundly criticised for not finding out who had taken responsibility for First Aid. He simply took it for granted that someone junior was appropriately in charge of Stephen Lawrence.

10.51 **The truth is, in a nutshell, that nobody did anything whatsoever for Stephen Lawrence except the small amount of testing to see whether he was still breathing and whether his pulse was beating. Officers who had allegedly been trained and undergone refresher training ought to have realised that the bleeding was such that there should be an immediate investigation in order to decide whence the blood was pouring, in order to try to staunch the flow of blood and if necessary to lift up the legs of the injured man. It is little consolation to Mr & Mrs Lawrence and the Lawrence family that nothing that anybody had done would have made any difference whatsoever. The fact that nothing was done is a source of understandable distress to them, to this day.**

10.52 As to the First Aid issue there remains to be considered the expert evidence that was called to assist the Inquiry in respect of measures which ought to have been taken by anybody trained in elementary First Aid at the scene. There were three witnesses who dealt with this area of the case. The most impressive was Mr Graham Cook, Fellow of the Royal College of Surgeons of Edinburgh, and Fellow of the Faculty of Accident and Emergency Medicine. He gave evidence on Day Five. He is a most experienced man and he is at present Director of Accident and Emergency Services at Maidstone Hospital. Furthermore, he is a Medical Consultant to Kent Constabulary and has, for a long time, been involved in the overseeing of First Aid training for police officers and others. His full statement is available as is the transcript of his evidence. But, in essence, he says that First Aid must be based on immediate assessment of the patient. The result of that assessment dictates the necessary activities and measures to be taken. **He introduced the letters "ABC" which form the fundamental basis of the initial check which must be made of any patient, namely the checking of the Airway, the Breathing, and the Circulation. He said that haemorrhage control does not require anything more than basic First Aid skills. He indicated that if there had been a blow to the head there could be substantial blood loss, but that would be clearly visible even in poor lighting. From the horrendous injuries suffered by Stephen Lawrence he was sure that there would be very heavy bleeding. He is sure that a properly instructed First Aider would and should have attempted to trace the source of the bleeding in order to take elementary measures to staunch the flow of blood. The right course was to staunch the flow and, said Mr Cook, to raise the legs to put more blood back into the system. Mr Cook asserted repeatedly that this was or should have been elementary to trained First Aiders. There is no doubt that the Inquiry had before it a witness of enormous experience and of practical skill.**

10.53 Recommendations will, of course, be made later in this report, but it will be apparent that the Inquiry criticises strongly the training of police officers in First Aid and the lack of any apparently successful or satisfactory refresher training.

10.54 The Inquiry heard two other witnesses in connection with First Aid: Mr David Sadler was until 1997 Branch Training Officer for the Kent Branch of the British Red Cross Society. He is a man of much experience in the field of First Aid. In cross-examination Mr Sadler did effectively agree with Mr Cook that the first priority was to check a casualty's breathing and make sure that there was a pulse and then to go to the bleeding. He did say that he would not want to move the patient once he knew an ambulance was on its way, but later he said that if there was any sign of profuse bleeding then the bleeding point should at once be ascertained, and it should be stemmed by direct pressure. To that extent Mr Sadler accepted the opinion of Mr Cook. His earlier opinion expressed to the Kent inquiry that reasonable steps had been taken by those present was based upon information which omitted reference to the visible blood loss and the possibility that there had been a blow with an iron bar.

10.55 Lastly Police Constable Stephen Hughes gave evidence before the Inquiry. He has been in the MPS since 1975 and he was for many years a First Aid instructor. He was called at the invitation of those representing the Commissioner to help with what the level of First Aid training was in the MPS in 1993. He served from 1989 in No 3 Area Training Unit. He said that from 1984 until 1994 there used to be *"an annual week long First Aider seminar"*. This was apparently discontinued in 1994 because the Force First Aid adviser retired and First Aid training was absorbed by the Occupational Health Branch who saw no need to continue the seminars. Prior to 1994 all uniformed Constables and Sergeants had to have a current First Aid certificate up to their twenty-first year of service. PC Hughes told us that now all officers up to but not including the rank of Inspector are required to have a First Aid certificate which covers them for the last year of service. In 1984 there was a three-day course with about eighteen hours training. That contracted in 1986 to two days ie. twelve hours training. Then from 1987 the course lasted one day and amounted to six hours training. PC Hughes said that it remained thus until the time with which we are concerned. PC Hughes indicated the nature of training which would take place including stress placed upon the importance systematically to search a casualty at skin level for major external blood loss. On finding bleeding students were told to control it by hand if necessary and to complete the search. PC Hughes agreed that if a person is obviously bleeding from the body then plainly the first thing that must be done is to control that bleeding by placing the hand over the wound and applying pressure. In cross-examination PC Hughes indicated that there were refresher courses, but no testing. He also told the Inquiry that one of the reasons for the reduction in length of First Aid courses was simply lack of resources. At one time a doctor examined students after the three-day course, and he had to be paid. There was no requirement in the regulations for a doctor to be involved and for that reason the services of the doctor were dispensed with. The MPS is not registered with St John's Ambulance in connection with First Aid instruction. Certificates come directly from the Health and Safety Executive.

10.56 **This evidence reinforced the Inquiry's views as to the lack of satisfactory and proper training in First Aid for officers of all ranks. Not only should officers be properly trained and be given proper refresher training at regular intervals, but it must be made plain that more senior officers need instruction just as much as junior officers. An officer in the position of Mr Groves must be able to ensure that what is being done by his juniors is proper and satisfactory and in accordance with well co-ordinated and directed training. The notion that it may be good enough simply to wait for the ambulance and the paramedics must be exploded.**

10.57 **The long and the short of it is that front-line police officers must be instructed to "think First Aid". They must be trained properly in basic steps to be taken to recognise and deal with what is discovered. It should be automatic that the Airway, the Breathing and the Circulation are assessed at once. With basic training the staunching of bleeding, the administration of mouth to mouth resuscitation, external cardiac massage and where heavy bleeding is seen, raising the legs to protect circulation should be as much a matter of second nature as it is to dial 999 or to radio for an ambulance.**

10.58 The strongest criticism in the area of First Aid must be made against Mr Groves. He received no reply when he asked what was going on, and simply left the scene because he believed that there had been some kind of fight. He was plainly casual and unprofessional in this respect. We are forced to the conclusion that his attitude and his dismissive conduct were contributed to, if not wholly caused, by unwitting but clear racism. He saw a young black man lying injured, and an obviously stressed and agitated young black man on the pavement nearby. It is plain to all of us that he was deflected by what he saw and by his wholly wrong conclusion, and that his whole approach to what had happened was thus undermined by racist stereotyping. We conclude that in this case it must be said that he reacted as he did simply because of what he saw, and that he would not have been similarly dismissive if the two young men involved had been white.

10.59 As to the others involved directly in the allegations as to First Aid we do not infer that their inaction was initiated or caused by overt or unwitting racism. We understand the reactions and strong feelings of Mr & Mrs Lawrence, but we are not persuaded that anybody involved in the immediate attention or lack of attention in connection with First Aid can rightly be accused of anything more than failure to heed such training as was given and of over-reliance upon the imminent arrival of the ambulance and the paramedics. We hope that our recommendations in this field will ensure that such failure and over-reliance do not occur ever again.

CHAPTER ELEVEN

INITIAL RESPONSE

11.1 **Anybody who listened to the evidence of the officers involved in the initial police action after the murder would, so all the members of the Inquiry feel, be astonished at the lack of command and the lack of organisation of what took place. Police officers who gave evidence before us believed that everything they had done had been properly organised and professionally carried out. That does not appear to us to be the position.**

11.2 **It is difficult to reconstruct with any accuracy or confidence what exactly was done and when it was done. This is because there is almost a total lack of documentation and record in connection with the whole of the first night's operations. Not a single police officer of any rank either made or initiated a log to record the decisions made and the actions taken. Mr Groves regarded this as unnecessary, because he believed that his own notes, made on his blue clipboard which he always carried with him, would provide the necessary record of what had happened.**

11.3 It does seem likely to us that Mr Groves had a clipboard with him, but we will never know what was written upon it. The Inspector says that his notes were copied and that the originals were taken to Shooters Hill Police Station some time after the night in question. Neither the original notes nor the copy survived for use by the PCA in 1997 nor by us in 1998.

11.4 Furthermore, each Territorial Support Group (TSG) vehicle should carry with it an action sheet upon which relevant actions are recorded shortly after they have taken place. PC Samantha Tatton (formerly Norrie) who says that she was on the first vehicle to arrive, indicates that there was indeed a sheet on her vehicle. She says that she believes that she used it in order to record the time of arrival and other short details which appear in her written statement. Those sheets have also disappeared. Mr Groves has tried to trace them from the relevant records section. Apparently documents of this kind are destroyed after four years. It is very surprising to the Inquiry that Mr Groves' notes and the sheets were not retained, since this case has been in the forefront of police consciousness since 1993.

11.5 **One officer produced a notebook with very short notes to which we will later refer. There was also an occurrence book relating to TSG activities in which there is a short entry signed by PSgt Clement indicating that carriers were engaged in a murder incident in the Plumstead section and that they *"assisted in cordons and search of scene and nearby streets"*. There are no timings in that record to assist us. No other notebooks or satisfactory contemporary records of police action at the scene exist.**

11.6 In parenthesis it should be said that we were unimpressed by the reference in cross-examination to the CAD message which suggested that the carriers had arrived at 23:45, namely almost an hour after the murder. That appears to us simply to be the official assigning entry, dealing with the matter in retrospect.

11.7 **It is a feature of the case that several of the officers appear to have decided together that the message reaching them alerting them to the murder came at 22:25. That was at least five minutes before the murder took place. One officer said that he had said *"at about twenty-five past ten"*, but that is clearly an incorrect time. The first message coming to a police control room was timed at 22:43, so that assignment of the first TSG vehicle could not have occurred until some minutes after that.**

11.8 PC Tatton said in her statement, and indeed in evidence, that she checked with the action sheet before she made her statement and that showed the arrival of her TSG vehicle to be at 22:57. Insofar as we can ever be satisfied of the time of arrival of the first TSG vehicle it appears to us that that is the most likely time. PC Tatton was an impressive witness, although her memory of events was clouded by the passage of time, in common with the memories of all the witnesses involved.

11.9 The next question to be resolved is who was on the first carrier and which carrier was it? It is really almost impossible to reconstruct with certainty, or even with reasonable accuracy, the list of officers on that carrier. It does seem likely, however, looking at the whole of the evidence, that Mr Groves was on that carrier and so was PSgt Clement and so were three or four other officers. There was even a contest between the officers as to who might have been driving the vehicle. In the result it seems to us most likely that PC Paul Smith was the driver. We will refer to his evidence later. PC Tatton in her statement referred to seeing Stephen Lawrence lying face down on the pavement. She also says that she saw about five males and females standing near him. She did not see Mr Brooks. She did not get off the carrier before it moved off from the place where Stephen Lawrence lay.

11.10 **In parenthesis it should be noted that Mr Brooks did himself say that he saw a carrier arrive. We are thus satisfied that at least one carrier arrived before Stephen's body was removed and before Mr Brooks went to the hospital.**

11.11 The likelihood is that Mr Groves and PSgt Clement did alight from this carrier and did go reasonably close to where Stephen's body lay. PSgt Clement then says that he left very shortly afterwards in the carrier, without Mr Groves, in order to carry out what he called a mobile search in the area in and beyond Dickson Road. He told the Inquiry that he was aware from a radio message that five or six white youths had been seen disappearing into Dickson Road. PC Bethel says that this information came from her. The more likely version is that PC Bethel passed that information on to PSgt Clement. Mr Groves himself heard nothing said by officers at all, and nothing said by Mr Brooks. We have already indicated in the First Aid section that he says that he asked if he could help and he asked other questions about the condition of Stephen Lawrence, but that he received no reply from anybody.

11.12 **What then happened is extraordinary. Without any clear information as to what had occurred Mr Groves went off with Police Sergeant Andrew Hodges, who was in 1993 a Police Constable, to the Welcome Inn Public House, which is situated to the north of the scene. He knew that this public house was the nearest one to the scene, and he resolved to go there to see if he could get any information about any violence that had taken place or any information as to possible witnesses of the incident. He left the scene without having established what had happened.**

11.13 **If he had stayed to ask further questions of the police officers at the scene he must have been told that the white youths had come from the direction of the roundabout and that they had been seen going down Dickson Road and away from the Welcome Inn. However, that is what he decided to do, with absolutely no result, because nobody in the public house had heard or seen anything suspicious. Mr Groves assumed that there had been a fight, without any basis for such a conclusion.**

11.14 PSgt Clement told the Inquiry that he went with other officers on the carrier down Dickson Road and did a short mobile search of some of the roads beyond Dickson Road, going as far as Appleton Road and then down into Rochester Way, then past the roundabout and up to the Welcome Inn. He says that he, with another officer, then went to the Welcome Inn Public House on a similar quest to that of Mr Groves, and with similar negative results. PSgt Clement did not see Mr Groves at the public house, and Mr Groves did not see the carrier there. It is difficult to establish when and where these actions took place, if they took place at all.

11.15 Having seen PSgt Clement for a long time in the witness box it did appear to the Inquiry that what he told the Inquiry about his actions was probably correct. He is marginally supported in his evidence by the driver PC Paul Smith who says that he did indeed drive into Dickson Road and who indicated that there was a measure of mobile searching done by the carrier in that area. The difference between them is that the driver thinks that he halted towards the end of Dickson Road, and was then told to go to Downman Road to block off Downman Road from Well Hall Road, where he parked his TSG vehicle. Indeed, he indicated that he went down Downman Road to Dickson Road when the search started. As Counsel pointed out, this was a peculiar route to take if the objective was to start the search in Dickson Road where the men had been seen running away. The entrance to Dickson Road was a turning off Well Hall Road almost immediately next to where the carrier must have been parked.

11.16 **It can be seen at once that the whole picture is one of disarray and uncertainty. What is certain is that Mr Groves never established any degree of direction or control, except perhaps in the ultimate dragon light search which did take place around midnight, when gardens and dustbins were searched with the help of police dogs. He had under his control probably four or five TSG carriers and thus about 40 officers. His prime responsibility as it seems to us was to establish as far as possible what had happened, and to take control of the scene, and to organise proper and co-ordinated searches of the scene and in particular the estate into which the attackers had run. He failed to find out what Mr Brooks had said, and that he was both a victim and a vital witness. He could have used Mr Brooks in connection with the searches. Who is to know whether properly organised action might not have resulted in contact with Gary Dobson, who left his house in Phineas Pett Road at about 23:45 to go to 102 Bournbrook Road, or Witness K who said to others that he went to visit 102 Bournbrook Road soon after hearing about the murder? This was the first opportunity to take positive action, and it was totally lost and indeed never got off the ground because of Mr Groves' failure. It is surprising that right up until the end of this Inquiry's hearings, the MPS still assert that *"officers at the scene were managed and directed satisfactorily"* and that Mr Groves "performed well, addressing each of the primary objectives for such an incident". We roundly reject this submission made to us at the end of Part 1 of our Inquiry.**

11.17 **That first mobile search was, as it seems to us, peculiarly pointless. Nobody seems to have stopped to think that the likelihood was that if the fugitives were on foot they might be caught, or might have been seen, at the far end of the estate, if they were aiming to leave the estate. Alternatively, if they were going into the estate because they lived there the likelihood would be that they might be in the houses within the estate itself. Sensible and calm co-ordination of what to do would surely have resulted in the use of all the TSG carriers in a search starting at the far end of the estate working back towards Dickson Road and covering the other possible exit routes from Dickson Road. The fact that this did not occur is entirely attributable to the failure by Mr Groves properly to establish facts which were readily available to him at the scene and logically to deploy his resources. Certainly the mobile search conducted by PSgt Clement and**

his team produced nothing. The driver, PC Paul Smith, had no idea what he was looking for when he embarked down Downman Road in the direction of Dickson Road.

11.18 The other TSG vehicles, which came to the scene later, appear to have stopped near Well Hall Road roundabout. There is no indication from any document, or indeed from any satisfactory evidence, as to what the occupants of those vehicles did. Probably they took part in the later search, when the dragon lights had been obtained from Headquarters by one of the police witnesses. But in the first stages they appear not to have been used at all. Some enquiries were made by knocking on doors and by talking to residents who had come out of their houses close to the junction of Dickson Road and Well Hall Road. A local resident, Mr Nugent, was seen by Mr Groves, and he made a statement. He heard noise in the street and had seen youths disappearing down Dickson Road.

11.19 There is no proper record of which other houses may have been visited by police officers during the second phase of the TSG activity which involved the first house-to-house visits. It cannot be termed a house-to-house search. The evidence given to us does establish that some houses were approached by police officers in these initial information seeking visits.

11.20 One message (from DC Pye) timed at 08:34 on 23 April does indicate that TSG searched Dickson Road to the end, Downman Road to No 22, Phineas Pett Road to No 13, and Sandby Green to No 41. No details of the nature of that search are given.

11.21 **Thereafter we know that cordons were established near the place where Stephen had lain, and in the mouth of Dickson Road. Two officers gave evidence who were stationed on the Well Hall Road cordon. Some steps were taken to block off part of the roadway because there was blood on the road. This should have been done earlier. At least one vehicle, namely the suspicious red Astra to which further reference will be made, was able to drive both up and down Well Hall Road while the police were active in the area.**

11.22 Mr Groves' evidence and indeed his statements made at the time and to the Kent inquiry, show that there has been considerable confusion in his own mind about the order of events. He says that he or his Unit had been told that there had been a fight or a disturbance and that somebody had been hit over the head with an iron bar. He said that he made enquiries about Stephen Lawrence. He expressed himself to be satisfied with what was being done. He believed, when he gave evidence to the Inquiry, that he had asked Mr Brooks what had happened and whether he was all right. But he indicated that he got nothing at all from him or indeed from any of the officers at the scene. He said that the only information which guided him eventually to Dickson Road came from Mr Nugent, considerably later.

11.23 In his statement in 1993, he had indicated that the driver of his vehicle was PC Clutterbuck, which we have indicated must have been wrong. Furthermore, he said that he set about the business of erecting the cordon to seal off the immediate area at once. That is in conflict with the evidence which he gave to us, namely, that the first thing that he did was to set off up Well Hall Road to the Welcome Inn.

11.24 He agreed that he had got the events in the wrong order, and his final version was that he set up the cordons and followed the trail of blood and took the actions described near Dickson Road after he came back from the public house. When he returned from the public house, the ambulance had been and Stephen Lawrence and Mr Brooks had gone.

11.25 As to PSgt Clement's search, Mr Groves indicated that he had ordered that search, namely an immediate search of the area. Exactly what area he intended to be searched is mysterious, but he seemed to imply that the right thing might be to search with the van on both sides of Well Hall Road and in the *"adjoining streets"*. In fact PC Bethel had told PSgt Clement about the white youths and had directed him into Dickson Road.

11.26 **When Mr Groves got back from the public house, he walked with PC Bethel back down to Dickson Road, following the trail of blood and he saw local officers cordoning off in Sandby Green, Cobbett Road and other places. Then, for the first time, he obtained information from Mr Nugent, namely that four or five men had run off into Dickson Road. The men were white. One was in shirt sleeves, and they were *"not that old"*. Mr Groves indicated that then and thereafter he made notes on his clipboard of what had happened and what was done. These notes were later *"translated"* into his statement.**

11.27 Mr Groves was asked which other officers he had seen during the hours of his duties. He said that he saw Chief Superintendent Christopher Benn and that his Divisional Chief Superintendent (John Philpott) had arrived at the scene later. We know that Chief Inspector John McIvor came to the scene and so did Detective Inspector Philip Jeynes. But Mr Groves indicated to us that it was his belief that effectively he was in charge of what was happening during the hours up to about 01:00 when the TSG personnel went back to base and went off duty.

11.28 Mr Groves said that by about 23:45 he had heard that Stephen had died of stab wounds, and it was after that, probably from midnight onwards, that the dragon light search took place. He said that the search covered both sides of the road from Dickson Road into the estate. There is a record in a CAD message indicating the extent of that search. He says that that was a *"thorough structured search, very different to what happened earlier on and that absolutely everything was looked at, houses, dustbins anything that would have been of interest"*. He says that he was the only person recording notes and that these notes were comprehensive. Indeed, he says that he was *"challenged"* as to what he was writing by Mr Benn. When asked about this he said that he was writing Mr Benn's name down, and this seemed strange for some reason to Mr Benn.

11.29 Mr Groves said that while the dragon light search was going on his men had been *"instructed to look for suspects as well"*. No description of those involved had been given at all to any of the officers at that stage. This more co-ordinated search did not take place until after midnight. Mr Groves knew nothing at all about the red Astra car. He said that he was not with PSgt Clement and PSgt Hodges for very long, and that this might explain his ignorance of the incident involving the car. When asked by the Kent officers about there being no scene log of any kind he said that the concept of a scene log was not familiar to him. In evidence before us he said that there was no need to keep a scene log. He seemed satisfied that his own clipboard notes were all that were required.

11.30 **The actual cordoning of the two scenes, that of the attack and that where Stephen Lawrence collapsed, appears to us to be the only initial action which was properly conducted. From the evidence we heard it would appear that both scenes were taped off and preserved for evidential purposes. However, even this minor achievement was sullied by the failure to establish a scene log. It is our understanding that the creation of a crime scene log is a standard procedure to ensure that the area which is being preserved and is subsequently to be subject to forensic examination is properly protected and that movement of people in and out of that scene is limited and recorded** for evidential purposes and in order to prevent contamination. It is not simply a bureaucratic requirement that there should be a scene log; it is an essential step in police procedures that it should be set up and properly managed immediately a scene is cordoned off and preserved. Any officer of any rank and experience should have been aware of this. Mr Jeynes said that it was *"historical practice to maintain such a log"*. There should in addition have been an "incident log" either on paper, such as Mr Groves indicated he had begun to create, or on the computerised CAD system recording the various actions and activities undertaken by officers under the direction of whoever was the officer in command. We will have more to say about this later when we consider the position of the senior officers who did come to the scene. Some messages were recorded early on the CAD system, but there is no satisfactory running record of what was being done.

11.31   In cross-examination, Mr Groves became embroiled with Mr Mansfield in a good deal of verbal fencing. It is unwise to tangle with Mr Mansfield in this way, and Mr Groves' position and evidence were not improved by his attitude. It is a matter of surprise to the Inquiry that at the end of his evidence Mr Groves seemed still to be perfectly satisfied that he had acted with efficiency and thoroughness, and performed all the actions which were necessary at the scene.

11.32   **It is apparent to all of us that the direction and control exercised by Mr Groves at the scene was almost non-existent. Nobody gave proper instructions to the officers in the earliest stages of the investigation, and no plan was made which might have led to the discovery and arrest of the suspects who had run down Dickson Road.**

11.33   **It has to be said that even if the correct and full steps had been taken in this regard it might have led to no different result. But in the absence of proper police action during the vital two hours after the death of Stephen Lawrence it is not surprising that Mr & Mrs Lawrence, and the public, heard Mr Groves' evidence with some incredulity. Indeed the catalogue of errors must cause concern to all who heard it.**

11.34   **Mr Macdonald, on behalf of Mr Brooks, cross-examined Mr Groves at some length. Mr Groves had described Mr Brooks as being *"distraught"* in one statement and *"hysterical"* in another. Little is to be gained by discussing this distinction. Mr Groves had virtually no contact with Mr Brooks at the scene. He plainly should have made more effort to find out who he was and what his involvement had been in this attack. As a victim, Mr Brooks needed help from the police, and he was obviously a vital source of information. Indeed, as we all know, he turned out to be the only witness who could give identification evidence at the eventual trial of three of the suspects. Mr Groves had no idea that Mr Brooks was in fact himself a victim of the assault, and he took no steps to discover what part Mr Brooks had played in the affair. If Mr Brooks had been of a mind to leave and give no further help he could have done so, considering the lack of proper attention paid to him in the early stages at the scene and the hospital.**

11.35   Probably at about 23:30 the red Astra car with five youths inside it was twice seen being driven down Well Hall Road. The car was being driven first in the direction of Shooters Hill, and some minutes later it came back in the opposite direction. The laxness evident in the failure to stop the car and later (after it was seen again on 30 April by chance) properly to follow up and research its occupants is separately dealt with in Chapter 20. Mr Groves had no knowledge of the car at any time.

11.36 **The main conclusion that we reach is that the inadequacy of the steps taken was as the result of the failure of direction by supervisory officers. The standard of command and co-ordination during the first two hours after this murder was in the opinion of the Inquiry abysmal.**

11.37 Of the other officers involved in the TSG activity, mention has already been made of PSgt Hodges. He accompanied Mr Groves to the public house, with as little information as to what he was trying to achieve as was possessed by Mr Groves. He was present with PSgt Clement when the red Astra came by, and he took part in the later searches.

11.38 PC Paul McGarry told us that he was on the first TSG vehicle to arrive. He had thought that he might have been driving. But later it was pointed out to him that the likelihood was that PC Paul Smith was the driver. He had some memory of the presence of PC Paul Robson, PC Tatton and PC Smith on his carrier, but he really had very little recollection of where the carrier went and what was done. He was one of the officers who had indicated in his original statement that the time of call out had been 22:25.

11.39 PC McGarry said that it was obvious that First Aid was being carried out to Stephen Lawrence. It was plain when he was cross-examined that all he meant was that he had seen people near Stephen Lawrence, but that he had seen no actual steps in connection with First Aid being carried out. He said that he had at some stage been told about five white youths going down Dickson Road. It is of some significance that he had no memory at all of the carrier stopping outside the Welcome Inn. Like the other officers, PC McGarry saw no reason to make any note of what he had done. It was pointed out to him that there was a very good reason to keep a record, for example, of which gardens had been searched, in case something appeared in one of those gardens the next day which could thus be proved to have arrived only after the search made earlier on.

11.40 PC Robson was an unimpressive witness. He says that he saw Stephen Lawrence lying on the pavement from his position in the police carrier. He then indicated in his statement that he had gone *"to search the vicinity for suspects"*. Later, he says, that he took over the cordoned ground where Stephen Lawrence had been lying. He took over from PC Tatton at the scene.

11.41 On the next day officers were briefed in connection with the more detailed house-to-house inquiries which took place over the weekend. Evidence as to the detailed house-to-house inquiries was given by DS Donald Mackenzie. A large number of houses were visited and reference will be made in a separate section of this report to those visits (see Chapter 17). Before starting the inquiries the officers were briefed. PC Robson did, unusually, have a short note in his pocketbook about that briefing. It was, as he indicated, a somewhat unsatisfactory note, but it did contain the description of one of the assailants, so that it is apparent that the officers doing the detailed house-to-house inquiries had some material in that connection. The words appearing in the Police Constable's notebook are *"six foot, brown bushy hair, 19 years"*. This description was probably the description given by Mr Brooks at the hospital to PC Gleason which had by 14:00 on the Friday been in some way transmitted to the briefing officer who was Mr Bullock. It must be said that there is some mystery about this, since nobody remembers PC Gleason's description being broadcast on the night of the murder, and his notebook disappeared after 23 April and was apparently not seen again until it surfaced at the Kent inquiry. PC Gleason says that he gave a copy of the book to Mr Jeynes on 23 April. It may be by that route that the briefing did include that short version of the description given to PC Gleason by Mr Brooks at the hospital.

11.42   That information had not reached the officers at the scene on the night of the murder, since nobody referred to any description other than that the assailants had been white. PC Robson also indicated that the call out had been at 22:25. There seems little doubt that officers had spoken to each other before that clearly wrong time was entered in their statements. This is an unsatisfactory feature of the evidence of the officers involved.

11.43   PC Robson saw PC Geddis at the scene early on. That and other evidence does suggest that it is established that the first TSG on the scene was there before the ambulance came. As we have already indicated this is supported positively by the evidence of Mr Brooks. Otherwise the evidence of PC Robson was vague and unsatisfactory. We do not believe that he was inventing his evidence, but all that he said was symptomatic of the lack of direction and proper management exercised at the scene. He had very little idea where he had been or what had happened during the early stages. This appears to us to be a fault of the commander involved, namely Mr Groves, who should have ensured that his officers knew exactly what they were meant to be doing and where they were meant to be going in connection with any searches which were carried out.

11.44   **The impression we gain is of officers doing things without any real direction or information. Much of what was done was, in essence, doomed to be ineffective because of inadequate co-ordination or control.**

11.45   PC Tatton was one of the better witnesses in the TSG section of this case. We have already indicated that the time of arrival of 22:57 in her statement probably did come from some record still existing at the time when she made her original statement. Judging by the lack of note-taking of all the officers involved in this part of the enquiry, it is likely that the TAG sheet had few details upon it. But at least the time of arrival may have been properly recorded. This officer's part played at the scene was limited. She indicates that she was directed to stand at the cordon near the scene of Stephen Lawrence's fall, and that she was relieved at about 00:35 by PC Robson. She said that her job was simply to stand on the path to make sure that nobody walked over that particular area. She indicated that there was a rendezvous point at the Well Hall roundabout, and that she had no radio with her since she had left her radio for use by others in the carrier. Therefore, she was not in contact with other officers while she stood in the roadway.

11.46   While she was at the scene this officer said that she had no idea that she was involved in a murder case. She believes that she actually first became aware of that when she heard the radio or television news later on. She does confirm the evidence of PSgt Clement and of Mr Groves, namely that they were together on the same vehicle as her and that both of them got off the vehicle at the scene. She believes that she saw the two officers go to where the other officers were standing, and minutes later she remembered that the ambulance arrived and took away Stephen Lawrence and that Mr Brooks left the scene simultaneously. She says that the carrier remained where it was until the moment when she was asked to get off to stand at the cordon.

11.47   It seems likely that this happened before the carrier went off to Dickson Road on its unsatisfactory first mobile run. In cross-examination PC Tatton appeared to agree that the roadway had been improperly cordoned off, since no vehicle should have been allowed to pass up and down the street. She had no idea at the time why the TSG vehicles had been called out, except that it was *"some sort of attack, I believe, or an assault"*. This shows, yet again, how little information was given to the officers who were at the scene, many of whom appear to have been left in almost total ignorance of even the limited information which was then available.

11.48 Finally, PC Paul Smith, the driver of the first TSG vehicle to arrive, gave evidence. We have already indicated the part played by him in the mobile search. There is no doubt that his evidence was unsatisfactory. But it is the opinion of the members of the Inquiry that he simply played his part by rote. He did what he was told when he was asked to drive or move the TSG carrier, but he knew nothing of what was going on and had no real idea at all when he was assisting in searches that there had been an attack, let alone a racist attack made by five white men in the horrific circumstances of which we are all now aware.

11.49 Later in the evening he says that he knew that there had been a racist attack, but he indicated that when he was driving the vehicle he concentrated on the driving and took little other action in respect of the activities of the officers involved. He had never heard about the red Vauxhall Astra.

11.50 **In answer to Mr Yearwood, for the CRE, he seemed surprised that anybody might regard it as offensive to be addressed as "coloured" as opposed to black. Even after four and a half years service in Brixton PC Smith seemed oblivious to this insensitivity.**

11.51 **In summary, therefore, the evidence that we have heard in connection with the TSG activity showed almost total lack of direction and control. It was most disappointing to members of the Inquiry that those involved should, even now, believe that they acted with efficiency and skill, and that they should have no regret as to the inadequate nature of the actions taken during the first two hours of the initial response.**

11.52 **It may be that even if full and proper actions had been taken and had been properly recorded nothing would have been discovered. At least this would have been some consolation to the Lawrence family and indeed to the public, since it would have established that proper steps had been taken even if no result had been achieved at the end of the day.**

11.53 We must, of course, always bear in mind that it is now nearly six years after the event. The TSG officers were not involved in the court proceedings or the Inquest which have taken place over the years. They were seen by the Kent officers in connection with the PCA report in 1997, and reference has been made to the somewhat fuller statements of the officers who gave evidence before us compared with the short and somewhat sparse statements taken in 1993.

11.54 Allowance always has to be made for the passage of time when recollections are tested. The fact is, however, that the short nature of the original statements and the complete lack of any contemporary notes makes it difficult indeed for us to assess whether there was more activity than is reflected in those statements. Mr Groves' 1993 statement does contain some sections which appear to indicate that he was probably working from some note when he made his statement. There is, for example, a considerable section of reported speech set out in full, and the suggestion is that this must mean that it came from a contemporaneously recorded account of the conversations that took place. Furthermore, there is a record, both in the statement and in CAD messages of the extent of the final dragon light searches which were controlled by Mr Groves.

11.55 There is, however, considerable confusion in Mr Groves' statements, as we have already indicated. What his notes did contain will never be known, because they have disappeared. We have no reason to believe that they have been wilfully destroyed, since they would plainly assist the officer if he was ever asked to reflect on what had taken place. The disappearance of those notes does make it difficult to test whether Mr Groves' recording of what took place was satisfactory throughout the important first two hours after the murder.

11.56 There is not much reference in this summary to the activities of the other carriers which arrived at the scene. Mr Groves believes that he called them up when he arrived in Well Hall Road. This may well be so. There is no record of the time of arrival of those carriers or their position or activities. There appears to have been a rendezvous point at the Well Hall roundabout, and the statements of some of the officers on the other carriers suggests that for a time at least they remained aboard the carriers and did not dismount. More than one officer indicates that the carriers were used for a measure of mobile searching, but it is likely that any tour around the relevant area was as unsatisfactory as that of PSgt Clement with his carrier.

11.57 In the end it seems likely that these officers would have been used on the later and somewhat more controlled dragon light search of the gardens under Mr Groves. They too would probably not have known what had happened and might in all probability have been acting in ignorance of relevant information which was by that time available. If officers were looking for a murder weapon they appear not to have known that Stephen Lawrence had died from stab wounds, nor that an early description of a weapon used was that it had been an iron bar.

11.58 **It is the case that numerically there were plenty of officers at the scene to conduct the searches and operations which were necessary as immediate action after this murder. The presence of satisfactory numbers of officers means nothing if they are not properly directed and supervised and asked to do the proper tasks which might have led to further information and a measure of success.**

11.59 **We stress yet again that it can never be said what might have been seen or heard or found if the searches and "knocks on doors" had been carried out at once starting with, for example, the far end of the estate and working back towards Dickson Road. This does not detract from the necessary criticism of the actions taken in the hours immediately following the murder of Stephen Lawrence. A marked lack of co-ordination and attention to detail seem to have been the features of these early hours.**

11.60 **We have felt it necessary to cover this part of the investigation in detail, because we have to say that we disagree roundly with the conclusion reached by Kent which positively commended the initial response and the early actions taken at the scene in the first hours after the murder. Furthermore the MPS in their final submission still sought to justify their actions during those vital hours.**

CHAPTER TWELVE
I ARRIVAL AT THE SCENE OF SENIOR OFFICERS
II THE HOSPITAL
III ARRIVAL OF THE CID

12.1 **While the local officers and the TSG personnel were at the scene performing their limited activities there arrived a series of senior officers and members of the CID. The Kent Report indicates that a large number of officers and some more senior officers did come to Well Hall Road. Some of them were in the witness box for considerably longer than they were present in and near Well Hall Road.**

12.2 The first of these more senior officers to give evidence was Chief Inspector Jonathan McIvor. He was the most senior uniformed officer on duty for 3 Area during the night of 22/23 April. He indicated that his role was *"essentially a public order role"*. He said that unless there were public order implications he would not have any direct responsibility in respect of a murder that might happen on his Division whilst he was on duty. He was also manager at Plumstead Divisional Headquarters. He heard that there had been a stabbing in Well Hall Road at about five minutes to midnight. The CAD message seeking him is timed at 23:51. He arrived at the scene probably between 00:15 and 00:30.

12.3 The first policemen seen by Mr McIvor were stationed at a cordon at the junction of Well Hall Road, near the Welcome Inn Public House. As a result of talking to Mr Jeynes, who was already present, Mr McIvor became aware that Mr Benn, a Chief Superintendent, had been at the scene already and had *"made some arrangements, or had added to the arrangements for area searches"*.

12.4 Mr McIvor states that he satisfied himself that all local enquiries were being carried out, or had been carried out, and this appears to refer to some house-to-house enquiries about which he had been told by Mr Jeynes. Mr McIvor thought that the scene *"appeared to me to be well conducted, with Mr Jeynes in charge."* He was aware that a Senior Investigating Officer had been called and was on his way. He indicated to the Inquiry that he was essentially superfluous at that time, and that he had his own duties to perform away from the scene.

12.5 **This is a matter of considerable surprise since we regard Mr McIvor as an important person in the chain of command. As the senior Divisional uniformed officer on duty it is our view that Mr McIvor was the man who ought to have taken charge and ensured that there was co-ordination and correlation between those present as to the steps which were being taken at the scene.**

12.6 Mr McIvor said that a formal document referred to as a Scene Log was, in his experience, not a document in existence or use in the MPS at that time. He says that comings and goings to a scene in 1993 were usually recorded on the CAD messages.

12.7 Mr McIvor appears to have been preoccupied with the possible public order and local community relations aspect of the case. He said that he spoke to Mr Philpott, when he came to Plumstead Police Station, in order to discuss what response needed to be made in respect of possible public order consequences. That was the concentration of Mr McIvor's thoughts on the night of the murder.

12.8 Mr McIvor had only been at Plumstead for about four months, but he does seem to have been less aware than we would have expected of other racist incidents and violence which had taken place on his Division. The position seems to be that Mr McIvor thought that things were under control, although he received little information from others present at the scene. For example, he did not know that there had been an eye witness to the murder. He knew

72

that TSG carriers were on the scene, as he had seen one in Well Hall Road and understood that there had been a full search.

12.9 **As to dealings with the family, Mr McIvor said that** *"whoever is in charge of the investigation at the time"* **should have the responsibility of ensuring that the victim of this or any murder should be identified and should ensure that the victim's family were contacted and properly informed of the circumstances.**

12.10 It is a matter of surprise to us that Mr McIvor stood back from the management scene and concerned himself only with possible future public order implications. Exactly what these were it is difficult to establish. He left the scene at about 00:55 and returned to Plumstead Police Station.

12.11 Mr McIvor clearly sought to distance himself from any operational responsibility for the incident on the night by defining himself as a "manager" with a purely Area responsibility for public order matters and therefore no Divisional operational responsibility. He used the phrase and concept of *"manager"* rather like a shield to defend himself from any suggestion of operational responsibility.

12.12 Mr McIvor did in our view fail to meet his responsibilities and to co-ordinate action at the scene in the immediate aftermath of the incident. The fact that he had such responsibility was made clear by his Divisional Chief Superintendent, Mr Philpott, who under direct questions on these issues stated that Mr McIvor's role was for the Area in relation to public order and *"to take over uniformed ground control of that* [the Stephen Lawrence] *incident"*.

12.13 Despite the fact that he was actually on duty physically in Plumstead Police Station and contactable by radio or telephone he did not arrive at the scene until after Mr Jeynes who was called out from home.

12.14 Mr McIvor had then immediately at his command resources from his own Division, CID officers from his and adjoining Divisions and the TSG who quite clearly required direction and co-ordination. He states that he made some cursory inquiries from Mr Jeynes regarding activity in relation to searches and house-to-house inquiries and then returned to Plumstead Police Station.

12.15 Mr McIvor states that he did not think about contacting the family, and that in any event that would have been the responsibility of Mr Jeynes and the CID. This is despite the fact that he knew prior to attending the scene that Stephen Lawrence had died. Mr Jeynes was not in fact so aware until 00:30 or later. Mr McIvor did not check that Mr Jeynes knew of Stephen's death, and that the duties in relation to the family were being discharged. He was not aware that the Lawrence family were at the hospital.

12.16 Mr McIvor was apparently not told of Mr Brooks' existence as either a witness or a victim, nor did he inquire about other witnesses or descriptions to satisfy himself as to the nature of the searches which had taken place. Mr McIvor did not make any notes personally at the time, nor did he ensure that an "incident log" (ie. a CAD or paper based record of actions and events) was kept. He did nothing in relation to checking whether a scene log was in place. Some five months later on 7 September 1993 he made out an incident report booklet apparently triggered by the fact that a review was taking place.

12.17 **Mr McIvor must be criticised for a) his failure to obtain full information of the incident; b) his failure to co-ordinate activities at the scene; c) his failure to command and direct resources; d) his failure to record activities personally and to ensure that there was some form of log of activities taking place for those who would subsequently take command; and e) his failure to consider the family.**

12.18 Chief Superintendent Christopher Benn is now attached to New Scotland Yard. In April 1993 he had recently been appointed Chief Superintendent in charge of the Operational Support Unit for the Area. His job included responsibility for Traffic, the Territorial Support Group, the Dog Section, the Mounted Branch and other support Units. Mr Benn had not been in uniform or on the operational side for some years. He happened to be accompanying a dog handler on duty during the night in question, as part of his learning process of the activities of those under his command. He told the Inquiry that he made some notes after the event, but these were what he called *"purely personal development notes"*, which had no evidential value and were simply *"for his own learning processes."* They were destroyed later, so that he has no document to help him in connection with the activities of the night.

12.19 Mr Benn believes that he arrived at the scene probably at about 23:45, since he knows that the call received by his dog van was recorded at about 23:26. He went to the scene simply because he happened to be with the dog van and dog handler. When he arrived he was the most senior officer present. Mr Groves identified himself to the Chief Superintendent, and Mr Benn says that he dealt with Mr Groves on and off for the time he was there. It will be remembered that Mr Groves says that he wrote the Chief Superintendent's name on his clipboard notes when he was introduced to him.

12.20 **In his statement, and in other documents, Mr Benn was very ready to accept that he personally was in command at the scene. He indicates that he bore responsibility for the actions of all officers who were there. At the bottom of the complaint form raised on behalf of the Police Complaints Authority, he indicated that *"any omissions are my responsibility not theirs* [that is the junior officers] *and I propose to make a full statement under caution for this Inquiry at any time"*.**

12.21 In a sense Mr Benn was too ready to accept responsibility, since he was only present by accident, and he was not truly in the chain of command of the operational or CID officers who attended the scene. He had little knowledge of Plumstead and its problems and of the area generally, since he was acclimatising himself to his role which covered a wide area of south-east London. He received little information about what had happened at the scene, and, for example, he had no knowledge of what Mr Brooks had said to any of the officers present, although he knew that he had been a witness of the murder. Mr Benn deserves some credit for having at least temporarily inserted himself into the chain of command and encouraged some actions which were sensible. But he failed to bring together the officers who were present. As a result there was no cohesive action.

12.22 When Mr Benn left the scene he went back to Plumstead Police Station in order to scan the CAD printout, and also in order to speak to Mr Brooks, who was obviously the most important person in connection with the investigation of this case. He did not take this or any further action at Plumstead, because he spoke to the Divisional Chief Superintendent, John Philpott, who was by then at Plumstead, who told him that the local officers would *"take it from here"*.

12.23 Mr Benn indicated that while he was at the scene he had been able, with Mr Groves, to *"check and verify everything that had been done up until that stage"*. For example, he ensured that the search of the area with the lights and dogs was properly carried out before he returned to Plumstead.

12.24 Mr Benn believes that both Acting Inspector Little and DC Pye were acting responsibly at the scene, and that Mr Groves was co-ordinating what was happening. He said that part of his briefing with Mr Groves was to go through what the officers had already done, for example in connection with looking for suspects. He was also surprisingly congratulatory or thankful in respect of Mr Groves' visit to the Welcome Inn.

12.25 Mr Benn indicated that Mr Groves would have had the management of the scene all the way through the time they were both present. His job on arriving at the scene was not to take that away from Mr Groves, as Mr Groves seemed to be someone who was well versed in what he was doing. Mr Benn saw his role as being to check and verify what had been done and to *"add those bits which I felt I could add"*.

12.26 Mr Benn was present at the scene for about 45 minutes. DC Pye did not remember seeing him at the scene at all. It does seem that Mr Benn concentrated his attention upon Mr Groves and his activities. Mr Benn did not, as was elicited in cross-examination, follow up any possible lines of information or intelligence while he was there. Indeed, perhaps understandably, it was his contention that since there was an experienced Detective Inspector, namely Mr Jeynes, present at the scene, that was a matter for the CID.

12.27 One of the steps taken by Mr Benn was to stop any further house-to-house enquiries, after the end of what he referred to as the dog search. He says that he was concerned about scientific evidence and its preservation, and that Mr Groves knew that it was his wish that there should be no further enquiries made from house-to-house. There was, as we have already indicated, only a limited house-to-house operation during the night, focusing on the area of Well Hall Road and the junction with Dickson Road and progressing into Dickson Road itself. This decision to stop further inquiries is strangely in conflict with Mr Jeynes' evidence which suggests that such inquiries were in fact *"widened"*. This reflects the essential failure to bring together the other officers, who were to all intents and purposes acting independently.

12.28 Mr Benn said that he believed that he had taken responsibility more than adequately for the scene management while he was present, but that he was neither competent nor qualified to carry out further detailed investigation, that being a matter for the SIO. Mr Benn indicated that he had been given a reasonably comprehensive account of what had happened by Mr Groves, including the information that this was an attack by white youths on two young black men, and that the white youths had made off along Dickson Road. There seems to be some doubt as to the source of any information given to Mr Benn, and certainly he had no fresh or further information to assist him in adopting the responsibilities which he says fell upon him at the scene.

12.29 Mr Benn summarised the position, namely that he was *"very keen and very thankful that Mr Groves had carried out the work that he had done before his arrival"*. He also seemed satisfied that everything that should have been done on the night in question, insofar as he was concerned with it, had been properly done.

12.30 **We feel bound to say that we were not as impressed as the Kent inquiry seems to have been in respect of the evidence of Mr Benn. He himself indicated that he probably should not have been adopting an active role at the scene but that he should have been at Plumstead Police Station, presumably liaising with the senior officers there. The result is, as we see it, that Mr Benn's presence at the scene added little to the control or co-ordination of all that took place.**

12.31 Mr Benn had no real role as a link in the chain of command at the scene. He can take credit, to a limited extent, together with Mr Groves, for the dog and dragon light search, which seems to have been reasonably carried out. But like the other officers, he did nothing to extend at once, and energetically, the search for suspects and the collection of intelligence and information which might have been used. Nor did he provide or ensure co-ordination of the activities of all the officers present.

12.32 **In summary we feel compelled to say that Mr Benn's part in this affair was no better than the somewhat unsatisfactory parts played by the other senior officers who were present. We are surprised that the conclusion of the Kent Inquiry was that everything during the initial response phase of this matter was properly carried out, and that Mr Benn played a distinguished part in it. Our conclusion is contrary to that of the Kent Police. All of us, having seen the relevant officers for a considerable time in the witness box, have to record this dissatisfaction.**

12.33 Inspector Ian Little was called before the Inquiry. He was promoted to Inspector in 1997. On 22 April 1993 he was a Police Sergeant at Plumstead, and he was Acting Inspector on the nightshift. Plainly Mr Little had limited experience at the time, although it was his job as Acting Inspector to take overall control of the uniformed officers on his shift at the Police Station. Mr Little was referred to the relevant CAD messages which were coming in after the attack, for example the message at 22:51 from the scene asking that the arrival of the ambulance should be speeded up.

12.34 **He says that he arrived at the scene after the ambulance had left, but probably before 23:15. He remembers that the information given to him on arrival was that it was believed that the victim had been struck on the head, and he says that he was aware at some stage, although he cannot remember when, that the assailants were five or six white youths who had apparently run off down Dickson Road. When he got to the scene Mr Little says that he did not see anybody else who appeared to be in charge.**

12.35 He says that his priority was first of all to establish the extent of the scene, and he discovered that there were *"two separate locations"* with which he had to deal, namely the place where Stephen Lawrence fell and the mouth of Dickson Road. He says that his initial reaction was to ensure that the scene and the immediate vicinity were contained for forensic examination. Mr Little has very little memory of Mr Groves on the night, although he believes that he did see him. He can remember no conversation with the Inspector, so that the amount of liaison between him and Mr Groves was plainly minimal. He says that the officers under his command and present at the scene were in the main on the cordons, and that the TSG men were elsewhere in the side streets so that he had no people under him to conduct house-to-house enquiries.

12.36 Certainly Mr Little gave no directions about any enquiries which should be made, and he seems to have concentrated on the very limited activity of the preservation of the two sites in question.

12.37 Mr Little was probably only at the scene for about half an hour. It must be said that there is considerable conflict as to the time when he left the scene and went to the hospital. He says that he was aware that PC Gleason had left the scene with the ambulance and was at the hospital on his own. He went to the hospital because information had been received after 23:30 to say that Stephen Lawrence had been certified dead and to say that some people had arrived at the hospital and that there was a potential witness there with PC Gleason as well. That, of course, was Mr Brooks. He says that he went to the hospital initially in order to support PC Gleason and to establish what the situation was there and to help PC Gleason with the people who had arrived at the hospital. Mr Little felt that there was nothing more that he could personally do at the scene since everything appeared to be under control. His contribution to what happened at the scene was very small, even on his own account.

12.38 **Mr Little was cross-examined at length both about the hospital and about his presence at the scene. He remembers no part of any conversation that he may have had with PC Bethel, and it is apparent that he failed to acquire any of the necessary information in order to discover for himself what offence had taken place. Both before the Kent inquiry and at the Inquest he has never been able to recall anything said to him by anybody at the scene. Questioning by Mr Mansfield did seem to establish that Mr Little did not have until much later any idea that there had been a group attack on Stephen Lawrence. When he was questioned by the Coroner at the Inquest Mr Little said that when he spoke to Mr Lawrence at the hospital he did not know about the group of men who were alleged to have attacked Stephen. When questioned about this he said "No, not at that stage. We knew there had been an attack, but the details were extremely sketchy at that time, so we had to close everything". Certainly, he accepted that he never said to Mr & Mrs Lawrence, even if he spoke to them, that there had been a racist attack.**

12.39 Mr Little, in common with most of the other officers, made no record of his own at all. As was pointed out to him, he did not know how the matter was going to develop, either at the scene or at the hospital, and it is most unfortunate that no record was made by him of anything that took place.

12.40 **As to his presence at the scene Mr Little's recollection is extraordinarily vague. He says that he saw one TSG carrier, and that he recalls speaking to a TSG Sergeant, but he cannot recall his name or the task that he was asked to perform. He has no recollection of how many officers he had under his command or available to him. He does say that TSG Units were "directed through me through the Control Room to go around the streets". He made no house-to-house enquiries because he said that he did not have the manpower immediately with him at the scene in order to perform this task. Even though he believes now that this was a racist attack he himself did nothing to activate any information gathering or intelligence sourcing which might have assisted.**

12.41 Mr Little had no knowledge at all of any sighting of the red Astra car to which reference has already been made. Once he returned to the Police Station with Duwayne Brooks he indicated that he dropped out of the picture, since he went back to his general duties as Acting Divisional Inspector.

12.42 **We have to say that we were unimpressed by the evidence of Mr Little. He added virtually nothing to the activity at the scene, and certainly he exercised virtually no control over what took place there. Initially he indicated that he had not spoken to Mr Groves. We believe that he probably did see and speak to Mr Groves, but without much effect or purpose. Mr Little was, as we see it, another weak link in a weak chain.**

THE HOSPITAL

12.43 As to Mr Little's visit to the hospital there is a fundamental conflict of evidence between himself and Mr & Mrs Lawrence. Mrs Lawrence was distraught and remembers little about any police officers or police activity at the hospital while she was there. That is wholly understandable, and is in no sense any kind of criticism of her. Mr & Mrs Lawrence both deny that any officer spoke to them at any time during their stay at the hospital. Mr Little says that when he arrived he discovered from PC Gleason that some property found on Stephen Lawrence's body had indicated that he was *"related to Mr & Mrs Lawrence outside, which is how things were beginning to develop together"*. He says that he spoke to both Mr & Mrs Lawrence and in his own words *"basically I identified myself to them and explained the situation, namely we've got a youth in the resuscitation room who has died and the indications were that he was their son, but we need a confirmation"*.

12.44 **In his interview by the Kent Police Mr Little said that he did not recall actually speaking to Mrs Lawrence, but that he had spoken to Mr Lawrence who was plainly the calmest of the group of relatives and friends who were present. In that interview these words appear, "....... *certainly one of us said to him* [Mr Lawrence] *'we've got a young lad in there, he is dead, we don't know who he is, but we would like to clarify that point. If it is not your son then all well and good, but we do need to know. I am sure you would like to know as well'."***

12.45 **If these were his words then it has to be said at once that this was a grossly insensitive and unsympathetic approach. Although Mr Little agreed that any dealings with Mr & Mrs Lawrence in the circumstances needed careful, delicate and sympathetic handling he did not seem to realise that the approach made by him (if it happened) was insensitive and clumsy and only capable of misinterpretation and difficulty. Mr & Mrs Lawrence, particularly Mr Lawrence, says that nothing was said at all by Inspector Little to him, and that he never made any visit to the resuscitation room either with one or two police officers in order formally to identify his son.**

12.46 PC Gleason had accompanied the ambulance to the hospital, and he says that he was the only officer there, until Mr Little joined him. Later on PC Bethel and DC Pye went to the hospital, and dealt with Stephen's clothing and exhibits.

12.47 No instructions were given to PC Gleason as to what he should do or how he should deal with the bereaved relatives who were inevitably going to attend. PC Gleason accepts that at no time during his stay at the hospital did he speak to Mrs Lawrence. She was understandably in a state of extreme distress. He does say that he spoke to Mr Lawrence, and that he can remember speaking to other members of the family as they left the hospital later in the morning.

12.48 **We should say at once that it does appear to us that PC Gleason probably did attend the resuscitation room with Mr Lawrence at 00:02. The visit may have been very short, and simply an extension of an earlier visit which had been made by the family when the body was seen after the doctors and nurses had done all that they could. There is an entry in PC Gleason's pocket book showing that he did go to the resuscitation room in order that there could be an identification of Stephen Lawrence. We can see no reason why PC Gleason should have invented that evidence, and made up that entry, nor any motive for so doing. Indeed there was no evidence before us of any formal identification made in the presence of hospital staff or police officers other than that short visit at 00:02 hours. The likelihood is that it took place but, wholly understandably, Mr**

Lawrence has no memory of it now. The events of that night must have excluded his memory of what took place.

12.49 It should be noted that PC Gleason spent more than half an hour at the hospital with Mr Brooks. He was still distressed and upset, for obvious reasons, and he was at first silent. When he heard that Stephen Lawrence was dead he did almost literally "climb the walls" of the hospital in his anguish. Later PC Gleason indicated that he managed to calm Mr Brooks down and he took a statement from him which is recorded in his pocket book. This is the first statement made by Mr Brooks and it is a most important document, since it contained the first full, or reasonably full, information as to what had taken place. There is no need to record the terms of the statement, which was recorded there and then in PC Gleason's notebook. That short statement contained a description of one of the youths seen by Mr Brooks. He said that *"one of the youths who had blue jeans, his hair was bushy light brown and stuck out, he was about 19 or 20"*. He further said that he saw that youth, who was in front of Stephen, strike down with one of his arms on Stephen's head. This may well have been a mistaken impression of the actual stabbing of Stephen Lawrence. PC Gleason says that he passed that information over his radio. No message has been traced indicating that this was done

12.50 Later on in May 1994, PC Gleason was asked about his dealings with Mr Brooks and he indicated that Mr Brooks was highly excitable both at the scene and in the hospital, and that to start with he was very unco-operative with police until he, PC Gleason, was able to obtain a statement from him in his pocket book at the hospital.

12.51 Although Mr Little in his evidence adopted the short entry in PC Gleason's notebook indicating that the identification had taken place at 00:02, it has to be noted that he had not countersigned the note and had no note of his own in order to refresh his memory. He said that he spoke to Mr Lawrence outside the resuscitation room and that Mr Lawrence said *"Well, what happens next?"* Then Mr Little says that he explained to Mr Lawrence as gently as he could what needed to be done during the coming hours, and indicated that a post mortem would have to take place. He says that he took the opportunity *"to explain to him [Mr Lawrence] briefly leaving out the lurid details that the body, clothing etc would have to be preserved for the investigation."* Mr Little says that Mr Lawrence then looked him directly in the eye and said *"Do what you have to do"*. He did say that there was little more conversation, but that he offered perhaps a few words of comfort. He could not recall the conversation word for word and he had no contemporaneous note to help him, nor any statement made very close to the time. Mr Little did accept that *"like anything, I am sure what I done could have been a little bit better, but I felt I had done a reasonable job if you like without wishing to impose on their grief any more than necessary"*.

12.52 Thereafter Mr Little went back to Plumstead Police Station with Mr Brooks. It was roundly suggested to Mr Little that this was bad practice, and that Mr Brooks was effectively kept at the hospital and made to remain there without any comfort or assistance until he was taken to Plumstead. Indeed the lack of attention to Mr Brooks might have resulted in his departure, since he was left apparently entirely on his own. Certainly Mr Little did take Mr Brooks to Plumstead, and he indicated that during the drive Mr Brooks was reasonably calm, and nothing was said, apart from some small talk. Mr Little rightly indicated that it was better that he should not talk to the witness en route to the police station where Mr Little believed that a full interview was to take place. He said that Mr Brooks was fairly quiet, perhaps slightly agitated, but that he did not view him as any problem. He wanted to ensure that the CID officers had an opportunity to speak to him at length in order to obtain an accurate and a full statement from him.

12.53 **The Inquiry is troubled indeed about Mr Little's evidence as to his contact with Mr & Mrs Lawrence. On his own account what he did and said was grossly insensitive and unsympathetic. All his actions portray a total lack of sensitivity in dealing with a bereaved family and coping with a situation such as that which pertained at the hospital. Whether Mr Little was put off by the comparatively large number of people who attended at the hospital is a matter which we will never be able to solve.**

12.54 We have already said that it does seem likely that a very cursory visit may have been paid by PC Gleason with Mr Lawrence to the resuscitation room, since he spoke of this in his evidence and did indeed make one of the very few records in a notebook which has been put before the Inquiry. It is wholly understandable that Mr Lawrence has forgotten that visit, but we do believe that it took place. **That note includes a specific entry giving Mr Lawrence's telephone number. It seems to us likely that this came from Mr Lawrence himself.**

12.55 In the end we also conclude that Mr Little probably was also present at 00:02 when PC Gleason and Mr Lawrence paid their visit to the resuscitation room. It is pointed out that this is in conflict with the evidence of Mr Jeynes, who believes that he told Inspector Little to go to the hospital at or after 00:15. But Mr Jeynes' timings are unrecorded, and it seems to us that Mr Little's evidence, as confirmed by PC Gleason, cannot simply be rejected.

12.56 **There is no explanation as to why he should say what he did if he was not present, particularly in view of the fact that if his evidence is wholly accepted it reflects very badly upon his own performance. The phrases used by him in evidence, and in his evidence to the Kent Police, were insensitive to a degree, and grated upon all who heard them when his evidence was given to the Inquiry.** No wonder they have been excluded from Mr Lawrence's memory.

12.57 Mr Little was rigorously cross-examined about his treatment of Mr & Mrs Lawrence. He accepted that he took no steps at the hospital to check with the medical staff about the identity or condition of Stephen Lawrence. He believes that Mr & Mrs Lawrence were pointed out to him by PC Gleason, and he accepted that he took no further steps himself to ensure that he was speaking to the right people. No member of the hospital staff remembers any conversation with Mr Little.

12.58 **When Mr Little left the hospital he made no arrangements himself with Mr & Mrs Lawrence as to what was to take place later. He says that he left them in the hands of PC Gleason, and expected that the PC would have made transport arrangements for them. This was a totally inadequate response by a supervising officer. There is no doubt but that the prime responsibility for failing to deal properly with the family at the hospital is that of Mr Little.**

12.59 Mr Little was expressly taxed with one matter which looms large in connection with family liaison. A report reached officers at Plumstead that Mr & Mrs Lawrence were eventually going home and that they did not want to be disturbed at all during the night. When questioned specifically about this by Mr Mansfield, Mr Little said that the first he had heard of anything like that was during the Inquiry. Certainly Mr Little was never told that Mr & Mrs Lawrence were going home and that they did not want to be disturbed. Indeed, it is most unlikely in our opinion that this was said to anybody. Mr & Mrs Lawrence were keen from the start to know what had happened and to receive such information as was available. Somebody may have assumed that they did not wish to be disturbed, but certainly this was not their attitude, and they are rightly indignant that a message of this kind was somehow passed to headquarters when they had given no indication that this was their wish.

12.60 **As to the Mr Little's race relations awareness, it was apparent that he had never undergone any course to assist him in this respect. He considered that it was a possibility, when he arrived at the scene, that this was a racist attack, and he treated the matter as** *"a murder".* **He did say that** *"everybody should be treated the same",* **and that he tried to be as sensitive as he could be with everybody irrespective of who they were. Although he had worked in multi-cultural societies and areas throughout his service and believed that he treated everybody in the same way his lack of sensitivity and his inaction, particularly at the hospital, betrayed conduct which demonstrates inability to deal properly with bereaved people, and particularly those bereaved as a result of a terrible racist attack. He failed to deal with the family appropriately and professionally. This was unwitting racism at work.**

12.61 In connection with the evidence as to what happened at the hospital it is necessary to stress the testimony of Mandy Lavin. She was the Night Services Manager at the Brook Hospital in 1993. She was a qualified nurse, and she remembered that there was confusion, upon the arrival of Stephen into the resuscitation room, about the extent and nature of his injuries. Reports which initially reached the hospital indicated that he had been attacked with an iron bar and had head injuries. Later it became obvious that he was the victim of terrible stab wounds, and the staff in the resuscitation room did of course quickly appreciate what had happened.

12.62 Miss Lavin remembers seeing Mrs Lawrence at the hospital, in extreme distress. She remembers *"quite a large number of people"* attending the hospital, and the family being accorded access to the resuscitation room to see their son. Miss Lavin was very busy with her own duties, and she has no recollection of seeing or dealing with any police officers at the hospital. She has no recollection of giving permission for the identification of Stephen Lawrence to take place. Her recollection was simply of the more general visit to the resuscitation room by a number of members of the family. She remembered prayers being said and a hymn being sung during that visit.

12.63 We are not satisfied that Miss Lavin's evidence must mean that PC Gleason was inventing his visit to the resuscitation room with Mr Lawrence. As we have already indicated it seems likely that this did take place in company with Mr Little, and that Mr Lawrence has wholly and understandably forgotten the short insensitive incident.

12.64 **Miss Lavin was asked a number of questions about her experience in connection with the treatment of the victims of racist attacks. She told the Inquiry, as she had indicated in her statement, that it was** *"true to say that on occasion I felt a general sense of unease about the police approach to such attacks in that the police tended to assume that such attacks were drug related and therefore of less importance than other assaults".* **Miss Lavin did give one specific example, namely the case of an Asian lady who had been subject to threats to kill and who had been doused with petrol. The difficulty of that evidence is that of course it is impossible to give a time or date for that incident, so that nobody can meet the allegation that the police did not view the incident with the same degree of seriousness as Miss Lavin. She said that she felt that the police approach was** *"perhaps more relaxed than I might have hoped"*

12.65 Miss Lavin was referring incidentally in this context mostly to her contact with junior ranks of police officers. Generally it was the more junior officers with whom she had to deal at the hospital.

THE CID

12.66 The first detective to arrive at the scene was Detective Constable Steven Pye. His first statement was made at 08:35 on the morning after the murder. At least he did make a reasonably contemporary statement. He says that he made some notes or consulted somebody else's notes in order to make that statement. There are no surviving notes to confirm this. Since DC Pye's statement contains, for example, a substantial list of named or numbered officers, there must have been some record even if it was scanty from which he may have helped himself to make his statement. On arrival at the scene, probably at about 23:15, DC Pye says that he spoke to a woman PC, presumably PC Bethel. He says that she *"updated"* him as to what had happened as far as she knew it. He had very little recollection of what he was told. He does believe that he may have been told that five or six white youths had run off down Dickson Road.

12.67 To the Kent Police DC Pye indicated that he felt that his responsibility at the scene would have been *"scene preservation: try to identify witnesses: try to apprehend suspects, and searching for physical evidence"*. In essence, this probably was a summary of that which he could or should have undertaken. He said that there were a lot of uniformed officers present, and that parts of the scene had already been cordoned off, and that Mr Groves and Mr Little, *"seemed to be in charge"*.

12.68 Undoubtedly DC Pye did transmit some information back to Plumstead. For example, he reported the possible evidence which might be available from one or more bus drivers; and it was DC Pye who relayed back the sightings of the red Astra car. Other than that which is recorded in his messages DC Pye said that he had some recollection of the night, but that there were areas which he just simply could not remember. He recalls that house-to-house enquiries were being done and that Mr Nugent was spoken to by some officers. But his understanding was that the only witness available at the time was indeed Mr Nugent. Referring to the house-to-house enquiries, DC Pye said that these were being done by uniformed officers *"under the control of myself, Mr Groves and Mr Little"*. He believes that some record was made of what took place, but he made no record himself.

12.69 In due course he told the Inquiry that he heard of the death of Stephen Lawrence. He believes that at some point during the night he must have been told that Stephen Lawrence had been stabbed, but he could not remember when this knowledge might have been imparted to him. DC Pye was asked by the Kent officers about the chain of command, and he said that he felt *"responsible towards the scene"*, but added that he was obviously not the highest ranking person there. He had a recollection of the presence of Mr Benn, and certainly he remembers the arrival of Mr Jeynes. He could not say whether he had been there a long or a short time when Mr Jeynes arrived. He told the Inquiry that he *"updated"* Mr Jeynes and indicated that from that point onwards Mr Jeynes would take control of the investigation.

12.70 Later DC Pye said that he was aware that Detective Superintendent Ian Crampton had arrived at the scene, but he had very little recollection of what was said or done by him. He did recall that both he and Mr Jeynes had briefed Mr Crampton as to what had happened and was happening at the scene.

12.71 **Again the long and the short of it is that the Inquiry is unimpressed by what DC Pye was able to tell us about what he did during the three hours or more that he was present in Well Hall Road and thereabouts. At about 03:00 he went to the hospital, probably on the instructions of Mr Crampton. When Mr Crampton arrived DC Pye indicated**

that Mr Jeynes *"would sort of hand over responsibility to him"*. At the hospital, as DC Pye's notebook in fact records, he saw the body of Stephen Lawrence in the resuscitation room and he collected all the clothing and other items which had been left there and catalogued them. These exhibits were later sealed and their details are set out in DC Pye's statement.

12.72 DC Pye was aware of the nature of a scene log. Its purpose is to record the names and details of those who pass through the boundaries of a cordoned area, in order to ensure that such entry is strictly limited, and that there is a record of those who do enter for cross-contamination purposes. DC Pye's memory was that he told an officer called Morony to keep a log. No such record is available in the system.

12.73 While he was still at the scene DC Pye says that he remembers that a message came through indicating that the family were at the hospital and that PC Gleason was requesting somebody to attend to assist him there. He says that he was told over the radio by somebody that the family had gone home for the night and did not wish to be disturbed. He gave this evidence after he had indicated that there seemed to have been some friction because of the length of time that PC Gleason had been at the hospital. There is some mystery as to what this "friction" was. It may be that PC Gleason or somebody on his behalf was complaining about the length of time that he had been left on his own at the hospital.

12.74 DC Pye agreed that he would have expected such a message about the family to have been recorded on the CAD system, since any operator receiving that information would wish to make sure that it was recorded. How this misapprehension came about is a mystery, as we have already indicated earlier. Certainly Mr & Mrs Lawrence never gave such an instruction or indication. Maybe PC Gleason himself concluded that this might have been their wish. It is an unhappy feature of the case and in particular of the family liaison.

12.75 In summary, when DC Pye was asked what he had actually achieved during the night, he said that he was *"instrumental in arranging things that were happening along with Mr Groves and Mr Little"*. He said that he constantly liaised with both of them throughout the night, and to that extent involved himself in what took place. He also called out Mr Jeynes and the photographic and forensic personnel. He also ensured the recording and continuity of exhibits at the hospital. His understanding was that through the night Units were patrolling and he repeated in cross-examination that he acted in a sense as a team with Mr Groves and Mr Little. He was not aware of any records being kept by anybody, and certainly he had no memory of Mr Groves showing him any detailed set of notes.

12.76 As to his own knowledge of the area and other incidents that might have taken place which could have been relevant to this inquiry again DC Pye's evidence was vague. He believed that the Duggal case involved a fight and a murder that had happened *after* the Stephen Lawrence case. He realised that a wider search and more extended house-to-house enquiries might have produced more information, but he repeated that he acted in a sense in the shadow of Mr Groves and Mr Little who were senior to him and who had the necessary officers to do that which was done during the hours of his attendance at the scene. In cross-examination he indicated that it was his belief that the message about the family going home and not wishing to be disturbed had probably come from PC Gleason. He believes that he communicated that information to Mr Jeynes. No record of such a message appears in the system.

12.77 **As to this officer's racism awareness it was established that he was accustomed to referring to black people as *"coloured"*. He said to the Inquiry that he was not aware that this might be regarded by black people as insulting until he watched Mr Groves giving evidence on the screen at the Inquiry. This officer could not remember receiving**

any formal racism awareness training, although he said that he *"seemed to remember some training in this regard when he was a probationer at Catford"*. **This is yet another indication that the training of officers in this department of their activity and relationship with the community was almost totally lacking.**

12.78 It is of some significance that DC Pye did not recall the arrival of Mr McIvor as a senior officer on the scene at all. Nor did he remember Mr Philpott being present. DC Pye indicated when asked whether he would do anything different as a result of his experience in April 1993 that he would have welcomed the presence of a second officer to work with him. His own colleague or partner on the night in question was in fact at court and was not permitted to work on that night.

12.79 **All in all we were not assisted by the evidence of DC Pye. It is perhaps not his fault that so little investigative initiative was displayed at the scene. As we have already indicated, he was alone and inexperienced, until Mr Jeynes arrived on the scene.**

12.80 Philip Jeynes was until October 1997 a Detective Inspector in the MPS. He started at Plumstead as a Detective Inspector in about 1992, and he retired after having completed 30 years service in 1997.

12.81 Mr Jeynes made a written statement on 1 October 1993. It was apparent while he was giving evidence that his memory of events was in many respects unclear. He had made no notes showing his involvement in the Stephen Lawrence case, and he was not asked to look back to the events of April 1993 until more than six months later. Mr Jeynes was the Duty Detective Inspector on 22 April 1993 and he was at home in bed when he was telephoned at about 23:30. He says that he arrived at Well Hall Road at about 00:15 on 23 April. He saw a uniformed Police Constable manning a cordon. Mr Jeynes was, like DC Pye, familiar with the concept of the scene log as a necessary requirement at a major crime scene. He said that it was *"historical practice"* to keep such a log, and that such a log was for *"forensic purposes"*. Plainly such a log should have been kept and retained.

12.82 After seeing this uniformed officer Mr Jeynes went to speak to DC Pye. Mr Jeynes regarded himself at that time as the senior investigator at the scene, and he remained in that role until Mr Crampton arrived probably at about 01:45.

12.83 Mr Jeynes was asked by the Kent Police as to what would have been his priorities when he was thus in charge of the investigation side. He said that he would have to look *"at preserving the scene, looking for witnesses, ensuring house-to-house enquiries are completed, making sure that all the forensic services are notified, arranging for families to be notified and arresting any suspects."*

12.84 That is in a sense a comprehensive list of the things which ought to be done at once at the scene of a serious crime. Mr Jeynes has some recollection of being given a reasonably full account of what had happened to Stephen Lawrence and Mr Brooks. It is doubtful whether that full information was in fact given to him at once by DC Pye, since DC Pye was himself not aware of Mr Brooks' existence. He thought that Mr Nugent was the only available witness. Certainly while Mr Jeynes was at the scene he never knew that Mr Brooks had given a statement to PC Gleason at the hospital. So that he, in common with other officers, knew nothing of the description which Mr Brooks had given of one of the attackers. Such information was vitally important to those at the scene.

12.85　It is part of Mr Jeynes' evidence that he had a recollection of sending another officer, who must have been Inspector Little, to the hospital. Mr Jeynes is probably wrong about the timing of this order, for the reasons already given.

12.86　Mr Jeynes was told that there had been limited house-to-house enquiries done in Well Hall Road and that one man, namely Mr Nugent, was making a statement as to what he had seen and heard. He also knew from Mr Groves that a visit had been made to the Welcome Inn and that the relevant areas were cordoned off.

12.87　Mr Jeynes referred in his statement to some information that had reached him about PC Gleason being at the hospital and *"having a bit of a problem down there"*. He has no recollection of what the problem may have been, but he did recall that he thought that it was not right that a PC should be dealing with the relatives by himself, hence his instruction, as he remembers it, to Mr Little to go to the hospital.

12.88　Mr Jeynes said that during the night, probably at about 01:15, he was told that the parents of Stephen Lawrence were going home and that they did not want to see anybody until the morning. Mr Jeynes indicated to us that he now positively recalls that the person who relayed that information to DC Pye on his radio was indeed PC Gleason. He says that he was standing beside DC Pye when the message came over the air. We do not believe that Mr & Mrs Lawrence ever said that they did not wish to see anybody until the following morning and PC Gleason denies creating such a message. The mystery as to the transmission of this information will probably never be properly solved. As there is no CAD message recorded it appears that a myth or rumour possibly started at the hospital and developed into a supposed fact simply by repetition.

12.89　Mr Jeynes said in his original statement, and indeed before the Inquiry, that he himself *"widened the house-to-house enquiries"*, to include both sides of Dickson Road down to the first junction, as well as houses in Well Hall Road opposite to the Dickson Road junction. He was present and watched police officers going to the houses in Dickson Road. He remembered seeing officers walking down driveways or pathways to various houses, and says that this was done on his direction. He told us that the searching of the gardens with the aid of the dragon lights by the TSG personnel had been done before those house-to-house enquiries were made.

12.90　Later Mr Jeynes says that he saw that the scene had been photographed and that the relevant scientific work had been performed, after which he sent DC Pye to the hospital, and then he left the scene at about 03:00 in the morning with Mr Crampton, who had by then arrived. He went with Mr Crampton to the police station, where he was generally engaged with enquiries and dealing with the exhibits and paying a short visit to a room where he observed that Mr Crampton was speaking to Mr Brooks, shortly before a full statement was taken from Mr Brooks by DC Cooper. Mr Jeynes went off duty at about 10:00 and he played no other part in the actual investigation of the Stephen Lawrence murder.

12.91　His only other duty, on the instructions of Mr Philpott, was to contact PC Alan Fisher, who was the Racial Incident Unit Officer at Plumstead. Together with PC Fisher Mr Jeynes went to the home of Mr & Mrs Lawrence probably at about 08:45 on Friday 23 April. Mr Jeynes was off-duty between 06:00 and 08:30 and when he came back to the police station he left shortly after that to visit Mr & Mrs Lawrence. He remembers that visit as having lasted for five to ten minutes.

12.92 Mr Jeynes indicates that he answered such questions as he could, and told Mr Lawrence what had happened, so far as he knew the situation. By that time he had quickly looked at the long statement made by Mr Brooks at the police station, which was completed probably at about 05:00. Mr Jeynes had never seen PC Gleason's short notebook statement made by Mr Brooks until he was shown it before our Inquiry. He indicates that after a short time he thought that it was best that he should leave because Mr & Mrs Lawrence needed only their family around them. He told them where the Incident Room was going to be set up, and then he left.

12.93 The fact is that apart from confirming what other officers have told us about their actions at the scene Mr Jeynes did not initiate any investigative action himself through the Collator's Index or the Racial Incident Unit to seek intelligence which may have helped in connection with the pursuit of the suspects.

12.94 A much later survey of the houses in Well Hall Road and Dickson Road suggests that the house-to-house enquiries made shortly after the attack were inadequate. We are not persuaded that the reconstruction of this aspect of the case, as illustrated by the coloured chart which was used at the Inquiry, establishes much one way or the other. That chart was compiled from information obtained four years later when there had obviously been changes in the occupation of the houses involved.

12.95 **The impression gained by the Inquiry is that once again the actions of Mr Jeynes, in common with the other officers, suffered from lack of co-ordination and direction and he himself failed to supply any leadership. He remembers various senior officers arriving at the scene from time to time while he was there, but there is no indication that he or anybody took control or arranged for a comprehensive meeting and discussion between the various commanders in order to extend the search, with the use of information which might have been available at the police station, and also with the use of information which might have been obtained from PC Gleason at any time after midnight.**

12.96 **We do not believe that Mr Jeynes was simply content to do nothing, or that he was positively influenced by the fact that he discovered some time after his arrival that this was a racist crime. We simply believe that he thought that other officers were doing what was necessary in their various departments, and his presence at the scene added little to the achievement of the police who were present during the night.**

12.97 At the end of the questioning of Mr Jeynes, he was asked about the presence of the other officers, and in particular the arrival of Mr McIvor. Mr Jeynes agreed that logically he might have expected Mr McIvor to co-ordinate the Inspectors who were present at the scene. He indicated that historically it was in his experience left to the senior Detective at the scene to run the investigation, plainly in liaison with the uniformed officers who were there.

12.98 It should be recorded that Mr Philpott, the Divisional Commander, attended the scene, probably about two hours after the murder. He says that he spoke to Mr Jeynes, and obtained information from him, and that he was generally happy that everything seemed to be satisfactory. He also plainly failed to concern himself with any detail, including the care of the family, and in general terms seems to have contributed little to co-ordination and control during his brief visit. To that extent he too must be subject to criticism in connection with his limited part played in the early hours after the murder.

12.99 **Overall the presence of all these more senior officers, and of the CID, added little to the investigation. The lack of co-ordination and control of the varying activities at the scene by senior officers stands out and must be roundly criticised. PC Bethel's vision of senior officers standing around with their hands on their hips may not literally be true, but in a sense it usefully sums up the situation as it struck all of us during the prolonged evidence given by these witnesses.**

12.100 **The scene of a murder may well be hectic and initially disorganised. But it is surely vital that more senior officers grapple with that disorganisation and attack the situation with energy and imagination. The senior officers of Inspector rank and upwards at this scene signally failed to act in this way. The lost opportunities for full and proper searches and investigation during the first hours after Stephen Lawrence's murder are to be deplored.**

CHAPTER THIRTEEN

THE FIRST SENIOR INVESTIGATING OFFICER
DETECTIVE SUPERINTENDENT IAN CRAMPTON

13.1 **The Senior Investigating Officer (SIO) who is in post in connection with an Area Major Incident Pool (AMIP) investigation is of course a most important individual. There are senior officers above him in the hierarchy, but it is the SIO who makes the vital decisions on the ground at the relevant time. A typical investigation team drawn from the AMIP in 1993 was headed by a Detective Superintendent. Under him, in accordance with the AMIP policy, there should be a full team of police officers provided for the investigation. From the pool of available officers a team has to be hastily assembled.**

13.2 We were informed that 3 Area faced a particularly heavy workload at the time of Stephen Lawrence's murder. Information was given to us that ten other major crimes including three murders were being investigated. There was no information as to the nature of these murders and the extent to which they made demands upon personnel. Suffice to say that no-one suggested that any of the nine murders approached the significance of the Stephen Lawrence murder and would therefore be likely to challenge its priority in terms of commitment and resources.

13.3 **The first SIO appointed to deal with the Stephen Lawrence murder was Detective Superintendent Ian Crampton. He joined the police force in 1965, and he retired in 1995. In 1993 he had been a Superintendent for two years, and he had been in the CID since 1968. Mr Crampton was plainly a most experienced officer. In 1992 he attended the Serious and Series Crime Course at Bramshill Police College, which apparently lasts for ten days. Mr Crampton had not worked on a racist murder before this case, but he was aware of the ACPO definition of racist crime in general terms, and he had investigated crimes of all kinds for many years.**

13.4 **On 22/23 April 1993 Mr Crampton was Duty Detective Superintendent on call for major incidents. He was telephoned in the early hours of Friday, 23 April, and was told that Stephen Lawrence had been attacked *"a couple of hours earlier"* and that he had been taken to hospital and had died from his injuries. He knew at an early stage that Stephen Lawrence had been stabbed, although he does not seem to be entirely clear where that information came from.**

13.5 During the previous week Mr Crampton had, among other duties, been concerned with the impending trial of some men accused of a contract killing of a man called David Norris. We will refer to that man, and his possible connection with Clifford Norris (the father of the suspect David Norris) later, but at the time Mr Crampton did not believe that there was any close connection between the two men. The killing of David Norris was investigated in Deptford.

13.6 **On Monday 26 April Mr Crampton was due to go to the Central Criminal Court, since he was the officer in charge of that David Norris murder case. So that it is apparent that Mr Crampton was only available to be the SIO in connection with Stephen Lawrence's murder until around mid-day on 26 April. This double duty occurred because everybody was fully engaged in their own activities, and because resources were stretched. It is significant and most unfortunate that an SIO was appointed who was only going to be able to control the murder investigation for a little over three days. The handover at that stage in a murder investigation must be avoided wherever**

possible. The first days after a murder are of course vital days. Murders can be and are sometimes solved by very quick action in the early stages. Even if this is not the case the decisions taken in the early days after a murder can have a major impact on the subsequent investigation and must be made with thoroughness, speed and with the fullest possible information available to the SIO.

13.7 **This we stress because it has seemed to us throughout this Inquiry that in this case the early days were particularly important, and one of the main grounds of complaint made by Mr & Mrs Lawrence has always been that no quick action was taken to arrest the suspects. Eventually the suspects were arrested on 7 May 1993, so that a considerable time elapsed before they were taken into custody, and before the unsatisfactory searches of their premises did eventually take place.**

13.8 It is to Mr Crampton's credit that very early in his evidence, when asked by Mr Lawson whether there was anything now which he wishes that he had done differently, he said at once that *"The strategy that I adopted was unsuccessful. .....because it didn't work and I had gone for an option that hindsight would tell me that quite clearly the other option may well have worked"*. The strategy to which he refers is the decision taken by him, which he says that he made in consultation with his senior officer Detective Chief Superintendent William Ilsley, not to arrest the suspects during the first weekend. On the other hand Mr Crampton says that every decision that he took during the time when he was in charge was a considered decision, and he felt that he was dealing with things in a professional way and in the way in which matters should have been properly dealt with.

13.9 **The question of the early arrests of the suspects is, as we see it, central to the whole of this Inquiry. We reach the conclusion, as will emerge, that there was a fundamental error made in the judgement and decision making, both by this officer, by his successor Mr Weeden, and by his supervisor Mr Ilsley who carried on the "strategy" laid down by Mr Crampton in connection with the arrests.**

13.10 Before coming to that vital decision however, there are other matters with which Mr Crampton was concerned during the night after the murder. By 08:00 on Friday, 23 April he was busily involved in setting up the Incident Room, and in mounting the investigation, and we have no doubt that things were hectic. That does not mean, however, that there can be any excuse for making what appear to us to have been wrong decisions.

13.11 When Mr Crampton was summoned from his home he went first to Plumstead Police Station. He arrived there at about 01:30 on 23 April. There he saw and spoke to Mr Brooks. He had a conversation with Mr Brooks, and apparently Mr Brooks told him very briefly what had occurred, before he made his full statement to DC Cooper. He says that he made sure that Mr Brooks was all right and that he did not want anybody there with him. In fact Mr Brooks' mother had attended the police station. Mr Crampton satisfied himself about Mr Brooks and concluded that he did indeed want to make a statement. Mr Brooks was in fact keen to make a statement, and although he was offered the chance to go home he preferred to stay at the police station with DC Cooper until his full and helpful statement was completed.

13.12 Mr Crampton told us, and the Kent inquiry, that he treated this murder as a racist crime from the word go, once he had spoken to Mr Brooks. Mr Brooks had told him that the murder was totally unprovoked and that it was by white people who had called him a nigger. *"From that moment on until it could be proven otherwise in my mind it was a racist murder"*.

13.13 In Mr Crampton's policy file, initiated on 23 April, he recorded that the murder was one in which the identity of the suspects was unknown, and that there was a *"possible racial motive"*. He says that this entry was made simply because at a later stage if the murder turned out to have been committed for other than purely racist reasons he would not have totally committed himself by a different form of entry in the policy file. We see no great significance in this entry in the file, bearing in mind Mr Crampton's repeated and firm assertion that this was without doubt a racist murder.

13.14 **Mr Crampton has no memory of seeing PC Gleason's note, which plainly should have been drawn to his attention. That note contained the first version of the matter given by Mr Brooks, and it included what might have been a most important description of one of the attackers. The failure properly to register the existence of that first statement is a feature of the early hours of this investigation.**

13.15 From Plumstead Police Station Mr Crampton went to Well Hall Road. The area was still cordoned off, and Mr Crampton remembers speaking to Mr Jeynes. Mr Jeynes was there with DC Pye, and Mr Crampton arrived with a Detective Sergeant.

13.16 Mr Crampton's memory is that Mr Jeynes was *"apparently in charge"*. He saw no uniformed Inspector at the scene, and indeed his memory is that the only officers present were the two Detectives and some officers manning the cordon. Mr Crampton was told nothing about the Astra car that had been seen. He says that he was given some information by Mr Jeynes as to what had taken place. He knew that a search had been carried out, including the use of dogs. He knew that TSG Units had been involved and says that he understood that there had been an extensive search *"in the area in which the suspects were known to run off and in the surrounding streets"*. At 02:52 a message shows that Mr Crampton reported that the scene had been examined, and the road was re-opened.

13.17 **As to Mr Crampton's attendance at the murder scene, it has to be stressed that he did not arrive there until after all the limited activity had taken place. We are critical of the activity that did take place, and particularly its lack of co-ordination by senior officers. But that was not the immediate responsibility of Mr Crampton. Mr Mansfield suggested, among other things, that there should have been a search of a circular area around the murder scene, and in particular that the Brook Estate should have been included in house-to-house searches or at least "knockings on doors" during the night after the murder. That is a justifiable comment and criticism of those who were at the scene. Undoubtedly there is criticism to be made of the co-ordination and control in that respect. But by 01:30 and even more by 03:00 when Mr Crampton left the scene it does seem to us that such steps would have been impracticable. They should have been taken earlier. It does not seem to us to be a personal criticism of Mr Crampton that various steps were not taken in connection with this investigation on the ground and early on.**

13.18 Mr Crampton was told by Mr Jeynes that information had been received that the family did not want to see anybody until the morning. Mr Crampton was due at the post-mortem at 09:00 on 23 April, and he directed Mr Jeynes to go to see the family at about 08:30 on that Friday morning. He had given further directions at the scene that photographs should be taken before he returned to Eltham Police Station. A decision was made, in consultation with Mr Ilsley, probably at about 06:30, that arrangements would be made for the investigation team to set up its Headquarters at Eltham, using the Home Office Large Major Enquiry System (HOLMES). We were told by one officer that the very early stages were recorded on a card index system, and that there was a change over to the HOLMES system. Mr Crampton indicated to the contrary. Mr Crampton's assertion is supported by other evidence which satisfies us that the HOLMES system was in fact used from the outset, and that the officer indicating otherwise was genuinely mistaken.

13.19   There was in existence in 1993 a "job description" in connection with the tasks to be undertaken by a Superintendent acting as SIO on an AMIP investigation. This is a comprehensive and detailed document, setting out full duties and instructions, and indicating that the Superintendent will be in active charge, subject of course to the direction of senior officers. Those duties include taking control of the crime scene, gathering information, evaluating priorities and initiating all investigation activities. They also include making the relevant decision as to the *"initial scope and pattern of the investigation"* and *"ensuring the correct treatment of persons injured or affected by crime in accordance with the Victim's Charter"*. That of course encompasses the appointment of Victim Liaison Officers, and *"ensuring adequate briefing, support facilities and victim support for as long as necessary"*.

13.20   In this context Mr Crampton was responsible for the appointment of DS Bevan and DC Holden, assisted by PC Alan Fisher from the Racial Incident Unit, in order to care for the Lawrence family. He himself did not see Mrs Lawrence during his tenure of command, but he did see and speak to Mr Lawrence at 14:30 on Friday 23 April shortly before the press conference which was held in order to publicise the murder and thus to seek assistance from the public.

13.21   Mr & Mrs Lawrence indicated that Sunday 25 April was a day on which they would like to be left to themselves. There was comparatively little time or opportunity for Mr Crampton himself to visit the Lawrence family. Everybody has pointed out, and this we accept, that the early days of a murder investigation can be fraught with problems and multiple activity. But it would have been better if Mr Crampton had been able to keep his finger on the pulse of the family liaison, since it is apparent that from the very earliest times the connection between the police and the family went badly wrong.

13.22   Whether he would have been able to identify the trouble during his tenure is a matter of doubt. Family liaison is an important aspect of any case and it should have been regularly and positively monitored. Mr Crampton says that the feedback that he was getting from police officers was that they were finding it difficult to sit down with the family on their own *"because there was so many people there"*. He did not personally see that as a problem, and in his evidence to us he said that he thought that the fact that the family had much support was a good thing. Mr Crampton says that when he did speak to Mr Lawrence and when he explained what had happened at the post-mortem, and what was going to happen, Mr Lawrence thanked him for his attendance and said that they would wish to be left alone on the Sunday. He picked DS Bevan for family liaison because he believed that DS Bevan had some training in *"human awareness"*. He picked DC Holden because she was a woman, and it was felt desirable that there should be a woman involved in the liaison with Mr & Mrs Lawrence.

13.23   The AMIP directive indicates that there shall be briefings *"usually twice a day"*, in order to *"Review cases, canvass and assess opinions and suggestions, set out immediate and long-term actions and policies"*. Mr Crampton told us that a meeting was held once a day and we have the typed up notes of Mr Bullock in respect of those meetings. There has been considerable reference to these notes. They do form a written record setting out the activities of the team, and in addition we have the various actions and pieces of information which started to reach the team from Friday 23 April onwards which are recorded on the CAD system.

13.24 We know, and it is a striking feature of this case, that most important information was reaching the team on Friday 23 and Saturday 24 April 1993. By 13:50 on 23 April Message No 4 from an anonymous caller indicated that there was *"a group of youths on the Kidbrooke Estate who always carry large knives and threaten people. They may have been involved in last night's stabbing. Two of them are Neil Acall(sic) and Dave Norris"*. The address of 102 Bournbrook Road was included in that message. There is no indication that this message was referred to at the 17:00 briefing on 23 April. Mr Crampton accepted, as of course he had to, that that message ought to have been mentioned at the meeting, but it appears that it was not. Nor was the message drawn to his attention until 24 April. This is an early indication of the problems as to the flow of information within the investigation caused by inadequate staffing and lack of knowledge of the HOLMES system.

13:25 The most important information of all to reach the team during the first weekend came from a man whose identity was in fact established from the start, but who was for obvious reasons given a pseudonym, namely "James Grant". At 19:45 on Friday 23 April this young man, later described by DS Davidson as *"a skinhead"*, walked into Plumstead Police Station. Detective Constable Christopher Budgen had been recruited on that day as a member of the AMIP team. He was sent to see the young man, and the information received was vital and illuminating. The information (as necessarily edited) has to be set out. It is known as Message 40:

> *"A male attended 'RM'* [Plumstead] *and stated that the persons responsible for the murder on the black youth, are Jamie and Neil Acourt of 102 Bournbrook Road SE3 together with David Norris and 2 other males identity unknown. That the Acourt Brothers call themselves 'The Krays'. In fact you can only join their gang if you stab someone. They carry knives and weapons most days. Also, David Norris stabbed a Stacey Benefield a month ago in order to prove himself. Benefield was taken to the Brook Hospital and told police he didn't know who assaulted him. He then went on to say that a young Pakistani boy was murdered last year in Well Hall, that Peter Thompson who is serving life was part of the Acourts gang. That in fact one of the Acourts killed this lad. They also stabbed a young lad at Woolwich town centre called 'Lee'. He had a bag placed over his head and was stabbed in his legs and arms in order to torture him. Jamie is described as white, 17 years, about 5'9", black hair, medium build. Neil is described as white, also 17 years, about 5'5", black hair, stocky build. Both are 'twins', apparently the house they live in was occupied by their mum, who has since left. Believed identity of informant established."*

13.26 DC Budgen reported this meeting to Mr Bullock. The message was recorded in the CAD system, although Mr Bullock appeared to receive DC Budgen's news with some lack of interest simply telling him to put the information on a "green sheet" for entry into the HOLMES system. The SIO did not know of the message until 24 April.

13.27 **DS Davidson told us that he saw James Grant with DC Budgen on Saturday, 24 April, when virtually the same information was repeated verbally. No message or retained record sets out details of that meeting, but it was important confirmation of James Grant's information.**

13.28 Research was ordered as a result of Message 40. By the evening of Sunday 25 April a full statement was obtained from Stacey Benefield (later confirmed by Matthew Farman) naming Neil Acourt and David Norris as those involved in the serious stabbing of Stacey Benefield in March 1993. The attack had been reported at the time, but no names had been given then by Stacey Benefield. This was perfectly clear evidence of the involvement of these two suspects in a potentially murderous attack.

13.29 **Furthermore two "letters" were recovered during Saturday 24 April both of which were letters shown to have been written by the same person (known to us as Witness FF). Those documents were recovered from a local telephone kiosk, and from the windscreen of a police car upon which the document was surreptitiously placed. They are reproduced at the end of this Report. They too were of importance, and they confirmed much of James Grant's information.**

13.30 Other anonymous and attributable information echoed that already received. It would be tedious to set out each and every message recording the receipt of further information. This has already been done by Kent Police in connection with the PCA report. The truth is that although people were reluctant to give their names there was no "wall of silence". In fact information purporting to implicate the suspects was readily and repeatedly made available, albeit hard evidence other than that of Mr Brooks and later the three bus-stop eyewitnesses of the murder was lacking.

13.31 Mr Crampton told Kent, and us, that he realised full well that the information coming to the investigation, particularly from James Grant, had to be taken seriously and that it appeared to be good information. Mr Crampton says that the action taken was to research it and to make inquiries in order to try to turn the information that had been obtained into hard evidence. Stacey Benefield's statement was taken on 25 April by DS Davidson who indicated to us that he regarded the introduction into the system of that hard evidence of a very serious crime committed by David Norris with Neil Acourt as grounds for making an arrest in itself.

13.32 **At some stage on 24 April Mr Crampton says that in consultation with others, he made his positive decision that there should be no immediate arrests. He says that by Sunday 25 April a formal decision had been made to utilise the surveillance team in order to observe 102 Bournbrook Road, and if possible other addresses, in order to advance the case, particularly in connection with possible association between the named suspects.**

13.33 **In his evidence Mr Crampton was emphatic that a** *"strategical"* **decision was made that no arrests should take place, at least until after the surveillance had thrown up further information, or until further evidence had been gleaned, perhaps by other witnesses coming forward.** He had of course in his possession from very early on a full statement from Mr Brooks which indicated that Mr Brooks might well be able to identify at least one of the suspects. It was known that there were other people at the bus stop, namely Joseph Shepherd, who was a friend of the Lawrence family, and Mr Westbrook and Mademoiselle Marie. The investigation team must have known that there was at least a possibility that there might be an identification made by one or more of those witnesses. In fact in the early stages of this investigation nobody was asked to make an E-fit or photo-fit of those involved in the murder. Mr Crampton indicates that he would not in any case ask for this step to be taken until after identification parades had taken place. **Otherwise, said Mr Crampton, the identification at a parade might be tainted. We do not agree, and it seems to us that all steps ought to have been taken which might have led to the identification of those involved very early on, including E-fit or photo-fit sessions.**

13.34 Mr Crampton said that by the Saturday evening, 24 April, consideration had been given to everything which was available, and a strategy had been adopted, namely that there would be no immediate arrests. He says that at the Saturday evening meeting those present would have been told of the decisions made and the strategy adopted, and that *"we would have thrown it open for discussion and any ideas, anybody's comments"*. There is no record in the relevant note of the Saturday meeting in this regard at all, and Mr Bullock's notes simply indicate in respect of future action that consideration was being given to the setting up of an observation point *"on suspect address"*. The history of the surveillance is elsewhere set out, but it should be remembered that Mr Bullock says that contact was not made until Sunday 25 April with the Sergeant in charge of the surveillance team. He indicated that the team was otherwise engaged in what turned out to be a comparatively trivial case on 26 April, so that they could not formally start their observations until 27 April.

13.35 A basic difficulty in connection with the police contentions in respect of the arrests is the total absence from Mr Crampton's policy file and records of any reference to the decision that there should be no immediate arrests and a closely related failure to record the decision to institute surveillance. Mr Crampton made nine entries in the policy file, all of them short, dealing with relevant decisions. It seems to this Inquiry palpable that the major and most important decision made by Mr Crampton was that these young men should not be arrested. If this decision was truly made after detailed consideration and proper consultation it should undoubtedly have been recorded in the policy file. This is not a bureaucratic requirement. The policy file must record important, and indeed vital decisions of this kind, both for record purposes, and in order to set out the thinking that the SIO has applied to the case. More particularly when the SIO knows that he is going to hand over within 48 hours of making that decision it seems to us essential that the matter should be fully recorded so that the new SIO can see exactly upon what basis the decision has been made.

13.36 We have looked with anxiety at the question of the decision not to make arrests during Mr Crampton's tenure as SIO. In the end, we are firmly convinced that a vital and fundamental mistake was made in failing to arrest the suspects over the first weekend, and certainly by early on Monday morning, 26 April.

13.37 As Kent indicated there are points for and against the decision to make arrests upon "reasonable suspicion". However, we are unanimously of the view that without a policy log entry indicating the options considered, the benefits of each option and the final decision, no weight can be given to Mr Crampton's assertion that the decision was a strategic one. The inevitable conclusion has to be that the alleged strategic decision was at the least ill-considered.

13.38 Inevitably there are doubts in our minds as to the considered nature of the decision, both because the decision itself seems to us to have been mistaken, and because there is no reference at all in any document to comprehensive discussion and to the strategic decision that is said to have been made on Saturday 24 April. By that time James Grant had been seen by DS Davidson. Even if DS Davidson's part in the quizzing of James Grant is to be criticised, there was information coming in which plainly gave reasonable cause for suspicion in order to make arrests.

13.39 If the right decision had been made, then the consequences are obvious. Searches could have been done wholly in accordance with the law, of the premises of the suspects. Identification parades could have been set up at short notice so that the witnesses

attended while their memories were at their freshest. Interviews could have taken place in the more immediate aftermath of the murder, and the suspects might not have reached their own considered decision that they would make no comment and remain silent.

13.40 Gary Dobson and Luke Knight did later answer questions, but questions posed in the early days are often more effective than those given after suspects have had time for reflection, and perhaps advice to remain silent.

13.41 **We wholly understand that early arrests might not have led to the conviction of any of the suspects. The same situation in respect of the elementary problems as to identification by Mr Brooks might have still prevailed. Furthermore if the suspects are as streetwise as they appear to be there may have been removal of incriminating objects very early on. If the arrests had been made earlier, and if no scientific evidence was even so available, and if no satisfactory identification had taken place, then the prosecution would almost certainly not have proceeded either in public or private form. In this particular case the delay in making the arrests has led to the problems that have dogged Mr & Mrs Lawrence since the early days. We feel compelled to say that the failure to make early arrests was the most fundamental fault in the investigation of this murder.**

13.42 Mr Crampton indicated in evidence that his *"negative strategy"* involved trying to obtain evidence in order to arrest as opposed to arresting in the hope of finding evidence. He also justified the decision on the basis that the probability was that after 36 hours any obviously blood-stained clothing or weapons would have been disposed of in any event. But as was pointed out there is always the possibility that those involved in crime may not have taken the fullest steps in order to protect themselves from detection as a result of blood-staining. Speed is always of the essence in connection with the obtaining of scientific evidence, and the longer matters are delayed the more there will be an opportunity for those involved to take even further steps to prevent detection.

13.43 **When the young men were eventually arrested on 7 May 1993 a pre-arranged script was used which read as follows, *"You fit the description of the youths involved: you with others have a history of being involved in recent stabbings in the area, and we have received information from various sources that you were involved in this"*. Those grounds for arrest applied with just as much force on Saturday 24 April - Monday 26 April as they did on 6/7 May.**

13.44 We understand that Mr Crampton wished to obtain further evidence, and his hope that the incomplete information set out in the relevant notes and documents would have been amplified by further investigation in the early days. For example, in respect of the family headed by the Witness DD, which included FF, the author of the two letters, further investigation and interviewing might have led to what Mr Crampton called *"a potential real live witness"*. This is true, but it is of much significance that eventually the arrests were made without any significant progress having been made in developing the information which had literally poured into this investigation room in the early stages. It seems to us that this was in fact the main hope of the investigators, namely that a witness would 'turn up', and solve the case for them. We feel that this is further indication that the alleged strategic decision and the glaring lack of an entry in the policy log reflect the fact that no proper considered decision making took place, and the investigation was allowed to drift in the hope that a significant witness would emerge.

13.45 Mr Crampton was doubtful whether he would have been fully entitled to search in connection with the murder of Stephen Lawrence if he had affected arrests in connection with the Stacey Benefield stabbing. He seemed to believe that such searches, for knives and clothing, in respect of the Stephen Lawrence matter, could not lawfully or properly have been carried out if the arrest was made on the grounds of the Stacey Benefield stabbing. Of course deception must not be practised in connection with searches, but it is not only commonsense but also the law that if arrests had been made because of the Benefield matter the relevant houses could have been fully and thoroughly searched, both for evidence in connection with the Benefield stabbing and for anything that might assist the Stephen Lawrence investigation. Section 18 and 19 of the Police and Criminal Evidence Act expressly provides that this is so.

13.46 During the weekend David Norris' address was available to the investigation from the collator's cards which were held at relevant police stations, even if at that stage no photograph of him was available.

13.47 Another matter of complaint by Mr & Mrs Lawrence's team in this case is that a proper search of the intelligence files at Scotland Yard and at local police stations was not made at once, either by the officers in charge of the initial response, or by Mr Crampton and his team, in order to forge connection between these suspects and the Stephen Lawrence murder. They also point out the investigation of other racist incidents might have assisted, and a connection between the Brook Estate, to which these men had headed after the murder, and where at least three of the suspects lived could and should have been discovered. Luke Knight lived in Well Hall Road nearby.

13.48 In connection with the policy file it must be noted that Mr Crampton's entries were short and sometimes concerned with comparatively small areas of the investigation. For example, there is an entry in connection with the searching of drains. There is no entry at all in connection with the most vital decision made during those early days, not to arrest the suspects. There are two possible reasons for this. First that no real considered decision was made and the investigation was simply allowed to drift until 6 or 7 May. Secondly that there was a deliberate unofficial policy not to record the reasons for major decisions which might subsequently prove contentious in order to seek to avert possible criticism. The latter would be the more serious. It is also significant that the failure to make a policy log entry in relation to a vital and major decision was clearly contrary to the MPS policy as set out in the AMIP guidelines. Nevertheless the failure was acceded to by Mr Ilsley who was party to the decision and was clearly aware of the content or lack of content of the policy log. Equally importantly it is clear that no senior supervisory officer ever appears to have looked at the policy log or made any comments whatsoever upon it. Indeed Commander Hugh Blenkin indicates in his statement to the PCA that he did not know what a policy log was. The lack of knowledge, interest and supervision by senior officers is singularly evident in this context.

13.49 On Monday 26 April Mr Crampton handed over to Detective Superintendent Brian Weeden. They met at a general meeting of Detective Superintendents chaired by Mr Ilsley, which was a forum which was apparently used to update Detective Superintendents involved in differing investigations and to resolve resource and other issues. Subsequent to the general meeting Mr Crampton spoke personally to Mr Weeden with Mr Ilsley present. There exists a long note made in Mr Weeden's own hand of the information he was given. Nowhere in those notes is there any reference to the decision that had been made not to arrest the suspects or the reasons for it. Nor was there reference to the Stacey Benefield statement nor any suggestion that Mr Crampton's decision should be reviewed with Mr Ilsley. It does seem remarkable that if such a fundamental decision had in fact been made it was not mentioned by Mr Crampton, not mentioned by Mr Ilsley and not queried by Mr Weeden. In our view this reflects the fact that Mr Crampton in fact did not make any strategic decision but allowed the investigation to drift until the point at which he handed it over, that Mr Ilsley acquiesced in this and that Mr Weeden failed to pick up the central issues of the investigation with sufficient grasp and urgency.

13.50 Mr Crampton, in answer to Mr Mansfield, said that of course the decision made as to the arrests was a flexible one that could have been changed at any time. That is perfectly true, but once the decision was wrongly made to leave these men at large it would be unlikely that the SIO taking over from the first "decision maker" would alter the decision already made, at least until there was some change in the circumstances, since the incoming SIO would not at once have a detailed knowledge of the investigation and, in this case regrettably no real knowledge of the basis on which the decision was made. When the handover took place Mr Weeden was consequently presented with a *"fait accompli"* in connection with the decision to arrest. He signally failed to focus upon this vital area of decision and to ascertain the reasons for it during his conference with the two officers responsible, Mr Crampton and Mr Ilsley, who must bear responsibility for not "bridging the gap" between the two SIOs and for not focusing upon the central question as to arrests.

13.51 **Mr Crampton was rigorously cross-examined by Mr Michael Mansfield on behalf of the Lawrence family. That questioning reinforced the strong view formed by this Inquiry that there was a fundamental misjudgement and mistake made during the first three days after the murder in connection with the arrest of the suspects. Furthermore, the poor processing of the information which had come into the Incident Room during the first two days after the murder is plainly a matter for criticism.**

CLIFFORD NORRIS

13.52 There has been much debate about the motive to be attributed to Mr Crampton. Mr Mansfield roundly suggests that there were plenty of grounds to arrest by 24 April and that Mr Crampton deliberately did not arrest. The suggestion made, in plain terms, is that *"What you were doing over that weekend was fudging it all, quite deliberately, and then you do exactly the same on the Monday morning so that you ensure no arrests and no identification"*. In other words Mr Mansfield suggested to Mr Crampton that he had for sinister reasons held back and formed a negative strategy, and that he had passed on this legacy to Mr Weeden, in the knowledge that it was likely that this strategy would be carried on. **This introduces into the case the prolonged and serious investigation of the possible connection between Mr Crampton and Clifford Norris, the father of the suspect David Norris. Mr Mansfield's allegation against Mr Crampton is clear and uncompromising. He says that either through fear of Clifford Norris, or for corrupt reasons, Mr Crampton was influenced by his knowledge of Clifford Norris and his probable connection direct or indirect with Mr Norris and his family.**

13.53 It is of course a notable coincidence that when Mr Crampton was given the short term duty of investigating the Stephen Lawrence murder he was actually engaged in connection with the trial of a man who was alleged to have killed a man called David Norris, an informant, sometime previously. The trial in connection with David Norris' death was starting at the Central Criminal Court, and it was to that trial that Mr Crampton had to go on Monday 26 April. That murder case involved drugs and was obviously in the high register of crime. Plainly the name "David Norris" must have been in the forefront of Mr Crampton's mind over the relevant weekend. Furthermore, Mr Crampton accepted that the *"Deptford Norrises with Clifford at their head were notorious at the time"*. In addition, Mr Crampton was of course aware of the suggestion that the dead David Norris was connected by some family relationship with Clifford Norris and his brother Alexander Norris.

13.54 Both Clifford Norris and Alexander Norris had become involved in allegations of major crime, involving drugs and murder, from around 1987 onwards. Before that the criminal records of Clifford Norris do not disclose that he was a major criminal, certainly in the sense that he had not been arrested for major crimes. But in 1987 and thereafter he became involved in high level drug activity. Alexander Norris was in fact arrested in 1988, long before Clifford Norris, and Alexander was sentenced to nine years' imprisonment in 1989. Furthermore, Alexander was ordered to forfeit more than £750,000 in connection with his drug dealing activities, and an alternative sentence of an additional five years was imposed upon him.

13.55 Clifford Norris had evaded arrest in June 1988, and in 1993 he was known by the police to be wanted by the Customs & Excise in connection with major drug offences. Eventually he was arrested on the orders of Mr Mellish in 1994.

13.56 During the investigation into the David Norris murder Mr Crampton knew that the dead man had claimed to police officers that he was a cousin of Clifford Norris. Indeed this matter was positively investigated, and statements were taken from the dead man's two brothers which have been seen by the Inquiry. Both brothers deny that there was any relationship between them and Clifford Norris. Of course this is not conclusive, since the two live brothers may be wrong and the dead brother may have been right. Searches at Somerset House do seem to confirm that there is no close blood relationship between the dead David Norris and Clifford Norris. Be that as it may it is plain that Mr Crampton knew that there was a suggested relationship in the sense that David Norris had claimed when he was stopped by police in the company of a man called Gary French that he was a cousin of Clifford Norris. Gary French's sister is apparently married to Alexander Norris. So that there was an oblique connection by marriage between the families involved.

13.57 **The real significance of this however is that Mr Crampton indicated emphatically to this Inquiry that he did not between 23 and 26 April make the connection in his own mind between the young 17 year old David Norris, who was named by several informants, and the villainous Clifford Norris. Mr Mansfield regularly returned to the suggestion that it was inconceivable that such a connection was not made. Mr Crampton was equally positive that he did not make the connection, although he accepted that he knew about the existence of Clifford Norris and his notoriety.**

SERGEANT XX

13.58 As the cross examination developed a further connection emerged, which is of great concern to the Lawrence family. Information from the Customs & Excise was given to the MPS in 1988, in connection with their investigation of Clifford and Alexander Norris, namely that Clifford and Alexander were associating with a Flying Squad Detective Sergeant who we have referred to as Sergeant XX. That Sergeant was seen on four occasions in company with one or both of the Norrises in public houses at a time when both Norrises were under observation and investigation by the Customs & Excise. That matter was reported to the MPS, and a comprehensive inquiry took place leading to disciplinary proceedings being brought against Sergeant XX.

13.59   It has to be noted that the disciplinary proceedings were not brought in connection with the association with Clifford Norris and his brother. Although Sergeant XX had been seen in most suspicious circumstances with the Norrises, that association was not the subject of a charge under the discipline code. The documents show that the Sergeant was warned as to his behaviour in that regard, and the facts of the association were thus never pursued in disciplinary proceedings. Sergeant XX denied any corrupt motive for the association and stated that he was seeking to develop Clifford Norris as an informant. Since this assertion was never tested in formal disciplinary hearings no firm conclusion appears to have been reached by the MPS as to the real nature and motivation of Sergeant XX's involvement with Clifford Norris. It seems to us right that we should register our concern that this aspect of Sergeant XX's association with Clifford Norris was not formally pursued and that the disciplinary penalties which were subsequently imposed appear lax, particularly since they resulted in the continued employment of Sergeant XX in the CID in the same area of London. Regardless of the fact that the association was not subject to formal discipline procedures it was plainly highly suspect.

13.60   **A connection between Sergeant XX and Mr Crampton was apparently known to his supervisors before this Inquiry, and emerged in the course of the evidence of Mr Crampton. It was discovered from the complaints file in connection with Sergeant XX that Mr Crampton had given a reference to the Disciplinary Board which dealt with Sergeant XX in 1989. That reference is in the form of a written statement, setting out a "professional" reference indicating that in Mr Crampton's view the officer was to be commended for his work, and indeed for his honesty during the time when he served under Mr Crampton in 1987. At that time Sergeant XX was stationed in south-east London, and he was serving immediately under Mr Crampton.**

13.61   Understandably this aspect of the case was pursued during our Inquiry over a considerable time. Furthermore, at the behest of the Inquiry all the relevant intelligence files in connection with Clifford Norris were obtained by the Inquiry, as were the personal files of the senior officers including Mr Crampton. These have been most carefully surveyed by all four members of the Inquiry team. These documents include a full report of the disciplinary investigation carried out into Sergeant XX by Superintendent Button. They also include the statement of Sergeant XX in connection with the disciplinary matters. Sergeant XX was in fact disciplined in connection with false entries on his duty state and other matters connected with his absence from duty, when he was supposedly at court, during the same period as he was associating with the Norrises. Sergeant XX was required to resign by the Disciplinary Board, but at a later appeal before an Assistant Commissioner he was allowed to continue his service, but was reduced to the rank of Detective Constable. We are bound to say that having seen the discipline file this appeal decision was unduly lenient. Assistant Commissioner Johnston appeared during his evidence to share our view.

13.62   The question of course is whether that connection between Mr Crampton and Sergeant XX involves any reverberation or connection which should persuade this Inquiry that Mr Crampton is more closely involved with Clifford Norris than he is prepared to say.

13.63   **Mr Crampton's evidence in this regard is categorical. He says that he simply did not know of the association between Sergeant XX and the Norrises, since of course the disciplinary proceedings did not involve that specific allegation. Mr Mansfield tested Mr Crampton strongly in this respect, and suggested that he must have known of the association.**

13.64 In addition to the question of the reference, Mr Mansfield also questioned Mr Crampton closely about his career and his positions both in SO11 (Criminal Intelligence Branch), and his professional positions in South London. SO11 is a section which deals amongst other things with intelligence as to criminals and their associates. The suggestion of course is that any police officer serving where Mr Crampton had served must have been alive to the existence and character of Clifford Norris, so that he could not possibly have failed to forge a connection between the suspect David Norris and his notorious father.

13.65 In the end we simply have to form a view of Mr Crampton based upon his own prolonged evidence and on what we have seen in the relevant documents disclosed during the days spent pursuing this important matter and searching the intelligence and other files to which we have referred.

13.66 **We understand the argument and suggestion made to Mr Crampton that it is strange indeed that the connection was not made in his mind. But we must also bear in mind the positive and indeed repeated evidence of Mr Crampton himself that there was in any event no kind of corrupt or improper holding back or fudging of his part of this investigation for any reason. Even if Mr Crampton had made the connection between the suspect David Norris and Clifford Norris at once, there is no evidence before us that Mr Crampton was himself fearful of what Clifford Norris might do, or that he was in contact with him in any way, or that he was or would have been likely to wish to hold back the prosecution of these vicious young men for any reason connected with Clifford Norris.**

13.67 We know that Clifford Norris, through his agent, is said to have become positively and corruptly involved in the prosecution of his son in connection with the attempted murder of Stacey Benefield, so that we have to bear that firmly in mind when looking at the whole picture in connection with the Stephen Lawrence murder. There is however no suggestion that any witness was tampered with or paid money in connection with the Stephen Lawrence case. There is the allegation that DS Crowley undermined the evidence of Mr Brooks, but this did not occur until weeks after Mr Crampton was wholly disengaged from the Stephen Lawrence inquiry.

13.68 **We are convinced that in spite of the connection which exists between Mr Crampton and Sergeant XX there is no proof that this connection or Mr Crampton's knowledge of Clifford Norris affected in any way his conduct. No allegation of this kind should be made lightly, and no allegation of this kind should be dismissed without the most careful and strenuous examination of the relevant documents and facts. However it would be wrong to make any conclusion or to draw any inferences against Mr Crampton without satisfactory proof that such a conclusion or such a deduction was justified. We do not believe that Mr Crampton was corruptly connected with Clifford Norris, or indeed that he acted out of fear or because of any other wrong motive in the actions that he took over the first weekend. It would be wholly unfair to Mr Crampton in all the circumstances to conclude or to hint otherwise.**

13.69 It should be added that during the hearings in connection with this part of the case Sergeant XX was at a fairly late stage represented by Counsel. In spite of the submissions made on Sergeant XX's behalf the Inquiry thought that it was right that the relevant documents should be used publicly in connection with Mr Mansfield's cross examination of Mr Crampton. Although disciplinary documents are usually wholly confidential, in our opinion justice required that they should be disclosed to the parties simply for the purposes of the Inquiry, and that they should be used by Mr Mansfield in his cross examination of Mr Crampton.

Mr Crampton was criticised for giving a reference without knowing the full and detailed account of the matter with which Sergeant XX had become concerned. We do not accept that that criticism is justified, although it is normally desirable that those giving references should be aware of the circumstances in which they are asked to give them. It does have to be said that our experience is that references are given, particularly references of the kind referred to in this case, simply as a general commendation of a man judged in connection with his professional activity. We do not believe that the circumstances established that Mr Crampton must have known or did know of the association between Clifford Norris and Sergeant XX. It does have to be noted that it is strange that this was not within Mr Crampton's knowledge. Rumours or talk about such things must have been rife, and Mr Crampton was concerned enough to give his reference. But we accept his evidence in this respect.

13.70 The matter has been one which required anxious and careful consideration by this Inquiry, since if there were improper influences bearing upon Mr Crampton that would most seriously affect the conclusion reached by us in connection with Mr Crampton's decisions made during his short tenure of office as SIO.

13.71 Kent were asked in September 1997 by Mr & Mrs Lawrence to investigate the possibility of police collusion or corruption. This matter had not been raised until then, and had not formed the basis of the original complaint made by Mr & Mrs Lawrence against the MPS. Until the end of September 1997 Mr & Mrs Lawrence did not in fact co-operate with Kent. After that they did register their opinion that the quality of the initial investigation *"could have been deliberately affected by collusion between one or more of the senior police officers with the prime suspects or their families"*. The fact that the matter was raised late does not mean that it could not be established. Now that the matter has been most thoroughly investigated, particularly in connection with Mr Crampton's part in the affair, we are convinced that there is no ground for a conclusion that collusion or corruption infected in any way the conduct of Mr Crampton.

13.72 **We saw him over a prolonged period in the witness box and we are wholly satisfied that his strong denial of the allegations made against him is to be accepted. As Mr Crampton points out his tenure of office was very short. There is no indication of any contact whatsoever between him and Clifford Norris. Furthermore he knew from the start of this high profile case that both he and his officers were acting under the closest scrutiny both from the media and indeed from the local community, and from Mr & Mrs Lawrence and those around them. We reject any suggestion that Mr Crampton was corrupt or that he acted in collusion with any member of the Norris family, or that he acted because of fear or because of the "Norris connections". His assertion has always been that he could have *"rushed in and arrested on no evidence and only on information"*, but as he has always said he sought to achieve the proper result in a different way, namely by waiting until there was firm evidence before making the arrests. This amounted to misjudgment and error, but there is no evidence that Mr Crampton was involved in corruption or collusion.**

13.73 A further limb of the cross examination of Mr Crampton involved the crime report which was completed in connection with the Stephen Lawrence murder. That is a document which is normally protected by public interest immunity, but it was disclosed and used in this case. The omission by Mr Crampton to indicate expressly on the form which was prepared by him that this was a racist incident is said to reflect the lack of importance given to the racist nature of the murder, as also reflected in the subsequently expressed views of several officers involved in the investigation that the murder was not racist, and the lack of urgency given to lines of investigation relating to the racist nature of the attack. Plainly this indication should have been given specifically upon the form, and similarly the relevant box indicating that this was a racist killing should have been ticked. This was not done. On the other hand the original form does bear a racist incident (RACINC) number, so that it is apparent that the matter was reported as a racist incident even if the form was improperly completed.

13.74 **It should also be stressed that in Mr Crampton's case nobody can suggest that he did anything other than conclude and assert that this was a purely racist murder from the start. We have already commented upon the entry in the policy file which might suggest some doubt about the matter. But having seen Mr Crampton and having heard him in the witness box we are convinced that he was wholly alive to the racist motive and nature of this murder throughout. He was undoubtedly not influenced in our opinion by the fact that the victim was black, and there would be no justification in the case of this senior officer for an assertion that he held back on racist grounds. It is perfectly true that Mr Crampton, like other officers, indicated that he had received little if any training in connection with race issues even at the SIO's course at Bramshill. Mr Crampton indicated that nothing was done in his day to deal specifically in training with racist matters or racist issues. This must of course be remedied. We will refer to this in our recommendations.**

13.75 Mr Yearwood, on behalf of the CRE, suggested that when statements were taken in the early days of this investigation from Joseph Shepherd and Stacey Benefield, more reference should have been made to the possible racist aspect of the case. For example it was suggested that Mr Shepherd should have been specifically asked about the racist remarks made by the attackers, and that Stacey Benefield should have been asked about his knowledge as to Neil Acourt and David Norris' racism. We see little ground for this criticism.

13.76 Mr Crampton was also cross-examined by Mr Macdonald on behalf of Mr Brooks. Mr Crampton indicated that he formed the view that Mr Brooks was doing all that he could to assist. Indeed both in his statements and in his evidence to the Inquiry he indicated that Mr Brooks was comparatively calm when he had contact with him and that he was satisfied that Mr Brooks was giving all possible assistance to the police. Indeed, he accepted in terms that Mr Brooks came over as *"quite a decent lad who appeared to be truthful and helpful"*.

13.77 Mr Macdonald appeared to suggest that there was some criticism to be made of Mr Crampton because of his failure to refer in his early statement, made before the Inquest, to the racist motive of this crime. This seems to us to be an unjustified criticism. Mr Crampton was simply making a "potted version" statement of what had happened factually. In any event reading Mr Brooks' statement alongside Mr Crampton's statement it is obvious that there was nothing but racist motive in this case, as Mr Crampton readily accepted. He was certainly not one of those who ducked the issue in connection with the motive of these white youths, and we see no grounds for criticism in connection with the making of his own statement.

13.78 **Mr Crampton was taken with care by Miss Sonia Woodley QC on behalf of the SIOs through each aspect of the case as it concerned Mr Crampton. He pointed out and stressed the basis on which he formed his strategy both in connection with the scientific or forensic matters and particularly in connection with his view that *"there were people or persons out there who did have that information and we were going to get to it and we felt that the delay and to try and get that was worthy of waiting. It was a risk but that was the decision we were going through"*.**

13.79 Miss Woodley stressed that Mr & Mrs Lawrence had asked to be left alone on Sunday 25 April, so that the available time during which he could have visited Mr & Mrs Lawrence was very limited. Furthermore he had established the family liaison team, and had instructed Mr Jeynes to go to visit Mr & Mrs Lawrence at the time when he was attending the post mortem at 09:00 on 23 April. We understand that point, but in a case as sensitive as this one it was absolutely essential that the SIO should take positive steps to ensure that nothing went wrong from the start. Both in connection with the arrests and in connection with family liaison the immediate decisions made and actions taken were of course vital. In spite of all the pressures upon him it would have been better that Mr Crampton had himself seen Mr & Mrs Lawrence.

13.80 In his initial interview by Kent, Mr Crampton indicated that *".... in my opinion I had more resources on that murder than I would normally have expected ... I was satisfied from the point of view of inquiry officers. If you want to ask me about was I satisfied with the amount of indexers [HOLMES team] I had then the answer was no."* According to AMIP policy the murder of Stephen Lawrence should have been classified as a "B" classification incident, but Mr Crampton said that the incident was not really formally classified as such and that lip service was paid to such classifications, and the reality of the situation was that Detective Superintendents were given such staff as was considered appropriate in discussion with Mr Ilsley. Had the incident been formally classified as a "B" then in comparison to the staffing levels recommended by policy there was a deficiency of two Detective Sergeants and a Police Constable in the Incident Room and the outside investigation team exceeded the specified levels by two Detective Sergeants and two Detective Constables. The view of "an expert" SIO from another force, Detective Chief Superintendent Burdis of South Yorkshire Police, indicates that in an investigation of this nature he would have required more than double the staff allocated to Mr Crampton (see Chapter 32). **Nevertheless the flawed decision made by Mr Crampton in relation to delayed arrests had nothing to do with strained resourcing. It is striking that this is another area where the MPS policy through its AMIP guidelines was clearly ignored with the apparent acquiescence of more senior officers. There is no indication that any senior officer took any direct interest in the application or otherwise of AMIP policy or in the adequacy or otherwise of staffing levels in this particular investigation.**

13.81 Mr Crampton had never previously used the HOLMES system in a murder investigation. He had had a two-day course on HOLMES in 1990, but it is plain that he and all those around him were remarkably untrained in connection with this computer and its operation. A separate section deals with this matter (see Chapter 32), but it is a matter of concern that this AMIP team was allowed to embark upon this murder investigation staffed by an SIO who had never run a HOLMES based incident, backed by a Detective Inspector with the same handicap, and initially assisted by a Detective Sergeant who had never been trained on HOLMES and had never run such an incident before.

13.82 On Monday 26 April Mr Crampton left the investigation of the Stephen Lawrence murder.

13.83 **We take into account all that Miss Woodley has said and written by way of submission on Mr Crampton's behalf. But we are convinced that a vital opportunity was missed, and that the failure to arrest by Monday 26 April, by which time Stacey Benefield's clear statement was in the hands of the team, must be primarily the responsibility of Mr Crampton. Mr Ilsley's acquiescence in Mr Crampton's decision is also the subject of criticism (see Chapter 27). This flawed decision appears to us to have been fundamental and most regrettable. Its consequences are plain to see.**

POSTSCRIPT AS TO GROUNDS FOR ARREST

13.84. As a result of the later submissions made on behalf of members of the Police Superintendents' Association (12 January 1999) we address specifically one of the central considerations in the investigation namely whether and when to arrest. We set out the grounds on which such a decision can be made, since there was clearly some confusion in the minds of more than one senior officer. Given the importance of the issue we summarise the considerations thus.

13.85 Section 24 of the Police and Criminal Evidence Act provides that *"where a constable has reasonable grounds for suspecting that an arrestable offence has been committed, he may arrest without a warrant anyone whom he has reasonable grounds for suspecting to be guilty of the offence."* *"Reasonable grounds for suspicion"* is not defined in the Act. It has been held (O'Hara -v- The Chief Constable The Royal Ulster Constabulary (1997) 2AC.286.) and other cases that an arresting officer must have formed a genuine suspicion that the person being arrested was guilty of an offence, and there must be reasonable grounds for forming such a suspicion. Such grounds may arise from information received from another (even if it is subsequently proved to be false) provided that a reasonable man, having regard to all the circumstances, would regard them as reasonable grounds for suspicion.

13.86 Having arrested on suspicion the police must then establish whether there is evidence sufficient to sustain a formal charge, in this case of murder. This is a subjective decision by the police initially, but the grounds on which they base their charge must subsequently pass the test applied by the Crown Prosecution Service (see Chapter 39, paragraph 12). Consequently police must have an eye to that test. In serious cases there is often discussion as to the grounds for charge with the CPS in advance.

13.87 In this case an early arrest between Saturday 24 April and Monday 26 April, would have had to have been made on the grounds of reasonable suspicion. Evidence would subsequently have had to be obtained to support the charge within 96 hours of the arrest taking place. Sections 41 to 43 of the Police and Criminal Evidence Act provide that a person shall not be detained for more than 24 hours without being charged. Magistrates, on application by the police, can extend this to a maximum period of 96 hours.

13.88 Whilst it is perfectly legal to arrest a suspect on "reasonable suspicion", consideration needs to be given to the likelihood of evidence being secured within 96 hours of that arrest and the impact of release without charge if such evidence is not forthcoming. If there is a better chance of securing evidence pre-arrest as opposed to developing it quickly after having arrested on "reasonable suspicion" then this may justify delay. There are no "rules". Each decision is different and more or less difficult according to the circumstances of the case. An SIO must make clear, logical decisions in this area. One would expect the issues considered, the reasoning and the decision to be carefully made and fully reflected in the policy log. In this case they were not.

13.89 The Inquiry asserts that the decision not to arrest by Mr Crampton and Mr Ilsley was a fundamental error. Our grounds for so asserting are clear. The first point at which we consider the decision to arrest could and should have taken place is on the late evening of Saturday 24 April. By then there were ten separate pieces of information, nine directly and one indirectly identifying the Acourts and their associates. In addition James Grant had given his initial information and had been seen a second time by DC Budgen and by DS Davidson. He had confirmed his information. The balance of considerations lay firmly with an early arrest, particularly with the possibility of obtaining scientific evidence. There existed "reasonable suspicion" par excellence.

13.90 **The balance continued to tip heavily in favour of a decision to arrest as time progressed through to Sunday 25 April when there is one further relevant item of information regarding the Acourts and, most importantly, the obtaining of Stacey Benefield's formal statement. At this point the balance in favour of action was in the Inquiry's view overwhelming.**

13.91. We recognise that on Sunday 25 April Mr Crampton was about to hand over to Mr Weeden. He may have felt reluctant to act at that late stage, unjustifiable though this is. However, by Monday 26 April when the handover took place in the presence of Mr Ilsley, the balance in favour of a decision to arrest was so clear that it should have been identified by Mr Crampton and by Mr Ilsley. An immediate review and assessment by Mr Weeden and Mr Ilsley should have been carried out resulting in a decision to arrest. We are conscious, in much of our Inquiry, that we may be accused of that fatal disease - hindsight. In this context we are certain we are not contaminated. The balance was clear to anyone who chose to look thoroughly and logically at the information available. The weight of the evidence in favour of decision to arrest should have been identified by all three senior officers, Mr Crampton, Mr Ilsley and Mr Weeden, not later than Monday 26 April.

13.92 **The lack of professional thoroughness and logic is demonstrated by the absence of any entry in the policy log. In the event there is nothing to justify inaction, and the conclusion must be one of drift rather than considered decision. In addition the fundamental mistake of delaying arrest is compounded by the abysmal nature of the accompanying surveillance.**

CHAPTER FOURTEEN

THE SECOND SENIOR INVESTIGATING OFFICER
DETECTIVE SUPERINTENDENT BRIAN WEEDEN

14.1 Detective Superintendent Brian Weeden gave evidence before the Inquiry for the best part of three days. When he was interviewed in 1997 by the Kent Police his interviews appear to have spanned four days. There is therefore a wealth of material available to the Inquiry dealing with Mr Weeden's involvement in the Stephen Lawrence murder.

14.2 **In 1993 Mr Weeden's senior officer summarised Mr Weeden as being** *"highly competent, sensitive, conscientious, thoughtful and caring"*. **Our impression of Mr Weeden is that he was a meticulous and fastidious man, who took upon himself much of the detail and burden of the investigation. But he was prepared to accept the situation handed over to him by Mr Crampton on 26 April 1993 without exercising his own critical faculties in order to test whether the right decisions had been made by Mr Crampton, both in connection with the strategy to be applied to the murder investigation and in connection with the allocation of tasks for which Mr Crampton had been responsible. Thus he perpetuated the wrong decisions made in the vital early days.**

14.3 On the morning of 26 April there was a long meeting of the Area Detective Superintendents, and later a handover by Mr Crampton to Mr Weeden. The nature of Mr Weeden's attention to detail can clearly be seen in the very full and careful notes made by him both on 26 April and thereafter. Much reference has been made to these notes which set out factual developments in the case, and which itemise each and every action which Mr Weeden required himself to perform. When a task was achieved he would rule a line through relevant action, to show that he had performed it.

14.4 Sometimes Mr Weeden's own thoughts are echoed in his notes. They form a revealing insight into Mr Weeden's mind. Part of the reason for making such detailed notes was, as Mr Weeden told us, his doubt as to the efficiency or efficacy of the HOLMES system which was set up to provide the full computerised record of actions taken and information gleaned and intelligence received in connection with this investigation.

14.5 **Mr Bullock had been appointed Deputy Investigating Officer. Mr Bullock was not HOLMES trained. Mr Weeden himself indicated that after speaking to Mr Bullock, who was not previously known to him, he appreciated that** *"accessing the HOLMES database was not going to be easy or certainly not possible in the early stages but he* **[Mr Bullock]** *was an officer with wide practical operational experience and I had hoped that in due course we may be able to perhaps get some in-house training so he would be able to use it even to a basic level"*. **An inauspicious start, considering that the HOLMES system was at the heart of the recording and processing of all information received and actions to be taken by the team.**

14.6 As to the manning of the investigation Mr Weeden's attitude was that he simply had to get on with the manpower which had been allotted to him. Like all the other officers he indicated that the team was undermanned, both in outdoor and indoor terms, although Mr Weeden agreed that in relative terms the Stephen Lawrence murder team was if anything generously empowered compared with other murder investigations current at the time.

14.7 **Mr Weeden was told, although this is nowhere reflected in his notes, that Mr Crampton had during his short tenure of office, positively decided that there should be no arrests. He was also told that the surveillance operation was formally to start on the following day. He also knew of course that DS Bevan and DC Holden had been appointed as family liaison officers.**

14.8 **In effect what Mr Weeden did was simply to adopt and continue the negative strategy, so far as arrests were concerned, which had been instituted by Mr Crampton. There is no indication that Mr Weeden brought his own judgement or instinct to bear in connection with the most basic decision of all, namely not to effect arrests at once.**

14.9 In the earliest hours of his command of this investigation there was available to him a full and detailed statement from Stacey Benefield, which provided the clearest evidence of the serious and almost fatal stabbing said to have been perpetrated by David Norris backed up by Neil Acourt. Mr Weeden was asked early in his evidence why that distinct case did not prompt arrests. His answer was that *"such a step would have made absolute nonsense of the surveillance operation. To have been seeking to establish associates of the known suspects while you have one or two of them in custody is going to frustrate the surveillance operation rather than assist it"*. **It seems to us that this reveals a basic misjudgement and a mistaken assessment of the relative importance of arrests and the opportunities that arrests would potentially provide, namely searches for evidence at the suspects' premises, and encouragement of other witnesses by the removal of the suspects, as compared with the surveillance operation with its limited objective of trying to establish association between some of the suspects.**

14.10 When he was cross examined by Mr Mansfield, Mr Weeden readily admitted that there had been a series of errors and omissions over the 14 month period when he was SIO. When asked whether there was anything that he might have changed, looking back on those months, he said this:- *"Well, with the benefit of hindsight I regret that the strategy which was developed during the weekend of 24/25 April and which I adopted and continued from Monday, 26 April was unsuccessful. At the time I honestly and firmly believed that the strategy of securing evidence before arrest was the right one, and offered the best opportunity of securing sound and successful convictions in the case. I had never before in any murder case arrested anyone for murder without evidence as opposed to information"*. He added that he shared the view that the best opportunity for securing scientific evidence had passed, and that there was a strong possibility that there could be witnesses who would give direct evidence, apart from the eye witnesses who had already been interviewed.

14.11 **This line of questioning led Mr Weeden to accept, with some reservation, that arrests could indeed have taken place certainly by 26 April, if not earlier. Almost in the same breath he said, *"I have always looked for some means of corroborating evidence corroborating information, and I have usually sought some evidence, but I do accept and without reservation that the position which exists is that there was reasonable ground for arresting at an earlier stage and arrests could have been affected"*. It also led to the astonishing situation revealed during the Kent inquiry, namely that Mr Weeden had told the Kent officers that he believed that he did not have the power to arrest until he had firm evidence.**

14.12 **If it was right that Mr Weeden believed in 1993 that he did not have the power to arrest upon the disclosure of reasonable grounds for suspicion then, as Mr Mansfield pointed out, it was indeed disturbing that a senior officer did not recognise *"a basic tenet of*** *criminal law"*. **Mr Weeden would not even accept that it was disturbing that this situation might have pertained; he indicated that he thought that it was regrettable. This was indeed an understatement.**

14.13 On the second day of Mr Weeden's evidence he sought to clear up what he called his *"thought processes"* and the answers given to Kent about his knowledge of his powers of arrest at the relevant time. He indicated to this Inquiry that the truth was that in 1993 he knew perfectly well what his powers of arrest were under the Police and Criminal Evidence Act and the criminal law, but that he simply chose not to arrest, continuing the strategy developed and agreed by Mr Crampton.

14.14 When seen by Kent Mr Weeden explained that since the decision about the delay in arrests had been the subject of much concern and criticism over the months and years that followed he had allowed himself to give a mistaken explanation of his state of knowledge as to his powers of arrest to Kent. He said that he had allowed his views in this connection to become distorted over the years, to the extent that he gave that wrong explanation.

14.15 **The picture is indeed confusing, and Mr Weeden has only himself to blame for the criticism and publicity heaped upon him as a result of his indication to Kent that he believed that he could not legally arrest upon reasonable grounds of suspicion. There seems to us to be a considerable degree of self justification by Mr Weeden, both in this respect and, as we shall see, in other fields.**

14.16 **The truth in any event is that Mr Weeden was both on and after 26 April, far too ready simply to accept the situation handed over to him by Mr Crampton. It may well be that his meticulous nature made it difficult for him to see the wood for the trees. It was essential, since he was from the morning of 26 April onwards in command, that he should review what had taken place and reach his own positive and correct decision as to what should be done. What in fact he did was simply to accept that the surveillance operation, with its very limited objects at the time, was an operation which should not be prejudiced. In fact there was a mass of information as to the association of the suspects, and positive evidence of their association if only as a result of Stacey Benefield's damning statement. Furthermore the surveillance operation was itself badly flawed, and Mr Weeden never exercised adequate supervision or control over the surveillance.**

14.17 The right course would have been to strike down the strategy which Mr Crampton was seeking to pass on to him, and to arrest at once. By 26 April of course yet more time had elapsed while Mr Weeden was *"reading himself into the case"*. We accept that as each day passed there was a greater risk that weapons and clothing would have been disposed of. But at least the opportunity could have been taken to make proper searches well before they were in fact made, and identification parades and interviews on or immediately after 26 April might well have been more productive. Furthermore, although this can never be established for certain, it seems to us more likely that witnesses would have been prepared to come forward if they knew that the arrests had taken place early on.

14.18 **The failure to make early arrests is, as in the case of Mr Crampton, the most fundamental misjudgement made by Mr Weeden. We will never know what the consequences might have been. We accept that it is possible that early arrests would have borne no more fruit than did the arrests ultimately made on 7 May. But at least, as we have already indicated, arrests on 26 or 27 April would have been markedly less subject to criticism, and might have ensured either that the case did indeed strengthen, or that it could be shown that the police had acted with sensible expedition.**

14.19   A further area of concern in connection with Mr Weeden's early days of command concerns the turning of information into evidence. Mr Weeden was on 26 April fully aware of the large amount of information which existed in connection with the suspects. At the heart of that information there was the man James Grant. As we know, Mr Crampton and Mr Bullock had passed this man over for investigation and research to DS Davidson. Mr Weeden was ready to accept both that he knew that James Grant was not an anonymous informer, and indeed that his information might have provided the key to the solution of the case in quick time. This was because James Grant's source was close to the suspects, if he was not involved with them himself. Both Witness K and Witness B could have been vitally important links in the chain. Eventually both of them were to make statements but they were not *'processed'* properly by the right people at the earliest opportunity.

14.20   The action allocated to DS Davidson to see Witness K was raised on 5 May. It is apparent that DS Davidson saw Witness K probably for the first time on 13 May. The statement made by Witness K was in fact made to DS Davidson on 17 May 1993. It is apparent from the Kent inquiry that James Grant was seen and interviewed by the Kent officers, and he told the Kent officers that he had told his handler, DS Davidson, the identity of his source at an early stage. When Mr Weeden was given this information in 1997 he said that he was *"staggered"* at the news. If that was true, and if the matter was not at once followed up there would indeed be grounds for heavy criticism. Since if DS Davidson was told that the source of Grant's information was Witness K that must have led to immediate action by Mr Crampton or Mr Weeden.

14.21   **DS Davidson denies that James Grant gave him direct information as to his source. DS Davidson positively said that Grant would not disclose that information, and in this he was supported by DC Budgen. Furthermore if that information had come to Mr Weeden he could not have failed to have acted upon it at once.**

14.22   **We believe that it is most unlikely that James Grant did in fact tell DS Davidson who was the source of his information. DS Davidson told us that in his quest for development of information he gave James Grant a hard time, and that Grant staunchly refused to take the matter further. It seems to us that this is likely to be true. As we have already indicated the information was so important and revealing that it should have been followed up by more senior officers, or at least by officers with characteristics different from those of DS Davidson.**

14.23   DS Davidson was a strong character, and he was given the heavy tasks in this investigation. Both in connection with James Grant and the other young and hesitant potential witnesses involved in this case much more care should have been taken in the selection of those allocated to develop the relevant lines of inquiry. For example, contact was made somewhat later in the investigation with Mr Noel Penstone of the Greenwich Council. He is known to be a man who is able to deal with members of the community who may be reluctant to communicate directly with the police. More co-operation with Mr Penstone and use of other more sensitive officers might have produced further evidence or fruitful information.

14.24   As to Witness B DS Davidson was tasked on 6 May 1993 with finding and investigating him. He was a witness who was reported to have said that he had seen four men running into Rochester Way when he was on top of a bus around the time of the murder. DS Davidson was, so his evidence has shown, given *"a name and a street in connection with B"*, by James Grant on a date which has never been established. Eventually as the official record shows, DS Davidson saw Witness B, but indicated on 19 May that he was a *"Walter Mitty"* and that his information suggested that Witness B's evidence would be of little value, since he was according to his mother a habitual liar.

14.25 Mr Weeden pointed out that a message on 4 May indicates that the girl who provided information about Witness B was going to try and find out his name on or after that date. This would be inconsistent with DS Davidson having already discovered the identity of Witness B by about that date. Mr Weeden said that it was *"crazy to suggest that we are raising actions to try and identify somebody who we already know"*. The suggested *"craziness"* of these conflicting actions may reflect the inadequate operation of the HOLMES system, and the lack of knowledge and control of information which resulted from inefficient use of the system. The counter to that assertion is the suggestion made by Mr Mansfield to Mr Weeden that the investigation of these witnesses was *"all a complete fudge"* and that the police were simply neither seeking nor indeed wanting to develop the information given by James Grant. Mr Mansfield alleged that the whole matter of James Grant and his information was being *"marginalised in importance and kept in the wings"*. Such are the stringent allegations made on behalf of Mr & Mrs Lawrence.

14.26 It is a feature of this part of the case that no documents exist in connection with the purported registration of James Grant as an informant. Nor is there a log of authorised visits which should exist if an informant is registered. DS Davidson and DC Budgen indicate that there was in existence an informant's docket which would have set out in some detail all that had taken place in the very early days in connection with the interviewing and testing of James Grant. They both say that the information was indeed properly and formally set out in a docket, and that the relevant papers were handed to the proper officer in connection with the registration of an informant, namely Detective Chief Inspector Leslie Owen at Greenwich Police Station.

14.27 **From there, as we were told by an expert in the field of informants, namely Detective Inspector Michael Barley, relevant inevitable steps would have resulted in that file being transmitted to the Area office, and from there at least a profile of the informant would have gone to New Scotland Yard. Searches have not revealed any documentation at all in connection with the registration of James Grant as an informant. This is a serious aspect of the James Grant affair, which creates obvious difficulties from the police point of view. If there were no proper documentation or registration that does support the suggestion made by Mr Mansfield that Grant's information was not properly dealt with.**

14.28 Later Mr Weeden did at the suggestion of DS Davidson forward a recommendation that £50 should be paid to James Grant, which Mr Weeden hoped might keep him interested and encourage him to provide further information for somewhat larger sums in the future. That action might be thought to support the suggestion that Mr Grant had indeed been registered. But as we will show the truth is that no registration was ever properly made, and DS Davidson appears wrongly to have been allowed a free hand to see James Grant without proper control.

14.29 **We accept that Mr Weeden was himself to be criticised in connection with the processing of the James Grant information. He was too ready to accept that DS Davidson was the right and the only person to be left in charge of that part of the investigation. We are not satisfied that Mr Weeden purposely ignored or delayed the investigation of Witnesses K and B and of James Grant's information, or that he did so for any ulterior motive. Whatever else may be said of Mr Weeden we are wholly convinced that it was his objective that the suspects or those involved in this terrible murder should be brought to justice. Mr Weeden's honesty and integrity are not impugned.**

14.30 Mr Mansfield pointed out correctly that during Mr Weeden's long interview with Kent the criticism was being made with justification that Mr Weeden did not reassure himself or take any positive action himself in connection with the James Grant information. As Kent pointed out this man might have been himself with the prime suspects at the time of the attack. Neither Mr Weeden nor his predecessor took any personal steps to focus upon James Grant. Coupled with the lack of any documentation from DS Davidson this gave Kent cause for concern. Energetic and direct contact by senior officers with this man should have been made as early as Friday, 23 April in the case of Mr Crampton, or Monday, 26 April in the case of Mr Weeden. Both SIOs were hoping for a witness or witnesses to provide them with evidence rather than information. Potentially James Grant could himself have been such a witness, or he could have taken the team to Witnesses K and B much earlier on.

14.31 **Prioritising James Grant and the earliest possible development of the evidence of Witnesses K and B might have led to the provision of some satisfactory evidence. In the end the evidence of Witness K as set out in the only written statement taken from him was of limited value, and he totally refused to co-operate thereafter. It has not been suggested that any further statement or information has been obtained from that witness which could have been used either in the original proposed proceedings or eventually in the private prosecution. Mr Mellish confirmed that Witness K was elusive and unco-operative. But he should have been seen and sensitively handled early on.**

14.32 **As to Witness B, his statement which was not available until November 1993 did suggest that he might provide valuable evidence, since he indicated that he had seen Neil Acourt and David Norris near the murder scene at the relevant time from the top of the bus. As it turned out this witness' evidence was virtually eliminated at the committal proceedings. He was unable to say that the Acourt seen by him in the street was Neil or Jamie. He indicated that he knew David Norris well and that he had seen him in the street. When an identification parade was arranged during the hearing at the Magistrates' Court Witness B was unable to pick out David Norris on the parade.**

14.33 Thus his evidence was rendered virtually valueless from that time onwards. He was, as we understand it, available at the Central Criminal Court. But once Mr Brooks' evidence had been rejected by the Court Mr Mansfield was not able to rely upon Witness B or upon any other evidence in order to go ahead with the case against those involved. Witness B had in addition told a wholly false story about the murder in his first account, so that his evidence was generally suspect for that reason alone. Again however he should have been seen earlier and should have been dealt with sensitively and carefully.

14.34 **It must be further said that even if Mr Weeden is subject to criticism as to the delayed arrest and in connection with the processing of the information available to him, there is no ground for alleging that these failures occurred because the victim of this murder was black or because Mr Weeden was in some way involved in collusion or corruption. Throughout the many questions put to him on the topic of racism and its possible impact on this case Mr Weeden rejected any suggestion that for racist reasons he had dragged his feet. We see no basis upon which it can properly be alleged that Mr Weeden acted improperly in his investigative duties because of racist attitudes. We were persuaded by Mr Weeden himself that he would not tolerate overt racism, and that he was not unconsciously motivated by racist prejudice in what he did or failed to do as SIO in his investigative duties. Different considerations plainly arise in connection with family liaison, as we will see.**

14.35 Furthermore, there is no ground in the case of Mr Weeden for any suggestion that he was in some way fearful of or linked to Clifford Norris. His evidence was that he knew from 26 April about David Norris' father, since his notes make positive reference to that fact. Thereafter he knew about Clifford Norris' involvement in serious crime, particularly because he indicated that Clifford Norris should be arrested if he was available when the arrests of the young men took place on and after 7 May. At least Mr Weeden realised that Clifford Norris should if possible be arrested. Strong action such as that taken by Mr Mellish in 1994 was required.

14.36 **Mr Weeden said that he did not know about Clifford Norris, and had no knowledge of him or his family until he took over on 26 April. Mr Mansfield suggested to Mr Weeden, as he did to Mr Crampton, that it was inconceivable that he had no knowledge of Norris as a criminal name in south east London. But we accept that Mr Weeden's answers in this respect were true. It was pointed out that to the Kent officers Mr Weeden had accepted that he was *"aware of his David Norris' father"*, but there is no indication that he told the Kent police that he positively knew of the existence of Clifford Norris before 26 April.**

14.37 In 1974, when Clifford Norris was 16 years old, Mr Weeden did in fact sign a document which effectively cancelled an arrest warrant in connection with Clifford Norris. This however was purely an administrative function which took place after Mr Norris had been arrested, so that the warrant inevitably had to go. It should also be said that the record of Clifford Norris, as set out in the criminal records, is not as substantial as one might imagine. He was being investigated by police over the years, and in 1983 or 1984 an intelligence marker was placed against him because he was suspected of being actively engaged in serious crime. Thereafter, from 1987 or 1988 he was plainly involved in high level crime, and he was on the run from 1988 until he was eventually arrested by Mr Mellish's team in 1994.

14.38 **We are not persuaded that the suggestion made by Mr Mansfield, namely that it was *"inconceivable"* that Mr Weeden had never before this case heard of Clifford Norris, has been established. Once he did know about Mr Norris, after 26 April, there is no indication that the existence of Clifford Norris or his influence in the case, and his part played in connection with the Benefield case, had any sinister impact in connection with Mr Weeden's part in this investigation.**

14.39 **Having seen Mr Weeden for such a substantial time we are convinced that he would not be a likely candidate for recruitment into a conspiracy to *"throw the case of David Norris and the other suspects"*. Mr Weeden himself described the allegations with some scorn as *"some ludicrous conspiracy theory"*, and it does seem to us wholly unlikely that Mr Weeden would have been involved in such a conspiracy. We conclude that Mr Weeden was an honest man.**

14.40 Furthermore, as Mr Weeden himself pointed out, positive steps were taken by his team to try to ensure that David Norris was prosecuted in connection with the Witham assault; and a re-trial had been demanded in the case of the unsuccessful prosecution in connection with Stacey Benefield. Clifford Norris' impact upon that case was disastrous. There is no evidence in our view that his influence affected Mr Weeden's actions in connection with this investigation in any way.

14.41 **The nature of the surveillance operation and the processing of its products is the topic of a separate chapter in this Report (Chapter 18). To the extent that Mr Weeden was in charge while the operation took place he must share the blame for its deficiencies. Indeed he was prepared to accept that it was extraordinary that there had not been the fullest investigation and identification of those who appeared in the photographs and their cars at an early stage. He believed that the lack of action taken, until later on, was probably caused *"because it was either overlooked or because people were overstretched"*. He is directly involved in this failure.**

14.42 Information could have been obtained by a careful and full analysis of these photographs as to persons connected with the suspects. Furthermore, and fundamentally, the lack of the ability to investigate what was being removed from the property speaks for itself. And even more eloquent is the known fact that in interview following his arrest Mr Dobson denied knowledge of David Norris, and yet these most important photographs showing them together were never made available to the officers who interviewed Mr Dobson, nor was a further interview set up of Mr Dobson in which these photographs could have been put to him to show that he was telling palpable lies.

14.43 **In the result Mr Weeden's attitude appears to have been that the failures in respect of the surveillance operation and the use of its products were the result of lack of manpower. He said that " *with everything else that was happening during that pretty hectic period it simply didn't get done"*. This is plainly a condemnation of this part of the investigation.**

14.44 **As to the red Astra car it is also palpable that the team failed properly to follow up that aspect of the case. When statements were eventually taken from three of the occupants of the car Kieran Hyland told the interviewing officer on 8 June 1993 that there had been five people in the car which visited and re-visited the murder scene soon after the killing had taken place. The other two occupants Messrs Copley and Goatley had said that there were only three people in the car which, so they said, passed the murder scene by accident. Mr Weeden accepted that the investigation was certainly unsatisfactory in this respect.**

14.45 **That is in our view an understatement. We fully understand that these people might not have *"supplanted the prime suspects"*, as Mr Weeden put it. But who knows what information might have been obtained if the matter had been pursued energetically at the relevant time. Nothing may have emerged, and there may have been no direct connection between the red Astra and its occupants and the murder. But it is not surprising that Mr & Mrs Lawrence feel that the failure to stop the car at once and to investigate the matter fully and at once betray inadequacies in the investigation of this case.**

14.46 The next suggestion made to Mr Weeden was that the ultimate decision to make the arrests, which took place on 7 May, was simply made on the spur of the moment because Mr Weeden and his team had become concerned about extraneous pressure, in particular the visit of Nelson Mandela to the Lawrence family and a planned demonstration in relation to racist murders and activity which was to take place on 8 May. In addition, it was suggested that Mr & Mrs Lawrence's meeting with Mr Ilsley on that day added to the pressure which resulted in the decision to arrest.

14.47 Mr Weeden says that by 6 May he was extremely disappointed at the progress that had been made, and that on that day he decided to make the arrests because his judgement was that additional matters had come into consideration which made it justifiable to arrest.

14.48　The three matters to which he referred were the finding of a knife in Wendover Road, the evidence of a lady who indicated that she had heard somebody call out *"J or Jamie"* on the night in question, and the arrival of the E-fits which had been compiled by Joseph Shepherd.

14.49　Mr Weeden says that the 13:30 meeting on 6 May, which makes no reference to any decision to arrest, was held so that he could review the evidence with his senior team members. After that meeting Mr Weeden says that he spoke with Mr Bullock and told him to bring forward and finalise the arrest, search and interview plans. Thereafter he was to indicate to his team in the afternoon that the arrests were to take place.

14.50　More than one member of the team indicated to us that they were completely taken by surprise by the decision to arrest made on that day, and Mr Bullock's note of the meeting of 6 May gives no indication that a decision to arrest had been made.

14.51　The suggestion made to Mr Weeden was of course that the arrests which were made on 7 May were simply a *"sham to satisfy the pressures"*. Thus Mr Mansfield roundly criticises the decision and doubts the justification for that decision, namely the arrival on the scene of the three somewhat tenuous strands to which we have already referred.

14.52　**To our mind the decision made on 6 May and the reasons given for it are further unsatisfactory features of the case. Virtually nothing had changed between 26 April and 6 May. While it was right that these men should be arrested the lack of any real change of circumstances by 6 May indicates and supports our conclusion that Mr Weeden did not properly review the strategy nor the decisions made as to arrest in the earliest days of his tenure of command.**

14.53　**If outside pressures did not contribute to the decision, there was no fresh reason to make the arrest and the justification for it is feeble. The probability is that by the afternoon of 6 May outside pressures did bear, even if unconsciously, upon Mr Weeden's mind, and we are not satisfied that the additional material could have been the spur which made it right to arrest on 6 May as opposed to 26 or 27 April 1993.**

14.54　Before turning to the important topic of family liaison it should be mentioned that Mr Weeden was asked for his opinion about the discontinuance of the prosecution of Neil Acourt and Luke Knight by the CPS in July 1993. It is apparent that Mr Weeden disagreed with the decision, in the sense that he believed that in spite of all the problems faced by his team there was a viable case to put before the court. Particularly as to Mr Brooks' evidence he believed that this would stand up in court, in spite of the obvious inconsistencies set out in Mr Brooks' series of statements, and in spite of his contact with DS Crowley.

14.55　Mr Weeden accepted that the decision was ultimately one for the CPS, whose task it was to put the case before the Court and to justify its prosecution. He realised that whatever his views might be it was in the discretion of the CPS to decide whether the matter should go ahead. In this context it should be noted that the discontinuance in July 1993 by the CPS was not in any event final. The CPS themselves indicated that the matter must be kept under review. The investigation team continued its investigations, as we shall see. In fact no further valuable evidence did emerge, with ultimate fatal consequences when the private prosecution was pursued. But in 1993 it is right to indicate that Mr Weeden still thought that there was life in the case, even though the CPS were not prepared to proceed to committal.

14.56 **Mr Weeden's part in the DS Crowley affair and the undermining of Mr Brooks' evidence is of significance. It is examined elsewhere (Chapter 22), but it is right to indicate that while Mr Weeden supports the version of events given by Mr Crowley in respect of the making of his statement on 3 June, he has indicated and does still indicate that he believed that DS Crowley might have misunderstood what Mr Brooks was saying so that he maintained his confidence in Mr Brooks as a witness.**

14.57 It is difficult to see how there was in fact any room for misunderstanding, since Mr Brooks' evidence and the indication given in his statement on 4 June was that he had not said all that DS Crowley reported him to have said. We do not understand Mr Weeden to be saying that he disbelieved DS Crowley, and in one sense his belief about the matter is of little consequence. The fact is that eventually the contest between DS Crowley and Mr Brooks has been held twice elsewhere, at the Magistrates' Court and the Central Criminal Court. We did not have the advantage of hearing the evidence of Mr Brooks being tested in cross examination before this Inquiry. We are thus left with the relevant inferences to be drawn and with the full account of the cross examination both of Mr Brooks and Mr Crowley at the Central Criminal Court, upon which we comment later in some detail.

14.58 Mr Weeden's evidence has a bearing on the dispute between Mr Brooks and DS Crowley. But in one sense the bearing is an indirect one. What can be said is that Mr Weeden confirms DS Crowley's evidence in connection with his arrival at the Incident Room and his instruction that a statement should be made there and then. On the other hand Mr Weeden's recollection was that what occurred might have taken place in the car on the way back to the Incident Room and not at Southwark Police Station itself. This was a misapprehension, since both DS Crowley and Mr Brooks (in his statement of 4 June) indicate that the material conversation that did take place between them was at the office at the Southwark Police Station after the identity parade. Mr Weeden instructed his officers to take statements on 4 June from Mr Brooks in respect of what DS Crowley had said, and it is evident that this was done. Mr Weeden believes that the officers may have visited Mr Brooks on 3 June and taken the statements on the next day. This was confirmed by the officers who visited Mr Brooks on 4 June, when two statements were taken from him, as we have already observed.

14.59 **One of the fundamental complaints of Mr & Mrs Lawrence is that nobody actually kept them up to date with the progress of the investigation during the first two or three weeks after their son's death. Mr Weeden's position in this respect is that he gave instructions to the family liaison officers to do precisely that, and he says that he was regularly reassured that this was being done. He directed that they should not give individual names, but he says that he instructed DS Bevan and DC Holden generally to offer what support they could, and if there were any contentious areas to let him know.**

14.60 He indicated to us that the most beneficial way of advancing family liaison would have been for him to meet the family himself. He said that he created the opportunities for that, but that the opportunities were simply not taken. On 27 April Mr Weeden says that he wrote a letter to Mr & Mrs Lawrence, at the same time that he wrote to both Mr Brooks' parents, which indicated in plain terms that DS Bevan and DC Holden were the liaison officers, but that if Mr & Mrs Lawrence wished to see Mr Weeden at any time all they needed to do was to say so. He says that the calendar of the first week involved on 26 April a verbal invitation to Mr & Mrs Lawrence through the officers for them to see Mr Weeden, followed by a verbal invitation and the letter on 27 April, and followed on 28 April by a note from a member of the family saying that the family did not want to be disturbed for the next two days unless there were developments.

14.61 Mr Weeden says that he had received two letters, two faxes and probably two telephone calls from Mr Khan asking that the liaison should be through him. Thereafter on 30 April another family representative communicated with Mr Weeden indicating that the family were going to be away for the weekend and that they did not want to be disturbed. He says that he had to balance his wish to make direct contact with the family's requests, coupled with the fact that it was likely to be seen as provocative and perhaps insensitive to sideline Mr Khan by going directly to the family.

14.62 **Mr Weeden says that probably on 28 April he telephoned Mr Khan's office and spoke to Mr Ratip, a solicitor working for Mr Khan, indicating that he would like to speak with Mr Khan. Mr Weeden believes that he made a considerable number of approaches and efforts, and he much regrets that they were not taken up. He believes that there was little co-operation and communication to ensure that this was achieved.**

14.63 When Mr Ilsley met Mr & Mrs Lawrence on 6 May the arrests were imminent. Mr Weeden says that he tried to contact Mr Ilsley, probably at his office, but he was unable to do so before the meeting took place. So that after the decision was made to arrest, Mr Ilsley was not in a position to inform Mr & Mrs Lawrence that this was to happen. In Mr Weeden's notes there is an entry saying *"inform them re arrests"*. But Mr Weeden also told us that it was never his practice to tell a victim's parents that an arrest was going to take place on the day before, presumably in case there was some leak of that information.

14.64 He says that he relies upon his notes of 7 May which indicate that the family representative was informed at 07:15 that the arrests had taken place only three quarters of an hour before. There is confirmation of this in a CAD message from DC Holden, although the timing of the entry of that message into the system is on the evening of the day of the arrests. It does however indicate that a message was sent at 07:15 . Mr & Mrs Lawrence say that they did not hear of the arrests until they saw the television or heard the radio announcement that they had taken place.

14.65 Mr Gompertz on behalf of the Commissioner put to Mr Weeden the content of two long briefing notes dated 13 July and 8 September 1993. The first briefing note was sent to the Commissioner to enable him to prepare for the proposed meeting with the All Party Parliamentary Group on Race and Community. The second briefing note was prepared to enable the Commissioner to respond to points raised in a letter dated 1 September 1993 from Mr Peter Bottomley MP.

14.66 **Those notes were self serving explanations of what had taken place in particular in connection with family liaison. Mr Weeden indicated that problems had arisen because of the large number of people surrounding Mr & Mrs Lawrence which tended to *"complicate and confuse matters"*. Furthermore, Mr Weeden indicated in the first note that it was in his view extremely rare for solicitors to act for a victim's family in such circumstances and that Mr Khan had been *"bombarding the Incident Room by letter, fax and telephone seeking detailed written information and so on"*.**

14.67 Indeed he said that the demands for information became such a distraction to the investigation team that on 30 April Commander Raymond Adams was enlisted to write to Mr Khan to ask that future inquiries should be addressed to him rather than the SIO and his officers.

14.68 Mr Weeden stressed in the first note that there had been many cancellations of meetings after 6 May, when Mr Ilsley and Mr Philpott had begun a series of weekly liaison meetings.

14.69 **The later note, dated 8 September 1993, referred to the family liaison arrangements and said that** *"in truth the family and their representatives have been dealt with sensitively, courteously and patiently by police throughout the inquiry and this will continue. The family and their representatives have had every opportunity to express their concerns and the two Chief Superintendents in particular remain receptive to anything the family have to say".* **This was not the true picture which has emerged during this Inquiry.**

14.70 Mr Weeden told us that he had tried himself to see the family but had failed so to do, and that in addition to trying to see them at home he had offered them an invitation to come to the Incident Room on their own, without their solicitor, so that he could meet them face to face and without the intervention of any other parties.

14.71 That invitation was turned down by Mr & Mrs Lawrence. They say that they had no wish to go to the Headquarters or to the Incident Room. Thereafter it is apparent that Mr Weeden lost patience with the Lawrence family, and in particular with their solicitor, Mr Khan. For example, he says that on Tuesday, 7 September, when arrangements had been made for a liaison meeting at Plumstead Police Station, Mr & Mrs Lawrence and Mr Khan were in fact giving an interview to LBC radio, and during that interview they were making *"the usual untrue complaints about police failures, disinterest and prejudice. This diatribe was accompanied by threats to sue the police".* The note ended with the following statement, *"Until recently the Senior Investigating Officer and his team have shown considerable understanding and forbearance in respect of the continuing irresponsible and damaging comments which have been made by the family and their representatives on radio, television and in print. However patience is now beginning to wear very thin in the face of frequently repeated slanderous and libellous remarks by the non family group especially Mr Imran Khan".*

14.72 Indeed Mr Weeden brought libel proceedings against a newspaper in connection with some of the publications said to have stemmed from remarks made by Mr Khan. An award was apparently made in his favour, but the publication went into liquidation and he did not receive his costs or his award.

14.73 **Those briefing notes grated upon the ears of the members of the Inquiry, since they show that Mr Weeden lost patience with the family, and in particular with Mr Khan. Mr Weeden's intentions may have been good to start with, but he never took positive steps to approach Mr Khan or indeed the family direct in order to ensure that a satisfactory meeting took place between them.**

14.74 As we have said in connection with the evidence of DS Bevan and DC Holden, the family liaison in sensitive and difficult cases of this kind has to be handled with great care and understanding. Things obviously went wrong from the start, and it was the duty of the senior officers in particular to take their own steps to ensure that alternative methods were followed in order to see that the family were kept properly informed and that their relationship with the investigation team was a healthy one. This they signally failed to do. Whatever the difficulties and whatever their cause the onus clearly lay upon Mr Weeden and his officers to address them. **They did not do so. In particular Mr Weeden never met the family face to face until over a year after his appointment as SIO. Mr Weeden allowed himself within days of taking over as SIO to be put off by Mr Khan. He wrongly assumed and said that Mr Khan was an Anti Racist Alliance member with his own** *"secret agenda".* **He distanced himself both from the family and Mr Khan when Mr Adams took over the correspondence with Mr Khan. He in turn must be said to have failed to act appropriately and professionally in connection with this grieving black family and their**

solicitor. He too readily allowed himself, as his own briefing notes show, to become involved in the negative and hostile stereotyping of the family and Mr Khan. He must be said to have been infected by unwitting racism in this regard. The formal intervention of Mr Ilsley into the liaison from 6 May cannot protect Mr Weeden from this measure of criticism.

14.75 **This aspect of the case, namely family liaison, is one in which important recommendations will be made since it is an essential part of the relationship between the police and the public that family liaison in cases involving racist incidents and crimes should be smooth, satisfactory and professional.**

14.76 In parenthesis it should be noted that Mr & Mrs Lawrence, during the course of this Inquiry indicated that they never received the letter of 27 April which Mr Weeden sent. There is some curiosity about this suggestion, since reference is made later to a discussion of that letter with Mrs Lawrence, when no allegation was made that the letter had not in fact been received. DS Bevan told us that he had delivered the letter by hand. It seems likely that the letter was actually delivered, but it seems also to be plain that Mr & Mrs Lawrence did not digest it. **Even if the letter was delivered and received the lack of any approach or response by Mr & Mrs Lawrence ought, as it seems to us, to have encouraged Mr Weeden to greater personal efforts to see Mr & Mrs Lawrence in order to make sure that the relationship between them and the police was satisfactory. There is no doubt that the relationship was from its earliest stages difficult and unhappy. This situation should never have been allowed to develop or to be maintained. The responsibility for this must be with Mr Weeden in his supervisory role in connection with family liaison.**

14.77 In answer to Mr Macdonald, on behalf of Mr Brooks, Mr Weeden agreed that he had always said that Mr Brooks was both helpful, truthful and co-operative. He said that to us, and he said it during the Kent inquiry. Mr Macdonald did however suggest that Mr Brooks was being patronised by Mr Weeden, because he had written two letters to Mr & Mrs Brooks on 27 April, indicating that he wished to make it clear that the police did not suspect Duwayne of any criminal involvement in this case whatsoever, and repeating that he has proved to be a helpful and truthful witness. It is not a valid criticism of Mr Weeden that he wrote those letters to Mr Brooks' parents, despite the fact that Mr Brooks was 18 years old. Mr Weeden said that it was indeed absurd to suggest that he was going over Mr Brooks' head and thus marginalising him.

14.78 Mr Weeden accepted, as had other officers, that the first statement made by Mr Brooks to PC Gleason had never been put before him. Comment has already been made about this unsatisfactory lack of processing of that first statement.

14.79 On 4 June 1993 Mr Weeden contacted Mr Medwynter of the CPS in connection with Mr Brooks' identification of Luke Knight and the trouble which had occurred in respect of the conversation between DS Crowley and Mr Brooks. Mr Weeden appears to have expressed the view to Mr Medwynter that notwithstanding the conversation between them Mr Brooks remained a credible witness. As we have indicated he gave his opinion that DS Crowley *"misinterpreted whatever was said by Brooks"*. Mr Weeden indicated that Mr Brooks continued throughout to be co-operative and helpful, making nine statements and giving evidence both at the Magistrates' Court and at the Crown Court and at the Inquest.

14.80 As to the pro formas which were sent out by the CPS in 1994 inviting officers to record the details of their dealings with Mr Brooks, some of which contained uncomplimentary remarks about Mr Brooks, Mr Weeden said that he agreed that those remarks were contrary to the views which he himself had expressed about Mr Brooks.

14.81 It appeared later that these forms, which are most unusual, were sent out by the CPS in 1994 when an indication had been given that Mr Brooks was going to plead automatism at his trial in connection with allegations made against him of riotous behaviour in relation to circumstances unconnected with the murder investigation. It was decided that if this was so any possible comments as to Mr Brooks' attitude and behaviour should be obtained from all those officers who had been in touch with him. Mr Weeden commented that the officers in question were simply reflecting their own personal dealings, some of which had taken place in very difficult circumstances on the night of the murder when Mr Brooks' behaviour may have been much affected by the appalling trauma to which he had been subjected.

14.82 **So far as Mr Weeden is concerned, those comments made by his officers cannot reflect against him. We do believe that Mr Weeden in his contact and dealings with Mr Brooks can be said to be the subject of some criticism. Mr Weeden did not positively offer special attention to Mr Brooks, because he believed that Mr Brooks was assisted by a solicitor early on, and he knew that later Mr Penstone became involved with him, so that he assumed that all necessary support was being provided for Mr Brooks. From October 1993 Mr Brooks was represented by Miss Deighton, who continued to be his solicitor during this Inquiry. Even if Mr Brooks was represented it was the SIO's duty to ensure that he was properly treated throughout.**

14.83 Mr Panton, on behalf of the London Borough of Greenwich, indicated that it was the Borough's view that the team had perhaps not used Mr Penstone enough in their dealings with the reluctant or young and sensitive witnesses from the Brook Estate with whom contact was made. Mr Weeden's answer to that was that he did not believe that those witnesses, such as Emma Cook, EE, FF, B and K were witnesses who would have been prepared to speak with any third parties. Indeed there were threats being made from time to time that if the police tried to see some witnesses they would be contacting solicitors on their own behalf. Mr Weeden must be subject to criticism for failing to try an alternative sensitive approach.

14.85 Mr Yearwood established, as he had with most of the officers called, that Mr Weeden had not been given any specific racism awareness training during the whole of his career. Mr Yearwood criticised the appointment of DS Bevan and DC Holden as liaison officers, and queried whether Mr Weeden had done enough to try to ensure that officers trained in race relations were used for this sensitive task. Furthermore, Mr Yearwood suggested that the officers involved had not focused on the racist aspect of the case when they were investigating the suspects and taking statements from witnesses who might have been able to assist in connection with the suspects' attitudes.

14.86 **In Mr Weeden's case the main criticisms to be made are that he failed to make his own decision on and immediately after 26 April as to the arrests and that he failed Mr & Mrs Lawrence and their solicitor. He worked very long hours and performed many detailed tasks in connection with the investigation, as his voluminous and meticulous notes show. But his decisions and his actions show lack of imagination and a tendency simply to allow things to drift in vital areas of the case.**

14.87 **To Mr Weeden's credit he stayed with the investigation until the summer of 1994, although he was due to retire in 1993. Little positive progress was made up to the date when he handed over to Mr Mellish in June 1994.**

14.88 We take into account all that has been carefully and helpfully said on Mr Weeden's behalf. But he must accept the criticisms which are set out above.

CHAPTER FIFTEEN

THE DEPUTY SENIOR INVESTIGATING OFFICER
DETECTIVE INSPECTOR BENJAMIN BULLOCK

15.1 Detective Inspector Benjamin Bullock gave evidence to the Inquiry over two days, Day 28 and Day 29. To our observation he was plainly a depressed individual. This is not surprising, since he has been involved in the Stephen Lawrence case since very early on, and has been thus a close observer of the failure of the case.

15.2 When Mr Mellish took over as SIO in 1994 he indicates, in a report on Mr Bullock, that the morale of the officers involved in the investigation was by then extremely low. Again this is not surprising since those who remained on the squad conducting the investigation had plainly failed to gather evidence which might support a prosecution. In 1993 and 1994 the CPS had indicated that the matter should not be taken forward. No further substantial lines of investigation had borne any fruit thereafter.

15.3 There was from the start intense media and indeed political pressure bearing upon the case. Mr Bullock had plainly found what he called the "hype" of the case by the media a burden and indeed an obstruction to the work being done by the squad. Thereafter in 1994 and 1995, the matter was handed over to the private prosecution team. Mr Bullock then saw that prosecution fail. In 1997 he was interviewed over a long period by the officers conducting the PCA inquiry. He is the only serving officer against whom it has been recommended that there should be disciplinary proceedings. Mr Bullock said during his evidence that he is a pessimist. This was apparent from the manner and content of his evidence. No wonder he is generally depressed about the case and its outcome and indeed his part in the matter.

15.4 Mr Bullock has nearly completed his 30 years service with the MPS. He was a Constable from 1969 until 1978 when he was promoted to the rank of Sergeant. He was promoted to the rank of Inspector in 1989. All his service as an Inspector has been as a CID officer. Mr Bullock had never been involved in the investigation of a racist murder before. It was wholly apparent from questions asked by various parties that he was not trained at all in matters of race relations, and he had no training of any kind in racism awareness. All murders must be investigated with skill and energy. But it is apparent, and should be known by all, that the investigation of racially motivated murders has special features of which officers must be aware. Mr Bullock's attitude was that a racist murder was just like any other murder. And he casually and insensitively referred to Stephen Lawrence and Duwayne Brooks as *"the two young coloured lads"*. He was oblivious to his own insensitivity in this regard.

15.5 Quite apart from lack of training in connection with race relations it is also apparent that Mr Bullock had never at any time, until his interviews with the Kent officers, seen the Metropolitan Police manual which sets out the AMIP guidelines in connection with the role which he was to adopt in connection with this investigation. Mr Bullock was the second in command of the AMIP team, both under the supervision of Mr Crampton and Mr Weeden. He was effectively the right hand man and the deputy to those officers. The AMIP manual sets out in detail the *"job description"* of a Deputy Investigating Officer (DIO). Mr Bullock's answers in connection with questions concerning this manual, both to Kent and ourselves, were most unsatisfactory. He said that the manual was not known to him until the Kent officers drew his attention to it.

15.6   It seems to us astonishing that a man who had been a Detective Inspector since 1989 and who had presumably been a DIO on previous occasions, had never seen the written version of his own job description. There is no need to refer to the details of the document. Paragraph 3.3 requires a DIO to keep himself aware of all policy decisions. He must, according to the document, be able to brief any appropriate person on the complete operation at any time. Furthermore the document decrees that *"Once a policy docket is opened ensure that every decision made is recorded with reasons and signed and the policy file is preserved according to the Senior Investigating Officer's instructions"*. Mr Bullock had no idea that that was part of his duty, indicating that in his view the policy docket was filled out by the SIO and was effectively not his business.

15.7   It is also an unhappy feature of Mr Bullock's evidence that he indicated that ignorance of the AMIP guidelines was not unique. Furthermore, Mr Bullock indicated that he had very little training or knowledge of the HOLMES computer system which was operating in this case. His training had been slight, and he said that the system was, certainly for himself, difficult to operate and indeed something of a mystery. Even now Mr Bullock says that HOLMES is *"a very difficult machine to operate and a system to operate"*. Only since he has been using the HOLMES system in order to research this case has he gained some recent experience.

15.8   Mr Bullock confirmed that in his view the manpower which was available in this AMIP team was inadequate in several ways. He said that there was a shortage of indexers, so that it was not possible to get the material on to the computer with reasonable speed. Furthermore he said that the Office Manager was really doing the majority of the work on his own, so that some of the messages that came in were not seen by himself or the SIO at times when they should have been seen.

15.9   **Mr Bullock worked extremely long hours over the early days of this investigation, and his memory of those days is that they were *"fighting for information, trying to get on top of what is coming in ....."*. It is perfectly obvious that the early days of an investigation will be hectic and extremely busy. On the other hand this is no excuse for failure properly to process the vital information that was coming in from the very first day after Stephen Lawrence's murder.**

15.10   As to the manning of the team it is sad to have to indicate that Mr Bullock's evidence is in tune with that of other witnesses who asserted that staffing resources were not made available properly to staff the AMIP teams operating in the Metropolitan Police Area at the relevant time. Both Mr Bullock and Mr Crampton indicated that for the Stephen Lawrence murder there was a comparatively generous allowance, but even then the manning levels were inadequate. The conclusion which was put to Mr Bullock was that if this was so then every major investigation team must have been seriously under strength in 1993. To this suggestion Mr Bullock and others agreed.

15.11   Mr Bullock had not worked with Mr Crampton before, although he knew him by name and reputation. Experienced police officers must of course be able to work together whether or not they have previously formed part of a team.

15.12   It is apparent, and was plainly apparent to Kent, that Mr Bullock did not see some of the early information coming into the investigation until too late. The early days are vital, for all the reasons previously set out. Unless the system ensures that the officers at the top receive vital information at once, there is bound to be a problem. Simply for example, Mr Bullock told us that he had never seen the first anonymous message on Friday 23 April, the day when it came in. He saw it later, but plainly as DIO that message ought to have been in front of him forthwith.

15.13 When James Grant came into the police station he was seen by DC Budgen. The DC says that Mr Bullock was told of the arrival of this man, and that Mr Bullock simply said *"Go and put it down on a 'green sheet'"*. There is some difference of opinion between Mr Bullock and DC Budgen as to what actually took place. DC Budgen said that there was a clash of personalities between himself and Mr Bullock in any event. Mr Bullock appears to have told DS Davidson to watch DC Budgen, which supports that belief. Mr Bullock's recollection is that he was shown James Grant's green form statement, and that James Grant had left the police station by that time. However James Grant came back on Saturday 24 April, when he was seen by DS Davidson and DC Budgen. It seems to us that the information given so fully by James Grant ought to have alerted Mr Bullock so that he saw James Grant himself. He never did see James Grant. It would be wrong to say that Mr Bullock took no interest in the information coming in, but it is apparent to us that he himself ought to have followed up such a vital potential witness, whose information raised the suspicion that James Grant himself might have been involved in the murder, or alternatively indicated that he was close to somebody who was involved either in the murder itself or with witnesses who might have given vital information about the murderers.

15.14 Mr Bullock was present at virtually every meeting of the team, and he made notes which were later typed up as an "aide memoire" of what had taken place. We have been using these meeting notes repeatedly during the Inquiry, and they have given a helpful indication of what was and was not said at the meetings. Mr Bullock was at pains to point out that these were really personal notes, and that there was no official status given to them. On the other hand, there is no record otherwise of what took place at the meetings at all, and plainly the notes are important. If these notes had not existed there would be another yawning gap in the documentation in this case. Such notes should have been taken as a matter of formal record of all discussions and decisions. They would then have been available to officers who had been away from the team or who were newly joining in order to bring themselves properly up to date.

15.15 The notes should probably have been included in the HOLMES material, but they were kept separate and they have survived. The original notes have disappeared. Mr Bullock says that the originals are simply mirrored in the typed up notes. There is one important gap in the notes, namely those which might have existed for 3 June 1993. That has some significance, since that is the day when DS Crowley came back to the station with his news that Mr Brooks had expressed his post-identification doubts to DS Crowley.

15.16 There is no need to go over yet again the arrival into the hands of the investigation of the succession of messages from various sources which seemed to *"put the finger"* on the Acourts, David Norris and Gary Dobson. Mr Bullock was fully aware of the anonymous letters recovered from the telephone kiosk and the Welcome Inn, and he accepted that by the Saturday afternoon or evening the investigating team as a whole was aware of what James Grant had said, and of those letters and the other anonymous information that had been received. This strengthens even more the importance of James Grant and the extent of the failure to deal with him as a matter of priority in order to maximise the profit from his information. His original information was confirmed by other albeit anonymous information. He remained the sole known and named informant.

15.17 Furthermore, the team knew of course by that time that there was evidence available in the shape of the detailed and vivid statement of Mr Brooks, and in Joseph Shepherd's statement. Some time later Mr Westbrook's evidence was available. Over the first weekend, as we have repeatedly seen, there was in the hands of the investigating team abundant information giving them reasonable grounds to suspect that the named suspects were involved in the murder. The Kent "diary" of events which appears in the Appendices to this Report sets out the details.

15.18 Mr Bullock does not remember whether there was any discussion at any team meeting in connection with the arrests. He said that he accepted that there had been discussions between himself and Mr Crampton and that the decision made not to arrest was because "*Mr Crampton wanted some evidence. We had no evidence up to then and it was looking like we were going to get evidence in so much as the Benefield case, but also because of the volume of information coming in we felt there was the possibility of an eye witness going to contact us*". In parenthesis this acceptance that there was a "*volume of information*" gives the lie to the subsequent suggestion (wherever it originated) that a "wall of silence" contributed to the ineffectiveness of the investigation.

15.19 Furthermore, Mr Bullock indicated to the Inquiry that it was his view that as the days went by firsthand evidence might come, perhaps from the DD family or from Emma Cook or from the Witnesses B and K. Mr Bullock's frame of mind was in reality that he "*felt there must be somebody out there that saw it*". He accepted at once that speed is of the essence in an investigation of this kind, and he like many others plainly regrets in retrospect that an arrest was not made over the first weekend, and certainly by Monday 26 April. Monday is of importance since it seems likely that the Stacey Benefield statement came from DS Davidson to Mr Weeden almost as soon as the changeover of SIO took place. Once the Stacey Benefield statement was available Mr Bullock believes that further delay took place because the team wanted the backup of Matthew Farman's statement, and because Mr Crampton had the idea that the two cases should be run in tandem after that evidence was available. In fact Matthew Farman's statement was taken on 28 April, so that its absence could not possibly have justified further delay after that date.

15.20 Mr Bullock's view of Mr Weeden is that he was considerably more cautious than Mr Crampton. Mr Weeden was, so to speak, inheriting the decision which had already been made in Mr Crampton's time, namely that arrests should be delayed. There is no entry of any kind in the policy file, as we have already pointed out, in connection with the decision not to arrest. It looks very much therefore as if the senior officers were burying their heads in the sand, and simply waiting in the somewhat forlorn hope that an eye witness would turn up.

15.21 The house-to-house inquiries had by Sunday night confirmed the information that the Acourts did live at 102 Bournbrook Road. Furthermore Gary Dobson's address was turned up during the house-to-house inquiries. David Norris' address could have been obtained quickly either from his own collator's card or from that of Clifford Norris, his father.

15.22 **Mr Bullock tended to say that the decision to arrest was not truly his business. But it appears to us that he was much too ready to go along with the wrong decision made by the SIOs. To his credit he was prepared to accept that if he were to be confronted with the same circumstances again he would accept that the team should have acted more promptly. As we have indicated in connection with the evidence of the SIOs the failure to arrest very early in this affair is the fundamental mistake made. When Mr Weeden took over Mr Bullock says that there was discussion about arrest, but that Mr Weeden "*wanted to follow along the same strategy*" which had been pursued by Mr Crampton.**

15.23 As to Clifford Norris, Mr Bullock indicated that he had had no dealings with this man. He was aware that Mr Norris was wanted for a large drug importation and that he had been involved in a shooting at some stage. Mr Bullock accepts that by the Monday after the murder David Norris' address was known to the team. Apparently nobody knew what Mr Norris looked like right up to the moment of arrest. Given that nobody in the team knew what Mr Norris looked like it was not possible to identify him in the surveillance photographs. On the other hand as soon as he had been arrested it must have been apparent that he appeared in the photographs. Yet as we know no use was made during Mr Dobson's interviews of the photographs of Mr Norris and Mr Dobson seen together outside 102 Bournbrook Road. Thus the valuable ammunition which should have been made available to DS Davidson then, or at a later interview which could easily have been set up, remained unused.

15.24 Our impression of Mr Bullock, both as to the happenings over the first weekend and up to the time of the arrests, is that while he was of course in the ordinary sense of the word busy and involved in what took place, he was often passive. This is highlighted when we consider the steps taken to see the people who might have led the team to some hard evidence. DS Davidson, probably the most experienced Detective Sergeant on the team, was given the task of managing James Grant. He also saw Emma Cook and Michelle Casserley and others, including Witness B somewhat later on. Most of these avenues did not lead to any evidence which could be used in criminal proceedings. As was pointed out to Mr Bullock it may well be that the approach to these people made by the stronger officers was mistaken. Witness B did eventually make a statement, and Witness K made a short statement. But careful consideration of the right approach to these witnesses or informants plainly might have led to much more valuable information or evidence. This is evidenced by the message from DC Keith Hughes and PC Andrews who when carrying out house-to-house inquiries came across the Witness DD and family and put into the HOLMES system the message, *"We both feel that a gentle approach when he is seen again would be the appropriate method of extracting information from him. He may also be responsible for the two notes to the Incident Room"*. Clearly no heed was paid to this information and in any event a gentle approach is something which was undoubtedly not in the armoury of DS Davidson.

15.25 As to surveillance it is apparent that there is considerable criticism to be made of the setting up and carrying on of the activities of the team brought in on Monday, 26 April. We deal with this in detail later (Chapter 18).

15.26 Mr Pitham's report (see para 18.17) plainly sets out the relevant documentation which ought to exist in connection with any formal surveillance operation. Apart from some surveillance logs and an unofficial notebook in which briefing notes were entered by one of the surveillance officers there is no documentation at all in existence. The truth is, as it seems to us, that the officers in charge including Mr Bullock simply drifted into the surveillance operation without much, if any, idea as to what it might achieve.

15.27 As to the two bloodstained tissues found in gardens in Rochester Way, Mr Bullock accepted that it was his decision to include in one of the reports to the CPS the facts in connection with their discovery, together with the conclusion that there would be no evidential value in submitting them for scientific examination since *"there is no evidence to suggest any of the suspects had been cut"*. He wholly agreed that exhibits should not in any circumstances be discarded, and he was not aware that one of the tissues was missing until this was pointed out during his Kent interview.

15.28 As to E-fits or artist's impressions Mr Bullock, in common with Mr Crampton, indicated that the policy was that such things should not be produced before identification parades had taken place. It is obvious that the value of such E-fits or body maps decreases the longer the process is delayed. Furthermore the decision not to ask Mr Westbrook and Mr Shepherd to make an E-fit or an artist's impression does not fit squarely with the decision which was made in connection with Mr Brooks, namely that he should make an E-fit on 5 May and that Mr Shepherd should make one on 6 May.

15.29 **The truth is that the earlier these steps are taken the better. Mr Bullock agreed that this was so but apparently doubted whether Mr Westbrook had been available, and he indicated that there was some problem in contacting Duwayne Brooks. The somewhat confused pictured conveyed by the evidence of Mr Bullock in connection with artist's impressions or E-fits confirms our view that the senior officers were in a sense allowing the tide to roll over them and that they were simply not analysing and planning the actions which should be taken properly.**

15.30 Good direction and control and properly reasoned decision making is not a feature of the activity of Mr Bullock or of the SIOs in this case. This is perhaps once more highlighted by the evidence of Mr Bullock about the period when Mr Weeden was unavoidably absent from duty for some days after 9 May 1993. Mr Bullock's indication to us, and to the Kent police, is that Mr Ilsley effectively became the SIO. Mr Ilsley says that that role was being performed during those days by Mr Bullock. There can hardly be effective leadership when two senior officers cannot agree on who is in charge. Once again the lack of any record being made of the decision not to arrest after the changeover from Mr Crampton to Mr Weeden is of significance. Mr Bullock says that the question of arrest was being regularly reviewed, but there is no note in any policy file or in any document that this was so.

15.31 **As to the Norris connection, it is apparent that Mr Bullock was aware early on of the influence of Clifford Norris, since he told us that *"there were some people going round warning off people in general on the estate"*. He believes that these people were connected to Clifford Norris, but of course he had no direct evidence of that. The suggestion made to Mr Bullock is that David Norris was favoured, or that the officers held off in their investigation of this case because of the existence of Clifford Norris, either through fear or for more sinister reasons. Nobody at this stage seems to have concentrated upon the obvious need to remove Clifford Norris from the scene, and to follow up those who appeared to be having such an important inhibiting effect upon potential witnesses.**

15.32 It is however of marked significance, as was pointed out by Mr Gompertz, that Mr Bullock was personally instrumental in resisting an application for bail for David Norris, and in taking positive steps to see that David Norris was prosecuted.

15.33 In connection with the aborted Stacey Benefield case a report was made by Mr Bullock himself to the CPS urging that an application should be made for a re-trial when it emerged that there had been problems in connection with the jury, following the attempted buying off of Stacey Benefield himself.

15.34 In connection with the Witham stabbing, said to have been perpetrated by David Norris and Neil Acourt, Mr Bullock also himself wrote a full report urging that the prosecution of the two men for that offence should be reinstated. A decision had been made earlier by the CPS that the prosecution should be abandoned, but Mr Bullock saw that case as a parallel to the Stephen Lawrence case and urged the CPS to reinstate the prosecution.

15.35 None of his actions in connection with David Norris appear to us to support any allegation that Mr Bullock was favouring that man. Indeed, our conclusion is that Mr Bullock's failings were not motivated by any fear of Clifford Norris or by any intention to hold off the prosecution of these suspects. They stem from inadequacy or inability to make the proper decision at the right time, as a result of Mr Bullock's make up and nature. He does appear to be limited in his ability to make decisions and to act positively in the way in which a good DIO must act, but there is no evidence at all that he was a dishonest man.

15.36 **Mr Bullock was cross-examined at length by Mr Mansfield and others. Mr Mansfield extracted from Mr Bullock a series of concessions as to the inadequacy of the work done by Mr Bullock in this investigation. He accepted that looking back he realised that the strategy followed by himself and the SIOs did not work. Earlier he said that he felt that he should have *"deployed somebody with the surveillance team"*. He says that he should have asked for assistance from the Witness Protection Scheme at Scotland Yard in order to deal with young witnesses who were obviously frightened and who did not want to get involved. Furthermore he accepted that during the whole course of his time with the investigation team he never met Mr & Mrs Lawrence.**

15.37 **Mr Bullock accepted without reservation that this was a racist crime, but as Mr Mansfield pointed out he simply did not appreciate that when such a crime is committed liaison with the family may have its own features, and that it is vital to monitor what is taking place in that regard. Mr Bullock's attitude was that since liaison officers had been appointed it did not in truth occur to him that he should himself go to see Mr & Mrs Lawrence. He regrets now that he did not do so during the whole course of his contact with this case.**

15.38 The truth is that Mr Bullock hardly seemed aware that there are particular sensitivities and issues which need to be addressed in connection with racist crimes. One of the vital matters is support for victims and of course for a victim's family. It simply did not occur to Mr Bullock that he might seek to overcome the obvious difficulties in relation to family liaison by influencing the SIO to visit the family or to seek, through the SIO, to visit the family himself in order to address the problems which were evident. He simply did not see it as his task to address such issues no matter how self evident they were.

15.39 Mr Mansfield also pointed out to Mr Bullock that junior officers appeared to be taking the view that this was not simply and solely a racist attack. Whether Mr Bullock can be held to be responsible for the views of the junior officers seems to us to be doubtful. It is however a feature of the case that the senior officers, including Mr Bullock, accept without reservation that this was purely a racially motivated attack, while the more junior ranks expressed their doubts in the wholly unsatisfactory manner which this Inquiry has observed.

15:40 **Mr Mansfield roundly attacked the decisions made by Mr Bullock, together with the SIOs, both on the grounds that they were ineffectual and pointless, and also on the grounds that they were motivated in particular because of the influence of Clifford Norris upon the case. We understand and to a considerable extent accept the criticism of Mr Bullock's decision making, of his failure to follow up himself the James Grant information, the failure and non-documentation of the surveillance operation, and the general "laissez faire" approach to the case, in particular of course the decision not to arrest. We do not conclude that there was any kind of sinister motive in Mr Bullock's action or inaction. He was plainly put off by the great degree of media and public attention to the case in the early days, and his training and his general ability were unsuited to a case of this nature.**

15.41 As to the surveillance operation we do not accept the suggestion made by Mr Mansfield to Mr Bullock that the surveillance was simply a sham, and part of a conspiracy to go easy on the investigation of these suspects. Such a conspiracy would entail the complicity and co-operation of a large number of officers. Mr Bullock of all people has, as we have indicated, shown that he had no inclination to favour the suspect David Norris.

15.42 We have already indicated that there are no notes of any team meeting on 3 June 1993. That was of course the day upon which Mr Brooks identified Luke Knight, and later, according to DS Crowley, registered his reservations about his own identification. Mr Bullock remembers no telephone calls coming to the investigation offices during that afternoon, but he does remember DS Crowley coming into the Incident Room and speaking to Mr Weeden. He could not remember the words used by DS Crowley, but believes that it was *something to do with the identification and the fact that Brooks wasn't sure or something like that who he identified*. The absence of any note of the meeting on that day may be accounted for, said Mr Bullock, by the fact that there was no formal meeting. He pointed out that in any event the fact was that DS Crowley made his statement on 3 June 1993.

15.43 **The long and short of it is that Mr Mansfield's cross-examination of Mr Bullock reinforced our view of him formed after Mr Lawson had concluded his questioning. We see no evidence that Mr Bullock was involved in any corrupt conspiracy. He does not seem to us in any way to be the sort of man who might be recruited for devious activity.**

15.44 As to Mr Bullock's scepticism about the HOLMES system Mr Gompertz indicated that training in the use of this system is now considerably more advanced.

15.45 **The somewhat swingeing conclusions of Mr Mellish as to Mr Bullock were referred to more than once during his questioning. Mr Mellish's criticism of the qualities of leadership of Mr Bullock and of his failure to produce *"innovative or positive strategy"* have to be echoed by this Inquiry. On the other hand it has to be noted that Mr Mellish added that in other areas of performance, such as policy docket detail and systems management and the major incident procedure, he found Mr Bullock to be thorough, and his attention to detail a vital asset and ingredient for such a high profile case. In a sense that confirms our conclusion that probably this officer, who is an honest man and a very long serving policeman, was appointed to act above his true station and in a position beyond his abilities. Criticism of him has to be considered in the light of that conclusion.**

15.46 The major responsibility for the team's failures lies with those who allowed Mr Bullock to occupy a position which was beyond his abilities, and who failed to supervise him. Mr Bullock is the only officer "available" for disciplinary proceedings arising from the PCA investigation. His seniors had by the time of the PCA investigation all retired.

CHAPTER SIXTEEN

THE INCIDENT ROOM, AND
DETECTIVE SERGEANT PETER FLOOK

16.1　Detective Sergeant Peter Flook joined the MPS in 1962, and after a short period he transferred to CID. He retired in July 1993. For four years before his retirement he had been a Detective Sergeant with 3 Area Major Investigation Pool (AMIP). Probably in about 1989, DS Flook did a week's training at Hendon in the use of the HOLMES system. He was never trained as a HOLMES supervisor, and it appears that he had been involved in investigations using the HOLMES system only on two occasions before the Stephen Lawrence murder.

16.2　In April 1993 DS Flook was attached or assigned to DS Weeden. In common terms he was Mr Weeden's *"bag carrier"*. That is a term expressly used in the MPS job description for a "Detective Sergeant assisting Detective Superintendent". This job description, together with all the others, sets out in comprehensive and indeed almost overfull term the tasks which it is expected that the person doing the relevant job will perform.

16.3　It is at the outset remarkable to record that DS Flook had never seen his own job description. For example that document requires a bag carrier to *"attend the SIO's briefing ensuring attendance by any office staff that can be spared. Take notes and make appropriate entries in action logs. Attend the meetings held by the Detective Chief Superintendent with AMIP personnel"*. When asked about this paragraph DS Flook said that it seemed to accord with his general experience, but that the taking of notes was normally done by the SIO or his deputy. In this investigation it is clear that no-one was formally delegated to take notes of such meetings and it is simply a matter of good fortune that the personal notes taken by Mr Bullock have survived.

16.4　On 23 April DS Flook was summoned to the newly set up investigation room. We have heard that DS Phillip Sheridan was the first office manager on the scene, but it was known by then that Mr Weeden would be taking over on Monday from Mr Crampton, so that DS Flook was to work in tandem at the very start of this investigation with DS Sheridan.

16.5　There is some mystery about the actual setting up of the office, since DS Sheridan indicated that at the beginning there had been a card index system for a very short time which was converted by the Saturday morning into HOLMES. The memory of DS Flook and others is that the HOLMES system was in fact set up on Friday, 23 April. By Saturday morning the system was up and running, in a comparatively small conference room at the top of the police station which was allocated as the Incident Office.

16.6　**The AMIP guidelines set out certain minimum requirements which are recommended for various types of inquiry. This murder qualified as a Category B investigation although it was never formally classified as such. The recommendation in the guidelines is that there should be three Detective Sergeants to fulfil the relevant inside tasks in connection with the management of HOLMES in such a case. DS Flook fulfilled four specific and fully described roles, namely those of Office Manager, Receiver, Action Allocator and Statement Reader.**

16.7 In addition to that he was Mr Weeden's personal assistant. On this Area DS Flook said that the manning levels had always been a problem. There was really no hope in 3 Area of obtaining or being given the kind of staffing level which ought to be available. Later, on 9 May, DS Flook said that an experienced Detective Constable named Sparrowhawk came in expressly to assist with the action allocating. But from the start and for 16 days DS Flook wore at least five hats as he sat at the hub of the investigation in the Incident Room. He has been described as the lynch pin of the investigation in connection with the processing of information. It is also of significance that when DS Flook took two days leave on 3 and 4 May, a crucial period prior to the arrests, his absence was not covered by any other officer, and the system was therefore left without anyone fulfilling the five roles.

16.8 It was his task in his varied and combined capacities, for example, to *read the documents generated through the Incident Room to assess the information, inform the SIO and keep him informed of the efficiency of the inquiry team and Incident Room staff*. The combination of the material set out in the job descriptions for the five roles to be occupied by DS Flook is voluminous. He had no knowledge of any of the prescribed tasks which are set out in those job descriptions, except as a result of previous experience.

16.9 **DS Flook was an experienced Detective Sergeant, but it is apparent that he was performing his job or jobs simply on the basis of his past knowledge and by the light of a measure of common sense. In his capacity as Receiver DS Flook was required to notify the Office Manager of any important development or evidence coming to his attention. Thus in this case he had to inform himself. Similarly, under the job description for the Receiver DS Flook was required to perform *"liaison with the Action Allocator"*. The Receiver is also described as *"acting as a sieve for the Office Manager"*. It can at once be seen, and is of vital importance, that the appointment of one man to these tasks made cross-checking of information coming into the investigation, which should have been a matter of standard routine, in fact impossible.**

16.10 During the first vital weeks, when the sorting and actioning of information is of paramount importance, DS Flook was absent from the office from 17:00 on Saturday 2 May until 07:30 on Tuesday 5 May. 4 May was a Bank Holiday. During that time there was no Detective Sergeant in the office. DS Flook said that one of the Indexers would have been able to perform his roles. Fortunately the Indexers do appear to have been efficient and experienced in their own field, but it is ludicrous to suggest that they could perform the essential supervisory roles.

16.11 **It is thus palpable that the HOLMES system was wholly inadequately serviced by responsible and trained and experienced officers. This may well account for the extraordinary lapses in time in connection with the processing of the large amount of information which came into the investigation room in the early days. There must be serious criticism of senior officers who allowed the system to operate in this way. Equally it must be of major concern that such ineffective operation was apparently the norm throughout the force.** DS Flook was working under Mr Crampton until Monday 26 April when Mr Weeden took over. DS Flook has no memory whatsoever of any discussion or of any positive decision being made not to effect any arrests under either regime.

16.12 DS Flook regularly indicated during his questioning that he could not remember things because *"it was all so long ago"*. To some extent he sheltered behind the passage of time. But it is right to indicate that he accepted at once that there were reasonable grounds for suspicion of the suspects and that they certainly could in his opinion have been arrested as soon as the Stacey Benefield statement was received on Sunday night or Monday morning.

16.13 **As to surveillance it appeared that DS Flook had virtually no knowledge of that operation. He said that there was *"surveillance done later on"*. But he had no recollection whatsoever of any documentation coming into the Incident Room. There is of course no formal record, as there should have been, of the instructions and orders given, nor of the arrival in the Incident Room of the photographs themselves.**

16.14 DS Flook did say in a further statement prepared for this Inquiry that the subject of arrests was discussed at office meetings. He accepted that there was no record of any decision in this regard. In his statement he indicated that *"finally I personally felt that outside pressure from other interested parties had an influence on the final decision"*. When asked about this statement DS Flook indicated that if he had been asked about this matter five years before he might have been able to give more precise answers.

16.15 DS Flook had no positive memory of the arrival of James Grant at the Incident Room on Friday 23 April. He agrees that he signed the relevant message and *"actioned"* it, so that he must have handled it, but he had no memory of the matter at all. He did indicate that he had done some research in connection with the registration of James Grant as an informant. The long and the short of it is that he found nothing to assist the Inquiry in this respect.

16.16 **When asked about the obvious and palpable delay in dealing with messages DS Flook was singularly unhelpful. Simply for example message 138, which deals with the DD family, was received at 17:30 on Saturday 24 April. Two actions were raised by DS Flook, namely actions 166 and 186, but these actions were not raised until 28 April and 30 April respectively. DS Flook could give no explanation for the delay in processing these matters. Plainly this showed that DS Flook was either incapable of giving proper priority to vital messages of this kind, or alternatively that he was simply going through the motions and not bothering to assess relevant priorities or to ask others for help in this important respect.**

16.17 The impression gained by this Inquiry is that DS Flook went through the motions and performed his task to the best of his inadequate ability, but that he was simply not capable of dealing with the information coming through his hands in a satisfactory manner. Provided he processed the information reasonably well in a mechanical sense he seemed satisfied to leave things to others.

16.18 **A classic example of the inefficiency of the system concerns the processing of the information in connection with the red Astra. We know that the first investigation of the partial registration number of that car resulted on 29 April in a downgrading of the inquiry to *"non-priority"* by Mr Weeden. On 30 April the car was coincidentally stopped by PSgt Clement, and the driver and a passenger were identified. That information was relayed on to the HOLMES system, but the relevant action to trace interview and eliminate the occupants of the car, number 460, was not raised until 7 June. That matter is dealt with more fully elsewhere in our report, (see Chapter 20) but DS Flook was wholly unable to account for the delay, or to deal satisfactorily with any of the actions taken or not taken in respect of that car and its occupants later on.**

16.19 When Mr Weeden gave evidence, in connection with the red Astra message, he said that the five week delay could have been accounted for by that message being stuck behind another piece of paper, so that it was simply missed. Mr Weeden said that that suggestion came from DS Flook. When he was asked about this DS Flook said that this was *"probably a throw away remark"*. He accepted in the end that the delay had been inexcusable and that in truth it simply could not be explained.

16.20 **Mr Kamlish's questioning of DS Flook was devastating, particularly in connection with positive and damaging statements made by DS Flook about the family and Mr Khan. The result was that DS Flook was forced to withdraw a series of assertions made in his statement to Kent, which plainly had no basis in fact. For example, DS Flook had recorded that** *"It was whilst the team were attempting to carry out the inquiries and keep information confidential that the same information had been passed to the victim's family. Subsequently they appeared to be discussing it freely within the community"* **When asked what was the basis of that statement DS Flook was readily compelled to say that it was his** *"recollection"* **and** *"If I am in error I am in error"*. **Thereafter the statement indicated that the Lawrence family were hindering the police in their investigations and preventing the police from targeting suspects. As soon as these sentences were quoted to DS Flook he said that he withdrew them and apologised.**

16.21 **In effect DS Flook appears to have put into his statement to Kent an amalgam or collection of gossip that may have been reaching his ears in the Incident Room. He had, as he accepted, a pivotal role in the AMIP team. It may well be that the worst aspects of the reactions of some of the junior officers are reflected in DS Flook's statement. He withdrew most of the allegations made, and there is plainly no substance in any of the matters to which he was referred. In answer to Mr Kamlish he said that officers were** *"coming and reporting conversations with people following inquiries, general things. You form an opinion. It is no more than that"*.

16.22 Furthermore DS Flook's strictures in respect of Mr Khan were plainly wrong. He said that he was in a position to observe what was going on and that Mr Khan seemed to be *"pestering the office continually, not me personally but the SIOs with messages and 'phone calls"*. When questioned about this he accepted that there were in fact only four letters written by Mr Khan, and he accepted readily that what Mr Khan was doing was justifiably seeking information that Mr & Mrs Lawrence themselves were not getting from the Family Liaison Officers.

16.23 How this statement to Kent came to be made is difficult to imagine. DS Flook said that he made a statement with a Detective Constable and a Detective Inspector from Kent:- *"They talked me through what I recalled of the incident, what I did, how the inquiry went. The high spots and low spots of the inquiry, and then it was turned into a statement"*. This suggests that the wording of the statement may not have been entirely that of DS Flook. Whatever may be the truth it is both revealing and unprofessional that DS Flook allowed himself to make the statements that he did.

16.24 Mr Kamlish continued to challenge DS Flook in respect of other deficiencies, such as the failure to obtain a photograph of David Norris by checking relevant information at Orpington Police Station. DS Flook confirmed again that he had seen no documentation in respect of the surveillance. He even seemed doubtful whether he had himself seen the photographs taken during the surveillance, and said that if the photographs had come to him they would have gone into the system either as an exhibit or as a document. In fact we know that the photographs were not documented or processed as they should have been at the time. Whether this is the responsibility of DS Flook or not is uncertain. The fact is however that he was in charge of the HOLMES system, and was palpably an important part of the organisation of this aspect of the investigation which was both inefficient and ineffective.

16.26 Questions from those representing the police officers in this case did little or nothing to reinstate our firm impression that the management of the HOLMES system and the control and command exercised by those senior to DS Flook in this regard were woefully unsatisfactory. Nobody seems to have been giving any proper supervisory attention to what was going on under DS Flook. This is yet another condemnation of the supervision and control and initiative exercised by more senior officers.

16.27 As to the racial aspect of this case again it is wholly apparent that DS Flook was untrained in this regard. He said that to his knowledge everybody accepted that this was a racist murder. He was undoubtedly unaware of the impact that this should have upon the investigation which was to follow.

16.28 **No wonder Mr & Mrs Lawrence and the community perceive, with justification, that the management of the case was deficient. DS Flook's attitude to Mr & Mrs Lawrence and to their solicitor, so vividly illustrated by DS Flook's critical remarks, must result in the conclusion that racist prejudice, stereotyping and insensitivity played its part in the lack of bite and energy devoted to the activities of the Incident Room. Unwitting racism was at work.**

CHAPTER SEVENTEEN

HOUSE-TO-HOUSE INQUIRIES

17.1 On Friday, 23 April it was decided that there should be formal house-to-house inquiries made on the Brook Estate. The policy file indicates the areas to be covered. The object of the exercise was formally to list those who were present in the houses on the night of the murder, and of course to elicit any information from householders which might advance the investigation. This exercise should not be confused with the informal "door-knocking" performed in order to try to obtain quick information on the night of the murder.

17.2 Detective Sergeant Donald Mackenzie was given the initial supervision of this task. On 24 April he was joined by Detective Sergeant David Kirkpatrick. Both were experienced officers. DS Mackenzie was involved until 30 April.

17.3 As the weekend progressed there was a flow of information reaching the AMIP team, and the two Detective Sergeants attended the daily meetings and briefings.

17.4 The officers involved in the visits to houses were Plumstead Crime Squad officers reinforced from the TSG. The teams involved would take with them a standard form, in order to list details of the occupants of each house and personal descriptions of those present. Strict instructions as to what is to be done are set out in the MPS directive as to such inquiries. The instructions include the identification of potential suspects as one of the purposes of such inquiries.

17.5 Experienced CID officers were detailed to conduct the visits to some sensitive houses, including 102 Bournbrook Road, known already as a result of information received to be the home of the Acourts. DC Keith Hughes and DC Graham Cook joined the team probably on 23 April. They organised the Plumstead officers and obtained the necessary documentation for the task. DC Hughes and DC Macdonald were the officers who visited 102 Bournbrook Road on Sunday 25 April, in the late afternoon. They conducted inquiries along Bournbrook Road in a sensitive way, so as not to arouse suspicion. Mr Crampton himself briefed these two officers, and told them to report back to himself what they had seen and heard. The visit to No 102 was in reality a subterfuge, to confirm the presence of the Acourts before surveillance took place.

17.6 At No 102 the officers saw Mrs Acourt and also Mr John Burke who apparently stayed part of the time there with Mrs Acourt. Mr Burke's form gives his personal description, and indicates that he was present at No 102 on 22 April but that he left at 21:00.

17.7 **Mrs Acourt's form indicates that she was at home and went to bed at 23:30 on 22 April. The occupants' form indicates that both Neil and Jamie Acourt and their half-brothers Scott and Bradley Lamb lived at No 102. Mrs Acourt gave unsatisfactory information about her sons' presence on 22 April, as follows:- "Neil, Jamie, Scott .... Bradley she states had 'flu. Friends came. Luke (Well Hall) - she states they were in all night. (Bradley could have been out). Scott may have come in about 10. Very unsure of movements. States Jamie was home."**

17.8 The officers saw none of the suspects on 25 April. Understandably the officers did not ask to go upstairs or to see whether any of sons were in fact present on the 25th. They cannot be criticised for this, since suspicions could have been aroused by further investigation or inquiries. The fact is however that the visit established that probably the Acourts and Luke (presumed to be Luke Knight, who did live at Well Hall Road) were together on 22 April 1993.

17.9 Mrs Acourt did not sign the form. This was an unfortunate omission. When it was pointed out to Mr Crampton he simply told the officers to record that fact in the Incident Report Book. DC Hughes told the Inquiry that he would have asked whether the young men were present, but he did not regard it as necessary to record the fact that they appeared not to be present on 25 April.

17.10 DC Hughes said that he did ask Mrs Acourt whether she had heard any *"rumours about the incident"*. She said that *"she had heard about it on the news, and she remembered that her sons had spoken about it."* She said that the whole house had to be redecorated, and there were obvious signs that decoration was going on.

17.11 Mr Mansfield suggested to DC Hughes that there were important omissions from the form and indeed from the inquiries made at No 102. We are not convinced that this was so. A further visit by DC Hughes, would simply have resulted in the obtaining of Mrs Acourt's signature. The first visit had confirmed the suspects' presence at No 102 on 22 April 1993.

17.12 When Gary Dobson's house (Phineas Pett Road) was visited by DC Cash at about 18:00 on 25 April Gary Dobson was present. At 18:20 DC Cash saw Mr Dobson go into 102 Bournbrook Road for about five minutes. The visit to Gary Dobson's home led to a conversation with Gary Dobson who said that he was at home all night studying, having arrived home at 17:30. His mother and father said that they were also at home. Association between Gary Dobson and the Acourts was established in any event.

17.13 DS Kirkpatrick was involved in other varied activities during the investigation. He arrested and interviewed Neil Acourt on 7 May. He saw and interviewed other potential witnesses, including Witness B. Throughout the early weeks he remained in charge of the house-to-house inquiries, which appear to have gone on into June 1993. A total of 829 houses were visited. There were 719 replies and 1,628 people were seen and spoken to. DS Kirkpatrick's job was to collate the information gleaned, and to pass on relevant information to the Receiver or Office Manager. We see no grounds for criticism of the method of carrying out of the house-to-house inquiries. DS Kirkpatrick was an experienced and impressive officer who seems to us to have performed his duties in connection with these inquiries fairly and professionally.

17.14 A limited area of criticism is the failure of either SIO to direct house-to-house inquiries in the areas from which the group of suspects may have emerged onto the scene of the attack, as opposed to where they ran after it. Such inquiries may have proved negative, but equally a witness may have been found who could have put the attacking group at the scene and who might have identified them.

17.15 Questioned about this Mr Weeden indicated that he thought this had been done. Mr Weeden's Counsel sought to sustain his recollection by identifying seven such actions. Only one was of relevance and that was limited to inquiries at Eltham railway station and the kebab shop on Tudor Parade. One of the few positive aspects of Mr Barker's activities in undertaking his Review was that he generated a number of actions for this purpose. Whether they were pursued, at that late date, is not known.

CHAPTER EIGHTEEN

SURVEILLANCE

18.1 **The story of the surveillance of 102 Bournbrook Road and of David Norris' address in Kent is a most unhappy part of this case. If a strategic and considered decision was taken by Saturday 24 April that arrests should be delayed, then the alternative road forward should have itself been carefully planned and recorded. As we know the policy file contains nothing to show when or why the decision not to arrest was made. Nor does the policy file contain any reference to the establishment of surveillance, which the SIOs indicated was to be part of the alternative way ahead. This in itself is a glaring omission.**

18.2 In Mr Bullock's briefing notes for Saturday 24 April the following entry appears:- *"Consideration being given to Observation Post on suspects address."* Other than this nothing is said in briefing notes or in the policy file about surveillance.

18.3 At some unidentified time on Sunday 25 April Mr Bullock says that Mr Crampton told him to make contact with the 3 Area surveillance team, which operated from the Force Intelligence Bureau (FIB) at East Dulwich. The team consisted of about ten officers. Detective Sergeant David Knight was the leader of the team, under Detective Inspector Cliff Davies. DS Knight was on leave until 27 April.

18.4 **If surveillance was a considered option by Saturday 24 April it is remarkable that the operation was not mounted at once on that day, or on Sunday at the latest. However it appears that the team probably did not operate at weekends in 1993. It also appears that the team was booked to observe a young black man on Monday 26 April. He was suspected of a minor offence of theft or *"theft from the person"*. If the surveillance for this murder was important it is remarkable that no formal or proper contact was made so that at least research for observation points could have been carried out over the weekend. Furthermore surely this murder must have been given priority over the minor offence referred to above. Such priority could have been arranged without doubt through Mr Ilsley who had the authority, should surveillance have been required urgently, to cancel any arranged surveillance in respect of some relatively minor crime.**

18.5 Mr Bullock said in evidence that he did go out on Sunday morning 25 April with Mr Crampton to look for *"an observation point to see if we could keep the premises under observation, but there didn't appear to be one that was useful to us ....."*. Furthermore Mr Bullock says that both he and Mr Crampton spoke to someone from the surveillance team on Sunday 25 April. There is a CAD message dated 26 April for Mr Bullock to *"Arrange for 3 Area FIB re suspects"*. Mr Bullock says that he wrote that message on Monday 26 April because Mr Weeden was about to take over. Plainly there was no urgency in any communication made on Sunday 25 April (if it took place at all), since the team did not carry out its planned observation of the theft suspect until 14:00 on Monday 26 April.

18.6 So much of the relevant documentation is missing that it is difficult to tell exactly when formal and effective contact was made. But PC Victor Smith (the team administrator) says that he received a telephone call at about 11:00 on Monday 26 April from DC Simpson or perhaps direct from Mr Bullock, that a surveillance team was needed by the AMIP team at Eltham. The result was that PC Smith arrived at Eltham at 12:15, where he saw Mr Bullock who told him what was required, and who said that what was wanted was evidence of association between the suspects, namely the Acourts, Gary Dobson and David Norris. Mr Bullock said that urgent action was needed, and that he wanted photographic evidence, because his team were not sure who was who. PC Smith was given some help as to Observation Point (OP) locations by DS Mackenzie, who had by then obtained information about the Acourts and Mr Dobson and their addresses. No written instructions or briefing were ever given. By this time 48 hours had elapsed since the making of the original note regarding consideration being given to the setting up of observation posts on 24 April. Such a delay is clearly inexcusable.

18.7   Checks were then carried out as to various addresses and their occupants, and by about 16:00 a point was chosen for observation of 102 Bournbrook Road. Peter Finch, the photographer, was by then present. PC Smith's very rough notes, recorded in his own memo book which was a wholly unofficial document, refer to his meeting with Mr Bullock on 26 April. More importantly they show that between 16:40 and 20:00 observation was kept on No 102 by himself and Mr Finch.

18.8   **At around 16:40 a young white man was seen to leave the house with what appeared to be clothing covered by a black bin liner. The camera was not set up, so that no photograph was obtained of this event. Nor was it notified to the Incident Room, since there was no means of communication from OP to Incident Room. The Incident Room was told of this event on the next day. We will never know what was removed from No 102 on 26 April. PC Smith's memo book records this event as follows:- "Silver Sapphire carrying dry cleaning". It is unusual to place a bin liner over clothes en route to the dry cleaners. After seeing that event Mr Finch took photographs, until he left for the police station at about 20:00.**

18.9   PC Smith and Mr Finch both returned at about 20:00 to the police station. The surveillance team had been there on that afternoon, but they had been stood down by 20:00. In the weekly return form for the surveillance team the only entry for 26 April refers to the theft surveillance, which lasted from 08:30 until 14:00 on 26 April. Surveillance Log 18819 confirms this. That log still exists, as do three other logs for 27 April (18821), 29 April (18843), and 30 April (18841). Log No 18820 is missing and there is no log for 26 April as to 102 Bournbrook Road. The Logs for 29 April and 30 April (issued in the wrong numerical order) show that an unproductive operation was mounted by the full team on David Norris' home at Berryfield Close on both those days, for only two hours and four hours respectively. Gary Dobson's address at Phineas Pett Road was apparently never surveyed.

18.10   **The only full team operation mounted on No 102 thus took place on 27 April. But extraordinarily the log shows that observation did not begin on that day until 19:47, and it ended apparently at about 21:10. The team was to be paraded on 27 April at 14:00, which is itself surprising, since the activity on 26 April suggested that full time observation might bear fruit. The full team operation at No 102 was therefore limited to <u>less than two hours</u>.**

18.11   **The photographer, Mr Finch, was however observing No 102 on the morning of 27 April, (although this is nowhere officially recorded). Between 08:00 and 11:00 he took some photographs. One of those (taken at 08:16) shows Jamie Acourt leaving the premises with a black binliner. There was no means of following him, because there was no communication and because the surveillance team was not on parade by that time. This shows a gross lack of planning and indeed of common-sense. If surveillance is to be fully effective there must be the means of communication from OP to base. There must also be arrangements in place for following those who leave in suspicious circumstances. When the full team was on duty in the evening at least one vehicle was followed, to a supermarket, so that such pursuit was in practice feasible.**

18.12 Many photographs were taken, which were processed and forwarded to the AMIP team in albums on 27 April. For 26 April there are pictures of various cars and of Zak Stuart, Jamie Acourt, Neil Acourt, Gary Dobson, Darren Davis (David Norris' cousin) and David Norris. Gary Dobson and David Norris appear together at about 19:55 in three separate photographs.

18.13 **There is no record of other surveillance performed by the team. Other photographs were taken at 102 Bournbrook Road on 5 May, which again showed both the Acourts carrying items of clothing (Neil) and a plastic bag (Jamie). Many other photographs were taken elsewhere in May 1993, but none of those appear to be of importance.**

18.14 Those photographs were never properly researched or used. They were at the Incident Room from 27 April, but nobody appears ever to have realised their great importance. Officers involved in all the interviews of those eventually arrested had little if any knowledge of the surveillance and its product. DC Hughes states that he was not sure if he knew that surveillance had taken place. DC Budgen was aware that there had been surveillance but he was not aware of its outcome. DS Bevan only knew about the surveillance in general terms. DC Chase states that he was not aware of the surveillance at all. Most particularly the photographs were not made available to DS Davidson when he interviewed Gary Dobson. Gary Dobson denied knowledge of David Norris. These photographs would have been a vital shot in DS Davidson's locker. If he had been able to confront Mr Dobson with them he would have established Mr Dobson as a liar. Who knows what effect this might have had upon Mr Dobson, who was ready to speak, and who was rumoured to be the one suspect who might crack.

18.15 **It appears that no other surveillance of any kind was ever mooted or carried out. So that the operation was limited and poorly planned and executed. The whole history of this surveillance reveals inefficiency and incompetence.**

18.16 Furthermore the documents which should exist in connection with the operation are conspicuous by their absence. We have already referred to the absence of entries in the policy file. The limited logs which are available are incomplete, since there is no log for 28 April. Yet the weekly return indicates that observation took place on that day with the result *"No movements at suspects H/A"*, [home address]. The hours worked are said to have been 06:00-14:00 on that day. Ultimately in evidence before us it was accepted that no surveillance did take place on 28 April and that it is likely that the day was spent in research for other unidentified OPs. Even that which is recorded is therefore grossly misleading.

18.17 Mr Philip Pitham is Head of Training at the Regional Crime Squad National Training Centre in Leicestershire. On 30 August 1997 he wrote a devastating report and critique about this surveillance operation. He is a most experienced ex-officer, now employed by the Home Office in respect of surveillance training. It would be tedious to rehearse the whole report, but Mr Pitham indicates that correct procedures were neither followed nor documented. Simply for example there is no tasking document, no management authority to deploy, no surveillance research material, no authority document for the use of technical equipment, no documentary proof of statutory requirements for the use of OPs, no operational briefing sheets. Furthermore apart from the logs referred to (which were incomplete and out of order) there are numerous other deficiencies of records during and after the operation. Mr Pitham poses many questions about the operation which are simply unanswered. And his concluding paragraph reads as follows:-

" Overall Conclusion

It is apparent however that the documentation that is missing from the file holds the key to the questions that I have posed.

Retained briefing material would have supplied the objectives to the individual surveillances, and given an insight into exactly what was required from the observations that took place.

The correct procedures in respect of the static observation post observations, and surveillance back-up or intelligence investigation could also have revealed the purpose of the 4 day surveillance operation.

The planning and preparation that did take place, according to the available paperwork was not of a standard that I would expect if the intention was to gain evidence to assist in a prosecution for murder.

Several important procedures have been apparently neglected (Recording of observations from OPs/Retention of material for disclosure/Recording of material generated by Surveillance) that in my opinion, the surveillance team appear to have been deployed in an 'ad hoc' fashion, with no apparent direction towards the achievement of specific objectives, or the collation of <u>evidence</u> to assist in the prosecution of an offence.

In my opinion, the surveillance has been used to 'trawl' for <u>intelligence</u> which may be of use to other more important lines of enquiry that were ongoing at this specific time in the investigation.

The procedures that were in place in relation to the issues of Surveillance log books 182, and the issuing register 128, within 3-4 Area FIB, at this time would also benefit by the production of the register, to counter suggestions of malpractice. "

18.18 The only identifiable follow up by the AMIP team seems to be one message raising an action about an Allegro car seen on 27 April, and requests from the SIO to retain the photographs, together with a request to DS Hughes from the SIO to complete a record of intelligence gained on the Acourts. No such record has been shown to us.

18.19 **The conclusion must be that this operation was ill-planned, badly carried out, and inadequately documented. If it was partly a substitute for arrests, as a matter of policy, then we conclude that the decision-making in this regard was flawed and incompetent. Furthermore the failure to use the material that was created by the operation, and the failure to have in position and available the means to check that which left the premises in black bin liners speak for themselves. All those who heard the evidence about this aspect of the case were understandably aghast. Furthermore the use of the surveillance team to observe a young black man suspected of theft in apparent priority to surveillance of the Stephen Lawrence suspects is remarkable. No explanation of this "priority" has ever been given.**

CHAPTER NINETEEN

DETECTIVE SERGEANT JOHN DAVIDSON
AND THE
HANDLING OF CERTAIN WITNESSES

19.1 The PCA Report rightly stresses that top priority should have been given to all the valuable and telling information which came to the Incident Room particularly in the early days. Between 23 April 1993 and January 1994 39 separate anonymous calls referring to one or more of the suspects were documented. The PCA Report points out that there are no recorded attempts to identify the callers, and no analysis was made to cross-check or properly to investigate the calls in a quest for fuller information. Failure to follow up the anonymous callers is plainly a matter for criticism.

19.2 **It would be pointless to try to deal with every part of this aspect of the investigation but some matters stand out and must be covered. There was and still is a lack of satisfactory evidence, but there was a generous flow of information from the start. Some of the information was second or third hand. It is a feature of the case that many of those who have been seen and interviewed were known to each other, and obviously there was much exchange of information and rumour on and around the Brook Estate after the murder. Prompt and efficient pursuit of such information can lead to evidence, and to further lines of investigation.**

19.3 We have already pointed out that the Acourts and David Norris were named in the first anonymous message at 13:50 on 23 April.

19.4 At 19:45 on Friday 23 April the man who was supposedly registered as an informant and who was given the pseudonym James Grant came to the police station. From time to time, and notably in the Barker Review, it has been said that this man was an anonymous source. This is not the position. His identity was known from the start. Grant was first seen by DC Budgen, who had joined the team on 23 April.

19.5 DC Budgen says that he at once told Mr Bullock about Grant, but that Mr Bullock seemed to show some lack of interest in the information. DC Budgen said that this did not surprise him. DC Budgen said that if he had *"recovered the Crown jewels it would not have made any difference"*. Mr Bullock simply told DC Budgen to put the message on a *"green sheet"*, so that it would enter the system in the usual way. It did enter the system and actions were certainly allotted as a result of that.

19.6 That message was not seen by Mr Crampton, the SIO, until Saturday 24 April.

19.7 DC Budgen says that he told Grant to contact him daily, and Grant was given telephone numbers for this purpose. Grant next came to the station on Saturday 24 April probably at about 16:30. On that day Detective Sergeant John Davidson joined the team.

19.8 **DS Davidson was an experienced detective officer. He retired in March 1998. He was a self-willed and abrasive officer who more than once became excited and angry in the witness box. Against him there were strong allegations made on behalf of Mr & Mrs Lawrence. Mr Mansfield alleged that DS Davidson was guilty of a combination of failures and mistakes which if unexplained were *"sufficiently fundamental that they provide a basis for inferring either gross negligence, or worse an attempt to thwart the effectiveness of the investigation"*. In those circumstances it is not**

surprising that the exchanges between Mr Mansfield and DS Davidson were acrimonious.

19.9   DS Davidson's duty state shows that he came on duty at about noon on 24 April. He was engaged in reading statements until 14:00. There is a record that at 16:30 he was *"engaged re informant"*. DS Davidson told us that he was in fact ordered to see the informant Grant with DC Budgen, since Mr Bullock regarded it as necessary for DC Budgen's activities to be monitored. DS Davidson told us that on 24 April Grant reiterated the information he had given on 23 April. He says that he questioned Grant as to where he had obtained his information and how he came by it, and that he checked as to whether or not Grant had any ulterior motive in visiting the police station. In general terms DS Davidson said more than once that he gave Grant a hard time during his contact with him in order to make certain that the information that he was being given was indeed genuine.

19.10   **DS Davidson says that there must have been a docket or folder which would have contained notes made of that interview on 24 April. He says that DC Budgen would have taken the notes and entered them into the docket. DS Davidson said that both that meeting and any other meetings at which he was present would have been recorded in this way. These documents have totally disappeared, or alternatively no notes were made other than those entered into the system. We believe that the latter explanation is more likely to be true.**

19.11   Part of the follow up performed by DS Davidson took him to Stacey Benefield, who was mentioned specifically in the information coming from Grant. DS Davidson saw Mr Benefield on Sunday 25 April. Mr Benefield had complained about a stabbing committed in March 1993 but he refused at first to say who had assaulted him. We now know that Stacey Benefield says that he was stabbed by David Norris. On 25 April Mr Benefield gave this information in a comprehensive but short statement giving a description of the attack made upon him by David Norris who was in the company of Neil Acourt. Mr Benefield appeared to DS Davidson to be a credible witness.

19.12   DS Davidson was satisfied as an experienced detective that quite apart from the information being received about the murder of Stephen Lawrence, the information set out in that statement from Mr Benefield would have justified the immediate arrest of David Norris and Neil Acourt. DS Davidson has no explanation for the delay in making the arrests, which was not his responsibility, but he believed that one of the reasons the arrests were held back was because it had been believed that Mr Benefield was reluctant to make or sign a statement or to give evidence.

19.13   In parenthesis it is established that DS Davidson did visit Lee Pearson, whose name was also mentioned in the Grant information as having been involved in an attack. He appears to have seen Mr Pearson on 30 April and also later. Mr Pearson gave a verbal account to DS Davidson of the incident, but was *"very reluctant to give a statement"*. Matthew Farman was also reluctant, but he did eventually provide a statement on 28 April which corroborated the evidence of Stacey Benefield.

19.14   **DS Davidson again saw James Grant on Tuesday 27 April. This was a meeting at a public house, together with DC Budgen. The CAD message in connection with that meeting is available. No further note or written information about the meeting exists, although DS Davidson says that in respect of each meeting with Grant there would have been a note made which would have been contained in the docket. That meeting is set out in Message 152. It reads as follows:- *"Met with informant known as James Grant in local public house. He states that the person who was approached by some blacks to find***

141

out the Acourts address then was threatened by the Acourts not to tell them. The lad in question is BB who lives in [**address protected**]. *He also stated that CC saw four assailants run past the house (ie. Dickson Road) after the assault. He left tasked to find out any more that he could. Grant then rang to say that he thinks he may have found a witness who stated to him that Neil stabbed him in the bottom part and David stabbed him in the top part. He said that this witness was on a bus, he is going to firm up the info and contact us on 28 April 1993. He stated earlier that the Acourts and Norris would probably say nothing and Dobson would crack up and probably tell all. He also said that there was a fifth blonde unknown kid present.*"

19.15   DS Davidson said that between 27 April and 6 May he is confident that he saw or communicated with Grant, but once again there is no document to support this nor any information as to what was said. At some stage DS Davidson says that Grant gave him a first name and a street name in connection with Witness B.

19.16   **The next recorded message from Grant is dated 6 May 1993. DC Budgen completed that message 276. That reads as follows:-** *"The above person stated that the Acourts have asked on numerous occasions whether they could purchase knives. They have a fascination with knives, that they usually hide them under the floorboards, that Lee Pearson was stabbed by Neil Acourt, also a Stacey was stabbed by Neil's friend. He is described as white 5'8" medium build mousy hair, curly. They the Acourts haven't been seen in the Well Hall area since the murder."* **That message is the source of information given to the team meeting on 6 May by DC Budgen in connection with the hiding of knives under floorboards. It is relevant in connection with the actions of all those involved in the arrests of the suspects.**

19.17   It is now necessary to refer to a most vexed part of the evidence in this case. DS Davidson says that he and DC Budgen decided that Grant should be registered as an informant. He was not strictly an informant in the ordinary sense of that term at all. He was somebody who was giving information, but there is no indication that he was habitually or even on this occasion seeking to give information for reward. However he wished to remain anonymous, and DS Davidson told us that he believed that he might be useful in the future, since he was so forthcoming in connection with the Stephen Lawrence murder. Be that as it may both DS Davidson and DC Budgen say that they assembled the papers, including such contact sheets and notes as had been created when Grant had been seen by them, and that they took them to Greenwich Police Station where Detective Chief Inspector Leslie Owens was in charge.

19.18   Both DC Budgen and DS Davidson have entries in their duty states which show that they did go to Greenwich on 28 April. Exactly what they did there is a matter of much dispute. DS Davidson said, both in his evidence early on before the Inquiry and when he was recalled specifically on this topic, that the documents were in fact given to Mr Owens for registration. He is adamant that this took place. Mr Owens for his part is equally adamant that he did not and does not know DS Davidson, and that no documents were ever left with him. If the matter rested solely upon the evidence of those two officers we would unhesitatingly prefer the evidence of Mr Owens. **It is palpable that in fact there was never any registration of Grant as an informant. Nobody has ever seen the documents in this connection, and we are wholly satisfied that there never was any registration. If there had been, the documents should have gone through the proper channels and they would have finished up with the relevant officer in Mr Ilsley's department, and at New Scotland Yard.**

19.19 The key to the matter may in the end be the evidence of DC Budgen. He says that he did go with DS Davidson to Greenwich Police Station with the papers which were in an envelope. He met Inspector Alan Buttivant, who was known to DC Budgen, and they were directed by Mr Buttivant to Mr Owens. They went to Mr Owens' office, but he was busy with somebody else. Therefore they went to the canteen and waited for some time and then the papers were taken down and left on Mr Owens' desk. DC Budgen says that there was no explanation given to Mr Owens, but that the documents were left there since they assumed that he would deal with them thereafter. There is some confirmation for this version of events since Mr Buttivant does remember seeing DC Budgen at Greenwich on that day. He had no idea why DS Davidson and DC Budgen were there, and no documents were given to him.

19.20 It is difficult to establish what motive DS Davidson may have had for giving us the clear picture of a formal registration which we do not accept. Even on DC Budgen's account of the matter the whole episode was lax and highly unsatisfactory, since sensitive papers in connection with an informant must always be handled with the greatest care. Whatever may be thought of DS Davidson in this regard we do not believe that DC Budgen has invented his version of events, and it is thus possible that there were documents which have gone missing simply because they were left without any explanation on or near Mr Owens' desk.

19.21 Later as has been established over and over again, DS Davidson wrote a letter to the SIO, Mr Weeden, suggesting that a reward should be paid to Grant. Mr Weeden endorsed this suggestion and proposed the sum of £50. These documents appear in an unregistered folder which contains the two documents. This folder with the two letters was found in the Finance & Resource filing system at Eltham Police Station during the course of the PCA inquiry.

19.22 Before us DS Davidson indicated that it was his belief that money was allocated to be paid in respect of his request. He told us that the money was available but that he refused to collect it because he thought that the sum was paltry. There is no evidence whatsoever that the money was in fact allocated. Mr Ilsley told us that he saw the request but that he did nothing to further it since he did not believe that the information given by Grant was particularly valuable since information of a similar nature had come from elsewhere.

19.23 **The whole episode of this alleged registration is highly unsatisfactory. It reveals certainly a woeful lack of attention to the steps which ought to be taken in respect of an informant, assuming that DS Davidson and DC Budgen genuinely believed that this man was an informant who needed to be registered. If he was registered on the 28 April any further contact with him ought to have been very carefully controlled and no contact should have been made with him without reference to the controller, a designated officer.**

19.24 Undoubtedly the episode reflects badly upon DS Davidson. On the other hand he is able to say that if he was in fact sidelining Grant, and that is the allegation made, he would surely not have sought a reward for him at all. Writing the letter asking for a reward would simply have highlighted at once the fact that Grant had not been registered. One strange feature of Mr Owens' evidence was that he did appear to have some recollection of a conversation in connection with the registration of an informant in a different case at about the relevant time. His written statement suggested that there might have been some connection with the Stephen Lawrence case in this regard. When he gave evidence he accepted that there was some room for confusion in this respect, but he reiterated that he had no recollection of seeing DS Davidson or DC Budgen at all.

19.25 What can and must be said is that it is plain that Grant was dealt with fairly roughly by DS Davidson. He said at one stage in insensitive but perhaps typical terms that *"this was simply a case of a skinhead turning up at a police station when a black has been murdered and wanting to know what is happening."* He repeatedly said that he had done his best to extract from Grant the name of the source of his most valuable information. Over and over again he said that he had never been given that information by Grant. Later when Grant was seen by Kent he indicated that he had told DS Davidson about the source, namely Witness K, while he was in contact with the team in April 1993. There is no record that this information was given by Grant on the system, and DS Davidson says that if the identity of the source had been given to him by Grant he would without doubt have followed it up and recorded it at once.

19.26 Information about Witness K came, as we know, from sources other than Grant. At one stage it did appear that DS Davidson was saying that he had heard about Witness K both from Grant and from other sources. This seems to have been an error, since DS Davidson consistently denied that Grant had told him personally who his source was. During his questioning DS Davidson had difficulty in remembering whether he had in fact seen Witness K or not. It is evident looking at the documentation that he did see him, and indeed he took a short statement from Witness K on 17 May 1993.

19.27 In connection with another witness, Witness B, there was more criticism of DS Davidson. He was the witness described by James Grant on 6 May. A name and a street were given to DS Davidson, so he said, by Grant at a later date and DS Davidson in fact traced Witness B. DS Davidson saw Witness B together with two other officers on two occasions. It is apparent that he formed a low opinion of Witness B, and the CAD message recording his visit indicates that he thought that Witness B was a *"Walter Mitty"*, and that he was most unlikely to speak the truth. Indeed he says that Witness B's mother indicated that he was open to suggestion. Witness B gave a version of the incident, namely fighting followed by his view of one of the Acourts and David Norris. He indicated that the incident took place near the Welcome Inn which is of course a considerable distance away from the location where the murder took place. DS Davidson's view was that Witness B was a very young witness who was prone to lie, and that this was confirmed by his mother. In fact Witness B was seen later by DS Kirkpatrick who took a statement from him which indicated that he knew David Norris quite well. Ultimately Witness B's evidence was wholly discredited at the committal proceedings because of his varied version of the events, and his failure to identify David Norris at a specially convened identification parade.

19.28 Mr Mansfield also criticised the handling of two potential young female witnesses by DS Davidson. One was Michelle Casserley. Entries found in her diary relating to the Acourts and others suggested that she might have some evidence to give, as did information received when her house was visited on the house-to-house inquiries. DS Davidson visited her and according to him in front of her mother she used *"the most venomous language I have heard from a young girl"*. This verbal abuse came apparently unprompted, and DS Davidson decided that he would make no progress with Miss Casserley. Incidentally Miss Casserley was seen later by a representative of J R Jones, Mr Khan's firm, when the private prosecution was launched in 1995. She then indicated that she could give no useful evidence and that it was not true that she had ever told anybody that she saw the Acourts on the day of the murder. She told the representative that she may have written the suspects' names in her diary because she knew those people and because everyone was saying that the Acourts and others had committed the murder.

19.29 **It seems doubtful whether she would have been a useful witness, but it must be said that it is likely that the general approach of DS Davidson was unhelpful. An over-robust senior detective was unlikely to be the best person to obtain information from young and reluctant witnesses.**

19.30 Another young witness visited by DS Davidson was Emma Cook who was said to have walked past the bus stop shortly before the murder. DS Davidson says that her father would not allow her to make a statement under any circumstances. In both these instances Mr Mansfield suggests that DS Davidson was marginalising or belittling the possible contribution to be made by the witnesses as part of his general lackadaisical approach to the case. Mr Mansfield alleged that DS Davidson dishonestly or alternatively for racist reasons was not bothering about the furthering of the investigation.

19.31 DS Davidson arrested Gary Dobson, and he interviewed Gary Dobson. Mr Dobson never made any admissions, but he did answer all the questions put to him by DS Davidson. A feature of those interviews involves a passage in which DS Davidson appears to be encouraging Mr Dobson by a suggestion that the murder had <u>not</u> in fact been a racist killing. DS Davidson explains this by saying that Mr Dobson appeared to be upset about the suggestion that he might have been a racist, so that the interview was conducted in order to go along with Mr Dobson in this vein in the hope that he would open up and eventually make some useful admission. This was a pragmatic stance in order to try to achieve an admission or information about the murder. On the other hand the method employed laid DS Davidson open to criticism in connection with his own misguided views about the motivation for this crime. It must also be noted that the Mr Dobson interviews were subject to criticism by Detective Sergeant Mould, an expert who examined all the interviews. He criticises the preparation of the interviewing officers, and in the Mr Dobson case he rightly points out that the questioning was "confirmatory", and not interrogatory in the true sense.

19.32 **We have already pointed out that DS Davidson was deprived of a most valuable piece of information during his interview with Mr Dobson, since he was not given the photographs showing Gary Dobson and David Norris together. As to this DS Davidson said that he was *"very annoyed, because whether it would have made a difference I don't know, but it would certainly have given me more of a lever when questioning him when he was denying association"*.**

19.33 DS Davidson was also involved in the arrest of Luke Knight, and he conducted the interviews with Mr Knight. Initially those interviews were conducted in the presence of Mr Knight's mother. Thereafter his mother indicated that she might be an alibi witness, so that it was unfortunate that she had been allowed to accompany Mr Knight to his interviews.

19.34 **A significant feature of DS Davidson's evidence concerns his view of the nature of this terrible murder. He was closely questioned as to this aspect of the case. He said that he realised that the initial description given to him might constitute a racist attack and he said that there was what he called a *"call out"* of a racist nature. On the other hand from the information which he obtained during the investigation he said that he believed that the persons involved were persons who would have killed anyone who had been in Dickson Road at the relevant time. Throughout his evidence he made it emphatically clear that he refused to recognise that the attack was purely racist. He accepted that there was a racist shout before the attack and that one essence of the attack was racist. But he added that *"because these lads had attacked whites before, very very similarly with a similar knife I believe this was thugs. They were described as the Krays. They were thugs who were out to kill, not particularly a black person, but anybody*** *and I believe that to this day that that was thugs, not racism, just pure bloody minded thuggery".*

19.35 **This is the same attitude shown by DC Budgen, DS Bevan and DC Holden. Officers indicate that as many as 50% of those involved believed that this was the true analysis of the case.**

19.36 The reason for stressing the racist aspect of the incident was, as Mr Mansfield put to DS Davidson, that where there is a racist attack it is vital to identify it as such because it will be important to look at what connection this attack may have had with other similar attacks or persons involved in such attacks. Mr Mansfield roundly suggested to DS Davidson that this attitude and the failure to follow up intelligence in connection with attacks was in itself an area of neglect. DS Davidson pointed out that other victims of these young men namely Stacey Benefield and Lee Pearson were white, and he said that he had only recently discovered that another young man attacked, namely Kevin London, was black. He says that he did not know when he was interviewing Mr Dobson that Kevin London was black and he said that Mr Dobson had not told him that that was the case.

19.37 **This attitude of DS Davidson and of other officers is to be deplored. Where any person alleges racist motivation it must have or should have been known to them all that the ACPO definition required the matter to be dealt with as a racist incident. The basic trouble with the officers' attitude is that any suggestion that this was not a purely racist murder is understandably anathema to Mr & Mrs Lawrence and indeed to the black community. They know, and so do we, that this was a totally unprovoked racist murder and consequently the obdurate attitude of DS Davidson and of other officers who took and expressed the same opinion must be severely criticised. It is insensitive and untenable to suggest that this was or might have been a motiveless crime or even a crime of mixed motives. To suggest that the crime was not purely racist can only lead to a conclusion in the minds of Mr & Mrs Lawrence that proper concentration was not brought to bear upon the investigation of the racist murder of their son, and that such an approach must have skewed the nature and direction of the investigation.**

19.38 **The senior officers, namely the SIOs, plainly regarded this as purely a racist murder. We simply do not understand why DS Davidson and others were unable to accept that this was the simple and uncomplicated position. We consider that their inability to accept that the murder was racist is a manifestation of their own flawed approach and of their own unwitting collective racism. DS Davidson and all the other officers indicated that within their limits they did do all that they were required to do and all that they could possibly have done in order to try to solve this murder and bring the perpetrators to justice. Unfortunately their attitude in regard to the racist motivation of this crime belittles their efforts in connection with the many actions which they were tasked to perform.**

19.39 Criticism of DS Davidson and his dealings with the very important sources of information and potential witnesses and of his attitude is justifiable. Our conclusion is that he was the wrong man to have been given many of the tasks that he was given although it must be said that DS Davidson and the other officers undoubtedly worked long hours and performed many actions and tasks with a view to solving the murder. Furthermore we do not believe that there is any strength in the suggestion that DS Davidson was affected by the aura cast over the case by the presence of the unarrested Clifford Norris. We do not believe that it can be or has been established that DS Davidson was influenced by the presence of Clifford Norris or by any connection with Mr Norris in respect of any of the actions taken or not taken by him during the investigation. DS Davidson was not part of Mr Mellish's team in 1995. But he was one of a group of Regional Crime Squad officers brought in at the final stage to help with the arrest of Clifford Norris. Mr Mellish was surprised to see DS Davidson, who did become thus involved simply in the actual arrest.

19.40 **The evidence of DS Davidson was undoubtedly unsatisfactory. Particularly in respect of his handling of James Grant and the registration, there is material upon which DS Davidson must be criticised. The question is whether any more sinister interpretation must be placed upon his conduct other than the comment that he was the wrong person to perform the tasks allocated to him. We are not convinced that DS Davidson positively tried to thwart the effectiveness of the investigation. It was he who took the statement from Stacey Benefield which effectively launched the prosecution of David Norris and Neil Acourt in respect of that gross stabbing of March 1993. He was in charge of the protection of the witnesses leading up to the trial of David Norris at the Central Criminal Court. That prosecution failed for reasons which cannot be attributed to any activity of DS Davidson. There is also no evidence that DS Davidson held back positively in respect of the lines of investigation which he followed in order to favour David Norris or indeed any of the other suspects.**

19.41 There was an overriding need in this investigation to turn information into evidence and to turn reluctant witnesses into willing ones in order to obtain the fullest possible information and evidence. There is no doubt that the investigation team felt rightly that there were witnesses who were saying less than they actually knew. Most if not all of these witnesses were young people, sometimes with a basic antipathy to the police. In these circumstances a tactful and sensitive approach to witnesses was needed. This is evidenced by the message of 28 April 1993 from DC Hughes and PC Andrews in relation to Witnesses DD and EE stating *"We both feel that a gentle approach when he is seen again would be the appropriate method of extracting information from him. He may also be responsible for the two notes to the Incident Room"*.

19.42 **DS Davidson was simply not the right officer to apply tact and sensitivity in his approach. This should have been known and recognised by his senior officers who deployed him as well as by himself. Our clear impression of DS Davidson was of a strong, self-opinionated character who would be inclined to seek to dominate witnesses in order to obtain information rather than solicit it in a more sensitive and sophisticated way. We are critical of both DS Davidson himself and his senior officers for the manner in which witnesses were approached and the failure to recognise the need to take steps to implement more sensitive methods.**

19.43 We do not consider that DS Davidson would wilfully cut off the investigation of witnesses with whom he was concerned or that he has pulled his punches or made any positive attempt to thwart the investigation. We do however firmly believe that his particular style of approach was likely to have been counterproductive in this case and that there was a failure to recognise and address this.

19.44 **Equally DS Davidson's attitude to the definition of this crime as racist or otherwise may well have affected his approach to the case. This is also clearly true of many other officers and in particular some of those close to him in the investigation whom he undoubtedly influenced. For example DC Budgen states that he regarded the murder as racist but changed his view subsequently to that expressed by DS Davidson. If officers expressed the view that they did not believe that the case was purely motivated by racism, when it so clearly was, then the perception of the black community in** particular, and of all who heard the evidence at this Inquiry is inevitably that such an unjustifiable stance reflects inherent racism in the officers involved and in the police service. DS Davidson and others have only themselves to blame for the perception that they were indeed "institutionally racist". This perception is justified in the sense that these officers approached the investigation in the wrong way and encouraged each other in their wrongful belief as to the motivation for the crime.

CHAPTER TWENTY

THE ELIMINATION OF SUSPECTS
AND
THE RED ASTRA

20.1 Both the PCA Report and the testimony and written submission of Detective Chief Superintendent Burdis (see Chapter 32) addressed the significant issue of the identification and elimination of "suspects" in the investigation into Stephen Lawrence's murder. In addition the "saga" of the red Astra motor car was highlighted both by Counsel for Mr & Mrs Lawrence and for Mr Brooks.

20.2 In any murder investigation a number of suspects can appear, some of obviously greater priority than others. They should be methodically and objectively eliminated as far as possible. The need to do this is reflected in the *"Elimination Codes"* which are a standard part of the HOLMES system. Six codes exist which are used to categorise the strength of the elimination. The codes are:-

Elimination
1 - Forensic (eg. DNA, blood, fingerprints).
2 - Description (on parameters set by the SIO).
3 - Independent witness.
4 - Associate or relative.
5 - Spouse or partner.
6 - Not eliminated.

An SIO can dictate as a matter of policy which codes he will accept as safely eliminating a suspect and define any specific criteria he wishes. In this case no entry was made in the Policy File in relation to elimination criteria by either Mr Crampton or Mr Weeden and the elimination code system was not used other than some suspects being shown as Code 6, not eliminated. Mr Weeden made individual judgements in relation to each suspect.

20.3 Mr Burdis identifies 75 suspects registered in the HOLMES system. In examination by Miss Weekes in relation to the use of elimination codes he stated *"well, there is tremendous confusion about the way elimination was handled..."*. In addition others clearly qualified as suspects but do not appear to have been classified as such. The occupants of the red Astra motor vehicle seen in Well Hall Road soon after the murder are in the latter category.

20.4 **PC Hodges was one of a number of officers in TSG Unit 326 who attended the scene of the murder shortly after it happened. Initially he went with Mr Groves, who decided to make inquiries at the Welcome Inn. About 30 minutes after arriving at the scene PC Hodges was standing near to the cordon at the point where Stephen collapsed. He saw an old style red Vauxhall Astra motor car, occupied by five white youths, approach the scene along Well Hall Road from the direction of Shooters Hill. The car slowed down at the cordoned area, and drove on in the direction of the Well Hall Roundabout. The occupants appeared to be laughing. PC Hodges caused a description of the vehicle to be circulated by radio through PSgt Clements who was standing with him. A few minutes later the vehicle came back, travelling in the opposite direction. PC Hodges, who was not in possession of radio himself, again caused the description of the car to be given out by another officer over the air. On neither occasion was the car stopped. No steps appear to have been taken to see that the car was followed. Most of the registration number was gained, and recorded as AGW 55 Y.**

20.5   PSgt Clement, who was PC Hodges' immediate supervisor on the night, confirms the initial radio *"circulation"* of the description of the car by himself. He also confirms the fact that both he and PC Hodges felt that the five youths in the car *"could match the description given of five youths together who were the suspects or indeed could have provided any further information"*. He also indicates that full details of the incident were passed to the investigation team.

20.6   The details do appear to have been passed to DC Pye, the Night Duty Detective at the scene. Message No 2, timed at 08:34 on 23 April records *"... uniformed officers noticed an old style Vauxhall drove past a number of times with a group of youngsters in it. They seemed to think something was humorous about this. The car had a part index AGW   Y. Uniform officers may have more detail"*. That message is marked to the effect that an action should be raised to identify the vehicle and trace the driver. There is some confirmation that the description of the vehicle was circulated over the air, since PC Robson testified that whilst manning a cordon at the scene he *"heard something about a red Astra ... I did not hear the full text of the message"*. Additionally PC Robson recorded in his pocket book these details:- *"Stephen Lawrence (v), Duwayne Brooks, description 6', brown bushy hair, 19 years, 6" blade knife AGW red Astra"*. He thought that he must have obtained these details when briefed on his return to duty at 10:00 on 23 April.

20.7   Action 20 resulted from Message 2. That action is endorsed by DC Doel some six days later on 29 April, showing that there were 28 Astras with AGW   Y registration. No further action seems to have been taken to check these vehicles, although this was a manageable inquiry in terms of numbers, particularly if taken on a local area basis. The SIO, Mr Weeden, classed the action as *"non-priority and no further inquiries to be made at this time"*.

20.8   **By sheer chance the vehicle, whose correct registration proved to be AGW 115Y, was seen by PSgt Clement on 30 April. He stopped it and obtained details of the occupants. Those details were passed to the investigation team and are recorded on Action 20. They showed that the driver was Daniel Copley, and the passenger was Kieran Hyland. Their addresses and dates of birth are given. A further action was raised to research Mr Copley and Mr Hyland.**

20.9   **There was no separate research section in the investigation team. Mr Weeden has indicated that he would have liked to have had one, but had insufficient manpower to create such a section. The action was then allocated to DS Flook on 1 May. DS Flook was of course already performing five separate tasks as Office Manager, Statement Reader, Receiver, Action Allocator and Bag Carrier. It was his task to prioritise this particular action and to allocate it. In fact there is no trace of the action emerging until 8 June, which is 39 days later. It was then allocated to DC Michael Tomlin. There is really no satisfactory explanation whatsoever for this delay. Mr Weeden felt that the delay might have been attributable to the misplacement of the paperwork, in that it might have been concealed or stuck behind some other document. This is pure supposition. Mr Bullock and DS Flook could simply offer no explanation at all for the delay. It is evident that the information flowing through the incident room and the resulting actions were markedly delayed. This is a classic example of such delay.**

20.10 Eventually the action requiring an officer to see Mr Copley and Mr Hyland was allocated to DC Tomlin at 08:26 on 8 June. DC Tomlin appears to have been assisted by DC Crane. Three statements were taken. DC Tomlin took statements from Daniel Copley and Kieran Hyland. DC Crane took a statement from Jason Goatley. All three men indicated that they had been drinking in the Wildfowler Public House at Thamesmead on the night of the murder. That public house appears to be a notorious haunt of racist white youths from Thamesmead. All three said that they left the public house in the red Astra at about 22:15 to 22:30 and that they had driven past the scene of the murder purely by coincidence in the course of dropping off Mr Goatley at his girlfriend's address. Mr Goatley and Mr Copley said that there were only three people in the vehicle. Mr Hyland however said that *"there were five of us altogether, but I don't want say about the other two"*. This palpable anomaly has never been addressed. When asked what he did to pursue this obvious line of inquiry DC Tomlin answered, *"What do you expect me to do"*. Later DC Tomlin indicated that he considered being asked why he had not investigated the differences between the statements as *"a silly question"*.

20.11 **DC Tomlin's attitude in the witness box was both condescending and casual. He had come apparently from abroad to the Inquiry and his contribution to the evidence was unsatisfactory. He performed such duties as were allocated to him, as the record shows, but it seems most likely that his casualness in the witness box was a mirror image of his activity during the investigation. Certainly this particular failure to follow up what could have been an important distinction between the evidence of these witnesses was serious neglect.**

20.12 This failure is made worse by the lack of any background research undertaken by DC Tomlin either before or after the statements were taken, and by the failure of his supervisors to address the obvious need for further investigation once the statements were logged.

20.13 It should be a matter of routine for obvious reasons, for an officer carrying out an action to research the HOLMES system in order to obtain any other relevant information relating to the subject matter of his action. This can be done by the officer himself, or it can be done on his behalf by the action allocator. This did not happen in respect of the red Astra during the investigation. Action Number 460 allocated to DC Tomlin showed no associated documents or linked actions, although Action 20 and Message 2 clearly existed and were relevant. DC Tomlin said in answer to questions before the Inquiry that he was not aware of the original sightings of the car on the night of the murder by uniformed officers. The Action simply stated *"TIE* [trace, interview and eliminate] *Daniel Edward Copley nominal 609 re knowledge of incident - drove past scene with Hyland nominal 610 in red Astra"*.

20.14 Furthermore simple local research would have established that Messrs Copley, Goatley and Hyland were well known in Thamesmead. They had convictions for racist attacks. Messrs Copley and Goatley had been arrested and convicted of threatening behaviour connected with the circumstances surrounding the murder of Rolan Adams. Mr Hyland had been convicted of a separate racist attack. All three were members of a local and notorious gang referred to as the NTO (Nutty or Nazi Turnout). As PSgt Solley, the local Community Relations Sergeant later testified, Mr Hyland was on record in the Racial Incident Unit at Plumstead, and all three were on record in the collator's index. The view of many of the team that the murder of Stephen Lawrence was not solely motivated by racism may well be reflected in this failure to obtain readily available local intelligence.

20.15 Even if this background had not existed the failure to address the differences in the three statements is inexcusable. The requirement placed upon DC Tomlin by the Action was to Trace, Interview and Eliminate. These three men were simply not eliminated by virtue of the statements taken. Indeed the opposite is the case. DC Tomlin should have pursued the obvious further inquiries which needed to be made. Furthermore the statements were seen by DS Flook in one of his five capacities, and by Mr Bullock and Mr Weeden, both of whom testified that they saw all statements. Nobody indicated the need for further investigative action, and the statements were simply filed. Messrs Goatley, Copley and Hyland were not eliminated despite having been near the scene in suspicious circumstances on the night of the murder.

20.16 It may be that the presence of the red Astra at the scene of the murder was entirely coincidental. On the other hand it is possible that the occupants of the red Astra had knowledge of or involvement with those who were involved in the attack upon Stephen Lawrence. One or more of the group responsible for the attack could, for example, have been dropped off by the red Astra. Alternatively the two groups may have been together before the attack. The crucial point is that such obvious and potentially significant inquiries simply did not take place. This shows professional incompetence of a serious nature by DC Tomlin, and an equally serious lack of supervision and management of the investigation by Mr Bullock and the SIO. DS Flook must also be criticised to some extent, but to a lesser degree because he was in the totally invidious position of having five separate functions to perform in the Incident Room.

20.17 **We have dealt in some detail with the history of the red Astra, since it is a signal example of the failure of the investigation team to take necessary action. It is no doubt too late now to expect any productive information to be gained by further interviews by the police of these men. We will never know what might have emerged if the task of investigating them had been properly carried out at the right time.**

20.18 The Kent Report lists eight suspects who were either related to or known associates of the prime suspects. All of these had simply been marked by Mr Weeden as *"No further action"* All were inadequately investigated and only two of the decisions were dated. Two prime examples are summarised here.

20.19 Blue Stuart was both a relation and an associate of the Acourts. He was named as a suspect by an informant to DS May, who passed on that information to the AMIP team. It did transpire later that DS May's informant might have been referring to a different murder. But Stuart was also identified, as *"Nickname Blue, blonde hair, Age 20"* on Mrs Lawrence's list given to Mr Ilsley on 6 May (see para 27.16 et seq). He was interviewed on 14 July 1993. He stated he had been drinking in the Crossways Public House until 23:00 on the night of the murder. He could not remember who he was with. On 13 August the girlfriend of one of Stuart's friends made a statement that she was in the public house until 22:30 on the night of the murder and that Stuart was there at that time. No further enquiries were made. Stuart was marked *"No Further Action"* and treated as eliminated. The decision was undated. Stuart's description fitted the general descriptions given by the three eye witnesses Mr Westbrook, Mr Shepherd and Mr Brooks of one of those in the group. In particular he had fair hair, a feature in all three descriptions, which does not fit any of the main suspects, as shown by the surveillance photographs and as acknowledged by Mr Weeden in his Kent interview. He stated *We didn't know what David Norris looked like but certainly none of them have fair hair and of course that was one of the reasons for continuing surveillance because we thought there may have been up to six people."*

20.20 Michael Bunn was an associate of the Acourts and identified as such by information received by DS Kirkpatrick on 28 April recorded as Message 238. Bunn's description also fits the general descriptions given by the witnesses Brooks, Shepherd and Westbrook and again, in particular, he is described as having blonde hair. He was seen on the 14 June 1993 and stated that on the night of the murder he was in the Brook Hospital Social Club with a friend whom he named. The friend was seen on 6 July and confirmed this, indicating that they arrived at the club at 21:30 and left by taxi about 23:00. The police examined the "signing in" book at the club and found that the entry for Michael Bunn was dated Wednesday 21 April not Thursday 22nd. There was a suggestion that the date stamp had not been changed, and was therefore wrong. However no further enquiries were made. Mr Weeden marked Bunn for *"No further action"* and he was effectively eliminated from further enquiry. The decision was not dated. When interviewed by Kent Mr Weeden accepted further enquiries should have been made at the club and with the taxi firm and stated *"...I accept that they were omissions and serious omissions."*

20.21 Other examples of persons named as suspects who Kent found to have been recorded as eliminated without full or proper enquiry were Bradley and Scott Lamb, the half brothers of the Acourts, who also lived at 102 Bournbrook Road. They were said by Mrs Acourt to have been present there on the night of the murder. Scott Lamb told the police that he arrived back at No 102 at 23:00 on the night of the murder. Bradley Lamb was never interviewed at all. Both had been named as suspects on 4 May 1993.

20.22 It is not always possible to eliminate suspects. A person may have, quite truthfully, been alone at a particular time, or an alibi supported only by a friend or spouse may be entirely true. Equally some suspects will be accorded greater priority in an investigation than others. In this case it is both self-evident and correct that the Acourts, David Norris and Gary Dobson were the prime suspects. But others, particularly those who were known associates, may have been directly or indirectly involved or able to give useful information. They needed to be thoroughly investigated and eliminated, particularly since the group attacking Stephen Lawrence was thought to have been greater in number than the initial four suspects.

20.23 **There is no evidence either in the policy log, the HOLMES system or the suspect documentation of the clear logic and reasoning on which elimination must be based. In the words of the PCA report *"...credible suspects were eliminated on spurious grounds"*. This is clearly the case and must be a cause of serious concern and criticism.**

CHAPTER TWENTY-ONE

IDENTIFICATION PARADES
AND
THE FAIR HAIRED ATTACKER

21.1   Identification Parades were held in connection with this murder on 7 May, 13 May, 24 May and 3 June 1993. All the parades were conducted at the area identification suite at Southwark Police Station. There was a permanent staff of police officers and civilians employed at the suite. There was no Inspector posted to the suite at the time and the practice was for the Division requesting a parade to supply its own Inspector.

21.2   In 1993 the suite was closed on Mondays for administration. Tuesdays and Wednesdays were primarily allocated for white suspects and Thursdays and Fridays for black suspects. The method of booking the suite involved the officer requiring a parade to take place contacting the staff, when a mutually agreeable date would then be allocated. Sometimes it was necessary to arrange a parade very quickly, and in every case speed is of the essence, since it is necessary to allow witnesses to view suspects who are arrested as soon as possible after an arrest.

21.3   **There is evidence before this Inquiry of laxness in connection with the running of the ID parades. There was plainly difficulty both in connection with the attendance of volunteers to stand on the parades and in connection with the alleged behaviour of a solicitor who was, so some witnesses say, difficult in connection with his demands.**

21.4   The first parade took place on 7 May 1993 and it involved the suspects Neil and Jamie Acourt and Gary Dobson. The witnesses were Joseph Shepherd and Mr Brooks. The Acourts and Gary Dobson had been arrested at about 06.30 on 7 May. Apparently Mr McIvor appointed Inspector Laurence Slone to act as Identification Officer on this and other occasions. Barry Nugent was a potential witness, but he declined to attend, stating that he would be unable to identify anybody.

21.5   The parade on 7 May was conducted by Mr Slone, who was approached on the afternoon of 7 May and told to conduct the parade. He was told that there were three suspects, but he had to contact the incident room at Eltham in order to ascertain information with regard to the offence which had to be entered onto the relevant form. There had been preliminary general contact made by Mr Bullock with Mr McIvor on 6 May as to the possibility of conducting parades in the future when suspects were arrested. Mr McIvor said that an Inspector would be appointed when the need arose. This approach was recorded before any decision to arrest had been made. The arrests of the Acourts and Gary Dobson took place at about 06:30 on 7 May. Mr Slone was given no warning of his appointment before the afternoon of 7 May. The lateness of this approach adds credence to the argument that the arrests were made because of outside pressures. Since 7 May was a Friday proper planning should have ensured that the identification parade suite was alerted at once to the need for parades including white suspects during 7 May. This was particularly important since the suite was not usually open at the weekend.

21.6   In the result the only suspect paraded on 7 May was Jamie Acourt, and neither Mr Shepherd nor Mr Brooks identified him. The failure to parade Neil Acourt and Gary Dobson is explained by Mr Slone on the basis that there was a lack of volunteers and that the hour was late.

21.7   **It was on this occasion that Mr Shepherd indicates that his name was *"inadvertently revealed to the persons taking part in the parade"*. Mr Slone told us that he did ask Mr Shepherd his name, but that he spoke quietly. However, the result was that Mr Shepherd refused to attend any further parades, since he was frightened that his name might be passed on. Such disclosure of names should plainly be avoided.**

21.8   The second parade took place on 13 May 1993. The Identification Officer on this occasion was Inspector John McIlgrew. Mr Shepherd refused to attend this parade, and his father indicated that he was in fear for his safety. The suspects on this occasion were Gary Dobson, Neil Acourt, Jamie Acourt, and David Norris. The witnesses in connection with the Stephen Lawrence murder were Mr Brooks and Royston Westbrook. Stacey Benefield and Matthew Farman were present as witnesses to the stabbing in March 1993 of Stacey Benefield by David Norris in the presence of Neil Acourt.

21.9   It was on this occasion that Mr McIlgrew indicates that he had difficulties with a solicitor, who wished to film the proceedings. As a result of considerable delays all round Mr Westbrook left the ID suite at 16:15, stating that he could not wait any longer. Mr Westbrook had been picked up between 09.00 and 10.00, and he was told that he would be wanted for about an hour. Not surprisingly he decided to leave when more than six hours had elapsed.

21.10   Furthermore, it was on this occasion that Mr Westbrook told us, in regard to the conduct of the parade, that during the day the witnesses were allowed to congregate unsupervised in a room before the parades took place. Mr Westbrook told the Inquiry about Mr Brooks in particular, indicating that he paced up and down the room, making other witnesses nervous. He also telephoned (within other witnesses' hearing), and appeared to be giving a running account of what was happening, probably to his solicitor. Then he spoke to Mr Westbrook, and later started asking for the addresses of other witnesses, to the consternation of Mr Westbrook and at least one other female witness. **No police officer was present while all this was going on. It is evident that this was a serious flaw in the conduct of the parade and of the arrangements on 13 May 1993, since witnesses should never be left together without police supervision. Any successful identification might well have been compromised because of this irregularity.**

21.11   Jamie Acourt did not take part in the parades on this occasion. Mr Brooks had failed to identify him already on 7 May 1993. There was apparently a lack of volunteers similar to Jamie Acourt.

21.12   **During the course of the parades Mr Brooks identified Neil Acourt, and he identified a volunteer on Mr Dobson's parade. Following this parade Neil Acourt was charged with the murder of Stephen Lawrence. David Norris and Neil Acourt were both identified by Stacey Benefield and Matthew Farman, and were later charged with the attempted murder of Stacey Benefield.**

21.13   A further parade was held on 24 May 1993, when the Identification Officer was Inspector Craig. The suspects were Jamie Acourt, David Norris, Neil Acourt and Gary Dobson. The witnesses were Mr Westbrook, Gurdeep Bhangal, Sandra Hood and Terry Witham. Mr Bhangal, Miss Hood and Mr Witham were witnesses to other alleged stabbings. Mr Westbrook was a witness to the Stephen Lawrence murder. Mr Craig has given a statement in which he sets out in considerable detail the problems which he encountered with a solicitor in which he states that these difficulties caused this parade also to take an excessively long time. Mr Westbrook attended the parade and viewed the parades involving Jamie Acourt and David Norris, both of whom he failed to identify.

21.14 **A further parade was held on 3 June 1993. Again Mr McIlgrew was in charge. The witness was Mr Brooks and the suspect was Luke Knight, who had with him a legal representative from a solicitor's firm. It had been the intention again to ask Mr Shepherd to attend, but he telephoned and said he was unwilling to attend any further ID parades. During this parade Luke Knight was identified by Mr Brooks and was subsequently charged with the murder of Stephen Lawrence. This parade and its aftermath is of very considerable importance in connection with the evidence given by DS Crowley, the escorting officer, to which we will refer later in detail (see Chapter 22).**

21.15 There were various attempts made after 3 June to hold further parades, but in fact no witness was called to the suite after 3 June. The only other parade which took place was on 5 September 1995, during the private prosecution committal proceedings, when David Norris was paraded for Witness B, who failed to identify him. That parade is of considerable significance in connection with the evidence of Witness B which is referred to particularly in the section dealing with the committal proceedings (Chapter 40).

21.16 Some criticism has been made of the failure to ask other witnesses to attend ID parades. It has been suggested that Mademoiselle Marie, the third eye witness at the bus stop might have been asked to attend, and that a witness who came forward in connection with a media appeal, having seen four white youths walking from Well Hall Roundabout towards Dickson Road, might have been called. Mademoiselle Marie indicated, however, that she was unable to give any description and could not recognise anybody. The other witness, who need not be named, only saw the youths from the rear. Although she was able to describe a distinctive jacket and gave some description of one of the youth's hair colour and style, it seems most unlikely that she would have made any satisfactory identification at a parade.

21.17 It has been said by the police that there was difficulty in contacting Royston Westbrook, both in order that he should attend ID parades and in order to provide photo-fit or E-fit evidence at an early stage. Any problem in this regard was simply due to the fact that Mr Westbrook did for some periods of time stay away from his home for perfectly good reasons. He is not to be criticised in any way. Indeed he gave very clear and helpful evidence to the Inquiry.

21.18 **As to the parades themselves the evidence shows there was improper control of the witness room before the parades took place. It must be most important to keep witnesses separate before they are taken to make their identification of possible suspects. The risk being that if witnesses are left unwatched they may talk about the case concerned and perhaps even give each other descriptions of the persons that they have seen in connection with the crime. Mr Westbrook himself discovered, *"through mixing with the witnesses"* that the other persons present were wanted for other crimes committed in Chislehurst and Eltham. These were crimes with which Neil Acourt and David Norris are said to have been associated. Such conversation carries with it built-in risks. In addition Mr Westbrook says that on both occasions when he was collected for parades there were other potential witnesses with him in the police van who were able to speak together without supervision. This practice is contrary to Code C of the relevant codes of practice, and plainly there was a risk of compromise should an identification have thereafter been made.**

21.19 The ID parades were delayed until about the middle or end of May partly because of the delay in making the arrests of the suspects. If the arrests had been made earlier it can be said that there would have been more prospect of successful identification, since the passage of time inevitably blunts the memory of the features or look of somebody who has been seen committing a crime.

21.20 **It may be that the person seen by Mr Westbrook was not on any of the parades attended by him. And a photo-fit or artist's impression of the man seen by Mr Westbrook might not have fitted the looks of any of the suspects with whom we are concerned. However it would have been far better if Mr Westbrook had been seen early on to make an artist's impression and if the ID parades had taken place sooner. If that had been done there could be no cause for complaint about delay even if in the end Mr Westbrook and others failed to identify anybody at the parades which they attended.**

21.21 We understand the many difficulties which can occur in the organisation of identification parades, particularly in relation to obtaining participants for such parades. Nevertheless where there are a number of suspects and witnesses and where identification evidence may be crucial this can only emphasise the extreme need for careful planning and foresight. In this case there was little evidence of either. As to the deficiencies of 7 May this may well be accounted for by the hasty and unplanned decision as to arrest which was made on the previous day.

THE FAIR HAIRED ATTACKER

21.22 It is a feature of Mr Westbrook's evidence that he is convinced that the white youths actually *"herded round"* both Stephen Lawrence and Mr Brooks, and that Mr Brooks managed physically to break loose before he ran. This does not accord with the evidence of Mr Brooks himself. Of course everything happened very quickly. Mr Westbrook said that the whole incident was over in 10-15 seconds. Those who observe an incident like this one often give conflicting accounts. That is the reason why such care has to be taken as to identification evidence.

21.23 Mr Westbrook did not hear any words used during the attack. Indeed he remarked upon the relative silence in which it took place. He heard only Mr Brooks calling out to Stephen to run. As he got onto the bus which came almost at once he felt a shiver of apprehension when he thought to himself that the attack seemed so motiveless that it might have been levelled at him if the two boys had not been there.

21.24 **Mr Westbrook described one of the attackers in considerable detail. He said that the man was *"about 25 years old, five foot seven or eight, stocky build, dirty fair coloured hair. I think it was wavy, it went up and back from his forehead, it was shorter at the sides although not shaved and in general not short"*.**

21.25 Mr Westbrook believed that he would recognise that man again. Indeed he said that he was confident about recognising him. In fact he made no identifications at any parade.

21.26 It should be noted in this context that during the Kent inquiry much comment was rightly made as to absence of any or any satisfactory follow-up of the person who became known as the *"blonde attacker"* or offender.

21.27 None of the five suspects appear to have had fair or light brown hair. The early descriptions given by Mr Brooks and Mr Westbrook both referred to the hair colour of the leading attacker. To PC Gleason Mr Brooks said on the night of the murder that that man's hair was *"bushy light brown. It stuck out"*. Mr Westbrook in his statement quoted above said that the leading attacker had *"dirty fair coloured hair"*.

21.28 Mr Brooks in his full statement of 23 April said that the man's hair was *"long over his ears and it was frizzy and stuck out of the sides"*. On 6 May 1993, when he compiled a computer image of that man he described the hair as being *"very light brown, fairly long, covered ears ...."*. Mr Brooks has indeed always said in evidence that one of the group had fair hair. His body map showed a man with fair hair. At trial the computer image was described as that of a man with *"peroxide blonde"* hair.

21.29 Joseph Shepherd described one of the offenders as having *"medium length fair hair which was frizzy"*.

21.30 James Grant told DC Budgen that he had been told that there was *"a fifth blonde unknown kid"* present at the time of the murder.

21.31 In Mrs Lawrence's note of possible suspects taken from her on 6 May by Mr Ilsley the name *"Blue"* is listed, with the word *"blonde"* beside it.

21.32 **As Kent pointed out the investigation at no time focused upon this. No line of inquiry was established to pursue the possible identification of the fair haired or blonde offender. There was no co-ordination or analysis of the various descriptions given. The fact that one of the attackers was fair haired should have been reflected in decisions made as to the elimination of suspects. The failure to deal logically with this line of inquiry must be another source of criticism of the SIO and his Deputy.**

CHAPTER TWENTY-TWO

DETAILS AS TO 3 JUNE 1993 AND
DETECTIVE SERGEANT CHRISTOPHER CROWLEY

22.1   Detective Sergeant Christopher Crowley gave evidence to the Inquiry over a period of a full day on 7 and 8 May 1998. He has been much involved in this case, and he gave evidence both at the committal proceedings and at the Central Criminal Court trial. His evidence is a matter of considerable controversy and criticism, and of much media attention. He has an outstanding libel action pending against the 'Private Eye' magazine. He has brought proceedings against 'The Caribbean Times' and Granada Television. Both of those cases appear to have been settled or to be in the process of settlement.

22.2   The allegations made against DS Crowley, both on behalf of Mr Brooks and on behalf of the Lawrence family, are serious. It seems right that these allegations should be set out.

22.3   Mr Macdonald, when he started to cross-examine DS Crowley, said that the first allegation was that the Sergeant was either lying about or had misunderstood what Mr Brooks said to him following the ID parade on 3 June. The allegation is that DS Crowley either on his own account or upon instructions undermined the credibility of Mr Brooks' identification evidence. Secondly, it is alleged that in connection with another case, involving the murder of Rolan Adams, this officer acted in a manner *"which had the effect of undermining the credibility of Nathan Adams, the principal prosecution witness, surviving victim and brother of Rolan Adams"*. It is said that the arrest and treatment of Nathan Adams by this officer on two occasions in 1991 were either *"deliberate, or the result of discriminatory conduct"* on the part of DS Crowley. It is also said that in taking witness statements in connection with the Adams murder, this officer failed to make an accurate record and *"failed to elicit evidence of racial abuse which was said to have been uttered on the occasion of the murder of Rolan Adams"*. Thus it was alleged that DS Crowley tried to thwart the success of both murder investigations.

22.4   **Mr Mansfield, on behalf of Mr & Mrs Lawrence, had cross-examined DS Crowley, both at the committal and the trial of the three suspects who were acquitted. He specifically adopted the allegations made by Mr Macdonald, but gave no separate notice of any *"charges"* to be made against DS Crowley. When this was dealt with during the evidence Mr Mansfield said, *"I am not suggesting that this officer is subjected to any Norris connection. What I want to establish through officers is the extent of the Norris connection with the squad, the extent to which the Norris family were known or it is denied that they were known in order to obviously ask questions of later senior officers, he was only in the inquiry for one day and his role was a pivotal one."* So that Mr Mansfield was both directly questioning the evidence of this officer in connection with his contact with Mr Brooks, and he was using the officer as a vehicle by which he introduced the suggestion that the investigating team, and in particular the senior officers, were favouring David Norris.**

22.5   This allegation was made on the basis that there might have been a number of motives for such favouritism. To quote Mr Mansfield *"It may be only one of a number of motives and clearly I am not going to be in a position to quote chapter and verse whether it is a question of race, whether it is a question of fear of the Norris family, whether it is a question of the influence of the Norris family or whether it is a question of the actual corruption of the Norris family or some other reason. We are not in a position to say more than that in relation to Mr Crampton but I have made it clear that I will put that into writing if that is what is required.*" This arose when there was considerable doubt as to whether proper notice had been given of such swingeing allegations to be made against the senior officers.

22.6 **It can be seen therefore that the attack upon DS Crowley was both direct and indirect, in the sense that he was expressly challenged as to his part in the case which was said to reflect strongly upon the conduct and the motives of both himself and the senior officers involved. Mr Mansfield plainly alleges that the conduct of the senior officers in connection with the Stephen Lawrence case, particularly as it concerned David Norris, was tainted by the officers' knowledge of and involvement with David Norris' father, Clifford Norris.**

22.7 Those then are the allegations. The evidence given by DS Crowley was in one sense perfectly simple. He says that he was nothing but the escorting officer appointed to his task by Mr Jeynes, because he was the only officer available to perform that duty. There seems to be no reason to doubt his evidence as to this, and certainly it is not proved that there was any ulterior motive in his appointment. He was not involved in the Stephen Lawrence murder investigation. At the time he was a Detective Sergeant at Plumstead Police Station, and he was in charge of a team of detectives who worked under him, and who performed their own individual duties in the criminal investigation field.

22.8 **The escorting of Mr Brooks to the identification suite on 3 June was the only duty done by DS Crowley in connection with the Stephen Lawrence murder. DS Crowley was to have collected Mr Shepherd also for this parade, but Mr Shepherd indicated that he would not come. Therefore the only passenger in Mr Crowley's car to and from the Southwark ID suite on 3 June 1993 was Mr Brooks. DS Crowley was not seen by Kent, but he made a statement for the benefit of our Inquiry simply to confirm the statement he had made in June 1993.**

22.9 There was cross-examination both here and elsewhere about the date of the statement made by DS Crowley, which was altered from 4 June to 3 June 1993. Similarly a short statement made by Mr Brooks at the ID suite was originally dated 4 June 1993 and was also altered to 3 June. It appears to us that there is in fact nothing sinister in the change of dates in these two statements. DS Crowley's own statement, which he says he made at Eltham Police Station, was taken to Plumstead Station by him on instructions, where the statement was "franked" indicating the "official" date as 3 June 1993. Later investigation showed that that stamping was certainly made after the statement was recorded. It had been suggested at one time that DS Crowley's statement might have been made on 4 June, on a form previously stamped and left blank on 3 June 1993. This allegation seems to have been exploded.

22.10 DS Crowley told us, and he has consistently said the same when he has given evidence on other occasions, that he was not involved in the Lawrence investigation in any way. Had he been so he would not have been eligible, because of the requirements of Code D under the Police and Criminal Evidence Act in relation to identification parade procedures, to act as an escorting officer or take a statement from Mr Brooks in these circumstances. The Code also requires an "identification officer" to be someone who is not below the rank of Inspector who is not involved in the investigation. Any breach of the Code may compromise an identification made thereafter. The identification officer in charge of the parade on 3 June was Mr McIlgrew.

22.11 The suspect to be put on a parade on 3 June was Luke Knight. DS Crowley says that he was not aware of this man's name until later on. The parade was held at about 15:55. Number 8 on the parade was identified, and Mr Brooks' signature appears on the page of the documentation indicating that this was so. Luke Knight was the person placed at number 8 on the parade.

22.12 After Mr Brooks had effected his identification, he came back, or was brought back by Mr McIlgrew, to DS Crowley. What happened after that between DS Crowley and Mr McIlgrew is contested. Mr McIlgrew says that as he went up to the administration area DS Crowley approached him and said something like, *"Was anybody picked out?"* Mr McIlgrew says that he answered, *"Yes, he picked the suspect."* Mr McIlgrew says that DS Crowley then said to him, *"I'm not happy. Brooks has said things to me that make me think he didn't see the suspect clearly."* **It is right to say that Mr McIlgrew accepted that he might have spoken to DS Crowley twice, once in connection with the actual identification, and then again in connection with the doubts expressed by DS Crowley. But his original statement is as set out above.**

22.13 DS Crowley's memory of the conversation is different. He says that he was informed by Mr McIlgrew, who was conducting the parade, that the witness had identified the man who was on the parade as a suspect. He says that Mr McIlgrew *".... told me that he had picked out number 8 of ten white lads which was the person the police had put on the parade"*. Thereafter, he says that he was with Mr Brooks in the witness waiting room and he took a statement from Mr Brooks briefly detailing his participation and recording his having picked number 8. DS Crowley says that at no stage did he tell Mr Brooks that he picked out *"the right person"*.

22.14 DS Crowley is adamant that Mr Brooks said that the only statement that he would make at any time during that afternoon was the short formal statement which is before the Inquiry indicating that he had picked out number 8 on the parade.

22.15 It was pointed out in cross-examination that at no time in that statement or anywhere else did DS Crowley record that Mr Brooks had refused to sign any further statement. DS Crowley accounts for this simply by saying that this was the fact, but that he saw no reason why that should be recorded.

22.16 **What happened immediately after that short statement was taken is the nub of this part of the case. It is perhaps important to note that there is in Mr McIlgrew's own evidence support for the fact that something strange happened, because on his account DS Crowley did say that he was not happy about things that Mr Brooks had said to him. It is apparent and seems to us to be plainly proved that DS Crowley did go to Mr McIlgrew to register his doubts. Indeed Mr McIlgrew adds in his statement that he said to DS Crowley *"Listen, I'm the ID officer, the parade went off correctly, if you have any doubts you must make a statement and contact the incident room."* It can be said that Mr McIlgrew would have been wise to record a note of what was said at the time, since this would have avoided some of the difficulty which has ensued. But no doubt Mr McIlgrew did not anticipate what would follow this seemingly simple identification.**

22.17 It is true that DS Crowley did not make a statement then and there. Mr Mansfield roundly criticised DS Crowley for having failed to tell Mr Brooks what he was going to do, and for failing to make a full statement there and then at Southwark Police Station. But DS Crowley said that as a result of what occurred he decided that he must not become involved at Southwark Police Station, and that it was his job to contact the incident room and to delay making his report until he returned.

22.18 **What happened is certainly unusual. DS Crowley says that Mr Brooks started indicating to him in the plainest terms matters which, if they were said, rendered his identification of Luke Knight and his earlier identification of Neil Acourt highly suspect.**

22.19 At the heart of the matter is the fact that DS Crowley says that Mr Brooks simply gave out the facts which are recorded in his statement, more or less as a monologue. He did refer to a *"conversation"* with Mr Brooks, but he says that he did not engage in any conversation with him in the ordinary sense, but that what was said was *"voluntary by him. He did all the talking."*

22.20 When asked repeatedly why he did not raise any questions with Mr Brooks about what he was saying he said that at the time Mr Brooks was telling him things which had a bearing on the investigation, so that he did not engage in any talk or conversation with Mr Brooks actually at Southwark Police Station, otherwise it might have been said that he had involved himself in the investigation itself. This may appear strange to outsiders, but in fact DS Crowley was bound to keep his distance from any involvement in the investigation, otherwise it might have been said that there had been a breach of the Code.

22.21 **DS Crowley was a dogged and somewhat unusual man. We can understand that he would have tried to keep himself aloof from the investigation, and he told us and repeated many times that what he recorded in his statement simply came from Mr Brooks himself. The central matters were Mr Brooks' own assertions, if DS Crowley is right, including the assertion that he could only remember the physical description and hair of the attacker, and that he did not *"in any way see the faces of the youths who were around Stephen Lawrence"*.**

22.22 DS Crowley knew that that was most important, as were all the other matters set out in his statement of 3 June. He also recorded, as can be seen, that Mr Brooks had told him that he had been prompted by a friend who said that he should know the suspects, namely the Acourt brothers, since they had attended the same school as him. This was not in fact the case, but that is what DS Crowley says was the effect of Mr Brooks' words, namely that a friend had prompted him in this way.

22.23 Furthermore, as the statement shows, he indicated that he had picked out one person on an ID parade because he had the physical appearance of having been kept in a police station, and was wearing tracksuit trousers, and *"had to be the one who had been put on the parade by the police"*.

22.24 If this were not enough he told DS Crowley that friends had prompted him as to the physical features and hair details of the Acourt brothers. He repeated that on the night of the stabbing he did not see any faces clearly enough to be able to identify them, but relied on the physical description and appearance and not upon facial identification.

22.25 **Mr Brooks is also recorded as having said that he hated the police, and wished to take revenge on them, because they had arrived on the night of the murder in place of the ambulance men. That last statement is among those accepted by Mr Brooks as having been said by him. It does seem most unlikely that DS Crowley would invent a statement of that kind. Such a conclusion is of course not available, since Mr Brooks admits that that is what he said.**

22.26 **Over and over again DS Crowley has been challenged about this development in the case. And repeatedly and doggedly he has denied the allegations made against him. He says that these things were indeed said, and that is why he reported to Mr McIlgrew at Southwark. There is considerable validity as it seems to us in this assertion, and as we**

have already indicated, Mr McIlgrew confirms that something was certainly said about the doubts in the mind of DS Crowley.

22.27 After this had happened, DS Crowley says that he telephoned to the investigation headquarters, in fact on two occasions, once from Southwark Police Station and once from Rotherhithe. He took Mr Brooks to Rotherhithe to collect a filofax which Mr Brooks had left there; he then took Mr Brooks to his father's address, near Deptford Police Station; and then he took him home. After that DS Crowley went to Eltham Police Station at once, where he saw Mr Weeden and others as well, and was told immediately to make a statement. He went into another room and made the hand-written statement which is the original of the version later set out in the HOLMES computer system. Then he took his hand-written statement to Plumstead Police Station for franking.

22.28 **There is of course a fundamental issue between DS Crowley and Mr Brooks as to the truth of DS Crowley's evidence. It is purposeless to rehearse all that took place at committal and trial. Anybody who wishes or needs to see the detailed evidence given on both those occasions can do so since the evidence is a matter of public record. Furthermore the cross-examination by Mr Macdonald and Mr Mansfield, pursued with considerable vigour and at length, is recorded in the transcript of this Inquiry.**

22.29 There are features of DS Crowley's evidence which are strange. To start with, it is certainly unusual that anybody should *"spout"* immediately after an ID parade, let alone that a witness should say the kind of things recorded by DS Crowley. Furthermore DS Crowley did not take a statement at the time, namely at Southwark Police Station. All this has been put to DS Crowley repeatedly.

22.30 Mr Macdonald alleges that there was no conversation of any kind at Southwark Police Station, but that such conversation as there was took place in the car going away from the ID suite. This has led some to compare the evidence of DS Crowley with the evidence of officers, in former days, as to what were known as "back seat confessions" made by suspects en route to police stations. Such evidence came to be familiar, and indeed notorious, before the passing of the Police and Criminal Evidence Act. Evidence of this kind was said to be given by officers allegedly to "nail" suspects unjustly.

22.31 On the other hand, in this case, Mr Brooks was not a suspect, he was a victim and a witness. And if DS Crowley had not written down what was said by Mr Brooks and recorded it fully, he could of course have been much criticised by those acting on behalf of the actual defendants, namely the three suspects who were eventually tried at the Central Criminal Court.

22.32 However, the most outstanding feature of the whole matter is that Mr Brooks does not deny by any means the whole of the "conversation". Not only has this been explored at the committal and trial, but again before us it has been pointed out with very considerable force, that in fact Mr Brooks has accepted enough of what DS Crowley says to undermine his identification in any event. The matter has been the subject of an internal inquiry for the MPS by Superintendent Selwood, who investigated this affair and, among other things, has produced a comparison in the form of a two column chart indicating the extent to which Mr Brooks accepts in his own statement of 4 June 1993 what DS Crowley says. **Furthermore, when cross-examined, particularly at the Central Criminal Court by leading Counsel on behalf of the defendants, Mr Brooks accepted important aspects of the evidence which was given in connection with this "conversation" by DS Crowley, to the extent that his own evidence was virtually destroyed. Mr Brooks' evidence at the Central Criminal Court did not support the thrust of his main contention made to us, namely that on the way home DS Crowley had simply said that Mr Brooks was** *"guessing"* about his identification, and that an argument had ensued, finishing with Mr Brooks getting out of the car and telling DS Crowley to "fuck off".

22.33 **It is most important to note that at the Central Criminal Court Mr Justice Curtis heard the evidence both of Mr Brooks and of DS Crowley. We have not had the evidence of Mr Brooks given in full and subjected to cross-examination. There is absolutely no reason to complain of this, and we do not do so. Mr Brooks has been subjected to the most terrible ordeal both because he was a witness to the murder of Stephen Lawrence, and a victim of the attack, and because of all that has followed. It is perfectly understandable that he is simply not able to give evidence in the full sense of the word before us. Therefore we have no means, other than by a survey of all the documents in the case, including the committal and trial documents and Mr Brooks' statements made to this Inquiry, to judge for ourselves this comparison between Mr Brooks and DS Crowley.**

22.34 **The significant fact is that at trial Mr Justice Curtis wisely did not act in connection with any of the contested matters. He took into account in reaching his conclusion on this aspect of the case only those matters which were accepted as having been spoken by Mr Brooks to DS Crowley. It was agreed by Counsel on behalf of the defendants that there was really no need to reach a conclusion on the contested aspects of the "conversation", since Mr Brooks had plainly accepted more than enough to damage the identification which he had made of Luke Knight on 3 June 1993 and also the earlier identification of Neil Acourt.**

22.35 However much Mr Macdonald and Mr Mansfield attacked DS Crowley, he stuck to his position and indeed was indignant, insofar as he showed indignation at all, that such allegations were being made against him as were roundly made before this Inquiry.

22.36 **We believe that DS Crowley's evidence was substantially correct. It is fruitless to go over and over all the ground covered by Messrs Macdonald and Mansfield. In the end we have to conclude whether or not we accept that which DS Crowley told us. He was tested in the firmest possible way in cross-examination. In our opinion he withstood the cross-examination, and his evidence is acceptable, applying as we do the standard of a high level of probability. This conclusion is made also in the light of the full evidence of DS Crowley and Mr Brooks given particularly at the Central Criminal Court.**

22.37 There is of course another part to the cross-examination of DS Crowley and the allegations made against him, both by Mr Macdonald and by Mr Mansfield. This is concerned with the allegations in connection with the *"favouring"* of David Norris. In Mr Mansfield's case, he expressly disavowed any direct allegation that DS Crowley was involved in skulduggery over the Norris connection. As we have already indicated, his contention is that senior officers were involved in the protection of David Norris, and thus of the other suspects, because of the spectre of Clifford Norris which hangs over this case and the case of Stacey Benefield. We doubt whether it was right that some of the questions put by Mr Mansfield, particularly in connection with Clifford Norris' relations with other police officers, should have been put to this witness at all. It is not right to "float" the possibility of corrupt or improper connection between a criminal and a police officer unless that connection has some direct influence on the case in question. There is no evidence that any of Clifford Norris' activities in the past have any connection with DS Crowley.

THE ROLAN ADAMS CASE

22.38 The second aspect of the saga concerning DS Crowley is his alleged activity in respect of the Adams case. Rolan Adams was murdered in April 1991 by knife wounds inflicted by a man named Thornborrow. We say this because Thornborrow plainly accepted that he inflicted wounds upon Rolan Adams and he was convicted of murder. In statements made to the police he accepted that he was physically responsible for those wounds. Both in his statement and at trial he defended himself on the basis that the wounds might have been inflicted by accident, alternatively in self-defence. Alternatively he said that there had been no intent to kill or to cause really serious harm. It was in fact not until well into the cross-examination of DS Crowley on this topic that the members of the Inquiry realised that this was the position. There are amongst our papers documents concerning this case. But until the matter was canvassed, and details were produced, we were not fully aware that this was the position. This is of considerable importance, since it is at once then apparent that the evidence of Nathan Adams, who was involved in the incident with his brother, was not central to the case. Indeed Nathan Adams was never able to identify any person as having been involved, and it is doubtful whether his evidence played much part in the case at all.

22.39 **Be that as it may, the suggestion made against DS Crowley is that in the case of Rolan Adams, just as in the Stephen Lawrence case, he attempted to undermine the evidence of an important witness. This is what Mr Macdonald said when introducing his allegations to DS Crowley at the start of his cross-examination.**

22.40 The suggestion is that DS Crowley was instrumental in pursuing criminal charges against Nathan Adams when it was unfair or incorrect to do so, so that the evidence of Nathan Adams at the trial of Thornborrow and others would be devalued. Nathan Adams was plainly adversely affected as a result of the terrible death of his brother, and we were told that he is alleged to have committed five crimes, including two robberies at knife-point after the murder and before the trial of those involved in this murder took place.

22.41 We do not propose to go into the matter in great detail, since it appears to us that there is little validity in the allegations made. Two particular instances were raised on behalf of Mr Brooks. The first involved an offence said to have been committed by Nathan Adams and another young boy against a man called Mr Cattini. DS Crowley accepted that he did indeed interview Mr Cattini both in connection with the murder of Rolan Adams and the later attack upon Mr Cattini himself. It had been intended to prosecute Nathan Adams, but not to continue any proceedings against the other young boy involved in the attack on Cattini. This, DS Crowley said, was not discriminatory conduct but was decided on the basis that there was no direct evidence of complicity by the other young man, whilst Nathan Adams' part in the affair was plain, since he had been identified as the attacker by Mr Cattini himself.

22.42 Mr Macdonald made much of the fact that in the second statement of Mr Cattini it had been stated that the witness was *"over 21 and a factory worker"*. Whereas only some weeks earlier it had been clearly said that he was only 15-years old. This seems to us to be a weak point, since the second statement clearly indicates at its foot that Mr Cattini was accompanied by his mother, and this would only be necessary of course for a juvenile. It was an unfortunate mistake that the words *"over 21"* and *"factory worker"* appeared at the top of the statement, but in our opinion this in truth takes the matter no further. We see no justification for criticism of DS Crowley in respect of this proposed prosecution which followed a charge made after consultation with the relevant Inspector.

22.43 As to the other offence with which DS Crowley's team was involved, this concerned a robbery at knife-point in June 1991, said to have been committed by Nathan Adams. The victim was a young girl travelling on a bus who recognised Nathan Adams as the attacker. What is said in this regard is that two officers under the command or in the team of DS Crowley arrested Nathan Adams on the very day after the Cattini case had been dropped by the CPS, in order again to have material by which to devalue the evidence of Nathan Adams. He was arrested for the robbery in Woolwich Town Centre by officers in DS Crowley's squad. But DS Crowley said that he had no part whatsoever in instructing the officers to make the arrest. They made the arrest independently, having seen Mr Adams in the town centre and having knowledge of the very serious crime he was said to have committed. That arrest took place on 12 September, which was the day after an indication had been given that proceedings in the Cattini case would not be pursued. DS Crowley said that he had in fact no knowledge that the trial of Mr Cattini should have taken place on 12 September, and the decision to terminate those proceedings was in fact a surprise to him.

22.44 Nathan Adams was bailed until 10 October in connection with the June robbery. Mr Macdonald suggested that this was sinister since the Rolan Adams case was scheduled to start on 11 October.

22.45 The fact is, however, that the trial of Thornborrow and the others, including two of those who were in the red Astra car on the night of Stephen Lawrence's murder, started on 7 October and finished on 16 October. Nathan Adams was not charged with the robbery until 22 October. Thus there is very little validity in the suggestion that the arrest was made, even if it was with DS Crowley's knowledge, as a means of devaluing Nathan Adams' evidence at the Rolan Adams trial. The robbery matter was unresolved and could not have been used to any effect during the Rolan Adams trial.

22.46 Miss Jane Deighton, the solicitor to Mr Brooks, also represented Nathan Adams. The information about the Adams case in the hands of Mr Macdonald came thus from Miss Deighton. There is no complaint about this at all. But it does seem to us unfortunate that this matter was canvassed as firmly and aggressively as it was, since in fact the evidence of Nathan Adams was simply not likely to be important in the Rolan Adams case. As we have already indicated, the trial did not depend upon identification or upon any fine points of evidence to be given by Nathan Adams himself. Indeed, it appears likely that the case could have gone ahead without the evidence of Nathan Adams, because of the admissions made by Thornborrow to the police which he accepted in the course of the running of his multiple defence at the Central Criminal Court.

22.47 **We see no validity in the suggestion that there is a parallel in the Adams case, in connection with DS Crowley's activities, which would reflect upon his part played in the Stephen Lawrence case. Furthermore it must be stressed that DS Crowley took nine statements in the ten days following the Rolan Adams murder from witnesses who were involved in the case and whose evidence was used at trial. There is no substantial complaint from anybody as to the taking of those statements, except in one instance. DS Crowley's part in the affair was limited to the taking of those statements, and of course to the parallel investigation of the allegations against Nathan Adams. There were in fact five allegations against that young man, and it is difficult to see how the police could have avoided charging Nathan Adams, since the offences were by no means trivial. The fact that Nathan Adams was never prosecuted came about because he was very young, he was much traumatised by what he had gone through, and Miss Deighton was able to obtain a comprehensive psychiatric report which indicated to the CPS that Nathan Adams should not be taken to court. We have sympathy with him, since like**

Mr Brooks he was a victim of the racist attack upon another, namely his brother. But we see no strength in the suggestion that DS Crowley's part in the Adams case should be used against him when attack is made upon his evidence in this Inquiry or elsewhere in respect of his part in the Stephen Lawrence investigations.

22.48 **Indeed, if Nathan Adams had been an important witness and had not been charged with this robbery and the other offences the suggestion might have been made that he had been shown favours by the police in order to keep him "on side" with consequent weakening of the force of his evidence for that reason alone.**

22.49 The express complaint about a statement taken by DS Crowley in the Adams case concerns the first statement taken from a witness named Mr Boland on 2 March 1991. That witness was in fact seen in the presence of his mother, a solicitor and Mr Penstone. Nothing appears in that statement to indicate that the gang of youths chasing Rolan or Nathan Adams were chanting racist abuse, and calling out, *"Get the nigger, get the nigger!"* The suggestion being made to DS Crowley was that for improper reasons he had left this out or not pursued this aspect of the case with the witness. DS Crowley said that there was no question of any omission by him, and that he simply wrote down what Mr Boland told him, and that all those present agreed that what Mr Boland had said had been faithfully recorded.

22.50 This is in fact supported by the contents of a second statement made by Boland on 23 April to another officer. In that statement the racist words were included, and the witness added that *"It was not in my earlier statement because I didn't realise the importance of mentioning racial matters. As this only sunk into me personally, and at the time of making my earlier statement did not seem very relevant."* Thus we do not see how this omission of the racist words can possibly be used as a criticism of DS Crowley's attitude or motives.

22.51 **We must add that we have set out the course of the evidence as to DS Crowley's involvement in the Rolan Adams case since it was much canvassed, and it would be unfair not to indicate our views on the topic. We stress that to his credit Mr Macdonald in his closing address said this:- *"We also accept that on the evidence that is before this Inquiry that no assistance on this matter can be derived from DS Crowley's role in the Adams investigation"*. That is a fair and important concession which must be noted.**

22.52 Mr Macdonald also fairly conceded that there was *"not enough to prove a racial motive or a corrupt motive"* as to DS Crowley's evidence about Mr Brooks. He argued that there was room for mistake or misunderstanding, or that DS Crowley might have *"sugared the pill"* because he did not like Mr Brooks or his attitude. We do not accept these submissions. We believe that DS Crowley gave on 3 June 1993 and to us an account which was substantially true, and which is to be accepted.

CHAPTER TWENTY-THREE

THE ARRESTS AND INTERVIEWS

23.1 Mr Weeden says that he finally made the decision to arrest at about 17:30 hours on Thursday 6 May 1993. He had previously spoken to Mr Ilsley (at about 13:30 hours), indicating that arrests were contemplated, but he did not go further than that. It is not easy to confirm from Mr Weeden's own notes when the decision was made, but he has consistently said that it was after the 16:00 team meeting. At that meeting those present gave their up-to-date information, and Mr Bullock's note ends with the words:- *"Review of evidence re suspects"*. There is no reference to any proposal as to arrests.

23.2 **What is significant is that DC Budgen at the 16:00 meeting gave information which had come from James Grant on that day, namely that *"They* [the Acourts] *are fascinated by knives. Tried to buy one. Usually hide them under floorboards"*. Anybody listening must have heard that recent important information.**

23.3 The decision to arrest plainly came as a surprise to members of the team, who can only have been contacted after the decision was made.

23.4 Search warrants were obtained at 20:45 from a Magistrate. Officers were alerted, and briefing appears to have been fixed for 05:30 on 7 May.

23.5 It seems certain that no proper steps were taken to ensure that the four suspects to be arrested were at home. In fact the Acourts and Gary Dobson were at their addresses when the arrests were made at 06:30 on 7 May. David Norris was not at home. His mother was seen at Berryfield Close, and he came to the police station with his solicitor on 10 May. Mr Norris' address was known much earlier, and indeed there had been surveillance at that address on 29 and 30 April. Nobody seems to have known what David Norris looked like. Plainly no proper steps were taken to try to identify him, perhaps from officers who had dealt with him previously. Until he was arrested therefore it was not known that there were in fact photographs of David Norris in the surveillance album, showing him clearly to be in the company of Gary Dobson. Those photographs were not shown to anybody who might have been able to identify the persons photographed.

23.6 The briefing notes set out the names of those who conducted the arrests. DS Bevan and DC Chase went to David Norris' home, with a full team of officers, including officers from the dog section and specialist search officers. DS Bevan believed that he had attended a meeting at 20:00 on 6 May, but there are no notes of such a meeting. He confirms that he briefed his own team at Eltham Police Station at or after 05:00 on 7 May.

23.7 **David Norris' mother was the only person present at Berryfield Close. She was annoyed by the visit. DS Bevan says that he stayed with her while the house was searched. In his statement to the Kent Police he says that *"A cursory search was made that involved looking in cupboards, wardrobes and drawers. Nothing was dismantled, carpets were not moved, floorboards were left alone, no panels or similar areas were troubled."* In evidence before the Inquiry DS Bevan indicated that the house was** luxurious and largely close carpeted. He seemed to say that any signs of removal of carpets might have been detected. But he could offer no explanation for such a negligent search. In view of the information given on the previous afternoon it is extraordinary that no steps were taken here or at the other premises to look under the floorboards. Whether or not the delay might have given the suspects an opportunity to remove incriminating items the fact is that the searches were incomplete and (in DS Bevan's case) admittedly *"cursory"*.

23.8 **DS Davidson with DC Hughes and DC Holden and officers of the area search team arrested Gary Dobson. The pre-arranged caution was read to him, and he was told that the *"grounds for arresting you are as follows:- 1. You fit the description of the youths involved. You with others have a history of being involved in recent stabbings in the area, and we have received information from various sources that you were involved in this."* It can at once be seen that exactly the same words could have been used if the arrests had been made over or soon after the first weekend. A knife was found in Gary Dobson's bedroom drawer. He said that it was one of the kitchen knives that he used for dinner.**

23.9 Neil and Jamie Acourt were arrested also at about 06:30 on 7 May. 19 officers went to 102 Bournbrook Road. Entry was apparently forced through the back door and also into a padlocked bedroom. No damage is recorded internally. It is accepted that neither here nor at Gary Dobson's address were any floorboards lifted. In view of the direct information about the Acourts' propensity to conceal knives under the floorboards this is to be deplored. No inquiry seems ever to have been made after the arrests as to whether this obvious task had been performed. So that it is palpable that the officers involved were not properly briefed or debriefed. This was the responsibility of the SIO and the DIO. DC Budgen, to whom the information about the propensity of the Acourts to hide knives under the floorboards had been given by James Grant, was present at No 102 at the time of the arrests. He said that he stayed in a bedroom with Jamie Acourt while the searching took place, and that detailed searching was the responsibility of the qualified search team. He had expected a detailed search, including the lifting of floorboards.

23.10 **At No 102 the officers found a large number of weapons. A knife was found behind a TV set. In the padlocked bedroom a Gurkha type knife was found. In the living room under the cushions of a settee there was a sword in a scabbard. There was a shoulder holster in a cupboard. There were knives in Jamie Acourt's bedroom, and an *"air gun type revolver"*. Neil Acourt was told that the officers held a search warrant. Neil and Jamie Acourt were cautioned with the same words used to Gary Dobson.**

23.11 The suspects were taken to separate police stations, where they were all interviewed. Of the four arrested on 7 May only Gary Dobson answered questions. He was interviewed by DS Davidson on three occasions together with DS Hughes. We have seen transcripts of all those interviews. Gary Dobson was attended by a duty solicitor, Mr Luckhurst, who never intervened.

23.12 Neil and Jamie Acourt were interviewed by DS Kirkpatrick and DC Canavan respectively. Neil Acourt's two interviews on 7 May lasted 14 minutes and three minutes. Jamie Acourt's interview lasted six minutes. Neil Acourt's third interview was held on 13 May and concerned the murder of Stephen Lawrence and also the Wimpy Bar stabbing and the Stacey Benefield case. Both Acourts were attended by solicitors from Henry Milner and Company.

23.13 David Norris, with Mr Milner himself in attendance, was interviewed on 10 May for 19 minutes, and on 13 May for six minutes, by DS Bevan and DC Martin Hughes respectively. On each occasion Mr Milner at an early stage said that he had advised Mr Norris not to answer any questions. Plainly the same advice had been given to the Acourts.

23.14 All these interviews have been the subject of much criticism, both by Counsel for Mr & Mrs Lawrence and by DS Mould, who gave "expert" evidence about them and who produced a very detailed report. He concludes that the officers were *"in the main doing their best with the information"*. He says that the interviewing officers' *"commitment varied, with DS Davidson and DS Bevan working hard to make the best of it, with the others showing a varied level of commitment, especially the two six minute interviews, who showed both a lack of skill and commitment. With higher skill levels all the interviews could have been far more effective and productive, but we will never know."*

23.15 To complete the picture we add that Luke Knight was arrested on 3 June, when he was identified by Duwayne Brooks. He was interviewed three times, for 25 minutes, 28 minutes, and 13 minutes respectively. He had a passive solicitor present. He answered all the questions put to him and made no admissions. Indeed neither Gary Dobson's nor Luke Knight's interviews could be said to have advanced the prosecution case at all. Both of them repeatedly denied involvement in the murder.

23.16 It is rightly said by DS Mould that all the *"no comment"* interviews of the Acourts and David Norris showed *"little system or method or depth that would indicate an objective based briefing."* Furthermore the six or seven minute interview of Jamie Acourt consisted of *"ineffective formalities with no other objectives than to go through the motions and get it over as quickly as possible"*. Certainly it is plain that there had been little if any proper planning of these interviews, which may well have been the result of the sudden decision to arrest. No doubt Mr Norris had been carefully instructed before he was arrested. Furthermore he had the benefit, as did the Acourts, of experienced criminal law solicitors who had plainly given firm advice to remain silent.

23.17 **Lack of planning and persistence are solid criticisms of these interviews. But it does have to be stressed that in 1993 the right of silence was absolute. Judges do not like police officers who go on and on at a person who is advised to remain silent and shows rigidly that he will not speak. Indeed such interviews were not put before juries, since the risk is that the content of the questions posed may be taken to have some evidential quality when it has none at all. The six minute interview of Jamie Acourt is plainly a "let off" in one sense, and the interview showed little if any evidence of preparation or technique. On the other hand Mr Acourt had spent an hour in consultation with his** solicitor prior to the interview and the solicitor had informed DC Canavan before the interview started that Mr Acourt would make no comment, and this proved to be the case. The officer would appear then to have made the pragmatic judgement that he was wasting his time, and he brought the interview to a quick conclusion. In theory we accept that he has given up too quickly and that there were things that could have usefully been put to Mr Acourt. In practical terms his judgement was probably right that it would have had no effect in any event. All in all the "no comment" interviewing therefore carries limited criticism compared with the other matters which are raised in this case.

23.18 Similarly the interviews of Mr Dobson and Mr Knight showed flaws in technique, and the use of closed or unproductive questioning, again without full or careful preparation. But those *"answering"* interviews read very much like many similar interviews put before the Courts. Police officers have and acquire skill in this field, but it is not an easy task, and if those being interviewed have their guard up and perhaps have had time (as these men had) to prepare themselves then it is not uncommon to read a *"blocking"* interview of this type.

23.19 The *"racist"* aspect of Mr Dobson's interview is addressed elsewhere (Chapter 19, paragraph 31).

23.20 The one plain obvious and glaring error lay in the failure to use the surveillance photographs which showed Gary Dobson and David Norris together on 26 April at 102 Bournbrook Road. Mr Dobson denied knowledge of David Norris repeatedly, and DS Davidson was rightly astounded to hear that this ammunition was not made available to him. **The failure to research and report fully those photographs, and the failure to use them later perhaps in another interview are gross errors for which there can be no excuse.** If Gary Dobson had been taxed with his lies about David Norris those lies would have been nailed. Whether that would have led to admissions is entirely another matter. In DS Mould's words, *"we will now never know."* Mr Dobson said to this Inquiry that he lied and would not admit knowing David Norris because Mr Norris had not been arrested by 7 May and he had in mind that he might protect Mr Norris in some way. That sounds unconvincing. In any event the lost opportunity to use the photographs was another serious error in the course of this investigation. That error must be laid primarily at the door of the SIO (Mr Weeden) and Mr Bullock who failed to ensure proper briefing, research and supervision in connection with the interviews and those conducting them.

23.21 Gary Dobson again answered questions when Mr Mellish took over in 1994. None of the others were interviewed then, and no doubt the decision rightly made was that interviews as late on as that would be unproductive.

CHAPTER TWENTY-FOUR

EXHIBITS

24.1 Detective Constable Robert Crane was throughout the relevant days the main Exhibits Officer to the initial investigation. He was appointed on 23 April, in the evening, and he started work on the morning of 24 April.

24.2 He performed other actions in connection with the investigation, including supervision of such things as the clearance of drains in order to check for weapons. He also did a variety of other tasks, including research of possible witnesses.

24.3 The main reason for calling DC Crane was in connection with the exhibits. There were very many exhibits collected in this case from many sources. There is a detailed register which sets out when and where the exhibits were found, and DC Crane has given a long statement dealing with the *"continuity"* of these exhibits.

24.4 One exhibit, namely a tissue, which was found on 23 April in or near the garden of 408 Rochester Way, has disappeared. It was found by Police Constable Marlowe, and handed in to DC Crane at about 18:30 on the evening of 23 April. That exhibit has been known as PM/1. Another tissue which was entered in the book as *"apparently blood-stained"* was found by Detective Constable Russell and marked KCR/1. That was found on the lawn near the front gate of 419 Rochester Way. The loss of exhibit PM/1 is inexcusable. No exhibit should be discarded or lost, since otherwise contentious issues such as developed in connection with this exhibit may arise.

24.5 **Furthermore, DC Crane's evidence about the lost tissue does have unsatisfactory features. When he was asked by Detective Inspector Newman of Kent, about the loss of the tissue he is reported as saying that any blood on both tissues appeared to be of old standing, and that because the place where the tissues were found was some distance from the scene of the murder they were not submitted for laboratory examination.**

24.6 It appears from the note made by Mr Newman of the interview that when he was seen in 1997, DC Crane was indicating that it was his belief that the tissue might have been tested for blood, using a simple system known as the KM test. He said to Mr Newman that his recollection was that the one that was not eventually put in the register, PM/1, offered visually to him the best chance of a result. He says that he believes that he had the test done by Sergeant Turnbull, who was the Laboratory Liaison Officer, with negative results. To Mr Newman he said that *"It was negative result and I can only imagine I have either discarded it then or not put it in the register on the basis that it was not blood."*

24.7 **DC Crane readily admitted that it was an error on his part that he did not put the tissue in the register and retain it.**

24.8 To the Inquiry DC Crane's evidence was firmer, in the sense that he told us that he was sure that the tissue, PM/1, was tested and that the result was negative.

24.9 The long and the short of it is that that tissue, PM/1, is not available, and has disappeared. This is plainly inexcusable, and it gives useful ammunition to those who questioned DC Crane about the system which he followed.

24.10   The other tissue, KCR/1, was eventually tested by the Home Office scientist, Adrian Wain. It was found to have blood on it, but the blood could not have been that of Stephen Lawrence. Otherwise the testing of that tissue did not advance the case one way or another.

24.11   The probability, as it seems to us, is that neither tissue would have assisted the investigation. But of course we can never be sure what the result of a full blood test of PM/1 might have revealed. We feel unable to rely upon the evidence given by DC Crane as to how he dealt with the tissue PM/1. There is no logic in having two bloodstained tissues, testing one rather than both, then failing to record and discarding the one which is tested but retaining and recording the one which is not. DC Crane is to be criticised for not keeping the tissue, since it is not up to an Exhibits Officer to make final conclusions as to the possible usefulness of any evidence which is contributed to an investigation by officers who search the area. The places where both tissues were found are a considerable distance from the murder scene, but of course each site was available to persons running from the scene should they have gone from Cobbett Road down to Rochester Way, and in any event both tissues were found within the area delineated for search by the SIO.

24.12   There was considerable controversy about the note made by Mr Newman, which was before the Inquiry. Mr Kamlish on behalf of Mr & Mrs Lawrence, indicated that it was their belief that there were further and more detailed notes of the interview which took place between Mr Newman and DC Crane, and that the summary which was before the Inquiry was exactly that, namely a summary, and not the full note.

24.13   This matter has never been satisfactorily resolved, but in the end we doubt whether the existence of further notes would have advanced our investigation of the loss of this tissue. DC Crane did not accept that the version set out in Mr Newman's note was accurate. Resolution of the difference between what Mr Newman recorded and what DC Crane remembers having said would not, as it seems to us, advance our Inquiry. The fact is that the tissue should not have been lost. The fact also is that it is unlikely that formal and proper testing of the exhibit would have led to any material advance in the investigation.

24.14   Another matter upon which DC Crane was questioned concerned the bags which had been put on Stephen Lawrence's hands, and which contained fingernail clippings, and which might have contained relevant fibres to connect Stephen Lawrence with one or more of the suspects.

24.15   Considerable cross-examination was also advanced on the basis that Mr Brooks' clothing should also have been retained in order to test whether there was any inter-change of fibres between him and the suspects. It is perfectly clear that Mr Brooks' belief, and indeed his evidence, was that he was never touched by any of the suspects. It seems to us most unlikely that there would have been any helpful evidence to have been obtained from his clothes. But witnesses did say that there had been contact from which Mr Brooks had *"broken away"*. Good practice would have suggested retention of his clothes.

24.16   As to the bags which were on Stephen Lawrence's hands, they were sent to the laboratory *"for retention"*. When exhibits are sent to the scientists, the SIO or a delegated officer, Mr Bullock in this case, liaises with the Exhibits Officer and decides in what category the various exhibits shall be placed. That is to say, there is an indication given at once that some must be tested, and some are sent for retention. This does not mean that the exhibits are not available for testing should the scientist decide that such tests were required. It is right to indicate that initially no tests were made in connection with fibres or other matters which might have been disclosed by an examination of what was in the bags.

24.17 Eventually at the behest of the lawyers involved in the second investigation there were most meticulous tests made in connection with the possible transfer of fibres between garments recovered from the suspects and the clothes of Stephen Lawrence. Furthermore, the contents of the bags were analysed and tested, and a very small number of fibres were found which could possibly have come from clothing owned by Gary Dobson. Their analysis produced *"some weak or very weak"* support for a case against Mr Dobson. Later Mr Mellish used that material when he interviewed Mr Dobson during the second investigation. In truth that evidence raised no arguable case against Mr Dobson.

24.18 Apart from the criticism in connection with the loss of the tissue and the failure to enter it in the register or satisfactorily to explain that failure we can see no further justifiable criticism of DC Crane's activity as the Exhibits Officer.

24.19 It is right to point out that he did not help himself in the eyes of Mr & Mrs Lawrence or of the black community, because when he was sent on 3 February 1994 to investigate some graffiti which had been put on a wall, he used the word *"Negro"* and *"Negroid"* in connection with what he saw. He saw no reason why the use of these expressions should be objectionable. DC Crane accepted that he had had no racism awareness training of any kind, and he did not seem to appreciate that such expressions might be offensive.

24.20 **DC Crane was yet another officer who drew the distinction between a purely racist attack and this particular attack upon Stephen Lawrence. He accepted that the individuals involved were racist and that there was *"a degree of racism"* involved, but he insisted that he could not convince himself that racism was the only reason for the attack on Stephen Lawrence. This collectively held view is a firm example of institutional racism, and how in a tightly knit group such views persist.**

24.21 DC Crane was questioned about his attitude to Mr Brooks. He had only a limited contact with Mr Brooks, but he was prepared in 1994 to indicate, on the form used in connection with the Welling prosecution, that Mr Brooks was *"unco-operative and surly"*. He said that he thought that he was unco-operative in as much as he did not turn up for meetings when asked to do so, and his memory of Mr Brooks' attitude was that he appeared to be surly. Of course this description coincided closely with that given by Mr Jeynes, who had indicated on a similar form, that Mr Brooks' behaviour was *"surly, non-co-operative"*. It is a feature of Mr Brooks' case that officers did seem to be prepared to give adverse reports on him when they had comparatively little contact with him.

24.22 It may be that Mr Brooks' behaviour, which was plainly much affected by the awful experience which he had gone through on 22 April 1993, was erratic and it is evident that he was liable to changes of mood. If the officers, including DC Crane, detected problems in dealing with Duwayne Brooks, it was undoubtedly incumbent on them to understand that he too was a victim of this terrible crime, and that his behaviour must have been conditioned by his experience and all that followed. Their expression of unjustifiable adverse views about Mr Brooks within the AMIP team lays them open to the accusation that they were stereotyping Mr Brooks in a racist manner and failing to be fair and objective about him.

24.23 DC Crane's only other relevant action in connection with the case is that he took a statement from Jason Goatley, one of the occupants of the red Astra car. He had very little recollection of taking that statement, but he was aware of the nature of the occupants of the car, and of the constant trouble which they caused the police.

CHAPTER TWENTY-FIVE

SCIENTIFIC EVIDENCE

25.1 The exhibits were forwarded to the forensic science laboratory, where they were primarily under the care of and under examination by Mr Adrian Wain. He has all the relevant qualifications as a forensic scientist, and he is plainly a most careful and expert man. Voluminous notes existed in connection with all his actions. He was able to refer to them and to his reports in order to assist the Inquiry.

25.2 Mr Wain believes that Mr Weeden was the senior officer throughout the time when he made his examinations, up until 1995. Of course most of the exhibits, particularly in connection with the suspects, did not start coming into the system until after the arrests and searches of 7 May 1993. This meant that the suspects, if they were involved in this murder, had more than a fortnight in which to remove offending exhibits and to secrete others. Mr Mansfield highlighted the problems which delay will inevitably cause in connection with the examination of exhibits. Shoes and clothing, and other possibly incriminating exhibits, may well disappear if delay occurs. Similarly fibre and blood traces may degrade or disappear.

25.3 **This seems to us to be self-evident, and to be relevant when we consider whether the arrests and searches should have taken place much earlier. Delay could not possibly be laid at the door of Mr Wain. Indeed in his cross-examination, Mr Mansfield accepted that there was no criticism of the scientist whatsoever. His criticism was that those who were responsible for holding up the process of the investigation, and the categorisation of some of the exhibits, should be called to account.**

25.4 Mr Wain did the most careful and detailed examination of a very large number of exhibits. For example, the two hand-written notes, which were found in the telephone box and on the officers' car at the Welcome Inn were examined by him. Many items of clothing were examined for blood-staining. Knives which had been found, which turned out to have no connection with the murder, were all examined.

25.5 It was also apparent that as the investigation proceeded, Mr Wain was encouraged to follow every possible avenue. Mr Wain was referred to a message in his own notes dated 8 July 1993 indicating *"DC Crane rang. Message from Superintendent Weeden. Everything that can be done should be done, regardless of my letter."* That is a reference to a letter not written by Mr Wain until 27 July but which he had told DC Crane that he was intending to send, which indicated his view that *"since the suspects were not arrested until at least 2 weeks after the event, I believe that looking at their clothes for fibres that could have come from Stephen Lawrence's clothes is not worthwhile at all."* Mr Weeden's general exhortation should have been followed up by some discussion as to whether the exercise might be useful. The matter seems to have been left to some extent hanging in the air.

25.6 Eventually the sum total of the evidence which could indicate any kind of connection between any of the exhibits and the suspects concerned fibres from the bags which had been placed over Stephen's hands, which were tested in 1994 and 1995. These meticulous tests went on for months and as Mr Wain indicated the extent of testing of fibres in this case was great, and the work involved painstaking and necessarily slow.

25.7   In summary, the conclusions of Mr Wain were really as follows:

> First, amongst the extraneous fibres removed from the bag from the right hand were two brown wool fibres that had the same microscopic and colour characteristics as those from Mr Dobson's cardigan. One of these had similar dye components as those from the cardigan. The other one was too small for dye testing.

> Also he found that one grey cotton fibre from Stephen Lawrence's jacket had the same microscopic characteristics as fibres from Mr Dobson's jacket. That discovery was made in June 1994. Also a single white polyester fibre found in the bag from Stephen Lawrence's right hand had the same microscopic characteristics as those from Mr Dobson's jacket. As that fibre was white no further relevant tests could be carried out.

25.8   The report of Mr Wain continued as follows ... *"Evaluation conclusions ... where fibres are found to match the component fibres of a garment, this does not mean that they necessarily came from that garment. They could have come from another garment of the same type or another source of similar fibres. **Therefore, in my opinion, there is weak support for the assertion that the two brown wool fibres recovered from the bag that was covering Stephen Lawrence's right hand came from an exhibit ASR/2, namely a cardigan recovered from Dobson's home"**, and that, **"there is very weak support for the assertion that the single grey cotton and white polyester fibres that were recovered from Lawrence's jacket and right hand bag came from item LA/5, namely a jacket found at Dobson's home."**

25.9   **This connection of fibres was of course the high watermark of Mr Wain's detailed examination, so far as connection between the suspects and Stephen Lawrence was concerned. Anybody familiar with the use of scientific evidence in court will realise that this degree of connection is indeed minimal. The use of the adjectives *"weak"* and *"very weak"* speak for themselves. Such "evidence" would never support a charge in itself and would have provided minimal support if other viable evidence had existed against Gary Dobson. There was no such evidence against him. Apparently Mr Wain was available at the Central Criminal Court when three of the suspects including Mr Dobson were eventually tried, but it would be very surprising if anybody should have argued that Mr Wain's evidence would truly have assisted the prosecution. Mr Wain was never called to give evidence.**

25.10   Mr Mansfield also pointed out that there had been no tests at all performed in 1993 on Stephen Lawrence's bag and strap, which were found at the scene. Nor were any tests performed upon a pair of gloves found outside 290 Well Hall Road, which were shown to Mr & Mrs Lawrence and to Mr & Mrs Taaffe. The ownership of the gloves has never been established.

25.11   Mr Wain was given Mr Brooks' statement, but not those of other witnesses who suggest that there was contact between the suspects and Mr Brooks, or that some kicking had taken place during the attack on Stephen Lawrence. Nor was he aware that there was a trail of blood from Dickson Road along Well Hall Road to the point of collapse, which would indicate there could have been deposits on the attackers. Mr Wain did standard examinations on the footwear for blood but not for hair, fibre or skin tissue.

25.12   In this context Mr Mansfield rightly questioned whether the system and criteria for selection and submission of items were thorough. It is clear they were not. Responsibility lies with Mr Weeden who, other than passing the message *"everything that can be done should be done"*, appears to have not exercised either thought or direction in relation to forensic submissions. Nor is there any evident thought or direction from his deputy Mr Bullock.

25.13   **Dr Angela Gallop was brought into the case on behalf of the Lawrence family by J R Jones, about August 1995. She was a most impressive witness, and her evidence very closely coincided with that of Mr Wain. She was instructed to read and to review the whole of the scientific work done up to August 1995 and to carry out any additional examinations which might be capable of establishing a link between Stephen Lawrence and the suspects.**

25.14   She accepted that the most important lines of analysis were blood and fibres. At the end of the day she indicated that there was *"Very little blood ... found on the suspects' clothing, and samples of it that had been tested to date either failed to give a result probably because there was simply too little blood for the purposes or were demonstrated not to have come from Stephen Lawrence."* She added, *"All in all there is no evidence of any of Stephen Lawrence's blood on any of the items of the suspects' clothing examined, but this is not a powerful point for the defence."* That is perfectly true, but the absence of blood meant that there was no scientific evidence to put before a court of connection between the suspects and Stephen Lawrence in this respect.

25.15   **Dr Gallop checked all the meticulous work that had been done on the fibres from various garments, and from Stephen Lawrence's fingernail clippings, and from the bags which covered his hands. She agreed that *"Even in combination these fibres provide only very weak evidence of any association between Lawrence's and Dobson's clothing."* In essence, her conclusions and findings as to blood and fibres did not differ at all from Mr Wain's. Dr Gallop said that she and he worked very much in partnership over this examination, and that this was necessary because there were many many weeks of work which had to be done in order to check all the earlier findings and to explore the matter anew. Many hundreds of thousands of fibres were in fact scanned, and 1,071 fibres were looked at in great detail.**

25.16   As to the tissues, Dr Gallop said, rightly, when she was asked about them, that their value and the possibility of any useful evidence in connection with them depended very much upon where they were found.

25.17   **The cross-examination of Dr Gallop did not in truth produce any further relevant material of assistance to the Inquiry. Dr Gallop's evidence was noted for its clarity and fairness. She did accept, as is self-evident, that the sooner exhibits are obtained the better, but by and large Dr Gallop's evidence wholly confirmed that of Mr Wain. Neither of them could, as it seems to us, conceivably have assisted to establish a case against the suspects should the opportunity have occurred for them to give evidence at the Central Criminal Court. They did not do so, because of course the prosecution was dropped after Mr Brooks' evidence had been rejected.**

25.18   In conclusion it should be noted that in answer to Mr Doyle, on behalf of the SIOs, Dr Gallop agreed that briefing officers should apply their minds to all aspects of clothing when instructing officers who were sent out to search premises. In this context it is fair to indicate that before the suspect houses were visited, Mr Weeden did in terms indicate that *"particular attention should be paid to footwear for blood ie. welts and laces, lace holes etc, as a considerable quantity of the blood was in the roadway at the junction of Dickson Road and the assailants were described as kicking victim".* He also warned the officers to pay particular attention to the waistbands of trousers and the edges of pockets where weapons may have been concealed.

25.19 **We have spent some time examining the evidence given in connection with the exhibits and their scientific testing. There can be no criticism of the scientists. There is a measure of criticism which can be elicited from the scientists' evidence as to the delay in making the arrests, inadequate searches of the suspect homes, the selection and submission of some items for inspection, and in the failure to provide all relevant background statements or information for the scientists' consideration.**

CHAPTER TWENTY-SIX

FAMILY LIAISON (until 6 May 1993)

26.1 **One of the saddest and most regrettable aspects of this case concerns the family liaison between the police and Mr & Mrs Lawrence. The two officers who were given the task of liaising with the family were Detective Sergeant John Bevan and Detective Constable Linda Holden. DC Holden told the Inquiry that she had liaised with two families in murder cases before she joined AMIP. She had been given an award for the professional manner in which she dealt with a rape victim. Those occasions were apparently in or about 1991. DS Bevan had not had any previous experience of acting as a Family Liaison Officer.**

26.2 The two officers were appointed to this task on Friday, 23 April, and they first visited the family on that evening. It has to be noted that DS Bevan was also in charge of a team in connection with the investigation of the murder itself. Both DS Bevan and DC Holden were later involved in the arrest and interviews of the suspects and much other general activity with the team.

26.3 **It is most unfortunate that there was this combination of tasks. Apart from the fact that their activities in connection with the investigation might detract from concentration upon their role as Family Liaison Officers, there must be a risk that a combination of several tasks will lead to confusion.**

26.4 Be that as it may there is no doubt but that the liaison between the two officers and the Lawrence family failed from the start. Both officers agreed during their evidence that this was so. Neither could give a satisfactory explanation for the cause of the breakdown. They both said that the liaison did not so much breakdown, but that it never got off the ground.

26.5 In addition to the task of family liaison with Mr & Mrs Lawrence, DS Bevan, with DC Holden, were made responsible for liaison with Mr Brooks. There is no need to go into the detail of that liaison since Counsel for Mr Brooks rightly indicated that there was no complaint in connection with that part of DS Bevan's activities. DS Bevan seems to have struck up a reasonable relationship with Mr Brooks, and to have kept regular contact with him during the time he was connected with him. From time to time there were disagreements between them, and they became somewhat fed up with each other, during what must have been a somewhat difficult relationship. By and large that part of DS Bevan's work could not be criticised. It is important to realise that the two officers were given this multiplicity of tasks during the relevant weeks. It must be partly because they were involved in these varying activities that their job as Family Liaison Officers to the Lawrence family suffered.

26.6 **Nothing was more important, as we see it, than that the police should establish a good and mutual relationship with Mr & Mrs Lawrence and those around them. It was a great disappointment to DS Bevan, and to DC Holden, that this was not achieved.**

26.7 When the family liaison began, DS Bevan did not know that there were guidelines in existence to assist officers in respect of family liaison. But he indicated that the title itself is *"explanation of what is required and what is needed"*, namely that of a Family Liaison Officer. It seems to us that this is an over-optimistic approach. Everybody needs training in the various roles carried on in life, and police officers plainly need training if they are to be involved in sensitive family liaison. The fact that guidelines exist is evidence of this, and it is an initial criticism that untrained officers unfamiliar with the guidelines were allowed to

179

take on this task. Neither DS Bevan nor DC Holden were truly able to get to grips with their delicate assignment.

26.8 DS Bevan says that he tried everything that he could to communicate with Mr & Mrs Lawrence. Before the Inquiry and to the Kent police he repeatedly said that he *"remained tremendously sympathetic"* to Mr & Mrs Lawrence to this day and that if he could help them now he would do so, even though the relationship in 1993 was almost non-existent. DS Bevan stated that he had mulled over the matter for the five years that have elapsed, but he could really not indicate at all what went wrong. He did say that there was *"a tremendous barrier to communication"*, but even with that indication he said that it was very hard to put his finger on exactly what it was. It is plain that he considered that *"lots of outside bodies who wanted to make their own statement"* had a considerable effect on the lack of communication. Very soon after the initial meeting both he and DC Holden were viewed with suspicion and mistrust. DS Bevan found this very sad. He was plainly never able to gain the confidence of Mr & Mrs Lawrence.

26.9 There is a detailed document setting out the "calendar" of attendance upon Mr & Mrs Lawrence by DS Bevan and DC Holden. The officers do not believe that it was composed by them. However, it does give an indication of the problems that occurred. For example, a note relating to 4 May indicates that DS Bevan attended with PC Fisher, the Race Relations Officer, when Mr & Mrs Lawrence's daughter, in front of a large number of people said *"Why hadn't we caught the man who murdered my brother?"* and then burst into tears.

26.10 **It is apparent that from very early on Mr & Mrs Lawrence and Mr Khan on their behalf were seeking more information. Indeed, as has been stressed by both the police and by Mr & Mrs Lawrence's legal team, there was unusual correspondence between Mr & Mrs Lawrence and the police very early on in the investigation. Mr Khan wrote three letters demanding information on behalf of Mr & Mrs Lawrence, and Mr Weeden replied. In his letter Mr Weeden indicated that he would be happy to go to see Mr & Mrs Lawrence himself. In fact Mr Weeden never did go to see Mr & Mrs Lawrence in connection with family liaison. Mr & Mrs Lawrence indicate that there were obvious problems, and Mr Weeden should have tried to sort them out. Similarly it seems to us that DS Bevan and DC Holden ought to have been prepared at an early stage to indicate that they were not the appropriate people to carry on with family liaison. It is all very well saying that one must not give up trying to achieve success, but where family liaison is concerned it seems hopeless to continue if there is plain and obvious mistrust from the start.**

26.11 Both from his long Kent interview, and in his evidence at this Inquiry, we formed the view that DS Bevan was an unusual man. His Kent interview betrays a strange use of words and language. In answers to Mr Kamlish we drew the conclusion that he was liable to say things which he did not entirely mean. For example, commenting upon arrangements which had been made on Saturday 24 April for Mr & Mrs Lawrence to view the body of their dead son at the mortuary he said that he felt *"quite elated"* at having assisted in achieving that visit. Furthermore, he said that Mrs Lawrence was *"aggressive"*, and he used many words which were inappropriate. Mr Kamlish accepted, whilst cross-examining DS Bevan, that DS Bevan and DC Holden had gone into the job of family liaison with perfectly good intentions, and we accept that as well. The fact is, however, that neither of them fully appreciated the way in which the family might have misgivings about white police liaison officers from the start after their experiences at the hospital.

26.12 **DS Bevan in common with other officers was not prepared to accept that the murder of Stephen Lawrence was purely a racist crime. It is difficult to understand how so many of the detectives working on this case were not willing to accept that this was so. Expression of that view at the public Inquiry did nothing to encourage Mr & Mrs Lawrence or indeed the black community to revise or review their opinions of police officers.**

26.13 As to the large number of people who surrounded Mr & Mrs Lawrence in the very early days, they were described by DS Bevan as *"hangers on"*. DC Holden said that she was not intimidated or upset by the numbers of people present. Both officers appear to have doubted the good intentions of those who surrounded Mr & Mrs Lawrence, to the extent that they both appear regularly to have asked people who were present to identify themselves, and to say from what organisation they came. Mrs Lawrence, in her statement, indicates that pressure groups did try to take a hand in the early days. **For example she was not happy at the arrival on the scene of the Black Panther representatives, and Mr Khan wrote to Greenwich Action Committee Against Racial Attacks, the Greenwich based organisation, asking them not to attend and threatening them with proceedings should they do so.**

26.14 **To that extent it does appear that there were more people around Mr & Mrs Lawrence than they themselves wanted. But it is not the job of Family Liaison Officers to query the activities of the family in this respect. Many members of the family, and other well-wishers, attended at the Lawrence house. A member of the family kept a detailed diary in a notebook of the comings and goings of those who were there.**

26.15 **Family Liaison Officers in these circumstances must blend in with the wishes of the family, and not be put off by the attendance of individuals or indeed organisations who seek to assist the grieving family. This shows a lack of training and sensitivity in understanding the way in which a black family may react to the terrible circumstances in which Mr & Mrs Lawrence found themselves.**

26.16 As to the information given to Mr & Mrs Lawrence, DS Bevan said that he made *"continual reference to the amount of people working and the fact that we were all working very hard"*. DS Bevan said that it was *"extremely difficult to know what actually I could tell them"*. The long and the short of it is that he ought to have been prepared to sit down and discuss in detail with Mr & Mrs Lawrence what were their anxieties and what information they were seeking. It seems to us that the indications are, both from what Mr & Mrs Lawrence say and from Mr Khan's letters, that Mr & Mrs Lawrence were not being given sensible or full information. DS Bevan said that police officers were *"working on suspects"*, and that he did not want to prejudice any impending or possible prosecutions. This does suggest that he held back in the giving of information which might have assisted Mr & Mrs Lawrence's anxieties.

26.17 That Mr & Mrs Lawrence were anxious about the matter is indicated both by Mr Khan's intervention, and by the fact that Mr & Mrs Lawrence consulted their MP, Mr Peter Bottomley, as to the lack of information which was reaching them. Mr Bottomley seems to have gone to the Commissioner, Sir Paul Condon, so that the matter was reported in the highest places. A letter to the Commissioner in June 1993 from Baroness Seear (representing the All Party Parliamentary Group on Race and Community) registered unease at the *"lack of sensitivity on behalf of the local constabulary towards the Lawrence family"*.

26.18 **DS Bevan furthermore found it difficult to deal with Mr Khan. He said to the Kent police that he was surprised at the intervention of a solicitor so early on in the investigation. He was surprised that *"the victims needed legal representation"*. He thought to himself *"What good is a solicitor going to do?"* He regarded Mr Khan as *"One more barrier to communication."***

26.19 **Again it is not the business of DS Bevan or DC Holden or indeed any police officer to criticise the arrival on the scene of a solicitor on behalf of Mr & Mrs Lawrence. That is another aspect of the case which the Family Liaison Officers had to accept, cope with and respond to positively.**

26.20 Many things done by the two officers seem in essence to have made matters worse. Of course it is necessary that the background of a victim must be investigated. Some investigation of the background of Stephen Lawrence might have led to information assisting the murder case. In fact all the investigation showed that he was an admirable and highly regarded young man. Such inquiries are a standard feature of any murder investigation. Any such investigation must only be done with the utmost tact and the fullest explanation to the family. That the family gained the impression that their dead son was under suspicion is a condemnation of the approach in this respect.

26.21 **Similarly, when a hat and gloves found at the scene were shown to Mr & Mrs Lawrence there should have been a very full explanation given that it was simply and solely the ownership of the gloves that was of interest to the officers. In the atmosphere of mistrust which existed it is perhaps not surprising that Mr & Mrs Lawrence's perception of the questions asked in connection with the gloves and hat was that some kind of suggestion was being made against their dead son. This was palpably not the truth, since it is the fact that everybody, including the two officers involved, agree that there was no shadow of suspicion against Stephen Lawrence. This displays the failure of the liaison officers to explain sensitively what they were doing. The officers were taken off their family liaison duties towards the end of May 1993.**

26.22 Even the telephone communication between the liaison officers and Mr & Mrs Lawrence and Mr Khan led to problems. Both officers used their own mobile telephones privately in order to help their liaison with the family. Indeed DS Bevan bought his mobile telephone expressly for this purpose. DC Holden already owned her own mobile telephone. Their intentions in this respect were plainly very good and intended to be helpful. But Mr & Mrs Lawrence found it difficult to get through on the telephone, and they believe, perhaps wrongly, that the officers were casual in their preparedness to talk to them, even on the telephone. Furthermore there was some reluctance to speak to Mr Khan on the telephone, although certainly DC Holden did give her mobile telephone number to Mr Khan himself.

26.23 When it was suggested that there should be visits to the incident room, in order to assist Mr & Mrs Lawrence's understanding of what was going on, a senior officer indicated that Mr Khan should not be allowed to attend. DS Bevan and DC Holden said that this was not their decision. It seems likely that they knew that the decision had been made. Certainly this exclusion of Mr Khan, Mr & Mrs Lawrence's adviser and solicitor, did not help relations between the police and Mr & Mrs Lawrence, and was inexcusable.

26.24 **From time to time Mr & Mrs Lawrence did indicate that they did not wish to be disturbed or contacted. This they were perfectly entitled to do, and their wishes in this respect cannot diminish the justifiable criticism of the family liaison.**

26.25 **It is plain from the policy file and the entries made by Mr Weeden, that the senior officers realised that it was important that proper information and support was directed to the family of Stephen Lawrence and, indeed, Mr Brooks. Mr Weeden's entry for 28 April shows that he wished to** *"Ensure that victim liaison is focused firmly on the Lawrence and Brooks families but not diluted or deflected in effect by various intermediaries who have now claimed to represent the family."* **This shows good intentions, but it also perhaps shows that the police view was that those surrounding Mr & Mrs Lawrence were to some extent an obstacle. This is not a justifiable attitude for the police to adopt. The family of Stephen Lawrence had to be taken as they were found, and as they chose to behave. They were entitled to demand to be dealt with as they were and according to their own needs.**

26.26 DC Holden's view of the problems which arose coincided closely with that of DS Bevan. She did not see Mrs Lawrence on the first day, because Mrs Lawrence was upstairs in the bedroom, and there had been a prescription of tranquillisers given to her by her GP. DC Holden did speak to Mr Lawrence, and she indicated that she tried to explain to him what the role of the Family Liaison Officers would be. But early on in her evidence she said that there were *"so many outside agencies from different sort of parties that I felt was sometimes giving their points of view that you couldn't really get a close relationship with the family because there seemed to be a lot of barriers put up"*.

26.27 **Furthermore DC Holden felt that Mr Khan was interposing himself between the family and the family liaison team so that this in itself created some kind of barrier. DC Holden said that she and DS Bevan tried as hard as they could to get a working relationship with the Lawrence family. It is wholly apparent that this was never achieved. DC Holden said that the problems were discussed at regular meetings with senior officers, and that the senior officers simply told the team to do their best and to keep on trying. This was an inadequate response by those officers.**

26.28 The accusation made against DC Holden by Mr Kamlish was that she and DS Bevan had been *"patronising"* either intentionally or unintentionally. She said that she and DS Bevan were *"Absolutely straight down the line with the family. Whatever they needed to know we told them."* DC Holden added that Mr Lawrence did not seem to understand the procedure, and that was why the family were going to appoint a solicitor to assist. There was plainly some frostiness in connection with Mr Khan, and DC Holden was prepared to say that she had not given him her own mobile telephone number. It was apparent, when a document was shown to her, that this was wrong. Even if there were a personal problem and some distrust between DC Holden and Mr Khan that had to be overcome. Mr Khan was acting on behalf of Mr & Mrs Lawrence and the family liaison team had a duty to do their best to get on both with the family and their representatives.

26.29 **DC Holden followed what in a sense appears to be the party line in connection with motive for this terrible crime. She seemed determined to stick to the proposition that she could not say what the motive of the young men involved was. It is clear that this was a racist crime committed by this group of white youths. They might have committed crimes against white people as well, but the facts of this case show with crystal clarity that this was purely a racist killing. As we have indicated before, the expressions used and the determination to water down the racist element of the killing offends Mr & Mrs Lawrence and the community, black and white.**

26.30 DC Holden was the person who actually took the hat and gloves to Mr & Mrs Lawrence. She says that when she talked to them about the hat and gloves, and they said that they did not belong to Stephen, *"that that was the end of the matter"*. It is accepted that there was never any positive suggestion that Stephen Lawrence might have been involved in nefarious activity, but the fact that Mr & Mrs Lawrence's perception was that this was so must demonstrate that the matter was not dealt with properly and as sensitively as it should have been.

26.31 DC Holden repeated, as had DS Bevan, that she and DS Bevan used to have conversations about their problems and meetings with senior officers to try to find ways of building up the relationship with the family. There is thus plainly material here for criticism of the senior officers, since if they knew that the relationship was as bad as it evidently was, immediate and comprehensive steps ought to have been taken to change the system. There were people, such as Noel Penstone, and Mrs Ros Howells and others who must have been readily available to help to cement a reasonable relationship very early on. The longer the difficulty and mistrust lasted the less likely was it that the matter would be remedied.

26.32 **A fresh approach and a fresh team ought to have been put into the role of family liaison very early on. As we have already indicated Mr Weeden's letter of 27 April 1993 expressed his own personal grief at Mr & Mrs Lawrence's loss and encouraged them to deal with DS Bevan and DC Holden, and suggested that he was prepared to visit them at any time that they wished. In fact it was incumbent upon the SIO to take the initiative as soon as he heard that the family liaison was so unsatisfactory. We are not satisfied that the family liaison officers devoted enough effort to overcoming what they saw as obstacles. They too readily stepped back from a situation simply because it was unfamiliar to them. More reprehensible is the failure of the senior officers, particularly Mr Weeden, to address the situation. It was evidently quite clear to Mr Weeden from an early stage that there were difficulties which demanded his personal intervention, apart from the common courtesy of meeting the family as the SIO in any event. Such intervention did not occur. It is difficult to understand Mr Weeden's inactivity in this regard and certainly it has to be a focus of major criticism. Indeed, as we say in Chapter 14 we conclude that this attitude betrayed unwitting racism.**

26.33 There was a press conference on the day after the murder, and Mr Lawrence had some short contact there with Mr Crampton who was at that time the SIO. But plainly Mr Crampton was in charge for such a short time that he may not have been able to divine what was going wrong with the family liaison.

26.34 When DC Holden was cross-examined by Ms Sikand, on behalf of the CRE, she stuck to her answers in connection with the racist motivation of this terrible crime, although Ms Sikand pointed out that even now her currently expressed view is not in conformity with the Association of Chief Police Officers' current definition of racially motivated crime or the MPS guidance manual of 1997.

26.35 **All in all the family liaison aspect of this case is much open to criticism. Ultimately on 6 May Mr Ilsley took over the role. By then serious damage had been done to the relationship between Mr & Mrs Lawrence and the police, and no proper steps were taken to "mend the fences" during the early weeks after the terrible murder of Stephen Lawrence. As will be seen the start of the family's dealings with Mr Ilsley was itself far from auspicious.**

26.36 During her evidence Mrs Lawrence was asked specifically whether racism had played its part in preventing a reasonable relationship being built between the family and the liaison officers. *"Racism is something you can't always just put your finger on"*, she replied. *"Racism is done in a way that is so subtle. It is how they talk to you ..... It is just the whole attitude ...... It was patronising the way in which they dealt with me and that came across as being racist."* **We accept, as did Counsel for the Mr & Mrs Lawrence, that the officers' intentions were good. Mrs Lawrence herself accepted in answer to Mr Egan's questions posed during her evidence, that DC Holden on 20 April took the trouble to deliver a birthday card to her daughter who was away on an outward bound course. Mrs Lawrence said that this was done because DC Holden *"wanted to be helpful"*. Regrettably the liaison as a whole failed, despite the good intentions of the officers involved.**

26.37 **Plainly Mr & Mrs Lawrence were not dealt with or treated as they should have been. Their reaction and their attitude after their son's murder were those of a grieving family. The fact that they were in their eyes and to their perception patronised and inappropriately treated exhibits plain but unintentional failure to treat them appropriately and professionally within their own culture and as a black grieving family. DS Bevan and DC Holden will for ever deny that they are racist or that the colour, culture and ethnic origin of the Lawrence family played any part in the failure of family liaison. We are bound to say that the conclusion which we reach is inescapable. Inappropriate behaviour and patronising attitudes towards this black family were the product and a manifestation of unwitting racism at work. Coupled with the failure of the senior officers to see Mr & Mrs Lawrence and to sort out the family liaison we see here a clear example of the collective failure of the investigating team to treat Mr & Mrs Lawrence appropriately and professionally, because of their colour, culture and ethnic origin.**

CHAPTER TWENTY-SEVEN

DETECTIVE CHIEF SUPERINTENDENT WILLIAM ILSLEY

27.1 Detective Chief Superintendent William Ilsley joined the MPS in 1963. He served most of his career in CID, and became a Chief Superintendent in May 1991. He remained Detective Chief Superintendent in charge of 3 Area until March 1995 when he retired. Effectively therefore he was involved in the Stephen Lawrence murder investigation until his retirement, although he indicated that during the second investigation he had only a minor supervisory role since Assistant Commissioner Johnston came to the Area. That second investigation was under the direct control of Commander Perry Nove and Detective Superintendent William Mellish.

27.2 At the time of Stephen Lawrence's murder Mr Ilsley had probably about 200 officers directly under his command. In addition to his responsibility for all AMIP inquires Mr Ilsley was also in charge of the Intelligence Bureau, the Drug Squad, the Crime Squad, the Child Protection Teams and, most significantly, the Surveillance Team for 3 Area.

27.3 It appears that in April 1993 the 3 Area AMIP was involved in ten major investigation, of which three involved murder. In answer to his Counsel, Miss Woodley, Mr Ilsley indicated that it would not be possible for him to have *"a detailed working knowledge of each and every murder investigation: that would be left to the individual Senior Investigating Officers"*.

27.4 Mr Ilsley was at pains to point out that he relied very much on the SIOs to tell him what was happening at their formal weekly meetings at Catford. He said that he would of course also attend regularly at the Incident Rooms involved in his Area. Because of the external pressures involved in the Stephen Lawrence murder Mr Ilsley indicated that he took a closer interest in this particular case than in some others. On the other hand more than once he told the Inquiry that he did not get involved in the *"nitty gritty"* of the case, and that his role was supervisory, and that he left the actual running of the Incident Room and the investigation to the SIOs.

27.5 He was of course responsible for the appointment of the SIOs, and he accepted that it was most unfortunate that there was a change over in this particular case within four days of the murder. Apparently Mr Weeden had been off because of an injury to his hand and leg during the week before the murder, so that Mr Crampton was the Superintendent on call when the murder took place. Mr Ilsley indicated that in those circumstances there was no alternative to the investigation starting under the leadership of Mr Crampton, but that he spoke to Mr Weeden to encourage him to take over as soon as possible.

27.6 **Obviously there may be circumstances where a change over is inevitable, but it is much to be deplored that there had to be a change over in this particular case, because it had serious consequences in connection with the negative decision as to arrest.**

27.7 Mr Ilsley is without doubt a somewhat verbose man. He accepted himself that he tended to *"ramble on"*. He has been described as a *"hands on"* man, but at the same time he did have a tendency to disconnect himself from the investigation where detail was concerned. Before us he tended to excuse what had happened on the basis that everybody did their best considering the resources that were available.

27.8   He told us that his team was under tremendous pressure, and that in the first year of his duty, for example, he had coped with 43 murders which was the highest in the MPS and the third highest in the British Isles. He was at pains early in his evidence to stress the lack of resources and the lack of staff available. He said that that was a known fact, and that he used to go to meetings regularly at New Scotland Yard with other Detective Chief Superintendents who would sing the same song, namely that there simply were not enough police officers to go round, and that the facilities and resources available were woefully short.

27.9   In a long answer Mr Ilsley indicated a comparison between his set up in 3 Area MPS compared with that which he found when he visited the Incident Room of a Sussex murder early in the 1990s. Mr Ilsley said that he would regularly discuss the totally inadequate resources and accommodation with Deputy Assistant Commissioner Osland and at meetings at New Scotland Yard.

27.10 **When Mr Lawson asked Mr Ilsley about the positions occupied by DS Flook, who had to cope with five separate roles bound into one in connection with the office management, he said *"It is not only poor, Sir, it is disgraceful, but it was something that we used to have to put up with all the time"*.**

27.11 It seems to us doubtful whether lack of resources accounted for the specific failings and mistakes which occurred in the investigation of the Stephen Lawrence murder in the early days, except perhaps as they concerned the operation of HOLMES and the Incident Room itself. Be that as it may, we formed the impression that Mr Ilsley did tend to try to pass off his own responsibilities, and perhaps to make excuses about manpower in order to avoid criticism. In parenthesis it should be noted that Mr Ilsley, in common with the other senior officers, confirmed to the Kent inquiry that this murder investigation was in fact better staffed than most, but that it was still woefully deficient.

27.12 **One of the first duties taken on by Mr Ilsley after the murder was the conduct on behalf of the MPS of the first press conference, which took place on Friday 23 April. Mr Ilsley indicated, as we have seen on the recorded television films of this occasion, that it was an outrage that two black youths had been attacked totally unprovoked by white youths. The 'Daily Telegraph' of the following day seems to suggest that he had also indicated that the attack was a purely racist murder. This is not reflected in the two recordings which we have seen. One was made at Plumstead Police Station at 14:30, and the other (for Newsroom South East) outside Eltham Police Station. The briefing notes indicate that *"If asked re motive believe it was racist attack"*. This may suggest that a decision had been made that the announcement should not include certainly at first blush the important indication that this was purely a racist attack. There is no indication of the reason why the motive was not positively identified. It may have been the desire to mask the occurrence of another serious racist incident in an area where there had been many. If this is the case it shows a lack of understanding of the concern and importance to the black community of recognising and acknowledging racial incidents as such.**

27.13 An important part played by Mr Ilsley in this case concerns family liaison. DS Bevan and DC Holden had been appointed from the start as Family Liaison Officers. It was considered to be inappropriate to appoint liaison officers from outside the ranks of the CID. Everybody accepts that from a very early stage there were considerable difficulties on this front. Mr Ilsley decided that he would take on the role from 6 May 1993. At some stage, probably before that date, Mr Philpott had offered to provide officers with experience and aptitude for dealing with minority ethnic concerns, but this was not accepted because DS Bevan and DC Holden were considered suitable. Exactly how and when this took place is uncertain, but it confirms our view that Mr Ilsley regarded himself and his staff as being more capable in this field than he should have done. It may also reflect a lack of real communication and co-operation between the uniformed staff on whose Division the murder occurred, commanded by Mr Philpott, and the CID staff commanded by Mr Ilsley. It is for example agreed between Messrs Philpott and Ilsley that Mr Philpott only found out about the family liaison difficulties through contacts in the community rather than any dialogue with the investigation team. It is certainly our impression that the AMIP team had little communication with the host Division and essentially operated as a force within a force.

27.14 Mr Ilsley says that by the time that he and Mr Philpott saw Mr & Mrs Lawrence on 6 May the question of appointing any family liaison replacement other than himself had passed. He told us that the way that he understood the situation was that Mr & Mrs Lawrence wanted more information, and that he was the person who would be able to give it to them, together with Mr Philpott. Mr Ilsley thought that the family had more support from other people than he had known in a murder investigation. Indeed he thought that there were too many people around them. He knew that their complaint was that they were not being given the information that they required as to the murder investigation. The short note in the policy file number 37, entered later, records that Mr Ilsley decided to *"take over the role of victim liaison"*. The reasons given for this were that *"At a meeting with the family and their solicitor, Mr Khan, they requested they didn't want any victim liaison apart from a weekly meeting with myself and Chief Superintendent Philpott"*.

27.15 Mr Ilsley never felt that he had achieved a close connection with the family, and he told us that he came away from the meetings that followed in a somewhat depressed state. Strangely enough there is an indication from a communication by Mr Khan that things were going reasonably well, as Mr Ilsley stressed. It may be that Mr Ilsley's attitudes and actions during the first meeting had in fact launched his era of family liaison on a bad basis.

27.16 **During the course of the meeting Mrs Lawrence handed a note to Mr Ilsley which contained a list of suspects, culled from notes made at Mr & Mrs Lawrence's home over the previous days. We have seen the note, and it contains a list of familiar names starting with the name of Zak Punt. The question of the handing over of this note has always been a bone of contention. In more than one statement Mrs Lawrence said that Mr Ilsley had *"rolled the piece of paper up in a ball in his hand"*. Various versions of Mrs Lawrence's statement were read before the Inquiry, and it is to be noted that she had also invariably said that Mr Ilsley folded the piece of paper up first. At the Inquiry Mrs Lawrence appears to have accepted that the paper was folded up tight, but was not rolled into a ball. Either way it seems to us that what Mr Ilsley did was insensitive, discourteous and unwise. There was no reason even to fold the paper up into a small packet; and the perception of Mrs Lawrence quite plainly was that he was doing this in a dismissive way. (The note is reproduced at the end of this Volume).**

27.17 Of course it is unfortunate that the particular phrase *"rolled the piece of paper up in a ball"* was ever used. But in the end now that that particular phrase is removed from the case we remain convinced that it was tactless at the least to fold the paper up so tight that Mrs Lawrence could conceivably form the impression, as she did, that the paper was of little consequence to Mr Ilsley.

27.18 **Incidents of this kind are obviously open to misinterpretation. Wisdom and sensitivity should have demanded that Mr Ilsley at least register his interest in the paper and indicate that it would at once have attention from the investigation team. What Mr Ilsley did was to put the paper in his pocket, without any expression of gratitude or interest to Mrs Lawrence. It is perfectly true that when he returned to the Incident Room he at once (at about 20:00) put the information contained on that piece of paper into the system. So that it is apparent that he did himself intend to transmit it to the SIO and the investigating team. But by then the damage had been done.**

27.19 **Mr Ilsley says that he would never criticise Mr & Mrs Lawrence under any circumstances for seeking information from the police. It is obvious that they believed that they were not being given any satisfactory account of what was happening, and this Mr Ilsley understood. On the other hand it is apparent that Mr Ilsley had no such sympathetic views in respect of the family's solicitor Mr Khan. He has alleged that Mr Khan was *"never ever supportive of anything we did"*, and he indicated that Mr Khan had a *"totally different agenda all the way through and was totally critical of the police for every single thing we did"*. Furthermore to Kent Mr Ilsley had said that *"his fear was that whatever police might say to the family, would be spread around and could hamper our inquiry"*.**

27.20 **This conflict between Mr Ilsley and Mr Khan never should have developed. To our mind Mr Ilsley exaggerated and distorted the problem that Mr Khan is said to have caused him and the police in general.**

27.21 At all events the 6 May meeting did not augur well for the continued relationship between Mr Ilsley and the family. Furthermore immediately after that evening meeting Mr Ilsley returned to the police station to be told by Mr Weeden that arrests were going to be made on the following day. He says that he was not consulted about the decision in advance, but was informed about it when he returned to the station. The reasons given were those already set out by Mr Weeden. Mr Ilsley says that it was pure coincidence that this decision was made immediately upon his return from the first meeting with Mr & Mrs Lawrence. Mr Ilsley says that something must have been said during his conversation with the family about the planning of arrests, and that he would simply have said that the matter was under consideration, but that he did not know when any arrests would be made.

27.22 It is of considerable significance that Mr Ilsley does have to accept and does in fact accept that he was consulted by Mr Crampton over the weekend about the decision that arrests should not be made at once. He said that the reasons for this were that time had elapsed so that suspects might have got rid of any suspicious weapons or clothing, that the identification evidence was weak, and that if the men were arrested there would be nothing substantial to put to them by way of evidence. Mr Ilsley agrees that this was a major decision. It was not entered in the policy file. He accepted at once that this should have been done, but he believes that this was simply an oversight. Policy files were, said Mr Ilsley, very much individualistic type documents within the MPS in 1993. That is no justification whatsoever for the omission of what was clearly the most central and major decision in the investigation. We cannot accept that this was simply an oversight.

27.23 **Thus Mr Ilsley has to be associated with what we believe to have been the vital wrong decision in connection with the arrest of the suspects. Given that it was not his own decision, but that of the SIO, it was still something which he as an active commander should have resolved in his own mind for himself. Mr Ilsley is plainly subject to the**

same criticism in this regard as Mr Crampton and subsequently Mr Weeden. Mr Ilsley says that the decision was positively renewed on Monday 26th, and that the decision was indeed reviewed all the time. When the time came for the arrests to be made it is of significance that the policy file indicates that there was a joint decision made in this regard by Mr Ilsley and Mr Weeden. Mr Ilsley says simply that he was agreeing with the decision, and that it was therefore appropriate that his name should appear in the policy file. On the other hand he also accepted, in the light of the policy file entry, that in terms of information that had been available there had been no substantial change in circumstances since the very early days. Therefore Mr Ilsley has to accept that if Mr Weeden's decision to make the arrests on 6 May was not prompted by new evidence or outside pressures those arrests could in any event have taken place on the same basis during the first weekend after the murder.

27.24 **It is an indictment of Mr Ilsley that he did not recognise and accept that there had been any deficiencies in the investigation carried out by the AMIP team until he saw the Kent conclusions. The deduction from that is that if there had not been a complaint by Mr & Mrs Lawrence leading to the Kent inquiry, and to this Inquiry, Mr Ilsley might still be saying that there was nothing wrong with the first investigation. Mr Mansfield pointed out that the Barker Review indicated that the first investigation was not to be criticised, and that Mr Ilsley had simply gone along with that report and made no comment to anybody that the Review was unsatisfactory in any way.**

27.25 **Somewhat reluctantly Mr Ilsley conceded to Mr Mansfield that in hindsight there had been deficiencies in the early days, citing surveillance, the searching of houses and the failure to make early arrests. Mr Ilsley was reluctant to accept that he had any responsibility for the failure to convert information into what he termed *"hard evidence"*. He accepted that it was *"regrettable"* that objects had apparently been moved in black bags from 102 Bournbrook Road during the week after the murder. He was not prepared to accept that the strategy adopted was *"a complete nonsense"*, and he roundly denied that he had known this to be so at the time.**

27.26 An important aspect of this case concerns the dealings of the team with James Grant. Both DS Davidson and DC Budgen indicated to us that they had together registered this man as an informant with Mr Owens on 28 April. They say that they applied to register James Grant in the normal way at Greenwich Police Station, and that the relevant documents were completed for this purpose. The fact is however that any documents, if they ever existed, have disappeared. Mr Ilsley was of course part of the chain of communication in connection with documents dealing with informants. He says that he had no idea what can have happened to the documents, and that his only contact with this matter concerned the submission to him by Mr Weeden of the request made later by DS Davidson and Mr Weeden for payment to James Grant for his services as an informant.

27.27 Mr Ilsley says that when he received the request he did not believe that any payment was deserved, because information had come from other people as well giving the same set of names and comparable information. This is plainly not correct since James Grant was the first and by far the most important informant, and he came to the police station personally on Friday, 23 April.

27.28 The unregistered cover with the letters attached suggesting that there should be a reward was found very much later on by Chief Superintendent Albert Patrick in preparation for the Kent inquiry.

27.29 The suggestion throughout this unhappy saga is that Mr Ilsley, in common with other officers, had no real interest in Grant, and that Grant was marginalised and kept out of the way because he knew too much and because the officers did not want to make arrests at all during the first weekend.

27.30 Mr Mansfield continued his attack in connection with James Grant, suggesting that Mr Ilsley himself, bearing in mind his own investigative skills and his position as a senior officer, ought to have personally followed up the Grant information, particularly in order to obtain from James Grant as much information about his own or his source's position in the matter. Mr Ilsley's counter to that was that Mr Crampton and Mr Weeden were the SIOs who were dealing with the matter, and that although he might have discussed the situation with them he would never have spoken to James Grant himself.

27.31 **It can be said that Mr Ilsley and the SIOs ought all to have interested themselves more in the James Grant information, and in what had been done to further that information and to follow up all that stemmed from it. We do not accept that there is any justification for the suggestion made by Mr Mansfield that Mr Ilsley slowed down the investigation for improper reasons. We find no evidence to suggest that Mr Ilsley was anything other than honest and well-intentioned.**

27.32 **Mr Ilsley does have to accept that he was associated with wrong decision-making and serious deficiencies in investigation and family liaison. We see no basis for any suggestion that he corruptly held back in his part in the supervision of the investigation. Mr Ilsley's angry rejection of such suggestions by Mr Mansfield was justified. No evidence was called to support the allegation.**

27.33 Mr Ilsley was also involved in the case involving the prosecution for the murder of David Norris. He was supervising that investigation which led to the prosecution in which Mr Crampton was involved at the time of Stephen Lawrence's murder. But he says roundly that he never made any connection between the dead David Norris and the David Norris who was one of the suspects in this case. He knew by the first Sunday that the suspect David Norris was the son of Clifford Norris, who was known to him as a south London criminal, but he had no knowledge of any alleged or claimed relationship between the dead David and Clifford Norris.

27.34 Mr Ilsley had himself in 1989 passed on information from one of his own informants in connection with allegations made against Clifford Norris, namely that he had been involved in the shooting of a woman who later refused to give evidence against the assailant. Mr Ilsley says that until this Inquiry started he had not even remembered that he had given that information. He reiterated that at first he did not even think of Clifford Norris when he heard that a 16 or 17 year old youth called David Norris had been named as one of the suspects.

27.35 Mr Ilsley was asked about the officer Sergeant XX, who figures in this case as a result of his suspicious association with Clifford Norris. Mr Ilsley says, and we believe him, that he did not know this officer and that he had never worked with him and would not know him if he walked into the room. As to Clifford Norris' position at the time of the Stephen Lawrence murder, Mr Ilsley says that he knew that Clifford Norris was a wanted man, but that he had no memory of the circumstances of Clifford Norris' evasion of Customs & Excise, and he said that it was not his task to take any steps in connection with the arrest of Clifford Norris, unless he turned up in the process of the investigation. **The case was a Customs & Excise matter, but it is extraordinary that no positive steps were initiated during the first investigation to seek out Clifford Norris and to remove him from the scene, since**

officers were aware of threats coming from him which were discouraging the witnesses who were so desperately sought.

27.36   By 25 or 26 April Mr Ilsley says that he probably did know that David Norris was the son of Clifford Norris, but this did not in itself spur him on to encourage Mr Weeden to arrest Clifford Norris in order at least to get him off the streets. The failure to address this inevitably fuels Mr & Mrs Lawrence's perception of collusion or corruption.

27.37   As to the house-to-house inquiries it was suggested by Mr Mansfield that another opportunity had been missed by Mr Ilsley's staff, because they failed to return to 102 Bournbrook Road in order to make some direct contact with the Acourt brothers and perhaps others who might be present. Mr Ilsley commented that he would have been very careful about that, because officers could get themselves into a difficulty by trying to trick the Acourts into saying something without administering a caution when in fact there was enough information already in existence to allow an arrest. In connection with the failure to obtain a photograph of David Norris Mr Ilsley said that he was not aware of the problem, and that in any event this was a matter of detail or *"nitty gritty"* which he left to his SIO.

27.38   Mr Mansfield questioned Mr Ilsley extensively about the decision to arrest made on 6 May. Mr Ilsley did not accept that the arrests were being carried out under pressure because of the visit of Nelson Mandela and the heavy press interest in the case which had developed. He simply says that the matter was entirely a decision for Mr Weeden who told him at about 20:00 when he returned from his visit to Mr & Mrs Lawrence that warrants were being obtained and that the team were going in on the following morning. Mr Ilsley says that Mr Weeden was in any event building up to the arrests and that it was no great surprise to him that this decision was reached coincidentally with the considerable outside pressures.

27.39   **Another justifiable criticism of Mr Ilsley concerns the failure by the investigating team either before or after the arrests had been made, to exercise or at least to consider some form of intrusive surveillance other than photography. That was of course done during the second investigation with marked success and with sophisticated equipment. Telephone tapping requires an express warrant from the Secretary of State, but no approach was apparently made to the Commissioner or relevant deputy for permission to "bug" premises occupied by the suspects during the first investigation. The grounds to do so certainly existed. Mrs Lawrence says that she raised this matter with Mr Ilsley, but that he indicated that this was not an acceptable tactic.**

27.40   As to the decision by the CPS in July 1993 to discontinue the proposed proceedings, Mr Ilsley agreed that both he and Mr Weeden were opposed to that, but he indicated that there was no mileage in registering opposition, since his experience was that once the CPS made its decision there was no going back. In our opinion Mr Ilsley cannot be criticised for failing to attempt to put pressure on the CPS.

27.41   As to the Barker Review Mr Mansfield roundly suggested that Mr Ilsley had indicated to Mr Barker that he was happy with his report because *"basically it kept the lid on everything"*, so that Mr Ilsley and his team were let off the hook. Mr Ilsley said that his initial response to the Barker Review was that he was not overly impressed by it, and that some of the recommendations seemed to be off key. He did not realise at the time that there were deficiencies in his team's performance, and he said that there was no reason for him to raise any opposition to the conclusions of Mr Barker. So far as the deficiency of accommodation and staff and money were concerned this was not raised with Mr Barker because that seemed to Mr Ilsley to be something which was common to everybody operating in the MPS.

27.42 **The unquestioning acceptance of the Barker Review by senior officers is a most serious aspect of this case. Mr Ilsley cannot escape his share of criticism in this regard, since he should have realised that the Review was flawed both in its recitation of facts and in its conclusions. The Review provided a convenient** *"shelter"* **to those involved. The failure of all senior officers to detect the flaws in the Review is to be deplored.**

27.43 Mr Ilsley was asked by Mr Mansfield about the attitude adopted by members of the team as to race relations and particularly as to the motive for this terrible crime. In particular the passage from the interviewing of Gary Dobson by DS Davidson in which DS Davidson and DC Hughes allege that the killing had *"nothing to do with colour"* was quoted to Mr Ilsley. He said that he certainly would never interview someone in that way, but that all that he could assume was that the officers were trying to get Mr Dobson to admit to the crime and were therefore *"going along"* with Mr Dobson in this regard. Mr Ilsley did find it incredible that officers under his command should try to make a distinction between a racist murder and a racially motivated murder. Mr Ilsley accepted that identification of a crime as racist would determine the kind of support that should be given to the victim and his family, and would and should condition the kind of effective action that might be taken to detect the crime.

27.44 Mr Ilsley never saw Duwayne Brooks, although of course he was very much alive to the statements made by him and to the evident co-operation of Mr Brooks with the officers in the investigation team. In many instances Mr Ilsley indicated that in connection with Mr Brooks he simply could not answer the questions put, because he was effectively being asked about matters with which he had not himself been concerned.

27.45 A relevant matter concerned the occupants of the red Astra car. Mr Ilsley accepted that in respect of the investigation of these men errors had plainly been made. He would not accept that this failure was, as Mr Menon, on behalf of Mr Brooks, put it, *"in effect deracialisation of this crime by the investigating officers"*. Mr Menon's suggestion was that *"race has been put on the back burner"*, by the team. Mr Ilsley rejected this suggestion. He said that this was clearly a racist murder in his eyes and that he had wanted nothing other than to arrest the people who had committed the murder in order to bring them to justice. We accept Mr Ilsley's evidence in this regard. Nonetheless unwitting racism within the AMIP team did in our view affect the way in which the investigation and in particular the family liaison were conducted.

27.46 It is right to point out that in answer to Mr Gompertz Mr Ilsley acknowledged the force of two messages which indicate that the more general criticism in connection with the care taken of Mr Brooks is exaggerated. We know that DS Bevan struck up a reasonable relationship with Mr Brooks, and furthermore there is information amongst the HOLMES system messages indicating that liaison took place, and that DS Bevan and DC Holden liaised both with him and with his mother and father, and *"made arrangements for someone from Victim Support to contact the family and Duwayne"*. On 1 May a further message indicates that Mr Brooks did not appear to be suffering from any untoward problems, and he was currently still attending college and was still happy to assist the police. The parents of Mr Brooks had, so the message relates, at each stage been informed of the progress of the murder investigation and again were happy to assist.

27.47 In addition we know that on 2 May Mr Khan went to see Mr Brooks, apparently in his capacity as his solicitor. Thereafter Mr Brooks was represented at least for some time by Mr Khan. At no time was any contact made with the Incident Room or with any of the police officers involved to indicate that Mr Brooks was not being properly looked after or needed any particular form of special counselling.

27.48   **Mr Gompertz dealt in detail and at considerable length with the suggestion made that Mr Ilsley was connected with or affected in some way by Clifford Norris, so that either through fear or corruption, or for racist motives, he had deliberately failed to take any steps in order to bring the suspects to justice. It does seem to us that in the case of Mr Ilsley these allegations were wide of the mark. Such allegations must not be made unless there is the material upon which to make them. In the two days spent in the witness box by Mr Ilsley there was no evidence that Mr Ilsley was connected with Clifford Norris, or affected by any knowledge that he may have had of Clifford Norris or his influence on others.**

27.49   Finally we must mention the perhaps revealing difference between Mr Ilsley and Mr Bullock in connection with a period of time when Mr Weeden was absent, owing to an unfortunate family bereavement, for eight days in May 1993. It was plainly Mr Ilsley's responsibility to determine who was in charge of the investigation during that time. Mr Bullock considered that Mr Ilsley was in charge, and Mr Ilsley considered that Mr Bullock had been left holding the temporary office of SIO. It is perhaps symptomatic of Mr Ilsley's lack of direction of his SIO that this confusion existed.

27.50   **Mr Ilsley allowed himself to go along with the weak and unenterprising decisions made by Mr Crampton and Mr Weeden in the very early days, so that the opportunities which an early arrest might have produced were missed. There was a tendency for Mr Ilsley to disconnect from the investigation in connection with justifiable criticisms, and to excuse any deficiencies on the ground of lack of resources. Mr Ilsley should have ensured that Mr Weeden was fully aware of the decision to delay the arrests and the need to review that decision, particularly in the light of Stacey Benefield's statement. He should also have been made aware of the surveillance plans. He had the authority to give immediate priority to the Stephen Lawrence murder investigation surveillance.**

27.51   **Mr Ilsley ought plainly to have been aware of the inaccuracies of the facts set out in the Barker Review and of the inadequacy of that Review, yet he allowed himself to accept the Review as it was and failed to bring its failings to the attention of his superior officers. This failure contributed to those officers being misled by the Review's falsely reassuring tones.**

27.52   **There was in our opinion failure to supervise and to manage effectively and imaginatively this highly sensitive murder investigation to the degree required by Mr Ilsley's position as Crime Manager for the Area. This conclusion is in tune with the conclusion of the Kent inquiry, with which we agree so far as it concerns Mr Ilsley.**

CHAPTER TWENTY-EIGHT

THE BARKER REVIEW

28.1 **In July 1993 the CPS indicated that they did not intend to proceed with the prosecution of Neil Acourt and Luke Knight. That decision is examined elsewhere (Chapter 39). There is no doubt that this left the investigating team disappointed and frustrated. They maintained that they had taken all the steps which were available to them to investigate the murder, and certainly at that date the officers in charge did not accept that mistakes had been made in respect of the activities of the team, or that wrong decisions had been made particularly in the very early days after the murder.**

28.2 It was decided by Mr Osland that there should be a review of this unsolved case. The provision for such a review appears in the AMIP guidelines to which much reference has been made. Section 8 deals with *"Reviews of unsolved cases"*. Section 8.1 reads as follows:-

> *"A review of undetected major crimes being investigated by AMIP will be instigated 10 weeks after the start of a live inquiry. Such a review may be started earlier if the Area Commander (Ops) considers it necessary. If the inquiry continues, a further review will be conducted every five weeks thereafter. Where a closed inquiry is reopened the review should be instigated five weeks after the start".*

28.3 There was a change in personnel of Commander (Operations) at the end of June 1993. Commander Gibson had until then been in that post, and shortly before the end of June he was replaced by Commander Blenkin. Mr Blenkin told us that in fact there was a swop of roles between himself and Mr Gibson, and he told the Inquiry that he took over his duties as Commander (Operations) for 3 Area on 28 or 29 June 1993. This was of course before the CPS had decided that the prosecution would not go ahead, but it was about nine weeks after the murder.

28.4 Mr Blenkin was not aware of the guidelines or of the positive duty imposed by those guidelines upon the Commander (Operations) to set up Reviews. Indeed Mr Blenkin told us that he had never set up or even heard of a Review taking place until this one was established. He told the Inquiry that he knew of only one other Review, namely that into the murder of Rachel Nickell, during his service. It is right therefore to indicate that a Review of an unsolved case was uncharted territory.

28.5 **There has been some disagreement as to who was responsible for setting up and establishing the terms of reference for the Stephen Lawrence Review. There is no doubt in our minds that the moving spirit in setting up the Review was Mr Osland. It has been suggested that Mr Blenkin was the architect of the terms of reference, but we accept his evidence that the terms of reference were in fact established by Mr Osland, and that Mr Blenkin's part in the establishment of the Review consisted of his acceptance, after consultation with Mr Osland, of the terms of reference proposed.**

28.6 We accept Mr Blenkin's evidence that at the relevant time he knew very little about the Stephen Lawrence investigation, so that it would have been difficult if not impossible for him to draft the terms of reference in respect of the Review. Mr Blenkin accepts that he signed the terms of reference, and that he handed them over to Detective Chief Superintendent John Barker, the officer appointed to conduct the Review. Mr Blenkin points out that the terms of reference are plainly signed by him as Commander (Operations) *"for DAC 3 Area"*.

He says that if these terms of reference had been of his own design he would simply have signed as Commander (Operations). Mr Blenkin says that he believes that Mr Osland went on leave at the relevant date, so that on 16 August 1993 he did indeed sign the terms of reference so that the Review could get underway.

28.7 Mr Barker was an experienced police officer. During his evidence he told us that he had occupied many important posts in the MPS. He has been head of the Flying Squad. He was Crime Adviser to the Deputy Assistant Commissioner for the North West Division. He has been involved in important criminal justice projects.

28.8 Mr Barker told us that he was the seventh officer to be approached to conduct this Review. Mr Ilsley confirmed that this was so, and that he had himself contacted six other police officers who had turned down the appointment before he approached Mr Barker. It is likely that Mr Barker regrets accepting the post, since both the Kent inquiry and this Inquiry have had no hesitation in roundly criticising the Review.

28.9 **The guidelines for Reviews are explicit. They appear in the detailed documentation available to the investigation. Coupled with the guidelines are the specific terms of reference to which we have already referred. There is no template for terms of reference, but it is apparent that the object of the Review is to conduct a detailed and searching investigation of all that has taken place. The guidelines require a detailed study of all the documentation relevant to the** *"scene and the police response"*. **There should be detailed verbal presentation from the SIO. The policy file should be studied with care. The guidelines (at paragraph 8.6) indicate that** *"The research into the documentation related to the main lines of inquiry should be an in depth study".*

28.10 The terms of reference speak for themselves. It must be said that they are in a sense negative and over retrospective. As Mr Kamlish pointed out the only positive progress proposed by the terms of reference is to *"Progress the investigation by endeavouring to identify persons responsible for the murder"*. Whatever else had been achieved it is obvious that the focus was upon the five suspects, and certainly by August 1993 they were the targets of the investigation. The other terms of reference required the reviewing officer to examine and evaluate what had happened in various fields. Although it is to be noted, for example, paragraph (vii) does require the reviewer to *"examine practices employed and make recommendations for the conduct of future investigations"*. The Terms of Reference of the Review are reproduced in full in the Appendices to this Report.

28.11 It should be noted that the terms of reference expressly required Mr Barker to liaise with the SIO, and to advise him of any matters which he considered might benefit the investigation. On the other hand the reviewing officer was expressly excluded by the terms of reference from taking any operational role in relation to the investigation. Mr Barker was required to forward a written interim report of his findings to the Deputy Assistant Commissioner 3 Area by 8 October 1993, and he was required to complete his report by 1 November 1993.

28.12 There was to be a major public demonstration on 16 October 1993, and the indications are that this had a bearing upon the dates by which the two reports were required to be submitted. Exactly what that bearing was is not easy to determine. One officer thought that a report made by 8 October might result in arrests, so that steam could be taken out of the demonstration because of those arrests. Another suggested consideration was that the report might indicate that matters had been satisfactorily carried out, with the same result.

28.13   There is a conflict of evidence as to what was said by Mr Blenkin when he gave the terms of reference to Mr Barker and launched the Review. Mr Barker has given several accounts of this aspect of the matter. It should be noted that he was the only officer summoned by the Kent inquiry who refused to answer questions at interview. He did submit written answers to questions posed by the Kent inquiry, and he has of course co-operated with this Inquiry and given a long statement and attended to give evidence and to face cross-examination. The reason for his refusal to be interviewed by the Kent officers is that he was advised by lawyers acting for the insurers of the Police Superintendents Association not to give evidence. Exactly why this decision was made and this advice given is obscure. It is however to Mr Barker's credit that he has remedied the deficiency by attending before us.

28.14   **The Kent inquiry focused upon the Review and produced conclusions which are condemnatory of the Review and its contents. Our own conclusions are similar to those of the Kent inquiry. Indeed during the hearing of Mr Barker's evidence we were convinced that Mr Barker produced a misleading and flawed Review, and that the Review was effectively indefensible. Mr Barker accepted that there were deficiencies, but by and large he still attempted before us to defend his Review.**

28.15   **We have to say that we found his evidence unconvincing and incredible in a number of important respects. However insofar as there is conflict between Mr Barker and Mr Blenkin as to what was said right at the start when the terms of reference were handed over we accept that there is room for misunderstanding.**

28.16   Mr Blenkin's evidence was that on 16 August he did tell Mr Barker that the Review was to be made into *"a particularly sensitive murder investigation"*. He also told Mr Barker that Mr Weeden and Mr Ilsley were somewhat unhappy that the Deputy Assistant Commissioner had decided on a Review of their investigation. Mr Blenkin says that Mr Weeden and Mr Ilsley had each expressed this view to him. Mr Blenkin says that he read through the terms of reference with Mr Barker and that he did not speak to him again. Mr Blenkin was specifically asked whether he had indicated in any way that Mr Barker should *"go rather gently with Mr Weeden so as not to cause him offence"*. He denied that he had made any such suggestion to Mr Barker. We do believe that what Mr Blenkin did say may have conveyed to Mr Barker the idea that he should not criticise the SIOs.

28.17   Mr Barker has said both in his statement and in evidence that Mr Blenkin did indeed warn him that the Review would have to be carried out with sensitivity, but he added that the purpose of this was *"to avoid undermining the position of Weeden who was still Senior Investigating Officer at the time"*. Mr Barker says that Mr Blenkin made it clear to him that the Review was not being welcomed by the investigation and stressed that the purpose was not to interview witnesses or take over the role of the SIO *"but merely to take an overview in accordance with the terms of reference"*. Mr Barker concluded that the clear implication was that he should ensure that the conduct of the Review was not to be heavy handed. The Review was to be constructive but was not to take the form of a complaints investigation.

28.18   Later in his statement and indeed in evidence Mr Barker said that he believed that his report was by necessity to be general in content, because he was conscious of the fact that in any subsequent criminal proceedings the existence of this document would be revealed and might be disclosable to the defence. It therefore seemed, said Mr Barker, to be inappropriate to record in the Review criticism of any specific officer which might be used by the defence by way of discrediting prosecution witnesses. Indeed Mr Barker says that he consulted with a lawyer involved in his other current activities in the MPS and that the lawyer told him that the Review might indeed be disclosable. Incidentally the AMIP guidelines confirm that this is so when in paragraph 8.8 they indicate that *"The report should be regarded as pertinent to the inquiry and may be the subject of debate in a court. It should therefore be filed with the case papers"*.

28.19 **It is apparent therefore that Mr Barker embarked on this Review with two inhibiting fetters imposed effectively by himself. First, in our opinion, he misinterpreted the words spoken to him by Mr Blenkin insofar as he believed that he should not undermine the confidence of the team and particularly the SIO. It is true that Mr Blenkin said that the Review was sensitive and that those involved had bristled to some extent when told that there would be a Review. But this is far from saying that a Review should be anything other than searching and hard hitting and critical, if the investigation showed that mistakes had been made.**

28.20 Furthermore it would be absurd to conclude that because the Review might be disclosable therefore things should be omitted from the written report or document which contained the conclusions of the Review. Mr Barker told the Inquiry that he had contemplated at one stage making some kind of second document which should be used for the eyes of the police service alone. He also said that there were substantial discussions during the course of the Review both with the SIO, Mr Weeden, and with Mr Ilsley and matters were examined and commented upon which were not reflected in the Review.

28.21 **Mr Barker says that he made notes and collected together documents which formed the basis of his written Review as the matter progressed. Presumably these discussions to which Mr Barker referred would be reflected in those notes. The box of documents which Mr Barker says that he handed over to the investigation team after the Review was completed has totally disappeared. So that there is no way of checking the background documents to see whether there was discussion of important issues and indeed deficiencies in the investigation which are not reflected in the written Review.**

28.22 Mr Barker was asked what was the relevance of disclosability if he had to produce an open-minded and unbiased report. He said that he *"took the view that if I was including in there confidential information and aspects perhaps that might be interpreted as procedural errors in a document that was then to come into the public domain that could jeopardise any future prosecution"*. He put the matter in another way during his questioning when he said, *"I am saying that if I was to criticise unduly the actions of officers in any procedural matter that might be construed later on to affect that prosecution so I had to be very guarded in doing it.*

28.23 **The implication here is both quite clear and unforgivable. It is that a senior officer in the MPS considered creating two versions of a Review document, the first to be disclosable to the defence and deliberately designed to mislead by omitting any adverse references to the investigation and the second to be an honest document indicating any flaws in the investigation which might be useful to the defence, but deliberately withheld from subsequent defence discovery.**

28.24 In the result Mr Barker produced an anodyne Review, such that those who read it and considered it uncritically might be lulled into a sense of false satisfaction as to what had taken place in the early weeks of the investigation. As was pointed out there is no significant criticism of any single decision made, and the general conclusion of the Review is that everything had been progressed professionally and efficiently and satisfactorily. There is mild comment about the failure to arrest in the very early days after the murder, involving the setting out of some of the pros and cons in that regard. In truth Mr Barker believed that the arrests should have taken place early on, but this view is nowhere reflected in the report and there is no out and out criticism of the decision that was made not to arrest, or of the absence of any record of that decision in the policy file. There is an indication that surveillance took place, but no detailed study and comment upon that plainly flawed operation which took place from 26/27 April onwards.

28.25 There are also factual errors in the Review, both in the interim document and in the final report. In its thrust the final Review matches closely the interim report which was delivered to the Deputy Assistant Commissioner by 8 October 1993.

28.26 As the Kent inquiry indicated, and as Counsel elicited before us, Mr Barker mistakenly said that upon arrest all the suspects except Gary Dobson had failed to answer questions. In fact Luke Knight also answered questions at interview, so that this statement by Mr Barker was simply wrong.

28.27 **Much more serious however is the complete failure of Mr Barker to deal satisfactorily with the whole topic of information that was reaching the Incident Room, and the failure satisfactorily to follow up that information and to deal with the potential witnesses revealed in the information which was reaching the investigation in the very early stages. The prime example of this is the situation in respect of James Grant. He was a vital potential link to those who may have been very close to this murder. The teams dealing with James Grant and investigation of those who had been involved with him was a most important aspect of the case ripe for investigation by the Review team. Yet Mr Barker's Review makes no reference to James Grant whatsoever, so that anybody reading the Review would think that Mr Barker had never heard of him. He referred to the fact that all the information coming to the investigation team was anonymous, and made express reference only to the two letters found near the Welcome Inn and in the telephone kiosk, which were in fact, as we now know, produced by the same author. James Grant's information was fundamental to this investigation and lack of any mention of it in the report is extraordinary. Mr Barker says that he took the view that it was inappropriate to refer to it in a document *"that could possibly come into the public domain"*.**

28.28 **Mr Barker did plainly in our opinion pull his punches, and he produced a report which simply gives no proper overview of the early days of the investigation, and which contains no criticism, although there was much to be criticised. Mr Barker accepts that this is so now, but he still appears to believe that the Review can be defended on the grounds that these matters of criticism and comment were discussed with Mr Osland and the investigation team and Mr Blenkin, and that it was therefore justifiable to leave them out of the Review for the reasons which Mr Barker has repeatedly given.**

28.29 **The result is that the Review and Mr Barker's *"observations"* at paragraph 2.3 started with the words *"The investigation has been progressed satisfactorily and all lines of inquiry correctly pursued"*. This is palpably not the true position, and Mr Barker ought to have uncovered the deficiencies and commented strongly upon them in any Review which was to be of value to those who saw it and who had the responsibility of making decisions as to the future conduct of this murder investigation.**

28.30 Mr Barker did rightly observe that liaison between the victim's family and the team had deteriorated at an early stage. He added that this affected communication and confidence between the two parties, and that the press and media relations were hampered by the involvement of active politically motivated groups although there is in fact no evidence of this. A substantial part of the written Review does deal with victim support and the liaison arrangements made for the family.

28.31 As was pointed out in cross-examination there are important factual mistakes in the account given by Mr Barker of the steps taken in connection with liaison. There is no purpose in reviewing that part of the questioning of Mr Barker in detail, but it does appear to us that Mr Barker was much too ready to accept what police officers told him in contrast to that which was indicated to him by Mr & Mrs Lawrence. Simply for example, Mr Barker indicates in his comments in paragraph 12.16 of his Review that it was *"appropriate to consider the events from Mr & Mrs Lawrence's perspective"*. But then he went on to indicate that *"their version is factually wrong on a number of important points and other events have been blurred or misinterpreted"*. One of the matters referred to states that *"they* [Mr & Mrs Lawrence] *do not remember being spoken to by Acting Inspector Little at the hospital, although the officer was present at the identification"*. That is a reference to the formal identification of Stephen Lawrence's body by Mr Lawrence which PC Gleason says took place at 00:02. That shows, as do other matters set out in paragraph 12.16, that Mr Barker was far too ready to accept what he was told by police officers, and not even to set out the disagreement that was evident as a result of his substantial interview with Mr & Mrs Lawrence which took place shortly before the interim report was produced.

28.32 **Another glaring example of misjudgement is set out in paragraph 12.17. There Mr Barker says, *"The enormity of the liaison officers' task in attempting to satisfy the thirst for information by the family, often generated by their solicitor, Imran Khan, which at times then became public knowledge, was beyond any previously experienced"*. It is not surprising that this comment is offensive to Mr & Mrs Lawrence. Why should they not have a thirst for information? Where is there any evidence that such sparse information as may have been given to the family or to their solicitor was ever leaked into the public domain by Mr & Mrs Lawrence or by Mr Khan? Where is there any evidence that their demands were other than reasonable? Mr Barker has simply taken the negative assertions of the team about this family and their solicitor and repeated them in emotive terms. He should not be surprised that we and those who heard the evidence regard this as another example of institutional racism at work. The collective failure to deal properly and sensitively with the family is a feature of the case. Mr Barker accepted without demur the criticisms of the family, who with their solicitor were regarded as troublesome and over-demanding. This was a flawed approach. Full warning was given to Mr Barker that he would be taxed with this criticism. By Notice dated 18 May 1998 Mr Kamlish, on behalf of Mr & Mrs Lawrence, indicated that *"The assertion that Mr & Mrs Lawrence allowed themselves to be 'used' and had 'myths implanted' in their minds by outside groups is false, patronising and insulting"*. Whatever his intentions may have been it is undeniable that the Review perpetuated the insensitive and patronising way in which the family and their solicitor had been regarded by junior officers, and in his turn by Mr Weeden. Mr Barker was in our view surely part of the collective failure which marks institutional racism.**

28.33 A further criticism of the Review, stressed by Mr Kamlish, is that anybody reading the Review would believe that nothing had taken place between 24 April and 7 May. In other words the Review is lacking in continuity, and there is little if any indication of the sequence of events and the processing of information that was taking place. A proper survey of the steps being taken, particularly involving the extensive use of DS Davidson during those vital days, might have indicated to Mr Barker that other steps should have been taken, such as the importation into the team of Mr Penstone or of other individuals more likely to be able to deal with the young and perhaps frightened and hostile witnesses on the Brook Estate.

28.34 In addition to other factual mistakes made it is also apparent that Mr Barker failed to indicate that there had been an identification parade on 7 May 1993. He says that a series of identification parades took place but he states positively that they were held between 13 May and 3 June. Thus an incomplete picture is given to any reader of the Review.

28.35 Furthermore there is no criticism whatsoever about the nature of the searches which were conducted at the houses of the suspects when they were arrested. A cursory reading of the relevant minutes should have alerted Mr Barker to that criticism which was indeed a serious one, and a matter which is of considerable concern to this Inquiry. Mr Barker says that he was more concerned with discussing this, and other matters, with Mr Weeden and getting his verbal view as to why such steps had not been taken. This in the opinion of the Inquiry defeats the object of the Review. Such matters should have been included in the written document.

28.36 Another example concerns the policy file. That document was plainly inadequately completed, yet Mr Barker makes no comment in that regard. He said to the Inquiry that his view was that he had discussed that with Mr Weeden, who was aware that other information could have been included in the policy file and that Mr Weeden accepted that it should have been more comprehensive. Yet there is no criticism of the policy file in the written Review, because, said Mr Barker, of its *"disclosable nature"*.

28.37 **The very nature of the document ultimately produced suggests that he collected information from doubtful sources, perhaps including DS Flook, in connection with some aspects of the relationship between Mr & Mrs Lawrence and Mr Khan and the investigation team. Furthermore his wholly mistaken approach in connection with his determination not to undermine the SIO and to consider disclosability as an inhibiting fact militated against a satisfactory report of any kind being produced.**

28.38 As was pointed out during Mr Barker's evidence before us there were many lines of inquiry still to be pursued by the team. Yet Mr Barker's conclusion as to examination of relevant lines of inquiry and decisions to curtail lines of inquiry are both short and incomplete. For example in connection with the decisions to curtail such lines all that is said is, *"All decisions to curtail lines of inquiry have been taken by the Senior Investigating Officer or his deputy. I am satisfied that a consistent approach has been adopted in these decisions"*. That is a somewhat meaningless sentence, and there is no indication of any proper examination of those lines which had in fact been curtailed.

28.39 **The Inquiry took the unusual step during the questioning of Mr Barker to indicate that in our view his value as a witness and his credibility in vital matters had been undermined, for reasons which would be obvious to anybody listening to his cross-examination. We adhere to this view. Some of the answers given and assertions made by Mr Barker, particularly in connection with his decision to produce a muted report, were in the full sense of the word incredible. Overall we also indicated that subject to further questioning by his own Counsel the Review *"was likely to be regarded by us as indefensible for what must be obvious reasons"*.**

28.40 When the Review was ultimately submitted to Mr Osland he produced a minute on 9 November 1993 which reiterated that Stephen Lawrence's murder was *"competently and sensitively investigated"*. He did refer to the recommendations made by Mr Barker, and indicated that these matters should be taken forward by Mr Blenkin at the regular meeting of Commanders (Operations). It is revealing that Mr Osland added after making various specific recommendations, that Mr Barker had commented *"on the confusion which surrounded some aspects of the initial action, but despite this I consider that the first officers on the scene were sensible, professional and compassionate"*. Even with this conclusion, as will have been observed, we are unable to agree.

28.41 **We have to criticise roundly and with emphasis the failures set out in connection with the production of the Barker Review. Mr Barker is plainly, as we have stressed, an experienced police officer. But on this occasion it is apparent to us that because of the self imposed shackles which he placed upon his consideration of the investigation he produced a flawed and an indefensible Review.**

RECEPTION AND RESPONSE TO THE REVIEW

28.42 The manner of the reception and response to the Review produced by Mr Barker is also a matter of concern. The Review was clearly initiated and *'owned'* by Mr Osland and, in normal circumstances, no-one else may well have been involved with its reception and examination, certainly not the Commissioner. However the Commissioner had become personally involved. As an example of his involvement his letter of 22 September 1993 to Mr Khan indicates *"May I assure you that I have taken a close personal interest in this case from the outset, and that I am absolutely determined that everything possible should be done to bring those responsible to justice"*. In the same letter the Commissioner indicates to Mr Khan that he has discussed the case with the All Party Parliamentary Group on Race and Community, with the Commission for Racial Equality, the Home Office and Mr Peter Bottomley MP. The same letter indicates to Mr Khan that *"a Review of the entire inquiry is being carried out by a senior officer ..... . I would not wish to comment on specific aspects of the investigation in advance of the Review being completed and even then we must of course be careful not to prejudice any future proceedings."* The Commissioner's involvement was therefore clear. He was aware of the Review and awaiting its completion.

28.43 Given the nature of the Lawrence investigation, the rarity of such a Review (in the MPS at least) and the level of external interest from the family and third parties, particularly Peter Bottomley MP, we would have expected the Review to be thoroughly scrutinised by those senior officers taking an active responsibility and interest in its production, in particular Mr Osland and the Commissioner himself. In addition it is not unreasonable to suppose that there would have been early communication with the family as to the contents of the Review, subject of course to any legal considerations.

28.44 In the event it appears from the evidence and documentation before us that not a single question was raised by any officer receiving the Review.

Some areas of the Review which generate obvious questions are set out below:

> Review para 7.4:
>
> *Fear and intimidation of witnesses underlines the overall lack of information and credible evidence in this case.*
>
> Query:
>
> What is the nature of this intimidation? Do we have any specific example? (Inquiry into this particular area may have led to a senior officer ordering the much earlier arrest of Clifford Norris).

Review para 8.1:

Where practicable the ACPO Guidelines and AMIP Manual of Guidance were followed ...... although the practicality of staffing the HOLMES Incident Room ..... was such that these levels could not be met.

Query:

What were the deficiencies, what was their impact? Could this not have been overcome?

Review paras 10.4 and 10.5:

Mr Weeden reviewed the decision not to search the Acourts' home or arrest them deciding that any advances to be gained had now passed and to continue the surveillance for known associates. These were not unreasonable decisions given the available information but we are bound to conclude that:

- *evidence may have been found connecting the Acourt brothers to the murder by an earlier search of their premises;*

- *an early arrest may have diffused the victim's family frustration of perceived police inactivity in not arresting people who are regarded as suspects from an early stage. The lack of a meaningful dialogue with the family compounded the issue reinforcing the myths implanted in Mr & Mrs Lawrence's minds by outside groups, of police disinterest in the crime;*

- *delaying the arrests may have enabled the suspects to establish alibis, albeit in the event that they refused to answer questions during interviews.*

Query:

This appears to be implicit criticism of the original decision. What were the grounds for the original decision and the advantages and disadvantages of arrest or delay, were the decisions well-founded?

Review paras 13.2-13.4:

Activity at the scene was hectic and information scarce. Four detective officers were present before midnight but attended the hospital only after DS Crampton arrived. PC Gleason was at the hospital unsupported until about midnight when Acting Inspector Little attended. He was then left on his own for a further two hours or more .... The officer had been attempting to debrief a highly emotional witness, reassure and answer questions from the Lawrence family, in addition to liaising with hospital staff particularly after Stephen had died. This placed considerable pressure on the officer who was acting also as a communication link with the scene. He responded well to the pressure. However a CID officer and a senior uniformed officer should have attended the hospital earlier to relieve this pressure, establish links with the family and attend to forensic evidence.

Query:

This implies some significant failures to respond adequately. What were their impact? Is this where the team lost initial touch with the family?

28.45 Mr Barker himself, responding to Mr Kamlish, indicated that whilst the Review, as he had accepted earlier, was toned down it should still have generated concern:

Q: *.... you had led the Commissioner and the Assistant Commissioner in your Review to the view that everything went fine with minor exceptions of staffing, family liaison. You did not criticise the investigating team on any important issue?*

A: *I think I did. I think I reflected to you on Thursday that, reading that (the Review) I wouldn't be totally comfortable as a senior officer with what I saw in it.*

Q: *You agree you have misled the Commissioner in one sense in believing there was no problem?*

A: *No, I did not mislead the Commissioner.*

28.46 Mr Osland, who clearly bears the prime responsibility in this regard, indicates that he circulated the Review to Mr Ilsley, Mr Weeden, Mr Blenkin and the Commissioner. However he convened no general discussion of the Review at Area level.

28.47 In response to Mr Chawla, on behalf of Mr Barker, Mr Osland did indicate that he discussed the interim report at some length with Mr Barker. Mr Osland was unhappy with the part of the Review relating to the timing of the arrest of the five suspects. He stated, *"On the one hand Mr Barker was saying these were not unreasonable decisions but then goes on to give three reasons why, in fact, a different decision should have been made"*. Nevertheless Mr Osland agreed that he did not explore this matter with Mr Barker or anyone else. Nothing was documented.

28.48 **Mr Osland indicated that in relation to the final report he had some discussion with Mr Blenkin relating to the recommendations, and that he discussed the Review with the Commissioner - *"not detailed discussions"* and *"sometime after"*. He stated that the Commissioner did not, to his knowledge, raise any specific questions. It is clear that the Commissioner saw the Review document on 17 November 1993. He endorses it *"Seen. Thank you."***

28.49 The general assertion has been that senior officers above Mr Barker were misled by the nature of the Review into believing that all was well with the investigation. However it is difficult to understand how senior officers involved in its reception could fail to raise at least some of the significant and obvious questions generated by the Review in order to satisfy themselves as to the adequacy of the investigation, and therefore of the adequacy and accuracy of the assurances that they might give to others based upon it. The fact is that they did fail to do so.

28.50 In relation to Mr Osland, but not to the Commissioner, an explanation is offered by Mr Barker. He testified that whilst his written report was toned down, an unexpurgated version of events was given verbally to Mr Osland, the investigation team and Mr Blenkin. This was not accepted by the supposed recipients and particularly by Mr Osland who stated *"No. I totally, absolutely deny that anything of that nature was passed on to me"*. There is no evidence to confirm Mr Barker's assertion. Thus we are left with the unedifying result that one senior officer is palpably wrong, and cannot be speaking the truth.

28.51 Within the document Mr Osland states *"I will visit the Lawrence family to inform them of the general findings after seeking advice of solicitors in view of the Lawrence family's threats to take legal action against the police."* The essence of that advice was that there was no legal objection to meeting Mr & Mrs Lawrence either before or after the Inquest. **But for whatever reason Mr Osland did not in fact communicate with the Lawrence family. Despite the recognised problem of lack of communication with the family in the initial investigation it was not until 3 May 1994, almost six months later, that the family were given information relating to the Review.**

28.52 **In the intervening period, November to May, there had been an exchange of correspondence starting on 14 January 1994 between Mr Khan, requesting among other things knowledge of the Review on behalf of the family, and the MPS solicitors. There was no mention of the Review in any of the MPS replies. Only when Mr Khan wrote directly to the Commissioner on 11 April 1994 was there a response. The Commissioner, to his credit, met with Mr & Mrs Lawrence and Mr Khan promptly on 20 April 1994 and the notes of the meeting show that in response to a direct request relating to the Review the Commissioner agreed that Assistant Commissioner Johnston would provide a summary of the internal Review** *"as far as this was possible without legal impediment"*.

28.53 According to the notes of the meeting on 3 May 1994, involving Mr Johnston, Mr Nove, Mr Weeden, Mr & Mrs Lawrence and Mr Khan, Mr Johnston *"briefly summarised the three conclusions of the Review by DCS Barker."* There are in fact no *"conclusions"* in the Review. The reference appears to be to three points in the *"overview"* (Section 2 of the Review) which, reproduced in full, state:

"•   *The investigation has been progressed satisfactorily and all lines of inquiry correctly pursued.*

   •   *Liaison between the victim's family and the investigation team deteriorated at an early stage. This affected communication and confidence between the two parties.*

   •   *Press and media relations were hampered by the involvement of active, politically motivated groups."*

28.54 **At the very least the paucity of information offered reflects a continuing lack of open and meaningful communication with the Lawrence family and their representatives. There is a lack of rigour in the reception of the review document first and foremost by Mr Osland, but also by those above him including the Commissioner himself.**

28.55 The issues are encapsulated in a question from the Chairman to the Commissioner (Part 2, Day 3, pages 303/4):-

Chairman: *"What still troubles me, Commissioner, is that it seems to me that that review is simply accepted at face value by everybody who saw it, not only yourself because you saw it, but particularly perhaps the senior officers who ought to have been responsible for those who made the vital wrong decisions in the early hours. I do not understand how they could have accepted it if they had been doing their job properly".*

Commissioner: *"If I may respond to that. With the benefit of hindsight, several years on I understand the force of what you are saying. .... Faced with a report that seemed to be diligent, that contained a number of recommendations that seemed to be acknowledging flaws, that is arguing for reform that had been carried out by a middle ranking officer, then I think that did lead people to take that report as it was set out. Now, I accept with the benefit of hindsight that can be challenged and people must make a judgment around that."*

28.56 Our judgment must be that at the time, without the need of hindsight, the Review should have generated questions from senior officers which may have uncovered the difficulties which have subsequently been revealed in this investigation.

28.57 **We have taken fully into account the Commissioner's comments on the Barker Review and particularly its reception set out in his letter of 12 January 1999, which was his reply to the Inquiry's letter giving him advance notice of some of the Inquiry's potential conclusions. The question and answer set out in Paragraph 55 above and most particularly the letter of 22 September 1993 and the notes of the meeting of 20 April 1994 show that the Commissioner was on this occasion involved in the reception of the Review. Ordinarily we accept that he would not have been expected personally to have been involved.**

28.58 It remains to comment shortly upon the evidence given in general terms by Commander Blenkin. We have already dealt with his part in the initial stages and the launching of the Barker Review. Other than that Mr Blenkin played very little part in the Stephen Lawrence investigation. It is somewhat surprising to learn that the Commander (Operations) did not have responsibility in the line of command from himself downwards to the Chief Superintendents. The Chief Superintendents reported and were responsible directly to the Deputy Assistant Commissioner in the established lines of command as they were in 1993.

28.59 An unfortunate aspect of the evidence of Mr Blenkin concerned his confrontation with the somewhat pungent views expressed by Mr Osland at the Kent inquiry as to Mr Blenkin's capabilities and faults. Mr Osland had expressed himself strongly in this respect, and had indicated that Mr Blenkin's main characteristic was that he would unquestionably side with "the troops". This attitude and indeed the criticisms made orally by Mr Osland to the Kent inquiry were considerably modified by him before us. Through Mr Gompertz Mr Osland accepted that the comments he made to the Kent inquiry were exaggerated and required alteration. Mr Osland and all members of this Inquiry accept that Mr Blenkin was an efficient officer.

28.60 Mr Blenkin, as with other officers before him, used the word "coloured" and was surprised that this expression was not acceptable to describe those from minority ethnic communities. It is evident that a lack of racism awareness and training extends from the bottom to the top of the MPS.

28.61 **Our overall conclusion is that Mr Barker's review must be condemned. We do not find evidence that its inadequacies were the result of corruption or collusion. Mr Barker's unquestioning acceptance and repetition of the criticisms of the Lawrence family and their solicitor are to be deplored. Others took the review *"as it was set out"*, in the Commissioner's words, and all allowed themselves to be misled.**

CHAPTER TWENTY-NINE

DEPUTY ASSISTANT COMMISSIONER DAVID OSLAND

29.1 Deputy Assistant Commissioner David Osland gave evidence for nearly two days before this Inquiry. He joined the police force in 1957 and became Deputy Assistant Commissioner for 3 Area in 1989. Mr Osland retired from the police service in March 1994. It is of some significance that Mr Osland had throughout his service been a uniformed officer. He said more than once that he had little experience of detective work, and he had never served in the CID.

29.2 In 1993 there were two Commanders serving under him. Mr Osland was somewhat confused about the exact dates of the service of the Commanders. It appears that Mr Adams was Commander (Support) until 4 May 1993. Mr Gibson was Commander (Operations) until he handed over to Mr Blenkin at the end of June 1993. Mr Gibson has not been called to give evidence. Mr Adams' part in the Stephen Lawrence investigation is separately considered. Mr Blenkin was Commander (Operations) at the time of the initiation of the Barker Review.

29.3 There is some doubt about the exact nature of the relevant chain of command in 3 Area at the relevant time. Mr Osland appears to suggest that the relevant hierarchy would have been himself at the top, then Mr Gibson/Mr Blenkin, then Detective Chief Superintendent Ilsley, then Detective Superintendent Weeden. Mr Blenkin, in his evidence, indicated that in fact he was not a direct link between the Detective Chief Superintendent and Mr Osland. This would mean that Mr Ilsley was responsible directly to Mr Osland, without the intervening chain in the line of command of Mr Blenkin. There is a strange confusion between the witnesses. The chain and line of command and control must always be clearly established otherwise confusion may reign. Furthermore the inactivity evident in command and control terms of the Commander (Ops), evident from the statement of Mr Gibson which was read to the Inquiry, may be symptomatic of the operation of the CID as a *"force within a force"* without adequate and necessary senior supervision.

29.4 **When asked what his own role and responsibility was as Deputy Assistant Commissioner in 3 Area Mr Osland said, *"The totality of my role really was this was where the buck stopped. My role was total responsibility for all operational and administrative activities that took place on the Area".***

29.5 Mr Osland gave interesting thumbnail assessments of those who served under him. He said that Mr Weeden *"was more considered in his approach"* while Mr Crampton was *"rather sharper and quicker and more spontaneous"*. As to Mr Ilsley, Mr Osland said that he had excellent interpersonal skills, that he was quick-witted, and that he would defend his troops to the hilt. Mr Osland said that Mr Ilsley had a very good record of major incident investigations, but he had a measure of weakness in his ability to manage resources or to grasp broad concepts.

29.6 As to the staffing of the Stephen Lawrence team Mr Osland's general view was that he did not believe, in the circumstances prevailing, that the investigation was understaffed. In respect of the *"totality of the manpower"* his understanding was that the staffing levels were adequate. He stressed that the MPS was of course in general terms always seeking more staff, but he believed that within the terms of the AMIP guidelines, taking everything into account, the investigation was as well if not better provided from the point of view of men than other investigations.

29.7 Mr Osland agreed that there was constant complaint across the Area about the shortage of manpower in general terms, but he said that nobody came to him and asked for more manpower for the Stephen Lawrence investigation. By the same token Mr Osland agreed that he had not himself asked the senior officers actually conducting the investigation whether they were satisfied with the manpower provided. Everybody simply accepted that there was little point in asking for more officers, since the general experience was that even in terms of the AMIP guidelines for the various categories of crime staffing would be uncomfortably low, but that this was in tune with the general situation as to the supply of manpower in the MPS. This was a complacent attitude. If more officers were truly needed Mr Ilsley should have asked for them, and the Commanders should have tried to obtain them.

29.8 The concern about under resourcing in general was a concern amongst the whole of the MPS, said Mr Osland. The Service had, in common with many organisations, been cash limited for years, and in the end *"our job was to manage with what we were given and that's what we did"*.

29.9 Mr Osland told us that he was in reasonably close touch with the Stephen Lawrence investigation after the first weekend following the murder. He would visit the Incident Room regularly, and he was closely in touch with Mr Ilsley.

29.10 Mr Osland had full responsibility for the whole of the MPS activity in south east London. Although he indicated that he kept fairly closely in touch with the Stephen Lawrence investigation, because it was of course a very high profile case from the start, Mr Osland also stressed on many occasions that he was not directly responsible for what happened in terms of the investigation itself. He rightly indicated that the relevant decisions as to arrest, and any other tactical matters, were exclusively for the SIO acting either on his own or in consultation with his Detective Chief Superintendent.

29.11 **It would be unrealistic to suggest that the Deputy Assistant Commissioner could be expected to bear responsibility for decisions on the ground in respect of the various investigations in progress, otherwise than as the person ultimately responsible for everything that took place in 3 Area. In this connection Mr Osland was asked, by Mr Lawson, whether there were major decisions made in connection with the Stephen Lawrence investigation with which he now disagreed. He said that he did not disagree with any of the decisions made, but he did indicate that *"On the decision to charge ...... to arrest and charge on the first occasion I felt that the evidence was weak"*. Mr Lawson pointed out that Mr Osland seemed perhaps to be confusing considerations of arrest with considerations of charge.**

29.12 Mr Osland said, when interviewed by Kent, that he was told that *"certain evidence was available that possibly indicated some suspects, but at that stage the evidence was by no means sufficient to justify an arrest"*. Later still, in a sustained cross-examination, Mr Osland was taken to task about his views as to grounds upon which an arrest can be made. It is plain that on several occasions Mr Osland confused evidence with information, and he accepted that he was at least guilty of careless wording in answers that he had given to Kent and indeed in answers given before this Inquiry. At one stage Mr Osland said *"My view is that if you are moving towards the position where reasonable suspicion exists there had to be something to support the suspicion and what supports the suspicion is evidence or facts"*. Furthermore Mr Osland had in his answers to Kent said that the matter was one of fine judgment to be made by those involved and that the question was, *"Do you make an arrest without the power to do so in order to secure evidence"*.

29.13 Mr Osland denied that he was suggesting that there was some merit in unlawful arrest. There was undoubtedly a measure of confusion in his mind since he said that he did *"realise that there is a view that there was sufficient evidence to arouse reasonable suspicion"*. This is to confuse evidence with information. He also said that *"information is what is supplied to police and it is converted into evidence through the work of the police in establishing the link with the crime"*. That again is strictly an inaccurate summary of the difference between information and evidence.

29.14 **Mr Osland was at pains to stress that he was not himself involved in the decision as to arrest. On the other hand it is vital that every police officer of whatever rank fully understands the grounds upon which an arrest can be made. It must be a matter of concern and criticism that such senior officers as Mr Osland and Mr Weeden seemed to lack a clear knowledge of basic police powers. It is difficult to see how they could make rational judgments on whether an early arrest should have taken place or not if they were possessed of such muddled thinking in relation to police powers in that context.**

29.15 Mr Osland never met Mr & Mrs Lawrence. It is a feature of this case that so many senior officers seem to have stood aloof from Mr & Mrs Lawrence, for various reasons. Mr Osland realised that the relationship between the police and Mr & Mrs Lawrence *"was deteriorating from the outset"*. By November 1993 he said that the relationship was so bad that if he had seen the Lawrence family there would have been little that he could have said that they would have believed. Furthermore shortly before the Inquest was to start in 1993 Mr Osland held off because he said that he had advice from solicitors which suggested that some *"legal consequences"* might develop from a meeting which would be unfortunate. The solicitors' advice in fact clearly states *"I do not think there is any legal objection to your meeting the Lawrence family before or after the Inquest."* His distancing himself from the family was simply a matter of his own choice.

29.16 Mr Osland said that normally family liaison was successful, in his experience. He said that he had never known a family liaison which had deteriorated as this one did. When asked what he believed was the problem Mr Osland said that when the media reporting indicated that there were cracks beginning to appear in the family liaison he started to ask questions. He was told by his officers that the liaison was extremely difficult and that it was not working out because of the problems which the officers were having with the Lawrence family and their advisers and friends. He never heard the other side of the story.

29.17 **On 8 September 1993 Mr Osland wrote an internal note for the Commissioner which indicated that he was *"totally satisfied that the Lawrence family have received a professional, sensitive and sympathetic service from police"*. He explained this by saying that it seemed to him that things were going wrong predominantly because of what was happening in the Lawrence household. Much later on, after Mr Osland retired, it is evident that he allowed his views about Mr & Mrs Lawrence and in particular Mr Khan, to develop. He wrote letters to newspapers, and provided information for public dissemination, which were highly critical of Mr & Mrs Lawrence and those around them. Such views were necessarily unbalanced, given his lack of contact with the Lawrence family.**

29.18 **Mr Osland has clearly accepted what he was told by officers involved in the investigation about the activities in the Lawrence household without exercising necessary objectivity. He has simply adopted the adverse views of officers involved in the investigation as to the attitude of Mr & Mrs Lawrence's supporters and of their solicitor without question and without the necessary balance that would have been** provided had he chosen to speak directly to the family in order both to obtain their views and to seek to address the overall problem. He now accepts that some of the problems of the family liaison were attributable to the police themselves, but he is not prepared to accept total blame in this respect. This is another example of a senior officer seeing a problem but failing to address it, and of failure of all those involved with Mr & Mrs Lawrence properly to deal with family liaison. Because of his unquestioning acceptance and repetition, even in the public arena, of the myths about family liaison, Mr Osland should not be surprised that some who heard his evidence might regard this as another example of institutional racism at work. Collectively the officers involved failed to treat the family and their solicitor appropriately and sensitively. The evidence that this is so is plain.

29.19 **It is a feature of the family liaison debacle in this case that senior officers do not appear to have got to grips with the matter thoroughly and satisfactorily from early on when the relationship was obviously deteriorating. It does appear that in common with others Mr Osland was too ready simply to allow the matter to drift and to accept what was passed on to him and to take no personal initiative in order to see that matters were corrected. The problem was not insoluble. Mr Nove demonstrated during the second investigation that appropriate and professional liaison resulted in open dialogue.**

29.20 Mr Philpott did early on in the proceedings offer two trained and perhaps more suitable officers for the role of family liaison. Whether these officers would have been more satisfactory than those actually allotted to the task it is impossible to say. But it is apparent to the Inquiry that the whole question of family liaison was allowed to deteriorate, with much too much stress being laid upon the possible blame to be attached to Mr & Mrs Lawrence's family and supporters and their solicitor. It is wholly incumbent upon the police to make sure that family liaison is sympathetic and satisfactory, whatever the circumstances.

29.21 **In connection with the vital decision whether or not an arrest should have been made in the first two or three days after the murder Mr Osland's evidence was unsatisfactory. He said that he did discuss the matter with Mr Ilsley and he said that he *"listened to the advice of Ilsley on this"*. But he said to Kent that *"one thing that sticks in my mind is that there was just not sufficient evidence to arrest. If an arrest was made it would be one that was made because the case was highly political, highly sensitive, and it would placate public opinion at an early stage if the arrests were made"*. When it was pointed out by Kent that the grounds for arrest on 7 May were much the same as had in fact existed early on, Mr Osland said that the conclusion that he would draw was that it might well be that pressure to arrest became so intolerable that it was decided to arrest on the same grounds as had existed during the first weekend. When Mr Osland was asked whether he appreciated that there were really from within the first 48 hours quite sufficient grounds to justify arrest his answer was that *"his involvement in those early times was not close enough to offer an opinion"*.**

29.22 **The difficulty which faces us is that Mr Osland was at pains to say that he was involved in almost daily visits to the Incident Room and conversation with Mr Ilsley in particular, yet he distanced himself from any decision made on the ground by the SIO, indicating that any tactical decision in connection with arrest and other steps to be taken in the investigation were not for him to make.**

29.23 When pressed by Mr Lawson as to whether or not Mr Osland regarded it as surprising that nobody consulted him in the early days over the most vital decision in the case, he said that he would not have objected to being disturbed over the weekend for such consultation, but that *"with a decision like this, this is a matter that the officer in command or the SIO would have discussed with Mr Ilsley and the two of them would have made the decision. They would have notified me I suspect of a decision to arrest but not notified me of a decision not to arrest".*

29.24 We accept that the responsibility for making a decision as to arrest lies with the SIO and the officers close to the investigation. Mr Osland's problem seems to us to be that he indicates close contact with the investigation, and yet he distances himself from the decisions made. In his own words, *"Because I had a hands on approach it does not mean that I was involved in the decision making. It was not my function, not my role to make decisions on arrest. I did express the view at the time when I was told that arrests were going to be made that I thought the evidence was weak".* Mr Osland's interview with Kent confirms a more than usual degree of involvement. In his interview he stated: " *... I do recall, as far as this particular case is concerned, that as there was pressure for early arrests, they* [Mr Weeden and Mr Ilsley] *came to me with their opinion that there was insufficient evidence to make an early arrest and when they came to me and said that arrests were to be made, my own views were that although I didn't have all the details it did seem a bit thin".*

29.25 **This does suggest personal input into the ultimate decision as to arrest, which is difficult to reconcile with Mr Osland's view that he was not directly involved. Mr Osland did accept that external pressures might have played their part in the ultimate decision, although he was in no position to comment on what in the end did affect the minds of Mr Weeden and perhaps of Mr Ilsley himself.**

29.26 **An important part of Mr Osland's evidence concerned the Barker Review. That Review was commissioned by Mr Osland himself. The primary reason for the Review was, said Mr Osland, to progress the investigation. Mr Osland told us that he made it quite clear at the beginning when talking to Mr Barker that this was the primary purpose of the exercise. He also pointed out to Mr Barker how important family liaison was; and because that appeared to have broken down the Review must help to find out why that situation had developed in order to try to improve matters. Mr Osland said to us that it was possible that Mr Barker came to the conclusion that family liaison was as important or maybe even more important than progressing the investigation. In one sense that conclusion is echoed in the nature of the ultimate Review produced by Mr Barker.**

29.27 Everybody agrees that in spite of the time limit and the guidelines set out in the AMIP policy this was probably the first Review that had ever taken place in 3 Area, so that Mr Osland and Mr Barker were sailing in uncharted waters. To the Kent officers he said that his main concern was to *"try and reassure myself first that there were no errors, no mistakes, because of the fact that .... I had no detective experience. I needed somebody to reassure me that this lack of experience, lack of knowledge on my part was not hiding problems for us for the future".* Mr Osland said that this attitude was conveyed to Mr Barker.

29.28 Mr Osland says that he made the decision to hold the Review and that he had problems in finding somebody to undertake it. In fact the actual telephoning to the six officers who would not accept the appointment was done by Mr Ilsley. Mr Ilsley also told us that he ultimately contacted Mr Barker, who agreed to undertake the Review. Mr Osland says that his Deputy Assistant Commissioner colleagues could not spare a Detective Chief Superintendent, so that he went eventually to Headquarters in an endeavour to find a man of the necessary quality to perform the task. According to Mr Osland Mr Barker came as a result of a recommendation by Assistant Commissioner William Taylor. Mr Osland believed that Mr Barker was going to undertake the Review full-time, although it is apparent from Mr Barker's evidence that he was only able to give part-time attention to the Review.

29.29 Mr Osland said, in answer to Mr Lawson, that while he hoped to obtain reassurance from the Review he also hoped that there would be constructive suggestions or proposals as to what might be done to further the investigation itself. Mr Osland told the Kent officers that his directive from the outset was that this Review should be carried out effectively, efficiently and sensitively, and he added that he supposed that he was hoping that the Review would justify the view that he had taken from the beginning namely *"that what we had done was right"*. He hoped that the Review would recognise all the intensive and dedicated work that had been done. He added that if there were problems the Review would find them out and make recommendations for the future.

29.30 Mr Osland saw both the interim report and the final report. Mr Barker came to see Mr Osland with the interim report and discussed it with him. There was no later discussion because Mr Osland said that the final report was essentially the same as the interim report. His reaction to the Review was a mixture of reassurance and disappointment. Reassurance because Mr Barker was saying that basically the investigation seemed to have gone along the right lines and that he could find no major criticism of what was happening, and disappointment because he felt that *"the methodology was not clearly set out"*. However there is no evidence that he sought to address his concerns over the methodology, or any other issue, with Mr Barker at the interim report stage. Again all the indications are that the Review was simply accepted without question.

29.31 **Mr Osland denied that any instructions had ever been given to Mr Barker to pull his punches in the Review, and he says that Mr Barker did not, as Mr Barker alleges, communicate to him criticisms which had not been included in the report. Mr Osland roundly denied that his interest was otherwise than to get to the truth. He says that he would not have tolerated any sort of cover up or whitewash, and if in fact Mr Barker had told him that there were criticisms which were not disclosed to him he would have insisted that they were contained in the report.**

29.32 Mr Osland said that he overheard conversations between officers in which it was made quite clear that they did not think highly of the Review, but he appears simply to have accepted Mr Barker's conclusions, as did everybody else involved, without any truly critical appraisal of the Review itself.

29.33 Mr Osland was at a disadvantage in this respect. Although we would have expected Mr Osland to have heard of James Grant on his visits to the Incident Room he told us that he had never heard the name James Grant in the whole course of the investigation, so that he was in no position personally to challenge the statement in Mr Barker's Review that all the information which had been received by the investigation team was anonymous.

29.34 Mr Osland said that he was in effect lulled into a sense of false security and satisfaction by the Review. He asked Mr Blenkin to take forward the recommendations made together with his fellow Commanders. Mr Osland did himself forward the Review to the Assistant Commissioner and to the Commissioner, indicating that by and large the Review reflected a satisfactory investigation as a result of an accurate and thorough Review by Mr Barker.

29.35 **Mr Osland accepts now that the Review was deficient and that the reassurance given to him and to others by the Review was unjustified. Mainly perhaps this is a criticism of Mr Barker, but uncritical acceptance of the Review does have to be laid at the door of senior officers. Mr Osland seems to have been unprepared to grasp the nettle and to question the conclusions or to seek further details. Through Mr Osland the Commissioner saw the Review and they personally discussed it, again without any** specific questions being raised. **Furthermore Mr Osland expressly reported to the Commissioner that the SIO routinely visited the family and advisers until the family's demands became so great that the SIO was *"eventually insulated from them"*. This is palpably not a true picture, as we know from the evidence of the SIO himself.**

29.36 There is no doubt, as Mr Kamlish elicited early in his cross-examination, that Mr Osland's position was that as far as he was concerned things were going well, even before the Review reassured him, except that he had to accept that no satisfactory result had been achieved by the investigation team.

29.37 We accept that Mr Osland did not know the details of the steps taken by the investigation team. For example he accepted in evidence before us that although he attended the Incident Room almost daily he had no detailed knowledge of what the surveillance produced or in particular failed to produce. Even before us Mr Osland appeared to be ignorant of the plastic bags which had left 102 Bournbrook Road during the surveillance. When this was pointed out to him he said, *"I must say in fairness to my own position that my role as the Area Deputy Assistant Commissioner was somewhat above the general level of these sort of activities"*. He was interested and inquired about trends, but not about details.

29.38 **Mr Osland's reaction to statements made by or on behalf of Mr & Mrs Lawrence in connection with the police have been most unfortunate and wounding to them. As early as 8 September 1993 Mr Osland wrote a note to the Commissioner indicating that he and others felt that their patience was *"wearing thin"* on 3 Area not only with the Lawrence family and their representatives, but also with self-appointed public and media commentators. The note continued, *"I am totally satisfied that the Lawrence family have received a professional, sensitive and sympathetic service from the police"*.**

29.39 When Mr Osland retired he wrote letters to the newspapers and gave an interview to The 'Croydon Advertiser' in which he roundly criticised claims said to have been made by Mr & Mrs Lawrence that the murder investigation had been hampered by racism amongst the police officers involved. Mr Osland referred to the PCA report, which was published in December 1997, which made stinging criticism of the police investigation, but which did say that the murder investigation had not been affected by racism. Mr Osland apparently said to the newspaper that his advice to the officers concerned would be that they should consider legal action. *"The Lawrences seem happy to accept the findings of the report where it suits them but not where it does not"*.

29.40 **These expressions made by Mr Osland, compounded by other letters to the press in 1997, are most regrettable. Mr Osland is of course entitled as a private citizen to say what he wishes, but his later attitude does reflect uncomfortably upon his approach and reaction to the activities of the representatives of Mr & Mrs Lawrence in 1993. He said positively then that the Lawrence family had received a professional, sensitive and sympathetic service from the police, although he was fully conscious that the family liaison had broken down early on. In evidence before us Mr Osland did say that he accepted that Mr & Mrs Lawrence had grounds for criticising the police, and that his 1997 reaction was simply because of public statements by Mr & Mrs Lawrence alleging that his police officers had been guilty of racism.**

29.41 Mr Osland accepted in evidence that there had been errors and omissions and mistakes made by the MPS. He added that Mr & Mrs Lawrence were entitled to an apology from the MPS. Mr Osland says that from the start he had total sympathy and compassion for the Lawrence family, but he could not bring himself latterly to condone the comments which were being made by Mr & Mrs Lawrence after the PCA report had been made. It is difficult to reconcile this assertion with his avowal of his *"patience wearing thin"* as early as September 1993 and the fact that he never met Mr & Mrs Lawrence. **Mr Osland did say before this Inquiry that he made it clear that he accepted that Mr & Mrs Lawrence had been let down by 3 Area, and he apologised certainly on behalf of his own command to Mr & Mrs Lawrence.**

29.42 **It is regrettable that Mr Osland's later pronouncements and attitude have understandably exacerbated the feelings of Mr & Mrs Lawrence towards the police which are expressed so pungently and so repeatedly by them and those who surround them.**

29.43 Part of Mr Kamlish's cross-examination of Mr Osland involved an examination of Mr Osland's annual report made in 1993 in connection with 3 Area activities in 1992. The report confirms the unhappy fact that Plumstead and Greenwich Divisions show the highest racist incident and crime rate in the MPS. It is of significance that the only Racial Incident Unit in 3 Area is situated in Plumstead and staffed by a minimal complement of officers. There is perhaps no need to enlarge upon Mr Osland's evidence in this regard.

29.44 A further area of cross-examination by Mr Kamlish involved Mr Osland's perception as to the problems arising from family liaison and the presence of Mr Khan and the other groups present at Mr & Mrs Lawrence's home. Mr Osland's view was that the family liaison system was always intended to be an informal system whereby police officers worked closely on an individual basis with victims and their families. It was his belief, plainly fuelled by information given to him by officers involved in the investigation, that his officers had been *"thrown into an unfamiliar situation"* which was to some extent intimidating and which impacted on the exchange of information which should normally be expected.

29.45 **Certainly some of the information given to Mr Osland about the nature of the relationship between the police and Mr & Mrs Lawrence was inaccurate or misinterpreted. As we have stressed more than once in this Report it is in any event the responsibility of the police to overcome problems such as those which were perceived by some of the officers involved. Any family is entitled to be represented by a solicitor and to have in their home anybody they wish. The police have to accept this, and if those involved are not capable at once of reaching a healthy relationship then steps must be taken positively and quickly to ensure that this is achieved.**

29.46 In summary it must be said that the result of questioning by Mr Lawson and Mr Kamlish was that this Inquiry is satisfied that Mr Osland should bear no direct personal responsibility for the mistaken decisions made in the early days after Stephen Lawrence's murder. Furthermore any flaws in the processing of information and the investigation of potential witnesses cannot be laid at the door of Mr Osland directly. Nor indeed was he himself immediately responsible for the breakdown in the family liaison arrangements.

29.47 **On the other hand it can and must be said that Mr Osland was much too ready to accept that things were going satisfactorily, both in respect of the investigation of the crime and in connection with the arrangements for family liaison. Also once the Barker Review was established Mr Osland was too ready uncritically to accept what Mr Barker reported, and to examine Mr Barker's conclusions and his factual findings without penetrating criticism.**

29.48 In answer to Mr Doyle, on behalf of the SIOs, Mr Osland indicated that his main regret, while reflecting upon the past, is that he *"did not look as deeply into things"* as he would now. He agreed that Mr Weeden was about to retire in 1993, but that he stayed on in order to try to assist in resolving the Stephen Lawrence murder. Mr Doyle also stressed that there was very little contact between Mr Osland and Mr Weeden himself, and that a considerable amount of the contact between Mr Osland and the Incident Room was with Mr Flook and not with Mr Weeden.

29.49 **Mr Doyle stressed that there were no realistic prospects of getting more men in order to relieve Mr Flook from his five-fold responsibilities, or to increase the power of the team investigating the Stephen Lawrence murder. Mr Osland accepted that there was really *"nowhere else for this team to go"* in connection with increasing its resources. The MPS simply had to get used to doing its task with what was available. There was little purpose in applying for more men since everybody knew that providing more manpower for any particular investigation simply meant taking it away from other areas of policing. It must be said that it was plainly in Mr Osland's power to have diverted resources to this investigation. There is no evidence that this step was contemplated. No wonder Mr & Mrs Lawrence feel that the murder of their son was not given the priority that it deserved.**

29.50 **Mr Osland accepted that Mr Ilsley made a significant contribution to persuading the MPS that there should be a permanent AMIP squad which provided a larger and better trained source from which teams could be produced for major investigations. In 1993 this system did not exist.**

29.51 Mr Osland accepted, when questioned by Mr Doyle about Mr Barker's Review, that he had not considered having a round table discussion with the SIO in order to cast a combined critical eye over the unsatisfactory and anodyne Review which Mr Barker produced.

29.52 Mr Osland had no direct contact with Duwayne Brooks. Mr Osland pointed out that his task was to manage relationships with community leaders rather than with individuals, and that the responsibility for managing the relationship with Mr Brooks lay strictly at a lower level. Mr Osland was wholly unaware of the criticisms made much later by some of the junior officers of Mr Brooks' attitude, since by the time the CPS was investigating the prosecution of Mr Brooks Mr Osland had retired.

29.53 **Our impression of Mr Osland in connection with his relationship with the London Borough of Greenwich was favourable. Mr Panton asked a number of questions in this regard, and it was evident to us that Mr Osland did his best to ensure that there was a good relationship with the Borough and with GACARA, the organisation partly funded by the London Borough of Greenwich.**

29.54 **Part of Mr Panton's questioning concerned the lack of intelligence available to the police in connection with the activities of people such as the suspects living on the Brook Estate. The valid suggestion was made that liaison with the local organisations and improvement of intelligence gathering might well have assisted in the early stages of the investigation of Stephen Lawrence's murder.**

29.55 Mr Osland accepted, both in answer to Mr Panton and Mr Yearwood, that there did exist in 1993, and today, a perception that black people are worse treated and more likely to be stopped and searched than white people. He stressed however, on more than one occasion, that it was necessary to look at the *"totality of interactions between police officers and members of the public".* He said that there was undoubtedly room for dissatisfaction in a minority of cases.

29.56 Mr Osland readily accepted that there existed and still exist clear differences of perception in the black community which make that community distrustful of the police in their investigation of racist incidents and attacks. He conceded that people could see what the police do often in a different light than that observed by the police themselves. Mr Osland accepted that it was part of the job of the police to try to inform people and to listen to what they have to say and to bring the two sides closer together without misapprehension and misperception.

29.57 In connection with "stop and search" Mr Osland accepted, from Mr Yearwood, that the figures show an unhappy situation and state of affairs both in Plumstead and elsewhere. He accepted that this was a serious issue which needed to be investigated and it was his memory that during his service an inquiry was set up to look into the whole matter.

29.58 **It has not been suggested that Mr Osland was in any way involved in any collusion or corruption to hold back in connection with the advancement of the investigation of Stephen Lawrence's murder. There would without doubt be no justification for any such suggestion against Mr Osland. He had faults in connection with the Stephen Lawrence murder investigation and in particular the relationship with the family which were attributable to his readiness to accept without qualification or inquiry that which was told to him by his own officers, and by Mr Barker in connection with the unfortunate and flawed Review. A more critical examination of that Review would have revealed its failure. Whether that would have led to any different result in the end is of course doubtful. But at least the situation would not have been accepted as satisfactory when plainly it was not.**

CHAPTER THIRTY

ASSISTANT COMMISSIONER IAN JOHNSTON

30.1 Mr Johnston is an Assistant Commissioner of the Metropolitan Police. In connection with the Stephen Lawrence investigation he became involved in March 1994, upon his appointment to be Assistant Commissioner for one of the five new Areas designated after the Area structure was reformed.

30.2 **At the outset of Mr Johnston's evidence he indicated that he wished to make a statement before his evidence began. The Inquiry had been given some notice of this request and of course acceded to Mr Johnston's wish. Thereupon, in the presence of Mr Lawrence, Mr Johnston made an abject apology for the failures of the MPS in connection with the Stephen Lawrence murder. Unfortunately Mrs Lawrence was not present, since the represented parties had no notice of what was to take place until the morning of 17 June 1998.**

30.3 **The full terms of the apology appear in the Appendices to this Report. It is right to indicate that the apology was full and wholly unconditional. Mr Johnston, on his own behalf, and expressly on behalf of Sir Paul Condon, the Commissioner, indicated deep regret that the police had failed Mr & Mrs Lawrence and indeed the community and said that they hoped that eventually they would be forgiven by Mr & Mrs Lawrence.**

30.4 Thereafter Mr Johnston's evidence was in a sense something of an anticlimax. But it was plainly his intention to indicate acceptance of the gross shortcomings of the investigation and roundly to state that it was the intention of the MPS to learn all possible lessons from this tragic case.

30.5 As to racism in the police service Mr Johnston was aware that nobody in this case suggests that any officer was guilty of overt racism. That is simply not the nature of the complaint made by Mr & Mrs Lawrence. The heart of their complaint is that the investigation was skewed and slowed down by racism, and that there has been consistent insensitivity to Mr & Mrs Lawrence, and that they have been patronised. Mr Johnston accepts that in this context the question of racism is sophisticated and elusive. He referred to a perceptive paper submitted by Dr Robin Oakley.

30.6 **Mr Johnston appreciates that a proper assessment of racism can be based upon** *"whether individuals constantly assess, reassess the impact that they are having on others and adjust their behaviour anticipating that perceptions of racism may arise from their behaviour".*

30.7 Mr Johnston indicated that advances are being made in connection with training as to racism awareness and the conduct of racist incidents. Again it seems to us purposeless to set out in summary form what Mr Johnston said. All these matters require the closest attention by the MPS, as Mr Johnston plainly accepts.

30.8 It should be noted that during his evidence Mr Johnston indicated that he had played a considerable part in the initiation of the second investigation. Together with Mr Nove he saw Mr & Mrs Lawrence and Mr Khan on more than one occasion. He worked closely with

Mr Nove particularly in connection with the family meetings and the attempts which Mr Nove described to regain the confidence of Mr & Mrs Lawrence. It should also be noted that Mr Johnston, in common with Mr Nove, became aware of the family's interest in a private prosecution and decided that the MPS policy would be to give the family every support in managing that prosecution. He indicated that he tried to explain to Mr & Mrs Lawrence that there would indeed be many legal difficulties and problems in the way of the prosecution. But his purpose, plainly expressed, was to let Mr & Mrs Lawrence know that *"if there were any hurdles that could possibly be jumped we were willing to jump them"*.

30.9   Mr Johnston believed that there was at least a measure of additional evidence available to the team by the end of 1994 which might allow the case to be given a public hearing. Mr Johnston accepted that it was a weak case, but from his perspective it seemed proper to pursue it. When the prosecution was over Mr Johnston wrote to Mr & Mrs Lawrence assuring them of his and the Metropolitan Police's collective continued support. After the Inquest Mr Johnston made a public pronouncement, a copy of which was considered during his evidence. That statement included the following phrases:-

> *"I am deeply sorry that Mrs Lawrence feels as she does about the police. I would like to say again that I believe right from the start we did all we could. ......*
>
> *We started the investigation immediately, that all we had that evening was one witness who was very emotionally affected by what he had seen. Two days later we received anonymous information which alone was insufficient to warrant an arrest, but we took immediate action on it. It was thoroughly researched and we mounted a full surveillance operation. ......*
>
> *We want to get across to the black community that we take crimes against them as seriously as we do any others. When someone is murdered we do not think of the colour of their skin."*

Mr Johnston should not have allowed that statement to include palpably inaccurate statements about the first investigation. Also racist crimes do have their special features and do have to be specially addressed.

30.10   **As to the Barker Review Mr Johnston was ready in this context also to accept strong criticism. When Mr Mansfield put to him that there was in effect an unexpurgated version of that Review, and that matters had been omitted for the reasons given by Mr Barker, Mr Johnston at once said that he was *"absolutely appalled"* by this revelation. He said that this was totally and utterly unacceptable. Indeed to his credit Mr Johnston was ready throughout his evidence to accept major criticisms of what had taken place. It was his decision that a round and complete apology should be given for all the mistakes made and that a statement should be made indicating that the MPS were determined to remedy errors by education and training, and not to shrink from criticism.**

30.11 Many of the answers given by Mr Johnston were long and involved. The strain and effort of having to give evidence for a complete day was evident in some of Mr Johnston's answers. We can understand why this was so, considering that Mr Johnston had been, so to speak, deputed to deliver the apology both of himself and Sir Paul Condon, and that it was in the shadow or context of that apology that questions were asked of him.

30.12 The truth is however that the majority of the questioning really took the factual investigation of Stephen Lawrence's murder little distance. A considerable part of the questioning consisted of Counsel asking Mr Johnston to comment on one or more aspects of the case and indeed upon other cases with little relevance to this case. Mr Johnston did accept that Mr Brooks had not been dealt with at all well by the police. He agreed that Mr Brooks had been let down, and he accepted that there were lessons to be learned in connection with the handling of victims.

30.13 Mr Johnston had the unfortunate experience of allowing himself to use the word *"coloured"* when describing people from various ethnic backgrounds. The word plainly slipped out wholly unexpectedly and mistakenly. We accept his explanation in this respect and believe that Mr Johnston would not otherwise use such an expression, which is now anathema, and that he would reprimand anybody who did use this word, which is notoriously offensive to black people.

30.14 All in all the experience of Mr Johnston in giving evidence before this Inquiry must have been a daunting one. Mr Mansfield thanked him for his support to Mr & Mrs Lawrence during the second part of the investigation. Certainly so far as his direct relationship with Mr & Mrs Lawrence and with the case are concerned there is no criticism which could be levelled at Mr Johnston. He did not make any of the relevant early decisions, and he brought in Mr Nove and Mr Mellish who did all that they possibly could to revive the stale and flagging investigation from the summer of 1994 onwards.

30.15 By then all the relevant mistakes had been made, and most of them were incapable of remedy. Mr Johnston had no responsibility of any kind for the 1993 investigation. We accept that there are strong signs from Mr Johnston's evidence that he will be committed to ensure that the MPS will do their best to remedy the failings of the past. Whether this will be achieved is a matter for the future.

CHAPTER THIRTY-ONE

COMMANDER RAYMOND ADAMS

31.1 Commander Raymond Adams gave evidence to the Inquiry on two separate days. On 4 June 1998 he was questioned by Miss Weekes on behalf of the Inquiry. At the mid-day adjournment, before his evidence was completed, an application was made on behalf of Mr & Mrs Lawrence to defer cross-examination of Mr Adams. Mr & Mrs Lawrence's lawyers wished to look into certain matters that had come to their notice. The application was at once granted.

31.2 Mr Adams came back on Thursday 16 July 1998 when he was cross-examined at length by Mr Mansfield. He was also questioned by Mr Doyle and Mr Gompertz.

31.3 It is of some significance that no questions were asked of Mr Adams on behalf of Duwayne Brooks. Notice had been given dated 3 June 1998 indicating that Mr Adams would be asked questions about the treatment of Mr Brooks *"as a victim of crime or as a witness to crime"*. It was also suggested that Mr Adams might be asked a series of questions on behalf of Mr Brooks in connection with racist crime and complaints against the police. We considered this matter in advance of Mr Adams giving evidence, and ruled that it was inappropriate to ask general questions such as were set out in the proposed list. Accordingly, and quite rightly, Counsel for Mr Brooks did not question Mr Adams. There never was any suggestion that Mr Adams knew about Mr Brooks or that he had any contact with him of any kind. On 4 June there was no notice of allegations to be made on behalf of Mr & Mrs Lawrence.

31.4 On the 14 July 1998 a notice of issues and allegations was delivered to Mr Adams on behalf of Mr & Mrs Lawrence. As will be seen Mr Adams' evidence given in June was that he had literally played only one part in the murder investigation, namely to sign a letter dated 30 April 1993 to which reference will be made shortly. Mr & Mrs Lawrence's lawyers were sceptical of this, since it seemed remarkable that Mr Adams should have been involved in the case at all if he had, as he told the Inquiry, virtually no knowledge about the Stephen Lawrence case and certainly no involvement in it. The fresh notice served on 14 July indicated that *"Given Commander Adams' seniority, his purported state of health and lack of knowledge or participation in the Lawrence murder investigation, it is not accepted that he would have decided to take on or been allocated the role of family liaison, nor that he would have been delegated the relatively menial task of drafting a letter on 30 April 1993 in the terms that appear"*.

31.5 The reference to *"family liaison"* refers both to the letter and to a Policy File entry dated 30 April which reads as follows:-

"SIO/Cdr.(Adams)   30/4

Cdr. to deal with future contacts with solicitors representing the family -
phone call and letter from Cdr. to family confirms this.

To enable SIO to concentrate on progressing the murder inquiry."

This entry appears in the Appendices to this Report (Decision No 17). Mr Adams did try to reach Mr Khan by telephone, but he was unable to make contact. We believe that this file entry did not indicate any intention to take over future family liaison by Mr Adams. It does refer to the letter, which specifies that future contact by the solicitor should be through Mr Philpott or Mr Adams. The terms of the letter appear below. There was never any proposal that Mr Adams should deal with family liaison as such.

31.6 The notice to Mr Adams went on to read as follows *"in the absence of any sensible explanation for this incongruity it will be suggested that the nominal role masked another purpose. The suggested purpose was to influence the investigation so that the suspects named over the first week end were not arrested expeditiously. A potential channel for such influence arises from Commander Adams' previous links with Kenneth Noye who in turn has links with Clifford Norris. It is understood that Commander Adams took long term sick leave in May 1993 and retired in August 1993 on medical grounds. Since then has Commander Adams been in employment? If so please give dates and nature of work?"*

31.7 We are satisfied that in fact the only part played by Mr Adams in the whole of this case was indeed the signing of the letter dated the 30 April 1993 which went to J R Jones, Mr & Mrs Lawrences' solicitors. It purports to be an answer to a letter written by Mr Khan to Mr Weeden dated 29 April 1993. That was the last of a series of letters sent by Mr Khan to the police, to which much reference has been made during the Inquiry. Those letters started on 26 April, and the effect of them was to seek information about the investigation in some detail. The comment has already been made that the steps taken were unusual, and plainly the SIO was upset and to some extent deflected by the course of that correspondence. Mr Weeden had already written a letter dated 27 April in palliative terms, suggesting that he was available to be seen by Mr & Mrs Lawrence if they so wished. The receipt of another letter dated 29 April, which followed a meeting on 28 April at Eltham Police Station, seems to have spurred Mr Weeden to recruit somebody else to help him in dealing with the solicitors' requests. At the meeting of 28 April it appears that *"concern was expressed that the murder investigation team were being inundated with inquiries from the many parties interested in the progress of the inquiry. It was said that the level of inquiry was distracting the team from the task in hand"*. That is a quotation from the letter of 30 April, referring to the 28 April meeting. Apparently Mr Philpott asked on that occasion that all such enquiries should be channelled either to a Chief Inspector or to himself.

31.8 Mr Adams says that Mr Weeden came to him, on 30 April and asked for his assistance. Mr Adams tells us that he would not normally have been connected to Mr Weeden in the line of command. Mr Weeden would be responsible to the Commander (Ops) who was at the time Mr Gibson. He could go straight to Mr Gibson or to his superior who was Deputy Assistant Commissioner Osland. On 30 April Mr Adams believes that Mr Gibson was away, and that Mr Osland was not available. Therefore Mr Weeden came to Mr Adams. Mr Adams must now wish that he had turned his back on the whole case, since he had an unhappy time in the witness box before this Inquiry. He did not however turn his back and he told the Inquiry that together with a staff officer, probably Mr Osland's staff officer, and with

Mr Weeden, a letter was composed which was eventually signed by Mr Adams. It reads as follows:-

"Dear Mr Jones

RE MURDER OF STEPHEN LAWRENCE

In response to your recent letters and in particular that of 29 April 1993.

As you are aware Chief Superintendent Philpott is the officer responsible for policing activity within Plumstead Division. The murder of Stephen Lawrence is being conducted on his behalf by DS Weeden. The appointment of a senior detective from the AMIP team is normal practise in these circumstances.

In the overwhelming majority of murder investigations liaison with the family of the victim is direct. It is most unusual for the appointment of solicitors to represent the family interest as there is no conflict of interest or purpose. Police are of course fully aware of the private and public concern and distress over the murder of Stephen. To address these concerns DS Weeden appointed liaison officers from within his team to deal with enquiries and concern from both Mr & Mrs Lawrence.

You are no doubt aware of the conference at Eltham Police Station on 28 April 1993 when Deputy Assistant Commissioner Osland, the officer commanding 3 Area, met with members of the Commission for Racial Equality, Bexley and Greenwich Councils. At the meeting concern was expressed that the murder investigation team were being inundated with enquiries from the many parties interested in the progress of the enquiry. It was said that the level of inquiry was distracting the team from the task in hand. Appreciating the genuineness of most enquiries Chief Superintendent Philpott asked that all such inquires be channelled to either Chief Inspector Whapham, Plumstead Police Station, or himself.

On reading your particular correspondence it occurs to me that whilst many of your questions ask about the sort of information that is generally provided to families of victims some is not. In particular the information requested at 1. of your letter dated 26 April 1993 is not material that is normally released.

I was concerned to read your comments in your letter of 29 April 1993 concerning the liaison arrangements with Mr & Mrs Lawrence. I have discussed this with Mr Weeden, the arrangements and briefing of the officers is being examined. We shall also be talking to both Mr & Mrs Lawrence to satisfy them of our earnest wish to do everything to keep them properly informed.

I think you will agree with me that we must all do everything in our power to ensure that those responsible for the murder of Stephen are brought to justice I ask that you resist the temptation to enquire direct with the Senior Investigating Officer or his team. Chief Superintendent Philpott is available as well as I to assist you and other interested parties.

I trust my comments assist you in your delicate task.

Yours sincerely

R Adams
Commander (Support)"

31.9 We set the letter out in full, because it does seem to us to show, from its terms, that Mr Adams' explanation of what happened is right. It is true that he does put himself forward as somebody who is prepared to assist, together with Mr Philpott, in the one but last paragraph. But by and large it does seem to us that this is a letter written simply to achieve what Mr Weeden sought, namely relief from dealing with the correspondence with Mr Khan which he plainly found irksome. Mr Adams over and over again indicated in evidence that this was literally the only step that he took and the only part which he played in the Stephen Lawrence murder investigation.

31.10 He said that he had not even heard the names of the suspects at the time. He left Eltham on 4 May, and did not know the names of the suspects until he saw them much later in the 'Daily Mail'.

31.11 **Mr Adams was asked many questions about the Norrises, both Clifford and the dead David Norris. He had dealt with David Norris as an informant, and he was reluctant to talk about that connection. But he repeatedly said that he himself had no contact with Clifford Norris, and that he simply did not know that one of the suspects was Clifford Norris' son. He did not even know the name Clifford Norris or anything about him until a few months before he came to give evidence.**

31.12 It transpired that Mr Adams was unfit in April 1993. He had had continuous back trouble, perhaps stemming from an unidentified fracture in his spine, for a considerable time. We have seen his records and they bear out what Mr Adams said. He told the Inquiry that he had been to his doctor in the week before 30 April, and by coincidence when he came back on 4 May 1993, after the Bank Holiday weekend, he went to see Mr Osland and told him what the present situation was. Mr Osland told Mr Adams to stop working and to go on long term sick leave. Mr Adams did that, and the records show that on 7 May 1993 he was recommended by the MPS Medical Officer for medical retirement on the grounds of chronic back pain. On 7 June 1993 the records show that it was reported that Mr Adams was likely to be in hospital for the next three weeks. His formal retirement was recorded as being on 31 August 1993. Somewhat scathing cross-examination about Mr Adams' condition seems to us to have been misplaced in the circumstances. We have been presented with no significant evidence to show that there was anything sinister in Mr Adams' departure on 4 May 1993 from his duties.

31.13 **Furthermore in spite of long and hostile cross-examination by Mr Mansfield we have no reason to conclude that Mr Adams gave evidence in connection with the signing of this letter which was otherwise than the truth. It is of considerable importance to note that during the whole of the cross-examination Mr Mansfield never put to Mr Adams the positive suggestions which had been set out in the second notice of allegations to be made against him. He was questioned at length about his possible knowledge of Clifford Norris, but it was never positively suggested to him that there was a sinister connection with Clifford Norris or the man Noye or indeed that what Mr Adams had done, namely signing the letter, was done in order to influence the investigation so that the suspect David Norris should not be arrested expeditiously.**

31.14 Mr Mansfield did suggest to Mr Adams that the signing of the letter and his intervention was a sham, and a nonsense. But this was never followed up with any suggestion or any direct questions suggesting that Mr Adams had played a positive part in trying to slow down the investigation or arrests. It may be that this was not done advisedly, because there was no information which Mr Mansfield could properly use in this regard. At all events such suggestions were not made, and therefore the second notice was without question not substantiated.

31.15 **We have looked with care at the whole of the evidence of Mr Adams. There are strange features to it - and it is indeed surprising that an officer of his status came into the case simply in connection with this one letter. In the end however we are satisfied that it is not established that Mr Adams did anything other than that which he told us that he had done. He signed the letter in the absence of those who were perhaps the right people to sign it, in order to be helpful, and in order to relieve Mr Weeden of the burden which Mr Weeden said he was bearing, namely the requests for information by Mr Khan.**

31.16 It should perhaps be added that at the end of Mr Adams' evidence, after he had been questioned on behalf of the MPS and other police officers, he was asked to remain behind since there might have been an application to recall him. No such application was ever made. His evidence therefore remains as given on the two days to which we have referred.

31.17 **Whatever may be the suspicions of Mr & Mrs Lawrence's legal team there was never any substantiation of the allegations which were made and which no doubt conditioned the nature of the long cross-examination by Mr Mansfield.**

31.18 **As we indicated above it may well be that Mr Adams wishes now that he had not signed the letter. But after all the sound and fury we do not believe that his evidence betrays dishonesty or collusion such as was alleged against him.**

31.19 **Mr Adams was defensive in the witness box. But we have seen nothing in the evidence or in the many personal and intelligence files which we have perused to suggest that Mr Adams was involved in collusion, or corruptly involved in efforts to hold back this prosecution. By 4 May 1993 he was off the scene.**

CHAPTER THIRTY-TWO

DETECTIVE CHIEF SUPERINTENDENT MICHAEL BURDIS, HOLMES AND RESOURCES

32.1 Detective Chief Superintendent Michael Burdis produced a report for the Inquiry on the use of the Home Office Large Major Enquiry System (HOLMES) and associated issues. In this he was assisted by Detective Superintendent Philip Jones and Detective Constable Michael Botley. We are indebted to all three.

32.2 Mr Burdis gave evidence based upon his report. He is an experienced CID officer having served in the CID of several forces for over 30 years. He has many years experience as an SIO personally investigating over 100 murders. He is currently the Head of CID in the South Yorkshire Police. He has served on national working groups defining standards for managing major incident rooms. The HOLMES system has been in use for all major crime investigations in his force since 1986. Since 1992 he has been involved in various national police groups related to HOLMES 2 (the next generation of the existing HOLMES system) and reviewing the way major crime is investigated.

32.3 Given the nature of his experience it is perhaps not surprising that the majority of his report and evidence was received without challenge. We were greatly assisted by it.

32.4 Mr Burdis informed us that following the difficulties experienced in the detection of the Yorkshire Ripper murders Police Forces defined and agreed Major Incident Room Standardised Administrative Procedures (MIRSAP). The procedures created protocols for handling documentation, indexing and for recording data. A number of key functions within the incident room were identified and defined. Amongst these are:

- SIO
- Deputy SIO
- Office Manager
- Receiver
- Statement Reader
- Action Allocator
- Indexer/Action writer
- Researcher
- Exhibits Officer
- Supervisor of House to House Inquiries.

32.5 The number of personnel required to perform these functions varies with the nature and size of the investigation. The system's flexibility is such that one person can fulfil a number of roles; those of Statement Reader and Receiver often being coupled in smaller investigations. A number of persons may fulfil a single role; for example in a larger investigation there may be several Receivers to cope with the workload of that particular role. The actual deployment to these roles is therefore a matter of judgment for the SIO and those supervising him.

32.6 **The HOLMES System brought the added benefits of computerisation to the MIRSAP process. It is a means of capturing data in a structured way by agreed rules and conventions, and allows data to be easily cross-referenced and quickly recovered.**

32.7 Mr Burdis identified for us that the principal objectives of the computerised incident room system are:

- to provide an accurate record of all relevant information;

- to show the number of outstanding Actions at any one time;

- to provide investigating officers with a ready means of acquiring all the knowledge in the system about their inquiry subjects;

- to facilitate the identification of suspect people, vehicles or other factors;

- to allow new or absent members of a team easy access to existing information and policy decisions;

- to ensure information can be readily retrieved to aid the SIO establish priorities, make the best use of staff and ensure that inquiries are made speedily and effectively and results are properly analysed.

Mr Burdis also indicated that the computerised system can fall behind the actual investigation, dependent upon the volume of incoming information and the staffing levels allocated to the Major Incident Room. The judgment as to staffing levels is therefore crucial if the practical benefits of the computerised system are to materialise.

32.8 The MPS AMIP policy specifies categories of investigation. The Stephen Lawrence murder investigation should formally have been a *"B"* category investigation. That is one *"where the victim is known but the motive and suspect are unknown"*. As far as the Incident Room is concerned this would have thus required the *"standard"* allocation of three Detective Sergeants as Office Manager, Receiver and Action Allocator; a further Detective Sergeant as Staff Officer to the SIO; four Constable Indexers/Action Writers; and a Constable Exhibits Officer. There is in the policy no allocation for the key roles of Statement Reader or Researcher. Such *"standard"* policy allocations are of course a guideline. Objective professional judgements must be made in the light of the actual nature of an investigation with staffing reduced or increased accordingly.

32.9 In the Lawrence investigation, whilst it is universally accepted that in policy terms the investigation was a *"B"*, no such categorisation was ever made. There is no record of the category in the policy log or any other document. More specifically when questioned on the use of such categories Mr Crampton stated that the issue of classification was not discussed with Mr Ilsley, and staff allocation was simply a case of *"what he could get"*. This was normal practice. Mr Ilsley confirmed this. The AMIP policy on resource allocation was not given active consideration by anyone initially, though Mr Osland indicated that he had subsequently sought assurance that the *"B"* allocation had been made.

32.10 **Regardless of the lack of regard for formal policy the essential question is - were appropriate judgements made in relation to staffing? Mr Burdis' view in his written report is unequivocal.** *"It is my opinion that given the circumstances of this murder and the number of immediate lines of inquiry, particularly knowing that a gang of five or six people may be responsible .... the staff allocation was inadequate and failed to give support to the SIO in the performance of his function. The allocation of officers to the major incident room is, in my view, derisory ..... . Equally, given the lines of inquiry generated by the media attention and the appeals for public support and assistance made by*

Mr & Mrs Lawrence those charged with outside investigations apparently could not cope in a timely way with the amount of work allocated to them".

32.11 Mr Burdis highlighted the lack of staff over the Bank Holiday weekend 1-3 May 1993 when investigating staff were reduced to nine officers, then six and, on 3 May just four officers. He also dealt with the details of additional staff and others being removed to other investigations. We see no necessity to rehearse that detail here. Mr Burdis' conclusion, and we endorse it strongly, was that the staffing level *"was far below that necessary to competently investigate this murder"*. Indeed he indicated that he considered 40 to 50 investigating officers for outside work, plus an incident room with each role individually staffed would have been appropriate. The reality was an incident room with DS Flook performing four key roles and an outside investigation team which varied in size, but which was in Mr Burdis' view never adequately staffed.

32.12 In addition Mr Burdis highlighted other facts. That with no staff dedicated to the role of "Research" the investigating team were required to carry out their own research function thus reducing the time for investigation. That additional indexers should have been considered to cope with the "hump" in initial workload which is common to all investigations. Most particularly he identified the fact that conjoining the roles of Receiver, Statement Reader and Office Manager meant that there was no cross-checking between the roles to ensure that information was properly prioritised and actioned. In Mr Burdis' words *"Not only could it have led to administrative delays within the incident room process, it also failed to provide an independent role designed to scrutinise the work of the Receiver and Statement Reader. That role would normally fall to the Office Manager but in this instance he was doing all three jobs."*

32.13 Delay or failure to raise and pursue actions properly because of the inadequate management of information through understaffing in the incident room is evident in the "Red Astra saga" addressed elsewhere. Mr Burdis identified several other serious instances in relation to the important statements of Duwayne Brooks, Joseph Shepherd and others. For example whilst the statements of Mr Brooks and Mr Shepherd were properly *"marked up"* for some initial actions to be carried out quickly other actions have been missed completely or confused. In the first of Mr Brooks' statements reference is made to four young people who were with Mr Brooks and Stephen Lawrence after school on 22 April. The four were indexed and entered as *"Nominals"* but no Actions were ever raised in relation to them. In the same statement Mr Brooks gives a description of *"the attacker"*. The described attacker is registered as Nominal 113 and the statement marked for an Action to be raised to TIE (Trace, Interview and Eliminate) the suspect attacker. No Action was raised or allocated. Subsequently Action 140 links a description of one of the attackers given by Mr Shepherd, the eye witness at the bus stop, to that given by Mr Brooks, clearly assuming that the descriptions are of the same person. Mr Burdis identifies in his report that in his view the assumption is mistaken and *"the error probably arose because Actions to identify these unidentified persons were never raised"*. He adds, further, that *"In my opinion one of the key factors leading to the successful investigation of major crime is to identify unidentified persons. Not enough rigour or energy appears to have been put into this important function."*

32.14 In connection with the handling of Witness B Mr Burdis also expressed surprise that there had been no involvement, recorded in the system, of the SIO or his deputy determining how to deal with Witness B. He found no material to indicate that the SIO or his deputy had tried to intervene or spotted that an important witness had not been progressed properly. It was Mr Burdis' opinion that the 'processing' of witnesses such as Witness B and Witness K, and other related inquiries, appeared to be incomplete, so that there was little prospect of the interviewing officers being properly prepared for their tasks once the arrests had taken place. Mr Burdis' conclusion in this regard was that if more staff had been allocated to this investigation *"many of the questions which remain unanswered today could have been resolved before any interviews took place"*.

32.15 Mr Burdis, in fairness, did identify that the database of the HOLMES system was correctly set up in accord with protocols, and that the indexing, the actual entry of detail on the computer, was correct and performed to a high standard.

32.16 **The conclusion however can only be that this investigation was grossly understaffed both in the incident room and externally. Indeed the lack of staff and the consequent serious mismanagement is so obvious that the question automatically arises as to whether senior officers took adequate steps to intervene and address the problem.**

32.17 Of the senior officers in a position to address or seek to address the staffing inadequacies Mr Bullock indicated that whilst he had had an appropriate two or three day training course to use the HOLMES system that course was some five years earlier and he had no experience of live use of the system. He acknowledged that information did not reach him as promptly as it should. Actions were not always raised or carried out as they should have been. There were insufficient staff in the incident room to cope with the initial workload. He had to organise unofficial internal training for staff to be able to access the system. He did not understand the priority allocation system on HOLMES. Initially at least he felt that the HOLMES system was a hindrance rather than a help. As a result he felt the HOLMES system was *"slightly chaotic"* and he reported his concerns to both SIO's, Mr Crampton and Mr Weeden.

32.18 Mr Crampton indicated that, like Mr Bullock, he had had a two day training course in HOLMES some three years previously but had never used the system in a live situation. Questioned by Mr Lawson his responses indicated that he was aware of the inadequacies but simply accepted them as a fact of MPS life:

> "Q: *Did you have enough people to run the HOLMES system effectively?*
>
> A: *Well, I never had enough to run the HOLMES system. You would never have enough to run the HOLMES system. Of course in the Met if you were running the card system you would still be short.*
>
> Q: *Did you ask for more resources?*
>
> A: *I had asked for as much as I could have and that is what I was given. So there was little point in asking for more."*

32.19 Mr Weeden for his part accepted without hesitation Mr Burdis' view of the inadequacy in numbers of both the outside investigation team and the incident room staff. He indicated that had he wished to complain about resources his *"line"* would have been to Mr Ilsley, but that Mr Ilsley *"was perfectly aware of the difficulties we often faced and, indeed, which were evident in this case"*.

32.20 Mr Ilsley testified clearly and forcefully that he was very much aware of the shortcomings. He described DS Flook's multi-role activity thus, *"It is not only poor sir, it's disgraceful but it was something that we used to have to put up with all the time"*. Similarly he wholeheartedly accepted Mr Burdis' assertions on staffing when questioned by Mr Lawson, *"Absolutely. It was just accepted within the Met that we just did not have the resources"*. He indicated, with equal force, that the difficulty with resources applied to all murder investigations, and that this was regularly identified to Mr Osland, the officer in overall command of 3 Area. In fairness he balanced this by indicating to Mr Lawson that *"we did put more resources on this inquiry than we did on any others"* but agreed with Mr Lawson that even so the staffing was *"still woefully deficient"*. Nevertheless he accepted that he did not seek additional staff from other Divisions, nor seek the assistance of his superiors Mr Gibson or Mr Osland to do so.

32.21 **Mr Gibson did not in fact give evidence to the Inquiry. He provided a short written statement which was read publicly indicating that as Commander (Operations) 3 Area from mid 1992 until 28th June 1993 he was responsible for all aspects of operational policing including AMIP investigations. In discharging the latter responsibility he had weekly discussions with Mr Ilsley and would visit AMIP incident rooms. He stated that, five years on, he could not recall any detail of the Stephen Lawrence investigation. He can remember pursuing the general problems of "resource" in relation to investigations but cannot remember specific details.**

32.22 **Mr Gibson's lack of recall cannot be held against him. However, we consider it is self-evident that, in a case as high-profile and significant as the Stephen Lawrence investigation, simply because of his position in the hierarchy, he could have identified the difficulties both in relation to staffing and to family liaison. Even if the topics did not feature in briefings by Mr Ilsley the difficulties were there to be discovered, and addressed by more senior officers, by the most cursory of inquiries or the most limited of active supervision. Mr Gibson had the power to acquire more resources from the 10 Divisions within the Area, and equally could have taken a positive initiative in relation to family liaison, as was indicated by Mr Nove in his explanation of the role of Commander Operations to Junior Counsel for the Inquiry, Miss Weekes. Mr Gibson has told us that he did himself see the family at Eltham Police Station. We readily accept from him that this was so.**

32.23 For his part Mr Osland testified that he considered that the investigation had been formally classified as a 'B' Investigation in terms of AMIP policy, that the totality of manpower available was sufficient, and that he was unaware of the lack of resource allocation, within that totality, to the incident room. He stated that *"In terms of manpower (generally) this was a constant complaint across the Area but nobody came to me and asked me for more manpower for the Stephen Lawrence inquiry."* He was however approached for more money to fund overtime working for the existing team, and he obtained £80,000 from central funds.

32.24 In response to Mr Doyle Mr Osland indicated that he visited the Incident Room almost daily. The SIOs in his Area could expect him, as part of his function, to find more resources for them. However, he may not have been asked for additional staff because they felt they were unlikely to get a positive response:

> "Q: *There was, was there not, at that time amongst SIO's a culture of acceptance that they had to do the best they could with what they had?*
>
> A: *Yes, I think that is fair."*

He specifically indicated that Mr Ilsley made no complaint in relation to staffing, that there were avenues Mr Ilsley could have explored within his Divisions, and if they did not respond he could turn to him or Mr Gibson. He did not do so.

32.25 Even more than Mr Gibson it is clear that Mr Osland had the opportunity, power and responsibility to ensure that the resourcing of the investigation was adequate. On his daily visits and briefings the situation must have been visible and known or discoverable with ease. A response made during Mr Osland's evidence is to be noted:-

"Q. *Again, quoting yourself earlier... "my function was to receive the information the SIO chose to pass on to me". Do you feel that is rather too passive an interpretation of your role and you do have a duty to enquire and reassure yourself in relation to the investigation ....*

A. *I suppose as when I was asked about what lessons I learned I suppose in retrospect I should have paid closer attention or gone into things in greater detail."*

32.26 During the course of the Inquiry there was a persistent defensive theme that the demands upon the MPS related to the resources available meant that the understaffing of major investigations was inevitable and unavoidable. Mr Bullock, Mr Crampton and Mr Weeden testified to this effect. Mr Ilsley went further, saying that resources devoted to major crime investigations in London were deficient compared with those outside London and that the chances of solving a murder in London would be less than elsewhere.

32.27 On the same theme when questioned by Mr Beer on behalf of the Commissioner Mr Burdis accepted that the policing by the MPS is unique, the pressure on resources is unique and the intensity of resources demanded is unique. He also accepted, from Mr Beer, that there were ten other major crime investigations, including three murders, ongoing in 3 Area. Mr Burdis did however indicate in his written report that he did not find the ten investigations unusual. The police strength of 3 Area in 1993 was in fact equivalent to a medium size force and indeed exceeded the entire strength of South Yorkshire Police, Mr Burdis' own force.

32.28 We are clear that it is not for us to make any formal judgement as to whether MPS is adequately resourced in relation to other forces, nor do we have the information on which to base such a judgement. However given the persistent general suggestion of unique demands and inadequate resources, but no actual figures or evidence to support the assertion, we have looked in a basic way to see if there is any obvious evidence of this. The Inquiry has examined police establishments, population, total crime and homicides for four forces in 1993 - the Metropolitan, West Midlands, Greater Manchester and South Yorkshire. The figures for No 3 Area MPS are also included. The comparisons are of course simplistic. We make no apology for that. It does however appear that, even allowing for the additional constitutional and public order functions performed by the MPS, there is no indication of an excessive imbalance in resources compared to other forces. The figures are shown at the end of this Chapter. They show that whilst the MPS had rather more than nine times the establishment of South Yorkshire, they had less than six times the population and crimeload, and slightly less than eight times the homicide rate. The suggestion that, in 1993, the MPS or 3 Area faced excessive demand with inadequate resources compared to other forces is not therefore compelling even allowing for the simplicity of the comparison and the additional policing factors which exist in London. If there are difficulties they may reflect choices in deployment.

32.29 **The stark conclusion must certainly be that there were insufficient officers available for the tasks they faced. In Mr Burdis' words** *"I genuinely believe that given three times the numbers of staff actually allocated to this investigation all the necessary evidence would have been captured in a timely fashion and would have played a very positive part in a subsequent prosecution".* **But simply increasing the number of officers involved in an investigation may not be the only solution. More fundamental in this case is the standard of direction and control and execution which those who were actually involved were to provide for the investigation, particularly in its early and vital days. This was undoubtedly compounded by the signal failure of senior officers to identify and respond to obvious shortcomings and thereby provide the leadership that was sadly lacking.**

FORCE	ESTAB. (POLICE)	POP (,000's)	RATIO ESTAB.	TOTAL CRIME TO POP	CRIMES PER OFFICER	HOMICIDES	OFFICERS PER HOMICIDE
MPS	28,244	7,446	1:264	910209	32	159	178
WEST MIDLANDS	6,918	2,649	1:383	330091	48	40	173
GREATER MANCHESTER	7,077	2,578	1:364	364858	52	41	173
SOUTH YORKSHIRE	3,031	1,291	1:426	157229	52	20	152
3 AREA MPS	3,149	1,163	1:370	144400	46	*27	*117

NOTES:

1. FIGURES FROM HOME OFFICE STATISTICS AND MPS 3 AREA ANNUAL REPORT 1993.

2. MPS STRENGTH MARCH 1993=27,867 (377 UNDER ESTABLISHMENT) OTHER FORCES NOT KNOWN.

3. ALL FIGURES CALCULATED ON ESTABLISHMENTS.

* 3 AREA ANNUAL REPORT HOMICIDE FIGURES ARE FOR 1992/93. OF THE 27 HOMICIDES 11 WERE INVESTIGATED BY AMIP AND 16 BY DIVISIONS.

CHAPTER THIRTY-THREE

THE SECOND INVESTIGATION

33.1 By June 1994 the investigation of the Stephen Lawrence murder was at a low ebb. The CPS had indicated twice that they did not believe that there was a case to take forward to the courts. Nothing fresh had materialised by way of evidence. Much publicity had been given to the case.

33.2 High level correspondence and conferences were held. The Commissioner was personally involved in the sense that he wrote letters about the case to Mr Khan and to Mr Peter Bottomley MP and to Mr Peter Lloyd MP, and it is plain that there was much interest in the case both before and after the Barker Review was completed, between September 1993 and the spring of 1994.

33.3 **Advertisements seeking witnesses were published in the autumn of 1993, and the investigation continued, to little avail. To his credit Mr Weeden delayed his retirement, in the hope that he might further the investigation.**

33.4 The documents show that there had been continued activity by the MPS during the latter part of 1993 and the early months of 1994. The Inquest was adjourned in December 1993, because Mr & Mrs Lawrence's legal team believed that further evidence might be available.

33.5 On 2 May 1994 Mr Johnston's command team was joined by a senior officer, who was at that time a Commander, named Perry Nove. Mr Nove is now Commissioner of the City of London Police Service. On 1 August 1994 the MPS was restructured and Mr Nove became the Deputy Head of the new South East Area which took in all of the old 3 Area and most of the old 4 Area of south London.

33.6 **Mr Johnston and Mr Nove decided that there should be virtually a fresh start with the investigation of Stephen Lawrence's murder. Mr Nove indicated that it was not easy to** *"do away with the bureaucracy at the stroke of a pen"*. **But he and the Assistant Commissioner decided that a second investigation needed urgently to be launched, and decided that whatever the second investigation needed it was going to get. Primarily of course resources come from the Area involved. But it is apparent that during the course of the second investigation Mr Nove did all that he could to ensure that the investigation's needs in respect of cash were satisfied. Mr Nove says that everybody insisted that the second investigation had to be fully resourced so far as possible.**

33.7 The man chosen to be SIO in the new regime was Detective Superintendent William Mellish. In 1994 he was a most experienced detective. Immediately before taking over the Stephen Lawrence murder case Mr Mellish had been involved with a team of officers in the reinvestigation of the murder of Police Constable Blakelock which took place in Tottenham. That investigation had lasted from 1992 until June 1994. During that investigation Mr Mellish had worked under Mr Nove, and it was at Mr Nove's behest that Mr Mellish became involved in the Stephen Lawrence murder inquiry. Mr Mellish continued as SIO until March 1995. Thereafter he continued to help Mr & Mrs Lawrence's legal team when they embarked upon the private prosecution. Summonses in respect of that prosecution were issued in April 1995. Day to day charge of the matter after Mr Mellish ceased to be SIO was in the hands of Detective Chief Inspector John Carnt.

33.8   Nobody queried Mr Mellish's record in terms of his police expertise or suggested for a moment that anything that he did might be influenced by racism. Indeed all the indications are that Mr Mellish treated everybody firmly but well.

33.9   The arrival on the scene of Mr Nove and Mr Mellish did give a fresh impetus to the investigation which had flagged badly in the 14 months since the murder. We have already indicated that Mr Mellish found a dispirited team. Although he speaks highly of some of the qualities of Mr Bullock, who continued as the DIO, he criticised the fact that Mr Bullock seemed to show no innovation or flair in any of the decisions or suggestions that he made in connection with the investigation.

33.10   **Mr Mellish was at pains to indicate that from the start he intended to look forward in the investigation. What he described as conventional methods of investigation had in his opinion been exhausted by June 1994. He understood that his role did not include reviewing or reinvestigating what he called the *"minutiae of what the earlier investigation had done or not done"*. He saw the Barker Review, but laid little store by the contents of that document. He said that he regarded the Review as a *"tick in the box"*. Meaning that he was prepared to accept that a line should be drawn under the earlier investigation, and that a fresh start should be made.**

33.11   Mr Mellish was asked by this Inquiry what his view was about the earlier activities of the team, and in particular the decision not to arrest in the early days. He said that it was impossible or unfair to try to make a decision about the previous SIO's activity unless one was *"privy to all the information that the SIO had at the time"*. Understandably he was unwilling to perform the task which has been entrusted to this Inquiry, namely to make a comprehensive judgment on all that took place from the time of the murder on 22 April 1993. He did however say that if the names of the suspects were enshrined in good information within the first 48 hours then if things went well, and if the suspects could be definitely placed in their homes, arrests might have been made by the Tuesday or Wednesday after the murder.

33.12   **Sensibly however Mr Mellish was not prepared to be drawn too much into expressing opinions as to the past. He was very keen to indicate that while he ordered many actions in respect of names of persons who had earlier been investigated the new investigation was to be of a different kind and character.**

33.13   Mr Mellish was briefed by Mr Weeden, and there are notes to show that the effective handover took place on and after 20 May 1994. By early June 1994 Mr Mellish was firmly in the saddle. In addition to briefings and meetings with Mr Weeden and Mr Peter Essex, a solicitor in the MPS, Mr Mellish had visited the Incident Room at Eltham Police Station and taken away relevant statements and documents. He had also read all the police reports to the CPS which had been rendered to date. During his phase of the investigation Mr Mellish himself had no contact with Mr Khan and Mr & Mrs Lawrence. It was expressly laid down and agreed that Mr Nove himself or alternatively Commander William Griffiths or Mr Johnston would undertake all liaison with the family and their lawyers.

33.14   **There was no doubt at all in Mr Mellish's mind but that this was a racist murder. His brief from Mr Nove was that there should be evolved a radical and innovative strategy in order to try to get the investigation back on the rails and in order to obtain evidence to take the suspects to court.**

33.15 Mr Mellish produced a diagrammatic document setting out the strategy that he proposed to follow, in conformity with Mr Nove's instructions and discussions between himself and Mr Nove. There were in effect three main lines followed by Mr Mellish. First and foremost it was decided that there must be sophisticated surveillance using all available techniques to observe the suspects. The intention was to monitor the suspects for as long as possible in order to establish what they were doing, and perhaps to arrest one or more of them for some other serious crime. Next it was hoped that one or more of the suspects could be *"rolled over"*, meaning that they might agree to give evidence against the others. In addition Mr Mellish intended to review the best witnesses. For example, Witness B was taken to Kings Cross Police Station where there is a modern video interview facility. The idea was to debrief the important witnesses and to check on the evidence available.

33.16 Early on in his investigation Mr Mellish focused upon the position of Clifford Norris. He was aware that Mr Norris was wanted for large scale drug importation and that *"his presence at large in South East London could have a significant intimidatory effect"*. He rightly believed that both witnesses and sources of information could be inhibited by the shadow of Clifford Norris. Nobody knew where Clifford Norris was in 1994, although of course it is evident that he had been in close contact with his son because of the history of the case brought against his son involving the attempted murder of Stacey Benefield. Before he became involved in this investigation Mr Mellish had not himself known of Clifford Norris, but he said that he was, as we accept, well known in south London. Furthermore, Mr Norris had been on the run since 1988. It is difficult to understand why he had not been more energetically pursued after that date. There is no true explanation of the lack of energy in this direction either by Customs & Excise or by the police. Mr Norris' brother Alexander had been sentenced in 1989 to a long prison sentence for involvement in major drug crimes.

33.17 A combination of surveillance and investigation led the team to some oasthouse cottages in Battle, Sussex.

33.18 Mr Mellish's account of the capture of Clifford Norris was factual but dramatic, and it was received by the Inquiry audience with applause. There is no need to go into the full details in this report, since they appear in the evidence on Day 42. The long and the short of it was that by 10 or 11 August 1994 it appeared obvious to Mr Mellish and his team that Clifford Norris was at the oasthouse cottages. Observation was continued there, and on the evening before his arrest Mr Norris and an associate went to a public house where they were positively identified by DS Knight. Permission to carry out an armed operation was obtained from the local constabulary who provided armed officers. Mr Mellish also contacted the local Regional Crime Squad, and a team of officers including DS Davidson was provided to him. Mr Mellish spent the night at the police station and briefed everybody at 05:00 on 11 August. Mr Norris and his associate Mr Stainer moved in the middle of the morning and stopped for breakfast at a local cafe, where they were arrested. They were in possession of loaded handguns. An Uzi sub-machine gun and a large amount of ammunition were found at the oasthouse cottage.

33.19 With Mr Norris safely removed from the scene Mr Mellish hoped that fresh information would emerge, and that he might be able to discover or develop some eye witness evidence. Unfortunately the fact is that no such evidence has been obtained either by Mr Mellish or thereafter. The limited amount of evidence available in this case is only too clear to all involved.

33.20 The next step taken was intrusive video and audio surveillance of a flat occupied by Gary Dobson. He had been given a flat in Footscray Road, Eltham, by the Social Services Department, and these premises were found to be suitable for insertion of a probe. An audio and visual probe was inserted in the premises, and over a considerable period during December 1994 films and recordings were made which we have seen. The details of these are dealt with elsewhere, but as Mr Mellish indicated they showed that those who were present in that flat, including all the suspects except Jamie Acourt, had *"a propensity for violence and the carriage of knives and raving bigotry"*. The young men made revolting and explicit racist comments and remarks repeatedly, and large knives were much in evidence. These knives were waved about and used to simulate stabbing. On several occasions knives were inserted in the waistbands of some of the young men who were seen to leave the premises and to return, depositing the knives back on the window sill. Jamie Acourt was in custody, having been charged with another offence involving violence.

33.21 **We do not here examine the full nature of these terrible recordings. The fact is however that it was apparent that the young men almost certainly suspected that they were being bugged. Whether they appreciated that there was a video camera installed may be subject to doubt. But it is evident that these men knew that they were being overheard. Not only are they proved by the recordings to be violent racists, but they are also defiant of anything that is done by the police or by authority in connection with their own activities and their own nature. The transcript of the recordings which were before us is in the Appendices to this Report.**

33.22 From time to time the men were at pains to indicate that they had not been involved in the Stephen Lawrence murder. They did this obliquely, but it is a significant element of the audio recording. How much can be divined from this is problematical. The fact is however that, as Mr Mellish accepted, the product of the probe was disappointing to him. He had hoped to obtain either some direct admissions, or at least admissions of other criminal activity which would have enabled him to arrest the suspects. Mr Mellish's own view strongly expressed, was that *"not one iota of evidence capable of being left to a jury to prove that these men were the murderers of Stephen Lawrence was obtained"*.

33.23 As a result of the earlier audio surveillance a small morsel of information had been obtained indicating that perhaps Gary Dobson could not *"hack the pressure"*. This information came from conversation overheard when the young men were visiting Jamie Acourt at the Remand Centre where he was detained. He had stabbed somebody in a night-club, and was held in custody in connection with that matter. The fact that undercover police officers present in the club had observed the stabbing may have been one of the contributory factors which alerted the young men to the fact that they were being watched and recorded.

33.24 It was Mr Mellish's view that their knowledge and their appreciation of the possibility of the surveillance came primarily from *"schooling"* from Clifford Norris before he was arrested. Mr Mellish believed that after their arrest in 1993 Mr Norris would have *"sat the boys down"*, as he put it, and instructed them to keep silent and warned them of the risk that there might be sophisticated surveillance of them in the future. This is a possible theory. Alternatively they may have been alerted by others. In addition the young men were aware from the very start, as the recordings show, that the landlord of the flat with somebody else had been let in by Gary Dobson and the direct statement is made in the very first recording indicating that some interference had taken place.

33.25 It may not matter in the end how they were aware of the surveillance. The fact is that they probably were aware of it and therefore may have avoided making any incriminating remarks. Their whole attitude and their denials may have been specifically intended to put the police off the scent.

33.26 When Gary Dobson was seen by DS Knight, who approached him on the softly, softly basis he made no admissions in a long conversation and produced no useful indication that he would be able to give evidence against the others. Later when he was arrested Mr Mellish interviewed him, and again Mr Dobson made no admissions and was not prepared to assist. Incidentally there was very little evidence ever available against Gary Dobson. He was not identified at any parade, and the only material available to the prosecution in the end was the weak or very weak evidence concerning the suggested transference of fibres to Stephen Lawrence's hand.

33.27 By the time Mr Mellish left the team there was really little advance, in the sense that no satisfactory additional evidence was obtained in order to assist the prosecution. Mr Mellish was very doubtful about the evidence of Duwayne Brooks, principally in his case because he felt that everybody should *be aware that his defence have used a psychiatrist who says that he was suffering from post traumatic shock at the time of the riot. If this is so what value can we place on his positive ID made just after the riot?"*

33.28 Mr Mellish did not wish to approach the case or the family or their lawyers on the negative basis that the case was hopeless. But it is apparent that Mr Mellish's view was that the case was very weak. Indeed he indicated this informally to some of those involved from time to time. It was not for him to make the ultimate decision as to whether the prosecution should go ahead. That was for the Crown prosecution team, and later for the lawyers advising Mr & Mrs Lawrence. The CPS had made their decisions in 1993 and April 1994, so it was for Mr & Mrs Lawrence's team to make a proper and informed decision as to whether the prosecution should proceed. Once it has been decided that there should be no prosecution by the CPS it is possible for a private prosecution to start, subject to any veto which may be imposed by the Attorney General.

33.29 Mr Mellish indicated that there was not the material upon which a jury might act, even if the Judge let in the vital evidence of Mr Brooks. Mr Mansfield believed that the surveillance evidence would be admitted. Mr Mellish did not agree. This of course was never tested at trial, although it is right to indicate that the Magistrate at the committal proceedings did allow the edited version of these terrible scenes and words to be given in court. He did not have to make any final ruling as to whether the recordings could be made available at trial.

33.30 Mr Mellish was asked about the resourcing of his inquiries. He gave evidence which reflects the position, namely that resources are always and were always tight, but that those above him were undoubtedly helpful in obtaining money for the initiatives which he wished to take forward. Mr Mellish did not complain that he was short of officers or short of funds in the result in connection with the initiatives and investigation which he had proposed.

33.31 As to Mr Brooks Mr Mellish noted that Mr Brooks had been acquitted in connection with the Welling disturbance on the basis of traumatic stress. And his logic was that Mr Brooks must have made his identifications when he was under the same traumatic stress and *"a half reasonable defence barrister would make mincemeat of him"*.

33.32 Mr Brooks had never formally become a protected witness, in the full sense of that phrase. By the time of the trial at the Central Criminal Court he was still a vital witness. He had given evidence at the committal, and there is no doubt but that anybody who decided to call him thereafter as a witness must have been apprehensive. At the time he was being advised by Miss Jane Deighton, a solicitor from the firm of Deighton Guedalla, so that in one sense he was in her charge. We are sure that if there had been any trouble or difficulty in connection with Mr Brooks and the giving of his evidence she would have been the first so to indicate.

33.33 It was thought wise however that there should be a police escort provided for Mr Brooks during and around the days of the trial, and that he should be accompanied to hotels to spend the night with officers nearby. Throughout the course of the trial namely from 17 April to 26 April 1996 there were police officer escorts provided. Mr Brooks was taken each evening to Snow Hill Police Station, near the Central Criminal Court, where he was collected by officers who were given the duty of looking after him for the night. A detailed survey has been made of the duty states of the officers allocated to perform this guard duty.

33.34 In his statement to the Inquiry Mr Brooks does complain that he was taken to an Eltham hotel, where he had little sleep and he says that this affected his evidence. In fact he went to an Eltham hotel only after he had completed his evidence in "the trial within a trial". It is perfectly true that he might have had to give evidence before the jury if the Judge had let his evidence in, but it seems most likely that after he had given his preliminary evidence the general expectation must have been that his evidence would not be put before the jury.

33.35 Mr Brooks gave evidence on 18 and 19 April. He then went away for the weekend to the West Midlands. He continued and finished his evidence in the "trial within a trial" on Monday, 22 April 1996.

33.36 One of the officers allocated to guard him on that night was DS XX, to whom much reference has been made. Anybody who is asked about this allocation accepts rightly that if the allocating officers had known about DS XX's past he must have been regarded as a wholly inappropriate person to guard Mr Brooks. Mr Mellish had no knowledge of the association of DS XX with Clifford Norris, which had taken place in 1987/88. DS XX had been left as a fully serving officer from the date of his discipline hearings. Mr Johnston was appalled that a man who had associated with a criminal such as Clifford Norris should have remained in the MPS.

33.37 That is a separate matter in a sense, since the fact is that he was originally required to resign, but on appeal that decision was upset and he was allowed to remain in the force, in the same Area, as a Detective Constable.

33.38 **So far as the guarding of Mr Brooks is concerned, while it is obviously undesirable that DS XX should have been anywhere near him, there is no evidence whatsoever that anything went wrong as a result of DS XX's presence. Again we reiterate that if there had been any suggestion that DS XX might have interfered with Mr Brooks' evidence in any way it would at once have been raised. We are convinced that there is no basis for any suggestion that the presence of DS XX had in fact any bearing on the evidence given by Mr Brooks or indeed upon the course of the trial.**

33.39 When the trial was over Mr Mellish himself wrote to Mr Penstone of the Greenwich Borough Council, on 9 July 1996, seeking a Community Care Grant for Mr Brooks. Mr Mellish confirmed that Mr Brooks had been under his care during the currency of the trial and he pointed out that Mr Brooks had undergone rigorous cross-examination and had been the focus of enormous media attention. He indicated quite rightly that these experiences had had a most traumatic effect on this young man, and he hoped very much that Mr Penstone and indeed the police could help Mr Brooks to readjust to his new life. He rightly pointed out that Mr Brooks had been under exceptional pressures and would need every support to cope with his new situation.

33.40 It is a pleasure to record that at the outset of Mr Mansfield's cross-examination he thanked Mr Mellish and expressed the appreciation of Mr & Mrs Lawrence for the way in which he had conducted the second investigation. Mr Mansfield then prepared the ground for the showing of the video of the Mr Dobson's flat. The Inquiry then saw the video highlights, as did the public and the press. Mr Mansfield rightly told the Inquiry that consideration had been given to the question of prosecution for possible offences arising from the video itself. Since the activities of these young men took place in a private flat there was in fact no appropriate crime with which they could be charged.

33.41 As to Clifford Norris Mr Mansfield pointed out that Mr Mellish had been able to obtain from intelligence dockets and other documents his information about Clifford Norris without difficulty. Mr Mellish had never associated DS XX with Clifford Norris, but at the relevant time he was aware that DS XX had *"met a criminal in bad circumstances and was disciplined"*. Plainly the tactic of arresting Clifford Norris could have been followed earlier by the Weeden team. It is surprising that particularly after the Benefield case no positive steps seem to have been taken to take Mr Norris out of circulation. He must always have been regarded as an evil influence hovering over the case and potentially over witnesses and those who might give information, most of whom had been known to one or other members of the gang.

33.42 As to James Grant Mr Mellish indicated that the name Grant was of course on the system when he took over. He also said that James Grant was, so far as he knew, an informant judging by the text of the message or the action which had identified him to Mr Mellish in the first place. He said that his officers tried to find the paperwork relating to James Grant locally and at AMIP Headquarters but that they could find no documentation whatsoever. He raised an action to try to trace James Grant, and he told the Inquiry that he knew that one of his officers had approached somebody who appeared to have been involved as a handler of James Grant who told him that there was an informant, but that he had forgotten his name except that it was *"something like an off licence"*. Mr Mellish sardonically indicated that the name of James Grant was the nearest that one could get to an off licence connection.

33.43 The action to trace James Grant remained open until the new year of 1995. James Grant was never traced formally as a result of that action, but it is interesting, and somewhat surprising, to discover that two of Mr Mellish's officers in fact by coincidence when visiting somebody else came into contact with James Grant, and also Witness K. There was some confusion in the evidence about this aspect of the matter, but a pocket book entry by the two officers shows quite plainly that James Grant was seen on 2 and 3 February 1995 by them and that James Grant made a limited verbal statement to the officers.

33.44 Mr Mellish believed James Grant to be a registered informant and he says that that interview would not have resulted in any formal record of what had taken place. As Mr Mellish points out James Grant himself never gave any indication that he was a witness, and the true value of his information both earlier and in 1995 was in connection with what witnesses such as K and B might have been able to say. Witness K had given a short statement to DS Davidson on 17 May 1993. He had said that he had visited 102 Bournbrook Road at about 23:30 on the night of the murder and that he had seen Jamie and Neil Acourt and Gary Dobson and that one of them had said *"It weren't us"*. One of them, says Witness K, had his T-shirt off. Thereafter Mr Mellish told the Inquiry that Witness K was of course a priority and that he and his officers spent *"an awful lot of time trying to track him down and get him back on side"*. There had been variations of versions of what Witness K might have been able to say. Plainly Mr Mellish was keen to get in touch with that potential witness. However he indicated that Witness K was *"not making himself available to us"*, and the long and the short of it is that Witness K disappeared, so that the only witness statement that ever existed was that taken in 1993.

33.45　As to the registration of James Grant Mr Mellish confirmed that there was no paper work anywhere, although of course there should have been if James Grant had been formally registered and if the relevant and proper steps had been taken in connection with the documentation.

33.46　As to the private prosecution Mr Mellish told Mr Mansfield that he had never wanted to be negative and he would have mentioned in conversation rather than at formal meetings that he thought that the case was not strong. It was, said Mr Mellish, the family's job together with their lawyers to make up their minds whether they were going to go for a prosecution. Mr Mellish regarded his own opinion as in a sense irrelevant.

33.47　**Mr Mellish was cross-examined by Miss Woodley, on behalf of the SIOs. Mr Mellish agreed with Miss Woodley that the circumstances under which he operated were different from and better than the circumstances prevailing in 1993. Simply for example there was a dedicated HOLMES suite at Shooters Hill Police Station in 1994, and indeed dedicated staff filled various roles which had been duplicated or triplicated in 1993. Furthermore it is evident, as we have already indicated, that Mr Mellish was provided with money from central funds, because a decision had been made in the higher echelons that the second investigation should be well supported in terms of resources. It must be said that it was open to the senior officers overseeing the first investigation to have treated that operation with a high priority and to have provided additional funding and staff. He also agreed that he had met very similar difficulties to those encountered by the first investigation in connection with, for example, eliciting information from witnesses such as Emma Cook and others, who had always been reluctant to co-operate with the police. In connection with Emma Cook Mr Mellish said that police officers were simply prevented from getting anywhere near her by her mother. There is therefore an echo of DS Davidson's encounter with that particular girl. Similarly Michelle Casserley, who by that time had her own solicitor, was seen by a representative of Mr Khan's office, with wholly unproductive results. This cross-examination did indicate that the second investigation was itself unable to advance the case or to obtain satisfactory evidence, otherwise than in connection with the video recordings.**

33.48　In answer to Mr Macdonald, on behalf of Mr Brooks, Mr Mellish reiterated that while the *"guardian"* officers would have known something about the case which was going on at the Central Criminal Court, they would not have known the details. By then Clifford Norris had been arrested, and David Norris himself was not on trial at the Central Criminal Court, so that the *"Norris factors"* in the case were in any event diminished.

33.49 In answer to Mr Brian Barker QC, on behalf of the CPS, Mr Mellish confirmed that Mr Youngerwood was anxious to see the investigation going forward as far as humanly possible. Furthermore he indicated that he was prepared to give Mr Mellish every support that he could from his professional position and that he would of course support a further step in connection with the prosecution if any hard useful evidence could be produced.

33.50 **Mr Mellish confirmed that he had not met Mr & Mrs Lawrence during the investigation. The connection with them had been firmly taken into the hands of Commander Nove. Mr Mellish had been told that there had been a lack of communication with the family and that Mr Khan had played an important part in that, and he added that Mr Bullock told him that the solicitor had effectively *"hijacked the family"*. In Mr Weeden's briefing note to Mr Mellish Mr Khan was described as *"closely linked to ARA. Within hours of the murder he interposed himself between the Lawrence family and the Police. Has turned the case into a political bandwagon"*. This is another example of Mr Weeden passing on deprecatory views which did not help the situation.**

33.52 Mr Melllish did all that he could during his time as SIO. He retired from the MPS in February 1998, after 33 years service.

CHAPTER THIRTY-FOUR

COMMANDER PERRY NOVE (now Commissioner of City of London Police)

34.1 We have already indicated that the strategy followed by Mr Mellish came jointly from Commander Perry Nove and Mr Mellish himself. Mr Nove was in close touch with Assistant Commissioner Ian Johnston from the start of his involvement in the case, and both the Assistant Commissioner and Mr Nove determined that whatever the second investigation needed it was going to get.

34.2 Mr Johnston had asked Mr Nove to take a completely fresh look at the case and to advise him whether there were any practical new steps that could be taken to bring the case to a successful conclusion.

34.3 The evidence of Mr Nove was refreshing, intelligent and clear. He told us how he saw the matter, and of his instructions and conversations with Mr Mellish. Thereafter Mr Mellish was the SIO, so that the practical application of the new strategy was down to Mr Mellish.

34.4 **Mr Nove personally took on the liaison with Mr & Mrs Lawrence and Mr Khan. It is illuminating to see the careful and full notes of the meetings which took place in this regard. There is no need to go through the notes in detail, but it is apparent that Mr Nove sensitively and fully went through the possible steps that might be taken in the second investigation with Mr & Mrs Lawrence, and did his best to remedy the deep damage that had been caused by the unsuccessful liaison between the police and Mr & Mrs Lawrence during the first investigation. He was able to reverse the negative attitudes which had been shown to the family, and to produce a positive relationship, for which the family thanked him.**

34.5 Mr Nove was particularly surprised to find that Mr & Mrs Lawrence had never met the SIO in charge of the case. He discovered the depth of Mr & Mrs Lawrence's dissatisfaction with the police. Mr Weeden was present at the first of these meetings and the note of the meeting of 3 May indicates that Mr Weeden showed Mrs Lawrence his letter written on 27 April 1993, inviting her to see him should she so wish.

34.6 Mr Nove and Mr Johnston discussed after the meeting the importance of trying to get some of the confidence of the family back. They appreciated that trust had been totally lost, and it was decided that Mr Nove would personally continue the necessary and vital liaison. Mr & Mrs Lawrence were in the summer of 1994 very disappointed and frustrated and bitter that the criminal justice system had failed to deliver the result which they so fervently hoped to achieve.

34.7 This was, said Mr Nove, the first major investigation in his experience where there had been no sort of reasonable relationship between the investigators and the victims. And he fully appreciated, as his minutes show, all the relevant and understandable complaints made by Mr & Mrs Lawrence. Mr Nove told us that in his view Mr & Mrs Lawrence were *"absolutely right about what they were complaining about"*. Furthermore he was critical of the senior officers above the SIO at the relevant time. He said for example that the Commander (Operations) for the Area should be wanting to seek regular briefing as to what was going on, in order that his influence as a more senior officer could be brought to bear. Commander Gibson's statement, which was before the Inquiry, made no mention of any activity to seek such briefing or to challenge the activities of the investigating team, with the assistance and input of the Deputy Assistant Commissioner, Mr Osland. It is right to say that Mr Gibson was not asked to look back upon the case until several years afterwards.

34.8 **The truth is that Mr Nove is a most sensitive officer who did all that he could to try to win back the confidence of Mr & Mrs Lawrence and indeed of Mr Khan. He never found Mr Khan to be obstructive. It was his skill and understanding that ensured a reasonable relationship between the police and Mr & Mrs Lawrence and Mr Khan in the lead up to the decision made by them to conduct a private prosecution. Early in 1995 Mr Nove left the MPS and he handed over his duties to Mr Griffiths.**

34.9 Mr Nove was of course not involved in the detail of the second investigation. That was left in the capable hands of Mr Mellish. So that Mr Nove himself did not know about James Grant, and other details of the investigation were not strictly a matter for him.

34.10 As to the Barker Review Mr Nove said that such a Review should be *"bold and probative"*. Furthermore at the end of his questioning by Miss Weekes in connection with that Review Mr Nove accepted that police officers do have a tendency to protect each other. This is what he called *"a cultural legacy of the old police service"*. Reviews are, said Mr Nove, becoming somewhat more frequent in police forces generally now. The police certainly in his experience are encouraging and supporting open reporting, and there is a strong move to break down the culture of self-protection *"by leadership, by stressing the importance of professionalism, and on each and every occasion stressing the importance of our duty to the victim and to the public"*.

34.11 As to the December 1994 surveillance Mr Nove indicated through Mr Mansfield that he had become anxious about the possible leak of information as to the surveillance operation. He believed that the suspects evidently knew that they were being bugged, and that this was the result of their knowledge of the sequence of interventions which had already taken place. He referred to the arrest of Clifford Norris, the arrest of Jamie Acourt after an alleged night club stabbing and the detection of the importation of drugs into the remand centre where Jamie Acourt was based. He believed that the suspects were appreciating that their fortune had changed, and that in addition they were deeply suspicious because the landlord had let somebody into the flat in their absence.

34.12 Mr Nove always accepted that this terrible murder was totally motivated by racism. Mr Nove expressed his anger about a minute which had been prepared by the MPS solicitor which might have suggested that he had different views as to this. Mr Nove was rightly indignant about any such suggestion, and he required the minute to be amended. We have no doubt whatsoever but that Mr Nove was both sensitive and alert to the necessity to treat crime motivated by racism with care and understanding. In his case the facts speak for themselves. He did manage to create a relationship with Mr & Mrs Lawrence and Mr Khan which is wholly to his credit.

34.13 Mr Nove confirmed to Miss Woodley that it was right to say that the second investigation was in a considerably better position from the point of view of resourcing than the first.

34.14 Mr Nove agreed, in answer to Mr Egan on behalf of the Federated officers, that his criticism of family liaison was primarily a criticism of the more senior officers. Junior officers do what they are told and adopt what he called the *"can do philosophy"*. It is the job of the senior officers to ensure that the proper people are performing the roles to which they are allotted, and that the roles are being satisfactorily carried out.

34.15 Mr Nove commissioned what has been called the Selwood Report. This is a report which was prompted by articles in 'Private Eye' and elsewhere about DS Crowley and his part in this case and in the Rolan Adams murder. Mr Nove asked Superintendent Selwood, who was a Complaints Superintendent in the MPS, to carry out an investigation and to report by 2 June 1994. Mr Nove was under no illusions about the fact that the Report was produced in *"short order"*. On the other hand the object of the exercise was to check out the facts and to try to establish quickly *"who said what, and with which and to whom"*.

34.16 **The implications were of course serious. Either the matter was as DS Crowley had reported it, in which case he would have been guilty of suppression of evidence in the most serious way if he had not passed on the content of his conversation with Mr Brooks; alternatively if he had deliberately contrived the situation to undermine Mr Brooks' credibility that would be gross misconduct. It is true that Mr Selwood did not consider the possibility of corruption or misunderstanding in his deliberation. But he did carry out a balancing exercise, including a comparison of that which Mr Brooks agreed that he had said compared with that which DS Crowley reported Mr Brooks as having said. The areas of disagreement were comparatively narrow, as we have observed elsewhere. Mr Macdonald examined the Report in some detail. Mr Nove very fairly accepted that there were limitations in a Report produced with such speed, and in the absence of any interviews with the two persons involved. Such interviews were of course problematical since an interview with DS Crowley would have had disciplinary overtones. An interview with a potential witness of the importance of Mr Brooks would also have had its own problems.**

34.17 **In our opinion the Selwood Report is with all its limitations a relevant document, which by and large supports DS Crowley. The real test however, as we have repeatedly said, concerns the evidence given by the two persons involved both at committal and in particular at the Central Criminal Court. There the differences between the two versions diminished even further. The Judge at the Central Criminal Court decided the case not on any decision as to credibility between the two witnesses but on the evidence which was actually accepted by Mr Brooks. There were further fundamental flaws in connection with Mr Brooks' evidence which allowed the Judge to reach his decision without any total resolution of the differences between Mr Brooks and DS Crowley in connection with the fated conversation.**

34.18 It is important to note that Mr Nove and Mr Johnston held similar views as to whether in the public interest the prosecution of Mr Brooks for his involvement in the events of 8 May 1993 should continue. Both of them saw value *"for community tension and the confidence in the black community in a discontinuance of the proceedings against Brooks"*. Mr Nove and Mr Johnston did appreciate that there might be problems in terms of the credibility of Mr Brooks if the proceedings were to be discontinued. The comment would have been available to the defence that Mr Brooks had been done a favour by the CPS in order to keep his evidence firm.

34.19 There are arguments both ways. Mr Nove realised that, although it was his view that the better course would have been to have discontinued the prosecution of Mr Brooks. The ultimate decision was a matter for the CPS, as Mr Nove rightly accepted. Mr Nove believed that there was a clear public interest in conducting a prosecution of the suspects in the Stephen Lawrence murder case. Inevitably the discrepancy between DS Crowley and Mr Brooks would be tested, as indeed it was at the trial. Mr Nove felt that the prosecution of Mr Brooks was a mistake. Mr Brooks, said Mr Nove, had been so traumatised and frustrated and dismayed by the murder that his actions could be interpreted as an unfortunate protest which had got out of hand, so that criminal proceedings seemed hardly justified.

34.20 Mr Nove accepted that most of the steps taken in the second investigation would in fact have been available during the first investigation, although he did indicate that there would have been some problems particularly in connection with the video surveillance which did not present themselves until Mr Dobson was allocated his convenient flat. Mr Nove also accepted that the prescribed obligation to conduct Reviews, set out in the AMIP policy, was honoured in the breach rather than in the observance in the MPS. There has never really been any satisfactory explanation given to the Inquiry as to why Reviews were not regularly and properly conducted. It remains a matter of serious concern that the MPS had formal policies which were simply not pursued.

34.21 The CPS had on 15 April 1994 reached for the second time the *"unavoidable conclusion ..... that there is no prospect of a jury convicting anyone on the evidence available"*. They gave such support as they could to Mr & Mrs Lawrence's lawyers. It was neither the task nor the privilege of the MPS to make a decision on behalf of Mr & Mrs Lawrence's lawyers.

34.22 **Mr Nove's part in this case is entirely to his credit. He did his best, with Mr Mellish, and with the encouragement of Assistant Commissioner Johnston, to salvage the sorry situation which met him in May 1994. That he was unable to achieve a successful prosecution was certainly not his fault. By the summer of 1994 the case was, as things turned out, beyond redemption.**

CHAPTER THIRTY-FIVE

CHIEF SUPERINTENDENT JOHN PHILPOTT
AND
THE RACIAL INCIDENT UNIT

35.1   A batch of witnesses gave evidence in connection with the establishment of the Racial Incident Unit at Plumstead Police Station, which took place in December 1990. The first witness to deal with this topic was Chief Superintendent John Philpott. He was in fact the uniformed Divisional Commander for the Plumstead Division at the time of Stephen Lawrence's murder. Mr Philpott retired from the police service in December 1994. The actual part that he played in connection with Stephen Lawrence's murder investigation was comparatively small. He attended the scene on the night of the murder. We will return to that later.

35.2   Mr Philpott was not directly concerned with the investigation, because that had been taken over by the AMIP team. Since he was in command of the Division he became involved in the field of family liaison, after Mr Ilsley took that aspect of the case out of the hands of the SIO on 6 May 1993.

35.3   Much has been said about the Racial Incident Unit at Plumstead during our hearings. Mr Philpott decided to set up the Unit because of his concern about increasing violence between groups of youths that appeared to be racist as well as territorially motivated. The laudable aim of Mr Philpott's initiative was to conduct high quality investigation into racist incidents on the Division and to reduce racism in the area.

35.4   Mr Philpott was not aware of another Unit elsewhere in London operating in the same way as he decided to operate. What he actually did was to put a trusted Police Constable full-time on to the investigation of racist incidents. Mr Philpott himself said that initially he appointed PC Alan Fisher to this task, and later he added another officer, PC Richardson, to the small team involved in this activity. Mr Philpott said that he had to call the two people something, so that rather than call them the Race Crime Investigating Officers he called them a Race Unit, or later the Racial Incident Unit. There was nothing grandiose in the title, and there was no set up of special premises and equipment.

35.5   *"It was"* said Mr Philpott *"an officer and subsequently two officers that were dedicated to investigating racial crime"*. Another function of the Unit was the gathering and disseminating of information about racist crimes and their perpetrators. A card index was to be maintained of suspects, victims and incident locations, which was intended to be available to all officers investigating crime on Mr Philpott's Division. His intention in setting up the Unit was to reassure minority ethnic communities that the police took racist attacks seriously, and he hoped to deter potential offenders by increasing the likelihood of detection and prosecution. PC Richardson was added to the Unit after the Rolan Adams murder.

35.6   Mr Philpott accepted that from the start there could have been no doubt but that the Stephen Lawrence murder was a racist incident. Since murder is the most serious of crimes it would of course be dealt with in 1993 by an AMIP team. Therefore the murder itself did not come within the remit of the Racial Incident Unit. Indeed Mr Philpott accepted, as did others involved, that the Unit should probably have been called the Minor Racial Incident Unit, since all serious crime was taken on by the CID and by the AMIP teams.

35.7 During most of Mr Philpott's evidence it was believed that the card index which had been in use up to 1995 had been lost. In fact the cards were at the Plumstead Unit all the time, and they were produced for the members of the Inquiry to see. They contained many names and addresses of suspects and victims, so that general distribution of the index was not possible. We have however examined the index, which probably contains about 1,000 cards. In the main the information contained in the cards came from the crime sheets which are prepared by all officers who investigate criminal activities. There is also a manuscript note consisting of an alphabetical catalogue of the victims of racist incidents. The information about perpetrators of racist crime and of those involved in racist incidents was in theory certainly available to all officers involved in the Division. Similarly, as Mr Philpott pointed out, the collator's cards were also available. We have already considered the obvious desirability of all information being available to every officer investigating crime. We doubt whether it was universal or indeed a general practice to search these cards thoroughly in order to obtain as much information and intelligence as they might reveal.

35.8 The statistics indicate that after the Rolan Adams murder in 1991 there were more reports of racist incidents made directly to the Unit. Furthermore, Mr Philpott said that gradually cases were referred to the Unit from Greenwich Council or GACARA, the Greenwich Action Committee Against Racial Attacks. That Unit was financed by the Greenwich Council, and it was victim orientated. That is to say workers for GACARA encouraged victims to come to them, indicating that people from the ethnic minorities, and in particular women, were disinclined to report to the police when incidents of harassment or racist violence or abuse took place. Between 1991 and 1993 there were roughly 300-400 incidents reported to the Unit each year. The figures in the annual reports indicate that about two thirds of those were substantiated.

35.9 **In 1993 the Parliamentary Home Affairs Select Committee investigated racial matters. Sir Herman Ouseley, the Chairman of the CRE, gave evidence before that Committee and he extolled the virtues of the Racial Incident Unit at Plumstead. He had visited the Unit, as had other members of the Committee, so that he was able to form a view of its activities. Maybe that 1993 boost or recommendation from the Chairman of the CRE gave somewhat more credit to the Unit than was due. It does however seem to us somewhat churlish to criticise the formation and activity of the Unit, particularly in its early days. After all, bigger things grow from small beginnings. Mr Philpott himself was the first to indicate that while a start was made by the Unit and its officers the scheme was not as extensive or as wide ranging as he would have hoped.**

35.10 PSgt Peter Solley was the Divisional Community Officer over the relevant years from 1991 onwards. He acted in a somewhat informal way as the Supervisor of the two Constables in the Racial Incident Unit. Mr Philpott had much trust in PSgt Solley, and indicated that he supplied *"hands on"* leadership and enthusiasm and real interpersonal skills. We have seen PSgt Solley and we fully understand and would endorse, so far as our experience goes, his commendation of PSgt Solley. We also formed a good opinion of PC Fisher. It should be noted that Mr Fisher was throughout a Police Constable. He did not seek promotion, and no more senior officers were allocated to the Unit in its early years.

35.11 One of the shortcomings of the Unit's activities was that it did not contain much useful information about possible suspects. The tendency was to report and to direct reports in connection with racist crime to the Unit. Most of the information held by the Unit came from Crime Reports on which officers were bound to enter in the relevant boxes if a crime had a racist content. Such cases would then be sent to the Racial Incident Unit and a Racial Incident Unit number would be allocated to the case.

35.12 None of the five suspects in the Stephen Lawrence murder had cards in the Racial Incident Unit index. The reason for this is that until the Stephen Lawrence murder there were no identifiable crimes committed by the suspects which were infected with racism. Only one of the three occupants of the red Astra, the members of the gang involved in the murder of Rolan Adams, had his name on the Racial Incident Unit list. All those appear in the records of GACARA, because they had been involved in racist and violent activity reported by victims to GACARA following their activities in Thamesmead.

35.13 The truth is that the Local Intelligence Officer's cards or collator's cards contained more general information about criminal activities than did the Racial Incident Unit cards. Both were available apparently in the same office, but there does not seem to have been much formal or even informal exchange between the two sources of information and intelligence. Advances may have been made throughout the country in this respect, and there is plainly more work to be done particularly in the field of computers. It is most important that intelligence on violent and racist individuals should be collected, so that those investigating crimes have ready access to information which may lead them to the perpetrators of such crimes.

35.14 It was plain during Mr Philpott's evidence that much of the information in the hands of the Unit was in fact contained in the memories of the two officers. There are obvious drawbacks to the system as it evolved in its early years.

35.15 **PSgt Solley reported as to the Unit's activities to Mr Philpott, and Mr Philpott was responsible for a considerable measure of liaison with Greenwich Council and with GACARA. The evidence from Mr Dev Barrah, of GACARA seemed to support the notion that Mr Philpott's influence was good in this department, and that he did form a working relationship with the voluntary bodies which were aiming in the same direction as the Racial Incident Unit.**

35.16 As to training in connection with racism awareness and the investigation of racist incidents Mr Philpott told the Inquiry that it was his responsibility to ensure that his officers received training. He indicated that this was done particularly by a series of talks by local people with expertise in racist matters. Mrs Ros Howells and others apparently attended in order to speak with the Divisional officers. PC Fisher and his colleague also talked to some officers. Mr Philpott said that he believed that he had achieved 85% success in respect of training. We doubt whether the measure of training described was adequate. Again it does appear that Mr Philpott's heart was in the right place, although the measure and regularity of training was not extensive and does not seem to have made the necessary impact.

35.17 Mr Philpott in fact attended the scene of Stephen Lawrence's murder about two hours after it had happened. He was contacted because the murder happened on his Division, and he arrived in Well Hall Road to find that the cordons were in position and Mr Jeynes was the officer who appeared to be in charge. No log was kept of any kind. Mr Philpott indicated that he would have expected to see a scene log (a log of people passing in and out of the cordoned area), as it was his understanding that such logs were kept in the MPS. However he would not have expected to see a separate "*incident log*" recording the movements and activities of officers elsewhere such as searching etc, though he did add that he thought it would "*have been a good thing to have done.*"

35.18 **It does not appear that Mr Philpott made much inquiry as to what had taken place at the scene or as to the actions which had already been taken by the officers involved. He believed that the matter was now in the hands of the CID, and after he had been at the scene he met Mr Crampton at the police station and accepted that AMIP was from then onwards in charge. He spoke to Mr Crampton and learned amongst other things that Mr Crampton was not going to be able to remain as SIO. Mr Philpott regarded his duties thereafter as being concerned with possible public order developments, and maintenance of the connection with those in the community who had to be told that this terrible murder had taken place. It is evident that local Councillors were informed early on, and offers were made of assistance from Mr Penstone and others.**

35.19 Mr Philpott had no part in the early days of the investigation, and he had many other duties to perform. He must have been aware of the high profile nature of the murder, since press conferences were held and appeals were made from a very early stage. Later, during the first week after the murder, Mr Philpott learned, particularly from talking to local people, that the family liaison with the police was giving cause for concern. He believed that this happened within the first week or two after the murder, and he heard also about the arrival on the scene of Mr Khan, and of the concern which this was causing to some of those involved in the investigation. It is somewhat surprising that Mr Philpott should learn of the problems experienced in a murder investigation on his Division from members of the community rather than from the investigation team. On 30 April Mr Adams wrote or at least signed a letter to J R Jones indicating that contact should be made by Mr Khan and his firm directly through Mr Adams or Mr Philpott. The object of this exercise was apparently to take the heat off the SIO.

35.20 **As to family liaison Mr Philpott did not himself believe that DS Bevan and DC Holden were the ideal or the best officers to have been appointed to this task. At one stage he offered to supply two officers who might be better able to perform the task. It appears that those officers were PC Fisher, in whom Mr Philpott placed considerable trust, and a woman police officer other than DC Holden.**

35.21 Mr Philpott discussed his misgivings as to the appointments of the two family liaison officers, and he was present together with Mr Ilsley at the meeting on 6 May 1993 when Mr Ilsley indicated that he would be taking over the role of DS Bevan and DC Holden. The policy log entry as to this take-over is dated 27 May. It appears however that this is a mistaken date, since the 6 May meeting initiated Mr Ilsley's participation in family liaison. We do not know how or why such a discrepancy in dates occurred.

35.22 **Mr Philpott had no particular memory of Mr Ilsley's action in folding up the piece of paper which Mrs Lawrence had given him, but he did remember that Mrs Lawrence complained at the time that Mr Ilsley seemed to be paying scant attention to the information which Mrs Lawrence was giving to him. Mr Philpott seemed to accept that Mr Ilsley's action could have been misinterpreted, but the meeting seemed fairly unremarkable to him.**

35.23 **Mr Philpott seemed to have no memory of the arrests being made on 7 May, and indeed his memory of the investigation generally is understandably poor. He has after all been retired for three and a half years, and he was, in a sense, on the fringe of the investigation, because of the strict demarcation of responsibility between the investigating AMIP team and the host Division.**

35.24 As to the Barker Review Mr Philpott indicated that he had never seen the Review document at all. He had not even seen it when he gave evidence before the Inquiry. He was asked some questions about the recommendations in connection with family liaison made in the Review, but effectively he could not assist in connection with Mr Barker's report. He did accept a measure of Mr Barker's conclusions about family liaison, indicating that he agreed that the SIO should in a traumatic case such as this one be able to make the relevant instant decisions as to the level of information to be given, so that the family were provided with more than might be thought by some to be desirable in order to gain confidence and allay their fears.

35.25 Mr Philpott's assessment of why things went wrong included his view that the senior officers had difficulty in dealing with Mr Khan in his capacity as representative for the family. They felt that he was *"attempting to direct the inquiry and rightly or wrongly this upset them and put them on the defensive"*. Mr Philpott thought that the senior officers may have been informed that Mr & Mrs Lawrence did not particularly want to see them or felt badly towards the officers investigating the crime. The senior officers wanted to concentrate on the investigation and in Mr Philpott's words *"they thought that the family liaison matters would take care of themselves"*. Provided there was a successful prosecution the family might then feel less bad about the situation. Mr Philpott might be right to some extent in his beliefs, and this highlights in our view a *"laissez faire"* attitude about the family liaison, and the failure to get to grips at once with the unsatisfactory situation which developed almost from the outset.

35.26 When cross-examined by Mr Kamlish on behalf of the family Mr Philpott accepted that he made no records or memos of the steps that he took during the night after the murder, when he indicated that he contacted local opinion-formers in order to tell them what had happened. It is clear that this contact was made by Mr Philpott, since the messages show reaction both from the Council and others in the early stages.

35.27 **Mr Philpott understandably reacted against Mr Kamlish's assertion that all that Mr Philpott was doing was to conduct a public relations exercise in order to keep people happy and make people think that the police were doing their job properly. Mr Philpott's job was partly to ensure that the community was kept informed of what was happening.**

35.28 It appears likely that during the night after the murder at some stage Mr Philpott did see Duwayne Brooks at Plumstead Police Station. Furthermore it is likely that he saw Mr Brooks with his mother who was present at the police station. On the other hand it is a regrettable aspect of the case that in his statement to Kent Mr Philpott said that he saw a young man being shouted at by a woman who he thought was Cheryl Sloley, Mrs Lawrence's sister. This proved to be wholly erroneous. He said that he pointed this out to the person taking his statement, but that person said that it ought to remain in his statement if that was what he thought at the time. Such a flawed conclusion and such an unsustainable statement are understandably upsetting to Mrs Lawrence and all members of her family.

35.29 Mr Philpott is somewhat vague about the details of the complaints made by Mr & Mrs Lawrence about family liaison, but it is of some significance that he accepted their complaints, including the allegation that the liaison was insensitive and patronising. Furthermore Mr Philpott had plainly heard of the justifiable complaint of Mr & Mrs Lawrence that the family liaison officers were asking people in the house who they were. He agrees that such an approach was inappropriate and could only be regarded as offensive.

35.30 It may well be that Mr Philpott first approached Mr Ilsley about the matter, and, after a discussion, the change of tack and of arrangements made on 6 May followed. Mr Philpott's own direct contact with the family was small in the early stages, but he certainly gained the impression from his contacts with the community and with others that the family did not consider that the police were being supportive or providing them with proper information concerning the investigation.

35.31 **All in all Mr Philpott's evidence substantially supported Mr & Mrs Lawrence so far as their complaints concern the failure of the family liaison.**

35.32 When he was asked whether PSgt Solley might not have been a good person to become involved Mr Philpott indicated that he might have been but that an injection of PSgt Solley into the chain of command, or into the system, would have been against the *"culture and the organisation of the Metropolitan Police at that time. Uniformed officers did not interfere in the way an AMIP inquiry was conducted"*. This is an example of the compartmentalisation of the MPS in 1993. Such a set-up militates against good communication with the host Division and prevents good use of local knowledge and resources. Consequently it can also militate against proper detection and action where there are difficulties such as occurred in this case.

35.33 **Mr Philpott had no problems with Mr Khan or his role, although it is right to say that in his statement he said that it was his belief that Mr Khan *"wanted to control and direct the investigation"*. Mr Philpott accepted that this came from others and that such a complaint was to some extent gleaned from police station gossip. Such a comment was unjustified and should not have been made.**

35.34 **We formed the impression that Mr Philpott did decide on his own initiative that something had to be done in order to try to improve the situation in connection with the reporting and investigating of racist crimes. We have already indicated that the beginnings were small, but it seems hard to criticise Mr Philpott unduly for that. At least he did initiate something, and he made a start. PC Fisher devised the card index system used to record racist incidents, and although the system had its faults and limitations it was at least a beginning.**

35.35 It seems to us that very little is to be gained by comparison of the numbers of recorded racist incidents in the Racial Incident Unit's index as opposed to the numbers counted and recorded by GACARA. It may well be that the basis upon which the two organisations ran was different, and Mr Gompertz pointed out that when the documents are examined the GACARA figures cover not only Plumstead but Greenwich as well, so that any comparison between the two on a purely statistical basis may well be misleading.

35.36 Mr Philpott realised the difference in approach between the Racial Incident Unit and GACARA, indicating that the Racial Incident Unit approach was *"evidence centred"* while GACARA were *"singularly victim orientated"*.

35.37 Mr Philpott was taken to task by Mr Kamlish about articles and publications for which he was to some extent responsible. For example, on 4 August 1993 in a local publication called 'The News Shopper' Mr Philpott had indicated that it was insulting to allege that the police had failed in the investigation of the Stephen Lawrence murder case. It is apparent that Mr Philpott was defending the activities of the police. In one sense that was his job. Not of course to misrepresent what had happened, but to try to reassure people that things were not as bad as they were painted. The risk is that later such words will be held up as insensitive and to some extent incendiary.

35.38 The same may be said of Mr Philpott's support of PC Fisher in connection with his family liaison after the Rolan Adams murder in 1991. We do not intend to go into great detail in this regard, since we are inquiring into the murder of Stephen Lawrence. It is however apparent that Rolan's parents believed that they were not properly looked after, and yet Mr Fisher was commended by Mr Philpott *"for his professionalism and exceptional sensitivity"*. Mr Philpott said that he knew that the relationship between PC Fisher and the parents of Rolan Adams went up and down, but he still believes that PC Fisher did a sterling job in difficult circumstances.

35.39 We did not call Rolan Adam's parents, and it would be wrong in our view to delve deeply into the details of the family liaison after that terrible murder. We accept that the whole question of family liaison needs the closest attention by police.

35.40 As to PSgt Solley Mr Philpott said that he acted as Mr Philpott's eyes and ears and on occasions as a mouthpiece within the community. Mr Philpott rightly had confidence in PSgt Solley.

35.41 Questioning by Mr Yearwood, on behalf of the CRE, echoed much of the evidence that had already been given. We have already indicated that it is somewhat strange that Counsel for the CRE has been somewhat scathing in his questioning about the Racial Incident Unit. Sir Herman Ouseley's reaction in 1993 had been supportive. Whatever the shortcomings of the Unit may have been, at least Sir Herman realised that this was a potentially productive start. Later it is of some interest to note that an award was given to the London Borough of Greenwich for its part in the expansion and encouragement of the Racial Incident Unit. Too much time was taken up during the Inquiry in disputing whether the award carried any commendation of the Unit itself, rather than a congratulation to Greenwich for the part played by the Borough in its expansion. Very little turns upon this supposed conflict.

35.42 Miss Woodley, on behalf of the SIOs, pointed out that PC Fisher had indeed played a part in the early days in connection with the family liaison, since he worked with DS Bevan and visited the family on a number of occasions. By 4 May PC Fisher was in fact off the AMIP investigation team, and the policy file indicates that he was released from the Incident Room because he was required for community work and for preparation in connection with demonstrations which were planned. Mr Weeden did rightly provide in his note that PC Fisher should maintain close liaison with the Incident Room and that he should attend briefings.

35.43 Mr Philpott did not know why Mr Weeden was not invited to attend the meeting with the family on 6 May 1993. He said that he would have been delighted to see Mr Weeden there. Presumably therefore Mr Ilsley decided that the best course was to limit the meeting to himself and Mr Philpott.

35.44 Miss Deighton questioned Mr Philpott on behalf of Duwayne Brooks. Mr Philpott at once accepted that Mr Brooks was not properly categorised as a victim. Certainly in retrospect he was, to his credit, prepared to accept that Mr Brooks was not offered or given necessary specialist assistance and support by the police, particularly in the early days after the murder. This was primarily the fault of the SIOs and their superiors. Mr Philpott was perhaps somewhat hard on himself in accepting a major share of the blame in this respect.

35.45 Mr Gompertz in his questioning highlighted the evidence which had been given before the Home Affairs Committee, to which we have already made reference. It may be that the praise given before the Committee to the success of the Racial Incident Unit was *"bullish"* and optimistic. But it does seem to us unfair to criticise Mr Philpott who did at least take the initiative in Plumstead Division in this regard. He said that the praise given to the Unit before the Committee might have been somewhat fulsome. But he indicated more than once that he would like to think that Plumstead were going some way toward improvement in the system of tackling racist incidents and racist crime by the steps taken in connection with the Racial Incident Unit and in the work done in bringing together the local communities and the police. Mr Philpott was himself offered an award by the London Borough of Greenwich in this respect, but he declined it because he was aware that a substantial number of black people felt that he should not receive such an award. He felt that he could not have been doing his job well enough if there was a body of opinion against him, so that he declined that award.

35.46 **Mr Philpott agreed that the task of the Divisional Duty Officer, Chief Inspector McIvor, would have been to take over the uniformed ground control of the incident. Instead, as we know, Mr McIvor visited the scene, but quickly returned to the police station in order to look into the public order ramifications of what had taken place. Nobody properly took over the reins of command during the initial stages of the operation, as we have already indicated in the Chapters dealing with that aspect of the case.**

35.47 **All in all Mr Philpott came across as a good senior officer who did take positive steps in Plumstead in connection with racist matters. He appears to have been considerably involved with community leaders during his years of command. He was in charge of the whole Division and thus in charge of all aspects of policing apart from the investigation of very serious crimes. There were informal contacts between him and the SIOs in charge of serious offences, but it is apparent that there were in 1993 in a sense two different forces which were to a considerable extent compartmentalised.**

CHAPTER THIRTY-SIX

HARCOURT ALLEYNE
DEV BARRAH, AND 'GACARA'

36.1 On Day 49 two witnesses gave evidence whose input was important in connection with race relations in Greenwich and the surrounding areas. The first of these witnesses was Mr Harcourt Alleyne who is and has been for some years Head of the Department of Race Equality of Greenwich Council. Before that he had held other posts within Greenwich Council and had worked for many years in local government.

36.2 **Mr Alleyne was an impressive and a careful witness and he prepared a perceptive report for the benefit of the Inquiry and the public. Broadly Mr Alleyne dealt with the steps which had been taken and which he believed might be taken by the Council with a view to alleviating at least some of the problems highlighted by his report. There was in the 1980s a rising level of reported incidents of racist attacks and harassment within the police Divisions with which we have been concerned. Mr Alleyne indicated that there were community concerns about the perceived ineffectiveness of the police in addressing the problem of such incidents. Furthermore Mr Alleyne commented upon the presence in the neighbourhood of Welling of the British National Party who were active in the area and who disseminated a substantial amount of literature which was a cause of real concern in the local community.**

36.3 Mr Alleyne referred to the setting up in Plumstead Division in December 1990 of the Racial Incident Unit, whose purpose was in his view to provide general support to victims, to liaise with other agencies and to investigate all but the most serious racist incidents reported either directly or on referral from others. Those referrals might come from the Greenwich Council itself or from GACARA (the Greenwich Action Committee Against Racial Attacks) which was a Council-funded organisation.

36.4 Mr Alleyne indicated that by 1990 or early in 1991 there was considerable concern that the level of interaction or liaison between the various statutory organisations covering in particular the Thamesmead area was very poor. One organisation did not seem to know what the other one was doing. Therefore in order to minimise that problem and to co-ordinate efforts the Thamesmead Race Liaison Group was set up which was an umbrella organisation for the various organisations active in the area.

36.5 That Group met from May 1991 until January 1992, and later there was formed a body which was termed a Community Safety Partnership, which came together formally in the middle of 1993, after Stephen Lawrence's murder. There was then liaison between the Racial Incident Unit and the Council, and an Asian legal executive was in effect dedicated to assisting with legal matters with the police force through the Racial Incident Unit. The object of the exercise throughout was in Mr Alleyne's view to meet the Council's concern that there was a necessity to improve not only the Council's performance but also the police performance in responding to racist violence within the community. The intention was to create a two-way process.

36.6 A police officer was seconded to the Council in order to try to increase the level of understanding between the two agencies, in addition to the seconding of the legal executive from the Council to the police. Thereafter, and indeed until 1996, the Council took the initiative in seeking to improve the situation. It is apparent that the CRE approved and encouraged the steps that were being taken, comparatively small though they may seem to have been, in creating liaison between the police and the Council and other local bodies.

36.7 Mr Alleyne had considerable dealings with PSgt Solley, who was in overall charge of the police Racial Incident Unit, particularly from 1995 onwards. By and large he agreed that this liaison did help to move things forward.

36.8 In 1995 a multi-racial forum for the Plumstead Division was established. Overall Mr Alleyne believes that the joint Units created between the Council and the police were certainly an improvement on what had existed before. The objective was to provide a more speedy response to victims reporting racist attacks and harassment, and to reduce some of the duplication which previously took place when people did report incidents, particularly Council tenants. Mr Alleyne stressed the importance that the Council attached to the issue generally, and he believes that the fact that there had been joint arrangements made had helped better to inform both agencies and to bring together a better understanding of the difficulties involved from both sides.

36.9 Again Mr Alleyne indicated that from his own perspective before 1992 or 1993 there had been a lack of accountability, which Mr Alleyne believes that the joint Unit is now attempting to *bring into the frame through the multi-racial forum which involves the community*".

36.10 **Mr Alleyne commented in his evidence on the problem posed by the unwillingness of members of the public to report racist harassment and violence, and upon the tendency in the police force to *"de-racialise"* racist incidents. He stressed the importance of encouraging people to have confidence in the new system and the importance of the police committing themselves to the important role which they had to play in developing joint co-operation schemes to help with racist harassment and violence and to ensure that there is proper accountability to the community.**

36.11 **Mr Alleyne indicated that he did believe that the senior officers with whom he had come into contact were taking the situation seriously, but he appeared to stress that there was a long way to go in the general development of co-operation in this field.**

36.12 The purpose of the multi-racial forum, which is Chaired by a distinguished and prominent member of the local community, was to confront matters concerning the local community and the police and the Council, and perhaps particularly to focus upon problems which arose from, for example, the issue of local stop and search, which is everywhere a matter of considerable concern to minority ethnic communities.

36.13 In answer to Mr Gompertz Mr Alleyne indicated that in his view the situation in 1990 had been very poor so far as partnership between the police and the community was concerned. He believed that there has been some progress, but he indicated rightly that there is still a lot more to be done. He believed that there has been improvement because of the sharing of information and the inter-connection between the police and the Council. Mr Alleyne accepted that the Racial Incident Unit had at least provided modest success, and he indicated that the Council was concerned to see that a better service was provided to victims of racist violence. He indicated that the Council would actively work with agencies like the police and GACARA and the Greenwich Council for Racial Equality (GCRE) and other bodies in order to achieve that objective.

36.14 GACARA, as Mr Alleyne told us, is an organisation which is both supported and indeed funded by the Council. This has been the situation since the late 1970s. Since 1992 GACARA has been jointly funded with GCRE. The staffing of GACARA runs only to three or four persons to this day.

36.15 Mr Alleyne was overall cautiously optimistic that the result of the multi-agency framework would be that the police and Council officers would do more and more to assist the process of improvement of race relations, although he accepted in his evidence that there was a considerable ebb and flow of the nature of the relationship between the police and the black community. He told us that incidents such as the failure to apprehend Stephen Lawrence's murderers, and the Commissioner's statement in connection with Operation Eagle Eye knock relations back considerably. Mr Alleyne believes that it is most important that people who have positions of responsibility should be seen to be doing the right thing and taking the lead properly in relation to these issues.

36.16 The nub of the matter, said Mr Alleyne, is about ensuring that perpetrators have proper action taken against them, that victims are supported, and that a general down turn in the trend of racist incidents is somehow achieved. Until those goals appear to be met Mr Alleyne would not feel that the current joint Unit was being successful.

36.17 Mr Alleyne accepts that his impression is that there was greater openness certainly in the case of senior police officers, including Mr Philpott, and more willingness to discuss issues and to recognise that all is not well in connection with racist issues within the police force.

36.18 In answer to Mr Yearwood, on behalf of the CRE, Mr Alleyne would not accept that Eltham was peculiarly or exceptionally bad in connection with its record on racism. But he did accept that the problems of racist violence and harassment were considerable. Mr Alleyne indicated that he believed that the Racial Incident Unit, as it has developed, represented *"a step along a path from very low beginnings"*. He stressed that it was important to develop the addressing of wider issues about dealing with victims more effectively, and responding to their needs. He also indicated that it was important that more perpetrators of racist crime should be satisfactorily brought to court, and also that a more effective and better role should be played in getting involved with young people, particularly perhaps children in schools, as a preventative aspect of the whole scene, and to work very closely in partnership with others in performing these tasks.

36.19 Mr Alleyne indicated that there was concern that the establishment of a Racial Incident Unit might marginalise the issue, since this might suggest that the only persons interested in dealing with racist incidents were the officers in the Units themselves. Ultimately Mr Alleyne believed that officers closely involved in racist incidents ought to be responsible for ensuring that all other police officers in the service were well equipped to deal with racist incidents themselves effectively and on all fronts. Certainly Mr Alleyne accepted and believed that the police officers had a role together with others in terms of education as far as racism is concerned, and that the police are very much a key part of the drive to deal with the problem of racist violence and racist incidents and to show the commitment that is necessary to deal with these issues.

36.20 **Lastly Mr Alleyne indicated that he had the impression that there was far too much *"canteen culture"* of racism within the police force. Officers feel that it is appropriate to say things within the confines of their own ranks and without action being taken by people to put a stop to it.**

36.21 **All in all Mr Alleyne was an impressive witness. His evidence indicates the need for much development of the relationship between the black communities and the local Council and the Police Service. Small beginnings are all very well, but they must be encouraged to develop if the situation between the black communities and the Police Service is to improve.**

36.22 The second witness in this field was Mr Dev Barrah who started as a full-time volunteer project worker and campaigner at GACARA. He has been a full-time volunteer and ultimately an employee since 1980. Before the Racial Incident Unit came into existence in Plumstead in December 1990 Mr Barrah had dealt with a police community liaison officer. Mr Barrah had some doubts about the Racial Incident Unit, particularly at the start, because initially that Unit consisted of simply one male officer. At that time one of the local troubles was that there were attacks upon women, mostly Asian women, and Mr Barrah thought that there would be problems in appointing a white male officer to deal specifically with such cases. Mr Barrah's view was that all officers ought to be trained to deal with racist incidents, because otherwise there was a risk of marginalisation of such incidents. Mr Barrah said that he had not been enthusiastic about the establishment of the Racial Incident Unit.

36.23 Mr Barrah remains critical of the Racial Incident Unit and of its response. He indicated that the creation of the Unit had tended to slow down the response of the police to racist incidents, in the sense that as soon as there was a racist incident or minor crime the victims would be told that nothing further could be done by the police who were initially contacted but that the matter would have to be referred to the Racial Incident Unit. That Unit of course was small and not always manned. Mr Barrah believes that the Racial Incident Unit is to some extent cosmetic, and that it should be used as an intelligence gathering organisation collating information which might help other police officers to get cases to court.

36.24 **Mr Barrah believes that GACARA receives far more complaints and gives more assistance to victims than the police have ever given. He also believes that the only real improvement that has taken place in recent years is that the Greenwich Council have taken more action against perpetrators than have the police. In connection with the multi-agency meetings most of the relevant action and initiative comes from the Council rather than the police. Mr Barrah believes that not much has been achieved in connection with the relationship between the police and the community as a result of police initiative and the establishment of the Racial Incident Unit.**

36.25 In answer to Mr Gompertz Mr Barrah was reluctant to accept that the Racial Incident Unit had achieved anything, although it was pointed out to him that in 1992 he had told 'The Voice' newspaper that there had been *"a new dialogue with the police because of the Unit and that while there was room for improvement the police are going in the right direction"*. Mr Barrah indicated that his approval of the Unit was limited.

36.26 An issue has arisen in this case as to whether GACARA attempted to intervene by visiting Mr & Mrs Lawrence early on after the murder. PC Fisher saw Ben White at 08:45 on 23 April outside the Lawrence household. Apparently Mr White never went inside the house, although it had been the intention of GACARA to do what they could to assist. This appears to some extent to have misfired, since we know that a letter was written by Mr Khan indicating that GACARA, and apparently other bodies, were unwelcome and that the Lawrence family did not wish them to intervene.

36.27 Mr Barrah was well acquainted with Mr Khan, in the sense that he had contact with him in connection with work which they both did in Newham, where Mr Barrah had seen Mr Khan on a number of occasions. There was however no direct connection between Mr Barrah and Mr Khan, and Mr Barrah did not connect Mr Khan with the Anti Racist Alliance (ARA). The only point of the questions put to Mr Barrah in this regard appears to have been to point up the fact that to Kent Mr Barrah had said that the support of GACARA was rejected in favour of the ARA who had already become connected with the Lawrence family.

36.28 When questioned by Mr Panton on behalf of the London Borough of Greenwich it appeared to the Inquiry that there is unfortunately some disagreement between the Council and GACARA as to the value of the Racial Incident Unit as it has developed. Mr Panton suggested to Mr Barrah that a successful Racial Incident Unit might mean that there was less for GACARA to do and that his organisation had something to fear in a sense from the success of the Racial Incident Unit.

36.29 This appears to us to be a strange development, since GACARA is funded by the Council and it would be most unfortunate if there should be any rift between GACARA and the Council or any fundamental difference in their views as to the value of the steps being taken to further race relations and to deal with racist harassment and crime within the Council's area.

36.30 We have no doubt that there is considerable value in the development and the extension of the work of the Racial Incident Unit and the multi-racial forum, and that GACARA has its own role to play which is of considerable value.

36.31 Mr Barrah was somewhat grudging in his response to the Racial Incident Unit and the officers comprising that Unit. He was to some extent supportive of PSgt Solley and Mr Philpott, in connection with their attempts to build a relationship with the community. He had no confidence that a greater understanding had been established between the local police and those who suffered racist harassment in the area.

36.32 **It is important that any competition in this area and any resentment should be resolved, since little progress can be made if bodies who are well intentioned and successful in their own particular area cannot or do not work together with the same objective. Issues which may be preventing agencies concerned to pursue racist incidents in partnership should be resolved.**

CHAPTER THIRTY-SEVEN

POLICE SERGEANT PETER SOLLEY

37.1 Police Sergeant Peter Solley has been Community Divisional Liaison Officer for the Plumstead Police Division for about 10 years. His role has developed as time has passed. When he first undertook the role he managed local beat officers in the Division, and he had responsibility for Neighbourhood Watch liaison and for general community matters. The role has developed since then and in particular it encompasses line management of the Racial Incident Unit which was established in December 1990.

37.2 As we know that Unit was involved with the investigation and the recording of all but the most serious of racist incidents reported in the Plumstead Police Division. PSgt Solley's task was to oversee the work done by the two officers in the Racial Incident Unit. PSgt Solley worked directly to Chief Superintendent Philpott, and he had regular meetings with Mr Philpott in connection with all aspects of community liaison.

37.3 **We should say at the outset that we formed a favourable view of PSgt Solley. He was a thorough and sympathetic man, and we are sure that within his powers he would have done all that was possible to further good relations in the community.**

37.4 We have already given an account of the formation of the Racial Incident Unit and of its activities. PSgt Solley in his evidence elaborated upon the evidence already given and spoke of the co-operation which should have taken place between the Racial Incident Unit and those who were investigating racist incidents in the CID. Plainly the system was not well developed by 1993, but PSgt Solley believed that it performed a useful function.

37.5 On 23 April 1993 Mr Philpott telephoned PSgt Solley at home and informed him of the racist murder of Stephen Lawrence. Mr Philpott said that he had contacted the leader of the Council and others. PSgt Solley was instructed to get in early and to ensure that everyone else who needed to be informed was informed. PSgt Solley himself believes that he spoke to the Greenwich Council for Racial Equality, and to GACARA, and probably to Harcourt Alleyne who was, and still is, Chief Race Adviser to the Greenwich Council.

37.6 PC Fisher was allocated to the murder investigation team from about 05:00 on 23 April, so that PSgt Solley believed that any relevant liaison with the Racial Incident Unit would be performed simply because of that connection. PSgt Solley's role was a wider one under Mr Philpott's direction and he was certainly partly responsible for the organisation of a meeting which took place on the evening of 23 April at which leaders of the community were present.

37.7 PSgt Solley pointed out, as had Mr Philpott, that the index and card system of the Racial Incident Unit was of course not foolproof or wholly complete, but he also indicated that at least the Racial Incident Unit had given a start to the necessary attention to racist incidents in the Plumstead area.

37.8 As to the connection with the Lawrence family, PSgt Solley had no direct role to play in this regard. However on the day after Stephen's murder he was instructed to go to the family home to arrange for an alarm to be installed within the house. Mr & Mrs Lawrence were there, but PSgt Solley did not actually speak to them. He indicated that there were many other people in the house at the time, and that he had simply one specific task to perform. Thereafter PSgt Solley did meet Mr & Mrs Lawrence when they came to the police station to meet regularly with Mr Ilsley. He was the officer at the front counter who escorted them up to Mr Ilsley's office. He had thus met both Mr & Mrs Lawrence, but was plainly not closely involved with family liaison or indeed with the murder investigation.

37.9 Later on, probably in September 1993, PSgt Solley did meet Mrs Lawrence at her home when he had a substantial conversation with her. Apparently Mr & Mrs Lawrence were moving house and there was a need for some steps to be taken in connection with the security of their new home. PSgt Solley had a general conversation with Mrs Lawrence, discussing their family and the pressures and stresses that there had been on the Lawrence family since the murder of Stephen. He discovered during that meeting that Mrs Lawrence's complaint was that the police officers with whom she had contact were insensitive. Sometimes they were not available when they were needed. On one occasion she had telephoned in the early hours of the morning when she needed help and advice, and it was not forthcoming. The conversation also turned to discussion of the immediate hours after the murder, and to the part played by PC Geddis and his wife. PSgt Solley told us that Mrs Lawrence asked him to thank PC Geddis for what he had done.

37.10 **PSgt Solley had little to add in his primary evidence, but he did indicate that he had always treated the murder of Stephen Lawrence as a racist murder. He had no specific training in his role as Community Liaison Officer, but he had developed local knowledge through his involvement with local minority ethnic leaders and community groups and he was well aware of the impact of racist incidents upon the black community.**

37.11 **But for the arrival on the scene of a somewhat remarkable document produced by PSgt Solley his evidence might well have been anodyne. He was plainly a man with sensitive intentions so far as community liaison was concerned. It seemed unlikely that there would be any contest as to the part played by him on the fringes of the Stephen Lawrence investigation. The only criticism there could be was of the scale and ambit and perhaps the amateurism of the operation of the index kept by the Racial Incident Unit. There seemed to be no prospect of personal criticism of PSgt Solley.**

37.12 No notice of any kind was given to PSgt Solley that he would be criticised, or that he would be the subject of hostile examination by any of the Counsel involved in the case. At the end of his questioning by Miss Weekes, Junior Counsel to the Inquiry, we adjourned because we were told that something had arisen which had to be considered before further questioning of PSgt Solley.

37.13 What had happened was that a document had been produced by Mr & Mrs Lawrence's legal team, and in particular by Mr Kamlish, which Mr Kamlish wished to use in cross-examination. There is no doubt but that this document was produced by PSgt Solley himself. He produced it on his word processor at work. The eight page document set out a series of questions which might be asked at the Inquiry, together with proposed answers. The questions were set out in an interrogative manner, for example, *"Did your relationship with the family break down?"* Answer: *"Say that you would not describe it as a breakdown of relationship ..... etc"*. The answers were done in various colours. It was certainly an unusual document. As to how the document got into Mr Kamlish's hands PSgt Solley said that a copy was taken without his knowledge by a friend *"not ... with any malice"*, but without his knowledge.

37.14 Exactly how and when it was obtained should not be explored here. Once it was in the hands of legal representatives it seemed purposeless to say that it could not be used. The result of this was that much time was taken up by Mr Kamlish and others in questioning PSgt Solley about the nature of the document, and indeed in challenging him as to its objective and its effect.

37.15 **PSgt Solley firmly said that there was no question of any outside "coaching" in connection with his evidence. He said that the document was produced by himself, but that its contents had been discussed with others including members of the Greenwich Council. PSgt Solley named a number of people with whom he had discussed the questions which were posed in the document, and he said that the answers produced were in a sense an amalgam of the views and ideas which those persons, both friends and community connections, had given to him. PSgt Solley also discussed the evidence that he was to give before the Inquiry with his wife.**

37.16 More than once it was suggested to PSgt Solley that *"this was a script, provided to you by others"*. PSgt Solley firmly denied that this was so, and we accept his evidence.

37.17 **PSgt Solley's evidence was largely uncontroversial, and many of the answers which he gave were in fact favourable to the case put forward by Mr & Mrs Lawrence and others. PSgt Solley came through his ordeal in the witness box, because that is what it was, with distinction. Indeed the result of the questioning of PSgt Solley strengthened our view that he was both a useful and a sympathetic and a well motivated officer. He plainly did wish to improve relationships between the black community and the police, and he was an asset to Mr Philpott and to those with whom he came into contact.**

37.18 **To his credit PSgt Solley agreed during his questioning that officers in the police force were inclined to stereotype those with whom they had contact in the community. He accepted that the perception was that officers were often involved in confrontational situations which led to stereotyping. He also accepted the criticism that is available about the stop and search statistics, which show that black people are more often stopped and searched in the street than white people.**

37.19 In this respect PSgt Solley indicated that concerns over stop and search had to a considerable extent been responsible within the Greenwich Borough for the setting up in about 1995 of a police/community multi-agency forum which had provided the opportunity to discuss openly and frankly issues of concern, including stop and search.

37.20 PSgt Solley was plainly alive to the problems which have bedevilled relationships between the black community and the police service, and he was and still is a part of the developing Racial Incident Unit and of the community efforts which involve liaison and combination with representatives of the Greenwich Borough Council.

37.21 Indeed the Racial Incident Unit in the area now consists of a combined Unit with officers from Greenwich and Plumstead Divisions, with a civilian input from the Greenwich Borough Council. The arrangement is still by no means perfect, but it is a developing scene and one which has within it prospects of success.

37.22 **We took the opportunity after PSgt Solley had finished his evidence to indicate there and then that we had received no evidence to suggest that PSgt Solley's document was the product of outside coaching by police or lawyers or anybody on the outside. The document was certainly unusual, and perhaps a little bizarre, but we have no reason to doubt that it was produced in the way which he had described to us. There is no reason why somebody who is to be called before an Inquiry should not discuss with others the content of his evidence. In the end he must give his own views and his own answers.**

37.23 **We do not believe that he trimmed his evidence or dishonestly altered any part of his testimony which would otherwise have been different.**

37.24 **PSgt Solley accepted that there was a *"canteen culture"* of racism within the MPS, but he indicated that it is his belief that things were changing considerably from the situation of the '70s and '80s. PSgt Solley appreciated that the perception within the black community was that the culture still rules. Of all the officers of his rank and below seen by this Inquiry we believe that PSgt Solley was the most committed to work which would improve the situation. As we have already said he is a sympathetic and well intentioned man. Plainly there are limits to what he can himself perform. His value to Mr Philpott and to the community was and is in our opinion considerable.**

37.25 In answer to Mr Panton, PSgt Solley agreed that the relationship between the MPS and Greenwich Council was good, and the Council and the Police have, as we have indicated, co-operated in the development of the Racial Incident Unit.

37.26 Mr Gompertz asked PSgt Solley a series of questions about the document which had been produced by Mr Kamlish, and there is no doubt but that the answers given by PSgt Solley to Mr Gompertz reinforced our view that the document was not a dramatic or deceitful attempt to mislead the Inquiry at all.

37.27 PSgt Solley is still in post as Community Liaison Officer in Plumstead. No doubt he will continue to be used in future as the Racial Incident Unit develops and enlarges. His contribution will, as it seems to us, be considerable and beneficial.

CHAPTER THIRTY-EIGHT

POLICE CONSTABLE ALAN FISHER
AND
THE INCIDENT IN SAINSBURY'S CAR PARK

38.1   Police Constable Alan Fisher was the officer appointed to be the Racial Incident Officer in Plumstead in November 1990. Mr Philpott was the moving spirit in the foundation of the Racial Incident Unit, and PC Fisher applied for the appointment.

38.2   PC Fisher was fully aware of the ACPO definition of a racist incident. He set up the Unit with these criteria in mind, and he indicated to us that he decided to record racist incidents by using a card index system. He set up categories within this system under the headings *"Victim, Race Code, Suspect Code, Venue of Incident, Offence Code, and Crime Reference Number"*. He allotted sequential numbers unique to the racist incidents. The card indexes were intended to be cross-referenced under these headings.

38.3   We have seen the surviving cards of the card index, which were produced somewhat late in the day for the scrutiny of the Inquiry. Since 1995 the index has been computerised, and it is plain that in the early days the index was somewhat primitive. That is not intended to be a criticism of PC Fisher since he did the best that he could to embark upon uncharted waters. PC Fisher had no training relevant to this work nor in race awareness before he started work at Shooters Hill Police Station. He was the only officer involved initially on full-time duty in this regard.

38.4   In fact as long ago as February 1983 a document was produced called *"Community and Race Relations Training for Police"*. That is a report of the Police Training Council Working Party, and it sets out the *"Requirements for police training in community and race relations"*. That document is an interesting and sensitive report which would plainly have been useful to PC Fisher. It stressed the need for officers to be alert to the sensitivity of local conditions and to their reaction to different cultural attitudes.

38.5   PC Fisher thought that parts of the document sounded familiar, but the truth is that he was left effectively to develop his tactics and his job without much direction and certainly without training. PSgt Solley and Mr Philpott to some extent supervised and oversaw the activities of PC Fisher, but it is plain that he was left on his own, and later with PC Richardson, to deal with the thorny problem of recording and dealing with racist incidents.

38.6   We are confident that PC Fisher did the best that he could from the start. But he was a junior officer, and he accepts that to a considerable extent in that position he did have to look over his shoulder and rely upon other people to assist him in carrying out his task. He worked from the beginning closely with Greenwich Council, and he paid tribute to Mr Penstone with whom he co-operated from the start. PC Fisher had valuable feedback from Mr Penstone, and he told the Inquiry that he frequently asked Mr Penstone to attend when a statement had to be taken in more difficult circumstances. He and Mr Penstone dealt with a number of cases in co-operation. PC Fisher also relied on information and help from GACARA and from Greenwich Council itself. He said that that was the only way in which he had guidance as to how to conduct his duties, together with his own ideas and those transmitted to him by PSgt Solley and Mr Philpott.

38.8   PC Fisher thought that in terms of investigating crime involving racist motivation the system worked well, but he accepted that there was a marked lack of training in racist matters both as to himself and other police officers.

38.9   As to the gathering of intelligence again there was no specific direction as to how this should be done by the Racial Incident Unit, but PC Fisher developed a system of identifying problems where there were groups conducting racist attacks, in order to be able to contribute to the sharing of information which was coming into the various agencies involved in racist affairs.

38.10   PC Fisher believed that his relationship with GACARA, and in particular with Mr Barrah, was quite good. To start with it appears that there was some tension between PC Fisher and Mr Barrah, but PC Fisher's comment was that things appeared to get better.

38.11   In 1991 Rolan Adams was murdered in Thamesmead. PC Fisher was appointed as Family Liaison Officer to Mr & Mrs Adams. It is to some extent revealing that this appointment was made, since it meant that PC Fisher was wearing two different hats, one as the only officer in charge of the Racial Incident Unit and another as the sole Family Liaison Officer to Mr & Mrs Adams.

38.12   PC Fisher accepted that the connection with Mr & Mrs Adams took a long time to develop. Sometimes the relationship was good, and sometimes it was very strained. No complaint was made about PC Fisher directly or indirectly in connection with his role with the Mr & Mrs Adams, but it is palpable that things did not go well in that liaison.

38.13   PC Fisher became acquainted with the names Goatley, Copley and Hyland (the red Astra trio) during his dealings with the Adams case. He had also been a home beat officer for three years in Thamesmead during which time he had come across those individuals. When he became a Racial Incident Officer PC Fisher remembers that at least two of those young men, namely Mr Hyland and Mr Copley, came to his notice in connection with other racist behaviour or incidents. The name Hyland appears on a suspect card in the Racial Incident Unit card index, but to PC Fisher's surprise the names Goatley and Copley were not in the index at all. He could give no explanation for that omission, and he remains convinced that there had been cards for those men in his system.

38.14   As to the spreading of information PC Fisher told us that in the early days he would give information to the collators at the relevant police stations. This would be done by filling in a green form, and later on a fresh form was devised in order to ensure the flow of information from his Unit to the collators' cards.

38.15   At about 05:00 on the morning of 23 April 1993 PC Fisher was contacted and asked to attend Plumstead Police Station. At the police station PC Fisher saw Mr Jeynes, who explained the circumstances of the murder of Stephen Lawrence. In this somewhat informal manner PC Fisher joined the AMIP investigation team, probably because somebody realised that there ought to be input from the Racial Incident Unit. PC Fisher remained with the investigation team until 4 May 1993. On that date the policy file indicates that PC Fisher was to be returned to the Racial Incident Unit because there were demonstrations and other activities which appeared to be about to take place, and it was thought that PC Fisher had to be back at his original duty in order to deal with these matters.

38.16   PC Fisher was attached to the AMIP team to help if he could, particularly in connection with any racist aspect of the case. As a non-CID officer his input would have been limited to specific racist aspects rather than to the general investigation. Thus a message was passed to

S012, the Special Branch Section at New Scotland Yard responsible for holding intelligence on extremist bodies, to the effect that *"in view of the possible involvement of serious right wing factions would you note our interest and ask our officers at that desk to liaise with us via PC Fisher the Racial Incidents Officer."*

38.17 On 25 April PC Fisher was expressly deputed to arrange a search of the Special Branch Index in connection with the names Dobson, Acourt, Norris and Goodchild. Also on 28 April the system records that Mr Penstone would be *"in contact with PC Fisher and supply all rumours"*. Thus Mr Penstone was connected through PC Fisher with the investigating team.

38.18 PC Fisher was never formally appointed as a Liaison Officer to Mr & Mrs Lawrence. That task had been expressly given to DS Bevan and DC Holden. It was plainly thought desirable that a Racial Incident Officer should go to see Mr & Mrs Lawrence, as a temporary addition to the formal liaison team. PC Fisher in fact went to Mr & Mrs Lawrence's home on Friday 23 April. There he saw Ben White of GACARA standing outside the front door. It appears that GACARA did not on that occasion enter the premises, since there were other people present.

38.19 Mr Fisher also attended the mortuary on Saturday 24 April. He remembers that DS Bevan and DC Holden went inside with Mr & Mrs Lawrence. He was there to assist if his help had been needed.

38.20 On 30 April PC Fisher went to investigate an incident which took place in the car park of Sainsburys at Woolwich. It occurred when Mrs Lawrence was in a car with her sister, Mrs Sloley, and with another woman. There was an incident involving their car and a trolley loaded with shopping which was being manoeuvred by two white women. There was an altercation, and it appears that the white women used foul language as a result of which the incident developed. The white women made very unpleasant racist remarks, and one of them appears to have taken something from the boot of her car. Mrs Sloley believed that she was threatened by the woman who appeared to be holding a brick in her hand. The woman says that this was a can of dog food which she took from the boot because Mrs Sloley and her friend appeared to be coming towards them in a threatening manner.

38.21 There was obviously bad language used on both sides and at one stage Mrs Sloley tried to get hold of that which the woman was holding. PC Fisher believed that there was enough material and sufficient evidence to charge at least one of the two white women. He completed a set of case papers for the CPS, and alleged that there had been an affray under Section 4, Public Order Act, 1986.

38.22 Later the file came back and the Crown Prosecutor, Mr Burns, indicated that both the parties to this incident became particularly upset, perhaps because of recent bereavements, and that there was aggression on both sides. *"I do not consider that any offence is properly made out and proceedings should not be brought against any party"*. Mrs Lawrence and Mrs Sloley plainly believed that this was turning the case upon its head. PC Fisher agrees with that, and indicated to the Inquiry that he believed that there should have been a prosecution in this case. There was no prosecution. The unsatisfactory outcome of this incident from the point of view of Mrs Lawrence and Mrs Sloley is that it has similarity with a series of examples and submissions made to us during Part 2 of our Inquiry. The suggestion made is that racist incidents are "turned on their heads" by police officers and others who tend to side incorrectly and insensitively with the perpetrators rather than with the victims of such incidents.

38.23 **When Mr Kamlish questioned PC Fisher he accepted, as he had from the outset, that he had not had any relevant training in the area of racist crime or race relations otherwise than through brief notes which had been given to him at some stage. This was yet another example of another officer whose heart was in the right place, but who had had no training to conduct the special activities which he was given by Mr Philpott. He tried evidently to base his Unit on the Domestic Violence Unit, and thought that this would be a reasonable framework to start with. He appreciated that the very existence of a Racial Incident Unit would tend to isolate racist crime, so that the risk of marginalisation existed. Nonetheless he was an enthusiast, and believed that his general training and police activity would allow him to develop his specialised role.**

38.24 When he was appointed to the Stephen Lawrence investigation, he believed that he was there because the murder was motivated by racism, and it seemed to be a good idea to attach him to the team simply for that reason. PC Fisher believed that he might have been designated as a Family Liaison Officer, for the same reason, but in fact his actual contribution to the investigation seems to have been slight. That is not PC Fisher's fault. He was not a regular member of the AMIP team itself, and of course he had no CID experience.

38.25 In answer to Mr Yearwood PC Fisher expanded upon his activities in the Racial Incident Unit. He told us how crime reports would reach him, after being filled out by the original investigating officer. And he told the Inquiry about the classification of cases and the way in which they would thereafter be investigated. To some extent the Unit did simply develop as time went along. There was no true guidance as to what PC Fisher was to do, or how he was to manage the Unit's affairs.

38.26 Mr Yearwood criticised to some extent the failure of PC Fisher to obtain information in his intelligence gathering role from local schools. How much this can be laid at the door of PC Fisher is in our view doubtful.

38.27 **All in all PC Fisher was a sympathetic and a careful witness, and we gained the impression that he did the best that he could in the circumstances. To some extent he was in a watertight compartment, and he was of course a junior officer and was conscious that he had to look over his shoulder in connection with his own activities. He worked with GACARA and the local community. He never received a formal complaint against the police in connection with his tasks, but he did hear that GACARA had information that the community were not totally happy with the service which the Racial Incident Unit was giving.**

38.28 During the time that he was actually serving on the Stephen Lawrence investigation he indicated that he did what he could, and that he was always available for the team to contact him if he needed to be contacted so that he could put the AMIP officer in touch with people that he knew in the various organisations with which he liaised.

38.29 **His positive contribution to the Stephen Lawrence investigation was probably slight, but we feel that the small beginnings conducted by PC Fisher and initiated by Mr Philpott were at least positive steps in the right direction. That is not to say that the collection of information and the handling of racist crime and racist incidents is even now satisfactory. But at least a start was made which is being nurtured by the police and by the local authority and other agencies.**

CHAPTER THIRTY-NINE

CROWN PROSECUTION SERVICE

39.1 For a time we wondered whether a Police Act Inquiry into policing should encompass evidence about the decisions in connection with the prosecution of the suspects. On reflection it was plain that the Inquiry would be woefully incomplete if the prosecution process was not examined. Furthermore the inter-relation between the police and the Crown Prosecution Service, as highlighted in this case, could lead to recommendations in connection with the future prosecution of cases of this kind. With these considerations in mind evidence was called on Days 51 and 52 dealing with the CPS' part in this case. In addition we have seen all the background papers relevant to the prosecution, including 18 successive reports prepared by the investigation team for the CPS, commonly called Investigating Officer's Reports.

39.2 Some of the evidence given by the witnesses in statement form was read to the Inquiry, and two witnesses were called to give live evidence. The first of these witnesses was Mr Philip Medwynter. He gave short evidence in the witness box, and his full statement was read out by Mr Brian Barker, on behalf of the CPS, as the record shows. Mr Medwynter is a Bachelor of Law and a Barrister. He had experience as a Court Clerk in the Magistrates' Court and in 1987 he joined the CPS. He is and was in 1993 a principal Crown Prosecutor. He was the principal Crown Prosecutor for the Camberwell Greenwich Youth Team managing three other lawyers when the team acquired the Stephen Lawrence case. He allocated the case to himself because he realised its seriousness.

39.3 Initially Mr Medwynter believed, after reviewing the available early evidence, that there was a case for Neil Acourt to meet, because he had been unequivocally identified by Duwayne Brooks. As the case developed Mr Medwynter discussed it with his line manager Graham Grant-Whyte, who was an Assistant Crown Prosecutor. Mr Grant-Whyte rightly proposed that there should be a case conference with the police in order to discuss the available evidence, outstanding evidence, other suspects and the nature of police investigation and inquiries. The role allocated to Mr Medwynter was that of collating the evidence submitted by the police, assessing it and briefing Mr Grant-Whyte as to the nature and quality of the admissible evidence. There were frequent discussions between Mr Medwynter and Mr Grant-Whyte about the case, and a constant review of the evidence and developments was made by Mr Medwynter on behalf of his superiors.

39.4 It is significant to note that Mr Medwynter and the other prosecutors were fully conscious that this was purely a crime motivated by racism.

39.5 Mr Medwynter appreciated early on that it was not his responsibility to make the ultimate decision whether or not to prosecute in the Stephen Lawrence case, because of the gravity and aggravating features of the case, and because the case had attracted national media attention.

39.6 Once the identification of Luke Knight by Mr Brooks had taken place on 3 June 1993 and the evidence of DS Crowley came before the CPS there was further detailed consideration given to.the case. Mr Medwynter told us of the written minute dated 15 June 1993 prepared by Mr Grant-Whyte for Mr Howard Youngerwood, the Branch Crown Prosecutor, seeking Mr Youngerwood's decision as to whether the case against Mr Acourt and Mr Knight for the murder of Stephen Lawrence should continue.

39.7 A case conference in fact took place on **9 July 1993**, and Mr Youngerwood told those present his view of the evidence as it stood at that date. We all know that the ultimate decision made by Mr Youngerwood was that the evidence against Neil Acourt and indeed against Luke Knight was in itself weak, and that the evidence of Mr Brooks was further undermined by the evidence of DS Crowley. The decision to discontinue the prosecution was taken on 28 July by Mr Youngerwood himself, and the decision was communicated to Mr Weeden and Mr Bullock by Mr Grant-Whyte at a further case conference. Mr Youngerwood attended the closing stages of that conference and explained to the police that if further admissible reliable evidence came to light the prosecution could be resurrected.

39.8 The records show that there were further case conferences on 27 October and 11 November 1993. The evidence was reviewed therefore after the initial discontinuance, but the advice given by the CPS was still that the totality of the available evidence could not justify re-charging any of the suspects, and in particular those identified by Mr Brooks.

39.9 **It should be noted that there was never any question in 1993-94 of the other suspects being charged, since in truth there was no evidence against any of them to justify prosecution. None of them had been identified at any parade, and there was no other evidence to establish their involvement in this terrible crime.**

39.10 Mr Grant-Whyte's statement was also read on Day 51. He has retired from employment with the CPS. He was a graduate of the University of Natal, and he studied law at Cambridge and was called to the Bar in 1963. In 1966 he joined the legal staff of the Department of the Director of Public Prosecutions, and in 1986 he was an Assistant Branch Crown Prosecutor. Mr Grant-Whyte became ill in December 1993, and he handed over his part in the Stephen Lawrence prosecution to Vivienne Pert.

39.11 Mr Grant-Whyte told the Inquiry in his statement that he worked closely with Mr Medwynter, who he regarded as a most competent and efficient lawyer. Mr Medwynter was the primary reviewing lawyer having the day to day conduct of the case, but Mr Grant-Whyte read all the papers and had frequent discussions with Mr Medwynter and indeed with Mr Youngerwood who was his superior.

39.12 **Mr Grant-Whyte referred to the Code for Crown Prosecutors issued under Section 10 of the Prosecution of Offences Act 1985. He usefully set out the two criteria which have to be considered in every case which is reviewed and conducted by the CPS:-**

> *"First the sufficiency criteria, namely is the evidence such as would ensure a realistic prospect of conviction? That is, would a jury or a bench of Magistrates properly directed in accordance with the law be more likely than not to convict the defendant of the alleged charge.*
>
> *Secondly, if the answer is in the affirmative the public interest criteria falls to be considered, that is although there is sufficient evidence does the public interest require a prosecution?*
>
> *Each case has to be looked at on its own facts and circumstances. If both criteria are satisfied then a prosecution should normally follow".*

39.13 Mr Grant-Whyte himself considered that the evidence in the case of the murder of Stephen Lawrence appeared from the start *"to be exceedingly weak"*. Mr Grant-Whyte on 15 June 1993 submitted a long memorandum to Mr Youngerwood indicating that in his opinion the evidence of Mr Brooks was in itself weak, and that it was further weakened by the evidence of DS Crowley. Rightly both he and Mr Youngerwood applied the test set out in <u>R v Turnbull 1977 QB</u> p 224 in connection with the basic identification by Mr Brooks of Neil Acourt and Luke Knight. This and subsequent cases spell out with emphasis the dangers of misidentification. Experience shows that where there has been a "fleeting glimpse" of a person, or a longer observation in difficult circumstances, the Court must (if the case goes to the jury) give recognised and careful warnings of the special need for caution. How long was the observation? In what light? What were the circumstances?

39.14 **An apparently clear identification can be mistaken. When the quality of the identifying evidence is poor and unsupported the trial Judge should withdraw the case from the jury, since experience has shown that misidentification upon poor evidence is a source of injustice. This case, and subsequent firm endorsement of its principles, must be particularly noted in the context of this case. Once the Judge decides that the identification evidence is poor and unsupported he has a duty to withdraw the case. The law is clear, and the Judge rightly enforced it.**

39.15 **Mr Grant-Whyte confirms that Mr Youngerwood's advice was that there was no realistic prospect of conviction based upon Mr Brooks' evidence, and that the case should be discontinued subject of course to the discovery of other credible evidence to support Mr Brooks.**

39.16 On 12 July 1993 Mr Andrew Mitchell, an experienced Junior Counsel, had been booked to conduct the committal at the Magistrates' Court. On 14 July information was received from the police that the last outstanding scientific evidence would not be available for some months. Further identification parades involving Luke Knight had been mooted, but his solicitor had indicated that Mr Knight was not prepared to consent to a further identification parade unless he was advised to attend one by Counsel.

39.17 **On 27 July 1993 Mr Mitchell telephoned Mr Medwynter and informed him that having read the committal papers there was not, in his own words, *"a cat in hell's chance of a conviction"*.**

39.18 **On 28 July 1993 Mr Grant-Whyte in fact signed the notices of discontinuance, after Mr Youngerwood had advised that this should be done. Those notices were posted on that day, and copies to the solicitors for the accused were faxed on the morning of 29 July. The proceedings were formally discontinued at Camberwell Youth Court on 29 July 1993.**

39.19 Thereafter on 1 September 1993, at the request of Mr Gordon Etherington, the Chief Crown Prosecutor for London, a detailed report was prepared by Mr Grant-Whyte in conjunction with Mr Medwynter.

39.20 **It must be stressed that discontinuance did not mean a final and irrevocable end to the case. Everybody knows that the police remained active during the later months of 1993 and in the early months of 1994. Their activity produced no fresh evidence, and there were meetings and conferences held by the CPS during the latter months of 1993, and**

advice was given to Mr Weeden that on the available evidence the CPS still believed that there was insufficient evidence to justify charging any of the suspects with murder.

39.21 The CPS witnesses dealt also with the case of Stacey Benefield. Mr Grant-Whyte formed the view that the Stacey Benefield case had to be treated as a separate matter from the Stephen Lawrence case. It should be said that we agree that in legal terms that conclusion was correct. There would not have been any prospect of the prosecution being allowed to join the Stacey Benefield case with the Stephen Lawrence murder.

39.22 Incidentally it should be noted that the CPS were asked to reinstate proceedings against Jamie Acourt and David Norris in connection with the stabbing of a young man called Darren Witham in Chislehurst in 1992. David Norris had been picked out by the victim of that stabbing at an identification parade. The matter had been discontinued on the basis of insufficient evidence. In spite of the police wish that the matter should be reinstated it was the view of the CPS that such reinstatement was inappropriate.

39.23 This was also the CPS view of the case concerning a young man called Lee Pearson. No realistic prospect of a conviction in that case was present, bearing in mind that Mr Pearson could not say who had stabbed him and also bearing in mind that he was reluctant to give evidence.

39.24 **It should be observed that Mr Bullock and Detective Constable Freeman composed a strong memorandum which was submitted to the CPS inviting the prosecutors to reconsider the case in relation to the Witham brothers and seeking its reinstatement. As has been pointed out this action by Mr Bullock is inconsistent with any suggestion that he was *"going soft"* on David Norris. It should be added that we ourselves have some concern about the CPS decision not to revive the Witham case. There was evidence that David Norris and Jamie Acourt had been involved in violence, and a knife and truncheon had been used. It does appear to us that there was the material available for a successful prosecution. We appreciate that the weight and quality of evidence has first to be assessed by the CPS, and that the judgement of the relevant CPS officer is involved. But it must certainly be in the public interest to ensure that prosecutions follow where there has been violence and dangerous weapons have been used, provided that the evidential test is met.**

39.25 When Mr Medwynter came into the witness box after the statements of himself and Mr Grant-Whyte had been read, it was apparent that it was his personal view that the prosecution of Mr Acourt and Mr Norris could have been pursued. On the other hand he accepted that the decision was not his to make. He believed that DS Crowley might have misunderstood what Mr Brooks was saying, and he would have liked the prosecution to go forward notwithstanding the evidence of DS Crowley. However Mr Medwynter quite rightly accepted that even when there were differing views amongst the ranks of the prosecutors the ultimate decision was for the senior prosecutor to make. Mr Medwynter agreed that by July 1993 the evidence of Mr Brooks was *"severely undermined"* by DS Crowley's evidence and he realised that tactically it would have been better not to pursue the matter at once, but to wait to see whether further admissible and reliable evidence emerged. In answer to Mr Brian Barker he accepted ultimately that discontinuance was appropriate, although it is apparent that he was more keen than others that the matter should be actively pursued.

39.26 **The crucial evidence on behalf of the CPS was in fact given by Mr Youngerwood, since he was the man who had to make the relevant decisions. He had many years of experience as a solicitor both with the MPS, with whom he worked for 16 years, and in** the CPS in its various existences. When he gave evidence he was retired, but he had been involved throughout with the Stephen Lawrence murder investigation. He was an impressive witness, and it was plain to the Inquiry that he had been worried and anxious about the case and the decisions which he had felt bound to make. By the end of June 1993 he was aware that Mr Grant-Whyte and Mr Medwynter were both acutely concerned about the state of evidence in the Stephen Lawrence case. He had been in touch with them as the matter developed, but it was in June that he became closely involved in the decision making. He asked for the committal file, and he saw the key unused material.

39.27 Mr Youngerwood told us that it did not take him long, on reading the full papers which were put before him, to realise that the situation was depressing. He realised and accepted fully that this was a wicked racist murder. But it was his duty, as he told us, first to consider the nature of the evidence which was available. Plainly there was evidence that five or six white youths had killed Stephen Lawrence in a joint enterprise, so that there were no problems in that regard. There was however, as Mr Youngerwood told us in vivid terms, a very considerable problem as to the quality of the identification evidence of Mr Brooks.

39.28 **Mr Brooks had, as his statements show, concentrated his attention on the person referred to as *"the stabber"* who appeared to be staring at him. At the identification parades he had indicated that the persons identified were simply part of the group and not the person upon whom his attention had been concentrated. Mr Youngerwood over and over again in his evidence indicated that he looked at the matter in two ways. First he looked simply at the quality of the identification; he did not believe that any criminal lawyer of competence could in all conscience have said that the identification in the circumstances described could possibly be considered to have been safe. And in addition there was the evidence of DS Crowley. The basis of the discontinuance notice, said Mr Youngerwood, was *"these cumulative factors"*. His decision was based on the initial unsatisfactory quality of the identification of suspects in the group. Plus, as he said, *"the even worsening assessment of what the lowest effect of Crowley's evidence might be"*.**

39.29 The long and the short of it is that Mr Youngerwood throughout his evidence indicated that he could not conceive that there would be a conviction upon the evidence of Mr Brooks. It was therefore his duty to make his own assessment of the situation and reach a decision as to whether the prosecution should go ahead. He chose to discontinue at the end of July 1993 and not to adjourn the case at the hearing before the Magistrates. Mr Mansfield cross-examined Mr Youngerwood at some length as to this decision, suggesting that the most that should have been done was to ask the court to adjourn. The suggestion being put to Mr Youngerwood was that it would be difficult to resurrect the case once there had been a discontinuance. Mr Youngerwood believed that it would be wrong simply to seek an adjournment, and that the only fair course to take was to indicate that in the state of the evidence as it was the case could not and should not go ahead.

39.30 **We fully understand Mr Youngerwood's reasoning and his decision, and we believe that his conclusion was correct. If further evidence came to light, either scientific evidence or further evidence which might have emerged as a result of the repeated pleas to the public for their assistance, then the matter could have been revived. But if the situation remained as it was there would be no prospect of the case being pursued satisfactorily.**

39.31 Mr Youngerwood in his evidence was more than once asked why it was not reasonable to allow a jury to decide whether they believed Mr Brooks or DS Crowley. He accepted that this was an attitude which was understandable, but, rightly in our view, he said that this was a *"call from the heart"* which he had to resist. His first duty was to look at the case and reach his own conclusions, bearing in mind the Crown Prosecutors' Code, as to whether there was the basic material to allow the case to go to court. He believed that there could only be a negative answer to the question *"Was there safe identification evidence to allow this case to proceed?"*.

39.32 **Mr Youngerwood was criticised by Mr Mansfield on the basis that he was taking over the role of the Judge or the jury, and that he ought to have allowed the case to proceed. We do not agree with this criticism. Mr Youngerwood was a highly experienced and responsible solicitor, and it was his duty to reach a decision bearing in mind all relevant matters. He was not allowed in accordance with the Code or in accordance with the law to float the case simply because of its importance and because of the racist nature of the attack, or for any other reason. He had to make an assessment of what probative evidence was available at the time that he considered the case, and he had to act properly and in accordance with his conscience after such consideration.**

39.33 It was further suggested to Mr Youngerwood that he ought to have gone to Treasury Counsel in order to obtain a further view of the strength of the case before reaching the conclusion as to discontinuance. In fact Mr Youngerwood had the oral and uncompromising view of experienced criminal Junior Counsel, namely Mr Mitchell. It is true that there was no written opinion given or written advice obtained, and no further reference to more Senior Counsel was contemplated. As matters stood in 1993 it seems to us plain that Mr Youngerwood was not only entitled to reach the decision that he did, but that he reached the correct decision. There was in July 1993 no prospect of a successful prosecution being pursued on the basis of the evidence which was then available.

39.34 It is right to say that there was no qualification in the actual identification of the two suspects by Mr Brooks. Mr Mansfield described the identification of Neil Acourt as *"a classic identification, subject obviously to the usual warnings that any jury and any Magistrates' Court would have to have in mind"*. Mr Youngerwood agreed that the identification was unequivocal, but pointed out, rightly in our view, that people are often convinced that they are right and make what can be termed a classic identification although the circumstances make it plain that such confidence is misplaced.

39.35 **That is the reason, said Mr Youngerwood, why so much caution has to be exercised and why injustice has sometimes occurred over the years. A clear identification may well be mistaken, and the circumstances must be looked at with great care before an unqualified identification is taken as gospel.**

39.36 Mr Youngerwood's view was that the identification by Mr Brooks of two people who were not *"the stabber"* was patently unsafe in the circumstances. There was no identification made by any of the other three witnesses who were present at or near the bus-stop at the time of the murder.

39.37 There is justifiable criticism of the police for their failure to act quickly, and thus to be able to organise identification parades at which Mr Westbrook and the others might have been able to identify the culprits. We will never know whether that might have occurred. It seems doubtful, because none of those witnesses was able to give satisfactory descriptions of any of those involved, and all of them agreed that the whole incident was over in a matter of a few seconds.

39.38 The fact is however that there was no satisfactory evidence to corroborate the doubtful evidence of Mr Brooks, and even without the matter being tested in court the statement of DS Crowley was a severe stumbling block.

39.39 **In the round Mr Youngerwood asserted and re-asserted that it was his duty to look at the case, as he did with his colleagues, in order to make a decision logically and objectively in relation to the prosecution code tests, the first of which was the evidential test. If the view of the CPS after careful consideration was that the evidence of identification was very weak or woefully inadequate, bearing in mind the guidelines set out in R v Turnbull then the CPS had no alternative but to exercise their judgment and make a decision about the continuance of the prosecution.**

39.40 **Discontinuance may seem to imply a permanent block upon the prosecution. This is not so, since if further evidence arose the whole situation would be changed. No argument that there was an abuse of process could in our opinion possibly have been mounted if, for example, other witnesses had subsequently identified Neil Acourt and Mr Knight as being present and involved in the murder.**

39.41 **The simple truth is that virtually no further viable evidence was ever discovered. An indication was given at the first hearing of the Inquest that there might be some new *"dramatic"* evidence. But nothing more was heard of that evidence. Witness B's evidence was available in 1995 at the Magistrates' Court. But Witness B was effectively destroyed as a credible witness, because of his failure to identify David Norris and because of his confusion over the presence of one or other of the Acourts when he said that he had seen them from the top of the bus. No other 'dramatic' evidence ever materialised.**

39.42 There was in 1995 available also the surveillance evidence of the suspects. Taking all that into account (and that was fresh material), the Magistrate decided during committal proceedings that there was a case for two of the suspects to answer. Gary Dobson was also separately committed for trial. The fact that the Magistrate decided to commit Neil Acourt and Luke Knight for trial does not mean that the earlier CPS decision to discontinue was flawed. Different considerations governed the two decisions, and there was material available to the Magistrate which did not exist in 1993/1994. Furthermore the ultimate result at trial shows that the CPS decisions were correct. We do not blame the Magistrate for allowing the case to go ahead against those two suspects, but in the end the Judge was correct to stop the prosecution in its tracks once he had heard the evidence of Mr Brooks, closely tested and indeed destroyed as it was by Leading Counsel for the accused.

39.43 **We have looked again and again at the evidence of the CPS witnesses. We are unable to criticise the decisions made by Mr Youngerwood. It seems to us that he reached careful and reasoned conclusions, and he defended his decisions roundly and satisfactorily and conclusively in the witness box at the Inquiry.**

39.44 Mr Mansfield suggested to Mr Youngerwood that it might perhaps be right that a case of this kind should go to a Special Case Unit for review, or alternatively that there should be some guidance as to the checking of an opinion made in circumstances such as those in which Mr Youngerwood made his decisions. There are however no laid down guidelines or rules designed to impose upon senior CPS officers an obligation to take a formal second opinion. Mr Youngerwood was a senior lawyer, and he acted within a team of lawyers. Mr Etherington, his own superior, agreed with what he had done, and so did Counsel.

39.45 Private prosecutions are not automatically "vetted" by any agency. But they can, if the need arises, be stopped by the Attorney General who has the power to make a formal order to check unwarranted prosecutions.

39.46 Mr Youngerwood was asked questions about the private prosecution. So far as Mr Youngerwood was concerned the decision to go ahead in 1995-96 was a disaster. We believe that Mr Youngerwood did telephone Mr Khan, probably on more than one occasion, in order to indicate his disapproval of what was happening. Mr Youngerwood told the Inquiry that when he heard that the private prosecution was being mooted he at once contacted Mr Khan, because he was very worried since it was his view that the prosecution was bound to fail, unless there was further evidence in the possession of Mr Khan. Mr Youngerwood told Mr Khan that it was hopeless to bring a prosecution, because of the R v Turnbull guidelines as to identification evidence and because of the insuperable difficulties in connection with Mr Brooks' evidence.

39.47 Mr Khan was apparently very polite, but he said little or nothing about the intentions of the legal team advising Mr & Mrs Lawrence. When it was finally announced that the prosecution was to go ahead in 1995-96 Mr Youngerwood was ill at home. He telephoned Mr Khan again and offered to speak to Mr Mansfield and said that he would provide the legal team with any key unused material so that they could see what the problems were, namely that there was virtually no evidence which would sustain a prosecution. When he finally heard that Mr & Mrs Lawrence and their lawyers had launched their prosecution Mr Youngerwood was dismayed.

39.48 Mr Khan never indicated to Mr Youngerwood any substantial measure of disagreement or dissent as to Mr Youngerwood's opinion. He was always polite on the telephone and in his correspondence, and made no comment about Mr Youngerwood's views. We have no doubt that these views were transmitted to Mr Khan by Mr Youngerwood. It was for Mr Khan and Counsel and Mr & Mrs Lawrence to make their own final decision. The truth is that viable evidence was in the end not available at the trial and the final outcome was that those prosecuted obtained, as a result of their acquittal, immunity from any future prosecution.

39.49 **Another aspect of the case which concerned the CPS was the prosecution of Mr Brooks in connection with the damage done by him during the May demonstration in which he was involved following the murder of Stephen Lawrence. Mr Brooks' part in the incident was not brought home to the police until September 1993, when a police officer who had seen the incident was able to identify Mr Brooks as the perpetrator of damage to a motor car during that disturbance. In October 1993 Mr Brooks was charged with an offence, and thereafter he was prosecuted, eventually appearing before His Honour Judge Tilling in the Croydon Crown Court.**

39.50 There was disagreement between the senior police officers, including Mr Johnston, and the CPS as to whether Mr Brooks ought ever to have been taken to court. By the time that this prosecution was launched Mr Brooks was being advised by Miss Jane Deighton of Deighton Guedalla. He had been diagnosed as being traumatised and much affected mentally by the experience which he had gone through at the time of Stephen Lawrence's murder.

39.51 We are not surprised that Mr Brooks was traumatised, and when the prosecution was mooted he was seen by doctors, who assessed his mental condition and who wished to be able to identify what that condition had been on 8 May 1993. Later it appears that the suggestion was made at a preliminary hearing at Croydon that his lawyers might raise the defence of automatism, quite apart from reliance upon medical evidence in connection with Mr Brooks' disturbed mental state. The Judge took the view apparently that material should be collected in order to assist him and/or the jury in their decision in connection with Mr Brooks.

39.52 Mr Youngerwood says that the Judge indicated that all the statements that the police had should be looked at and a summary should be drawn up to see if there was material available to assist in connection with Mr Brooks' mental state. Mr Youngerwood was told by Counsel that the Judge wished to see and to collect together any evidence or information which showed *"untoward"* or *"abnormal"* behaviour by Mr Brooks because of the defence which was being pursued. Mr Youngerwood passed on this requirement to the police who suggested that the best way of acquiring the information would be by questionnaires to all the officers who had contact with Mr Brooks. Mr Youngerwood agreed, and the MPS created and circulated the questionnaires. This exercise was much criticised by those advising Mr Brooks, who suggested that it gave the opportunity for racist stereotyping, since police officers were being positively asked whether they had noticed anything abnormal or out of the ordinary in Mr Brooks' behaviour, which might prompt unfortunate and ill-founded comments from officers who were not well disposed towards Mr Brooks.

39.53 Mr Youngerwood says that all that was done was done in order to assist the defence and effectively because of the request made by the Judge. He accepted that he had asked the police to send out questionnaires to all police witnesses who had any dealings, however brief, with Mr Brooks asking whether any abnormal behaviour had been noticed by them. At the time no protest was made by Mr Brooks or those acting on his behalf. Indeed on 20 May 1994 Miss Deighton wrote to Mr Youngerwood indicating that she would be grateful if the completed questionnaires could be forwarded to her office *"at Mr Youngerwood's earliest convenience"*. The purpose of seeking the information was, she said, to assist the expert, namely the doctor, instructed on Mr Brooks' behalf.

39.54 **It is a feature of the case that some of the officers saw fit to make strong critical comments about Mr Brooks. However, we do not believe that the existence of these questionnaires or their content can lead to criticism of the CPS, since they emerged as a result of the defence which was being raised by Mr Brooks, and as a result of the Judge's wish to obtain any information which might be useful to the defence.**

39.55 It is perfectly true that Judge Tilling thought little of the case which was levelled against Mr Brooks. He indicated early on that even if there were a conviction it would be likely that Mr Brooks would be discharged. But the CPS had reached their own decision, namely that the case should be put before the court. As we have already indicated many police officers and others believed that the prosecution ought to have been stopped. Mr Brooks was the only witness who could give direct evidence in the Stephen Lawrence murder.

39.56 There is perhaps some irony in the fact that the CPS deemed it right to proceed against Mr Brooks but not to proceed against the suspects. When the matter is examined however the logic of the two decisions can be seen. The view of the CPS, and in particular of those who had to make the relevant decision, was that if the prosecution was dropped the defence would have considerable ammunition to aim at Mr Brooks, upon the basis that he had been favoured by the CPS in return for his continued willingness to co-operate and to give evidence in the Stephen Lawrence case. To add to the frustrations of Mr & Mrs Lawrence not only did these two decisions of the CPS run counter to their hopes, but so did the decision over the Sainsbury's car park matter, which is referred to in Chapter 38.

39.57 In the result the Judge thought the same as the police officers about the case against Mr Brooks. The case against Mr Brooks was dismissed upon the defence submission that there was an abuse of process, primarily because of delay in bringing the proceedings. Mr Brooks' medical condition was also before the Judge. We do understand the CPS' argument. In the end we feel that it would have been better if the prosecution of Mr Brooks had been abandoned early on. But a decision of this kind is not an easy one to make.

39.58   The way in which the discontinuance was brought to the notice of Mr & Mrs Lawrence was most regrettable. Mr Khan was told probably after the event that the prosecution had been discontinued, and Mr & Mrs Lawrence heard the news through the media. There is criticism to be made of all those involved in connection with the transmission of the news of the discontinuance to Mr & Mrs Lawrence. It must have been a shock to them to discover that the matter had even temporarily been halted in its tracks.

39.59   **Most careful timing and most careful transmission of news of this kind to a bereaved family are vital. Scrupulous consideration must be given to the consequences of a decision of this kind and to liaison direct with the family before such a decision is implemented. It is undoubtedly unfortunate that the matter had to be decided in a hurry, and that there was failure on the part of the CPS and the police to ensure that there was time and opportunity to pass on the news of the decision to the family before the matter went to court. The reason given is that the decision was made only at the eleventh hour, and that the matter had to be mentioned in court and that there was not time to communicate satisfactorily with the family before the matter was resolved.**

39.60   **This is in our opinion no true excuse, since there must have been channels available in order to ensure that the family were found and told that the decision had been made and was imminently to be implemented. Mr & Mrs Lawrence were in Jamaica at the time. But every effort should have been made through Mr Khan or through diplomatic channels to ensure that they were contacted at once. Careful explanation must always be made in circumstances of this kind of the effect of the decision. Use of the procedure of discontinuance and the very word "discontinued" have unfortunate connotations. Eventually the family must have appreciated that if further evidence were found the matter might proceed. But much care and sensitivity must be exercised in transmitting a decision of this kind to the family in circumstances such as this in the future.**

CHAPTER FORTY

THE MAIN COMMITTAL HEARING

40.1   Luke Knight, Neil Acourt, Jamie Acourt and David Norris appeared before a Stipendiary Magistrate, David Cooper, on Wednesday, 23 August 1995 at Belmarsh Magistrates' Court. Gary Dobson was not involved in those proceedings. He was committed for trial later, after an "old style" committal at Belmarsh, having been arrested on 28 August 1995 (halfway through the main committal proceedings).

40.2   Luke Knight was represented by Mr T Kendal. David Norris was represented by Mr Bromley Martin. Neil Acourt was represented by Mr C Conway. Jamie Acourt was represented by Mr T Burke. Mr Mansfield led for the prosecution, instructed by Mr Khan; Mr Kamlish was his junior Counsel.

40.3   The proceedings started with objections raised by the accused, who did not wish the Magistrate to hear the case, because he had dealt with previous applications (including bail applications) and was thus aware of the antecedents and other information about the accused.

40.4   The Magistrate heard the argument but held rightly and robustly that *"not only is there no real danger* [of bias] *in this; there is no danger of bias whatsoever"*. He declined the invitation to disqualify himself.

40.5   From early on in the proceedings there were edgy exchanges between Counsel, and the defence were putting down markers as to the evidence which Mr Mansfield proposed to call. After preliminary discussion, the case was opened by Mr Mansfield. Even in the opening it was apparent that there was potential confusion in respect of Duwayne Brooks' identification evidence. But Mr Brooks had picked out two of the accused on identification parades, Neil Acourt and Luke Knight. So that there was that basic evidence for the Magistrate to consider.

40.6   The other identifying witness to be called was Witness B. Witness B said that he was on a bus travelling down Well Hall Road from the Woolwich direction at about the time of the murder. He made a statement in which he said that he saw David Norris and Neil Acourt from the bus near the Church on the corner of Cobbett Road and Rochester Way. They were, he said, in a group of four men.

40.7   **Mr Mansfield was himself plainly doubtful about Witness B and his evidence. There seemed to be some question even as to whether Witness B would arrive at the Court at all. And Mr Mansfield rightly included in his opening the known fact that Witness B had originally given a false statement to the police (because, he said, he was fearful for his own safety), saying that the only incident he had seen involved a fight between people that he did not know near the Welcome Inn, which is nearby but not close to the place where he later said that he saw David Norris and Neil Acourt. Furthermore, Mr Mansfield knew (and opened) the fact that Witness B was plainly confused as to which of the Acourt brothers he had actually seen and was able to recognise. Witness B was thus the kind of witness that a prosecutor could only put forward with some trepidation. Mr Mansfield's obvious reservations about Witness B were later proved to be more than correctly stated.**

40.8   Other than those two witnesses the material available to the prosecution was very limited, as we all now know. Mr Mansfield rightly referred to the weapons found at 102 Bournbrook Road. More contentiously he then opened the evidence about the December 1994 video and audio surveillance which (he said) would show " ...... *not merely propensity, that would plainly be insufficient in itself, but it indicates motive in this case.*" Because (said Mr Mansfield) the men were clearly expressing in language which is abusive and almost unrepeatable their hatred of the black population, and their desire to cut up and injure black people, while demonstrating with knives their wish and ability thus to act.

40.9   Mr Mansfield submitted that the video evidence went to motivation and to support the identification by Mr Brooks and Witness B. Furthermore he mounted a somewhat involved argument about the men knowing that they were being "bugged", and that they were "performing" in various ways from which inferences of involvement in the Stephen Lawrence murder might be drawn, if only obliquely, against them.

40.10   **Reading that part of the opening it is apparent that there were very real problems for Mr Mansfield and the prosecution to face, both as to the identification and the video evidence and as to the case generally.**

40.11   On the first afternoon evidence was called. PC Bethel set the scene, and spoke of her contact at the scene with Mr Brooks. She was not cross-examined.

40.12   **Then Mr Brooks was called. His evidence was long and detailed. It is purposeless to try to summarise all that he said. He gave his vivid account of the terrible murder of his friend. Perhaps most notably he gave evidence about the attacking group, and he gave descriptions of people which plainly conflicted with the material in his early statement. He also spoke of the later sightings of people who he said were involved, on what have been called the Starburger and public house encounters which occurred later in 1993, and thus long after the identification parades had taken place.**

40.13   Mr Brooks was cross-examined first on behalf of Neil Acourt. Mr Conway concentrated upon the obvious problems of the identification and the short shocking circumstances, including the fact that Mr Brooks had said in his first statement that he was *"running and jockeying back"* when he saw the murder and those involved. He was also closely questioned about the *"boy with the bar"* who (said Mr Brooks) had broken away and pursued him and then run back and *"whacked"* Stephen Lawrence on the head. In Mr Brooks' first statement there was no mention at all of that part of the incident. The only person who Mr Brooks described in that statement was the man who first attacked Stephen, the man later known as the *"frizzy"* haired man, with hair which was *"over his ears and stuck out over the sides"*.

40.14   Mr Conway raised the evidence and issue involving DS Crowley, indicating that the Sergeant was to be tendered or called, and that his evidence of what was said by Mr Brooks could of itself be fatally damaging to Mr Brooks' evidence.

40.15   Cross-examined on behalf of Jamie Acourt, Mr Brooks was again confronted with his variant descriptions of the first attacker, and the plain confusion which arose as a result. In his first statement he could only describe the frizzy haired man. Yet in his evidence he said that Stephen's attacker was of *"medium build .... short black hair .... black, black hair"*. When asked, *"The statement you gave to the police within 24 hours of the stabber, and the only one you could describe, is wrong?"* Mr Brooks simply answered *"Yes"*.

40.16 We know that Mr Brooks also gave an oral statement which was recorded in PC Gleason's notebook at the hospital on the night of the murder. This statement disappeared from view until it surfaced during the PCA investigation. Mr Brooks' only description in that statement of Stephen Lawrence's attacker was of a youth *"who had blue jeans, his hair was bushy, light brown and stuck out ....."*. A description inconsistent with that given in evidence, and not a description which matched either of the Acourts or Luke Knight.

40.17 Mr Kendal (for Luke Knight) continued on the same theme, focusing particularly upon the fact that Mr Brooks had to accept what he had said in his statement of 4 June 1993, namely that he had been told (before the identification parades) that *"the Acourt brothers were responsible for the murder"*, and that the only description given of any of the men was of that *"frizzy haired"* man referred to in his first statement.

40.18 The pathologist followed Mr Brooks into the witness box, to give evidence about the wounds inflicted upon Stephen Lawrence.

40.19 There was then a long discussion about Witness B, who was to be the last live witness called, and as to the need to preserve Witness B's anonymity as he gave evidence. The discussion was somewhat difficult, and the Magistrate sensibly reserved his decision as to what to do over the weekend and Bank Holiday which followed. On Tuesday, 29 August the Magistrate ruled that Witness B should give evidence screened, and that he need not answer any questions that would *"tend to prejudice his anonymity"*. As the Magistrate said this was a classic exercise of his discretion.

40.20 Mr Bromley Martin did not like the decision, and the case was adjourned so that an application could be made for judicial review to upset it. That application was accordingly made, and the Divisional Court refused leave to question the ruling.

40.21 In due course Witness B gave evidence. He said that he had seen David Norris and Neil Acourt from the top of the No 122 bus, as indicated earlier in this Chapter. He said (with a seemingly remarkable degree of accuracy) that he saw the four men for *"5-7 seconds"*, and that he knew and recognised the two named.

40.22 As to the Acourt identification, Witness B's problem (raised in cross-examination) was that in an earlier statement he had said that he believed one of the Acourts was there, but *"couldn't be sure which one"*. And indeed he confirmed in evidence that he still could not be sure, but that he felt that it was Neil, because he was *"bigger built"*. At the end of his evidence he agreed that his *"present state of mind"* was that he believed at the moment that he had seen Neil Acourt, but he could not be definite *"as it may well have been Jamie."* Hardly a promising basis for a case against either of the Acourts based upon Witness B's evidence of recognition.

40.23 Further evidence was read and given orally, including that of Mr McIlgrew, as to the identification parades.

40.24 On 1 September submissions were made about the admissibility of the video surveillance evidence. In a nutshell the argument from the defence was that the tapes were not admissible at all, or alternatively were so grossly prejudicial that they should not be used. Mr Bromley Martin said that he must argue that *" ..... the zeal with which this prosecution is being pursued has to some extent affected the judgment of the prosecution"*. And he said that the 1994 videos could have no possible probative value in a trial for the 1993 murder of Stephen Lawrence.

40.25 On Wednesday, 6 September the Court sat again. And the Magistrate was given news which illustrates how remarkable this case is at almost every turn.

40.26 **In his evidence Witness B had repeatedly said that he knew David Norris, and had known him for some years. He said that he had met David Norris on numerous occasions, knew his face well, but indicated that he had in fact only known him by name as "Dave", and that his knowledge of the surname Norris came from other sources.**

40.27 **The prosecution decided therefore that it would be wise to hold an identification parade in order to test Witness B's evidence. This was a most unusual step to take, but the advice was that it should be done. And so David Norris stood on a parade at Southwark Police Station between the two sittings of the Court. Witness B surveyed the parade - and probably to the consternation of the prosecution he failed to pick out David Norris, but picked out a member of the public as being the David Norris who was well known to him and who had been near the scene of the murder.**

40.28 This news was given at once to the Court, and as Mr Bromley Martin rightly said, it meant that Witness B's identification evidence as to David Norris was well and truly undermined.

40.29 Then the argument about the video evidence continued at great length. The Magistrate was indeed a patient man.

40.30 On 7 September the Magistrate gave his ruling. He had plainly given much thought to that decision. He admitted a substantial part of the evidence on the basis that it could *"show that the defendants had a clear racist motive to kill Stephen Lawrence"*, and to a limited extent on the *"similar facts"* basis, because *"I believe the videos are positively probative in that, taken with other evidence called by the prosecution, they might well assist the Court in reaching a conclusion ...."*. He was doubtful about the prosecution's submission that involvement in the murder could obliquely be inferred from what was said and not said during the surveillance. But he said that it would be for the trial court to decide whether *"having considered the relevant sequences as a whole, that they do amount to confessions"*. As to prejudice/probative value the Magistrate said that this argument was for the trial Judge and not for him, although he felt that *"on balance the probative value in particular as against Neil Acourt outweighs the prejudice"*.

40.31 And so the reduced tapes were admitted, after further discussion about the way in which they were to be played.

40.32 Almost immediately after the playing of the tapes Mr Mansfield said that his evidence was complete, and that he would be asking for committal of Neil Acourt, David Norris and Luke Knight.

40.33 **Mr Mansfield expressly excluded Jamie Acourt, and explained why.** *"The case against Jamie Acourt depended primarily on the Witness Mr Brooks, followed by Mr B, followed by an eye witness - perhaps an audio witness would be a better phrase - Maureen George, who heard a phrase in a road nearby. However, as it turned out Mr Brooks' - I put it in inverted commas - "identification" of the person we were to arrest was Jamie is not in accord with what had been said before by him. He was not in a position to remember who he picked out before and therefore I was not able to proceed with him further. Secondly, Mr B made it clear finally in his evidence that essentially he is not including Jamie in any assertion about who was present ..... Jamie is not shown in the video ..... I feel it would not*

be proper to ask you for a committal in relation to him". Mr Conway made some strong and justified comment, namely that the case against Jamie Acourt had always been the same and was "non-existent". Jamie Acourt was then discharged.

40.34 On the next day DS Crowley was called on behalf of Neil Acourt. This evidence and this aspect of the case are separately considered. Mr Mansfield cross-examined the Detective Sergeant in accordance with his instructions, emanating of course from Mr Brooks. Inspector McIlgrew was recalled. Then the evidence ended.

40.35 On 11 September submissions of no case to answer were made on behalf of Neil Acourt and Luke Knight. They were thorough and painstaking and long. The contention was (in summary) that the evidence was so weak or tenuous that no reasonable jury properly directed could possibly convict. The argument was double-barrelled - or even triple-barrelled. First, the very nature of the scene and the speed of events made any identification unsafe, in R v Turnbull (1977) QB terms. Secondly, DS Crowley's evidence, particularly to the large extent that it was eventually <u>accepted</u> by Mr Brooks, undermined Mr Brooks. Thirdly, the video evidence should not bite even though the Magistrate had admitted it. Both submissions were thus made substantially under what the lawyers called *"the second limb of R v Galbraith"*, on the basis that no reasonable jury properly directed could upon the evidence available safely or properly convict.

40.36 Mr Kamlish replied. His submission was that there was evidence for a jury to consider. Warming to his task he was prepared optimistically to say that there was " ..... *an identification supported by other strong evidence of motive as far as Knight is concerned, and as far as Acourt is concerned a whole category ... several categories of evidence which make the case against him an overwhelming one"*. It is hard to see how such a statement could be justified, but that was the submission made.

40.37 After an adjournment the Magistrate gave his ruling. He directed himself impeccably as to the law. Sensibly, and in accordance with usual practice, he did not go through the evidence or the arguments. He found Mr Kamlish's submissions compelling, and he found that there was sufficient evidence to put Neil Acourt and Luke Knight on trial for the murder of Stephen Lawrence. David Norris was not committed for trial. Thus both he and Jamie Acourt, if viable evidence is available, can be prosecuted again.

40.38 Mr & Mrs Lawrence's legal team can thus say that at least there was some hope of conviction, since the Magistrate ruled that there was a prima facie case. Later Gary Dobson was also found to have a case to answer, although the evidence against him was palpably weak.

CHAPTER FORTY-ONE

THE CENTRAL CRIMINAL COURT TRIAL

41.1   The trial of Neil Acourt, Luke Knight and Gary Dobson opened on 17 April 1996 at the Central Criminal Court. The Judge was Mr Justice Curtis. He was, and is, one of the most experienced Judges dealing with criminal cases in England and Wales. In April 1996 he was one of the presiding Judges on the Wales and Chester Circuit; but he sat in many other parts of the country in his capacity as a Judge of the High Court, Queen's Bench Division. Before his appointment as a High Court Judge Mr Justice Curtis had served as Recorder of Birmingham. His professional life at the Bar, during which he specialised in criminal work, both prosecuting and defending, was spent in Birmingham and on the Midland and Oxford Circuit, both as Junior Counsel and as Queen's Counsel.

41.2   From time to time most High Court Judges hear cases at the Old Bailey, the Central Criminal Court, where the major London trials are customarily held. Hence his presence there to try the case levelled against these three men in the private prosecution which was to be conducted by Mr Mansfield and Mr Kamlish instructed by Imran Khan.

41.3   We express unhappiness at the criticism of this Judge by Mrs Lawrence during the course of the television programme *"The Stephen Lawrence Story"*. The suggestion was made that the Judge had been in some way selected to try the case otherwise than impartially. We fully understand the disappointment of Mr & Mrs Lawrence that the prosecution failed. But having read and re-read the full verbatim record of the trial we are all convinced that no Judge could have reached any decision other than that made by Mr Justice Curtis. All the necessary evidence was called. All possible arguments were made and heeded. The prosecution was given every chance to make a case. There simply was not the material available to go to the jury. Mr Justice Curtis so found. We are convinced that he was right, as the following narrative will show.

41.4   The Defendants were all represented by experienced Counsel. Mr Batten QC and Mr Conway appeared for Neil Acourt. Mr Thwaites QC and Mr Kendal appeared for Luke Knight. Mr Stewart QC and Mr Wolkind appeared for Gary Dobson.

41.5   Mr Batten was the first to speak. He at once indicated that he proposed to argue that the evidence of Mr Brooks[1] should be excluded, on the grounds that Mr Brooks' *"purported recognition"* and identification of Neil Acourt was so far undermined as to render it of no value, and thus that evidence should be held to be inadmissible and should be excluded in the Judge's discretion under Section 78 of the Police and Criminal Evidence Act 1984. Mr Batten sought a preliminary hearing before the case was even opened by Mr Mansfield.

41.6   Mr Thwaites supported Mr Batten's application. He rightly said that the whole case pivoted upon Mr Brooks' evidence of identification of his client, and he cited the well worn and well known case R v Turnbull 1977 QB which states that a Judge should intervene in order to stop a case *"Because the identification evidence is so meagre and there is no other evidence properly capable of confirming the correctness of a weak identification"*. The case also sets out definitively the firm warnings and directions that must be given in every case involving identification evidence (see Chapter 39, para 13). Mr Thwaites also referred to Section 78

---

[1]   We use the correct spelling of Mr Brooks' name, although, where quoting below, we use the spelling "Brookes" as was recorded at the time

of the 1984 Act, and asked the Judge to hear DS Crowley's evidence at least in order to test its potency when looking at the identification issue.

41.7 Mr Mansfield urged the Judge to say that the question was one for the jury, or alternatively that the issue as to Mr Brooks' evidence should be decided at the end of the prosecution case.

41.8 In parenthesis we note that Mr Stewart held his fire and did not argue this point. His client Mr Dobson had of course not been identified at any parade. The evidence against him was very weak.

41.9 A long argument followed. The defence said that *"This is a case where the prosecution do not have an identification that will withstand judicial scrutiny if the evidence is heard ...."*. Mr Batten floated a further argument which was to involve objection to the December 1994 video evidence. Mr Justice Curtis ruled that the challenge to the identification evidence should be made when it was to be tendered, that is after the opening and during the taking of evidence generally.

41.10 Mr Mansfield reconsidered the position, and said that the defence objections to any mention of the vital evidence were so widespread that there was virtually nothing that could be opened to the jury, and he asked the Judge to deal with the defence applications then and there. This the Judge declined to do, and so the jury were sworn.

41.11 **There is no note of Mr Mansfield's opening to the jury. Indeed an opening is not usually transcribed. It was plainly short. On the next day (18 April) evidence was called. Alexandra Marie and Royston Westbrook gave their eye-witness evidence of the murder. Mlle Marie said that *"It happened very quickly and I did not realise. I didn't have a chance to look at their faces"*. Mr Westbrook gave his vivid account of the murder and said that he had not been able to describe the *"group of white boys"*. He said that he had been on identification parades and had not seen anybody that he could recognise. *"It was dark. It was 10:30 at night and it was over really ... it was really, really quick. I was surprised, you know, this had happened through the quickness that it had happened. It was like 10/15 seconds and he was away and I just thought, you know, they kicked him and he got off and that was it"*.**

41.12 Any lawyer knows of the difficulty involved as to identification during such a fast happening in the dark. The shadow of R v Turnbull 1977 QB was already upon the case.

41.13 Then Mr Mansfield called Mr Brooks. His evidence lasted for the rest of 18 April and until the short adjournment (about 13:00) on Friday 19 April. He continued his evidence on Monday 22 April. This Report has already dealt in some detail with the "management" of Mr Brooks. It is not surprising that by the time he left the witness box his evidence was valueless. It is pointless to try to summarise all that he said. The full transcript of his evidence is available upon the record. He was skilfully and wholly fairly cross-examined by Messrs Batten and Thwaites. They highlighted the following problems:-

    (i) From the start Mr Brooks had said (in respect of the leading man in the group) that the man's hair was *"....long, over ears, frizzy and sticking out"*. And he said (in his first statement) that *"He had an oval face. I can't really describe his facial features but I think I could recognise him again from his hair and general look"*.

(ii)   When Mr Brooks drew or described the first man to an artist he left the face of the man blank. And he then described the colour of the man's hair as being *"very light brown"*. And he said that he was not sure if he could identify the man again.

(iii)   At the committal proceedings Mr Brooks said that a man who he recognised in a public house (later on) was the leading man or *"the stabber"*. And he said that he had seen that man on another occasion also (at the Starburger bar), but that the man was not one of those who had been seen by him on any identification parade, because that man was *"Slim, short black hair, ... quite a long nose"*. Mr Brooks told the Judge that the man seen at the Starburger bar and the public house was very much like the brother of somebody he had picked out on one of the parades.

(iv)   DS Crowley's evidence (if accepted) was of itself fatal to Mr Brooks' identification evidence.

(v)   Mr Khan's intervention and interview with Mr Brooks on 2 May 1993 (noted by another solicitor, Mr Ratip) created its own problems. Particularly because the notes of this interview suggested that Mr Brooks had, before the identification parades, seen the statements of other witnesses. The suggestion being that those witnesses' descriptions had influenced, or might have influenced, Mr Brooks' decision and choice at the parades.

These were in themselves formidable difficulties facing the prosecution.

41.14   DS Crowley was called on 23 April. His part in this case has already been discussed. Mr Ratip (the solicitor notetaker with Mr Khan) was called. Other witnesses also gave evidence, including the Police artist (DC Leveson), and DS Bevan, who had been the liaison officer with Mr Brooks. Mr Khan was called and recalled. A medical report on Mr Brooks by Dr Stewart Turner was put before the Judge, dated 27 May 1994.

41.15   Submissions followed on 23 and 24 April. Mr Batten and Mr Thwaites marshalled their arguments at some length. Mr Mansfield replied, and argued that the matters raised were simply referable to the weight of the evidence and not to its admissibility. *"There is,"* he concluded, *"a great deal that can be said about the circumstances of the identification in terms of its weight but nothing in relation to admissibility that should deter your Lordship from admitting both of these identifications. That is the way in which I put it"*.

41.16   On 24 April Mr Justice Curtis gave his decision. It is not a long judgment. It seems to us right to set it out in full in this Report. He said this:-

> *"No-one disputes that on 22 April 1993 Stephen Lawrence was murdered in a public street in Eltham. He was, in fact, knifed to death by a young white man wielding a large knife and a group of four to six others were with him and are said to have taken part in the attack on Stephen Lawrence.*

As if what I have described is not intolerable enough it is clear that there was no reason why the victim was set upon. The irrational and violent behaviour was, in fact, made worse by racial prejudice as the remarks by members of the group and their behaviour show; clearly this makes the offence worse.

The attack was witnessed by Lawrence's young friend Duwayne Brookes, who was also attacked but mercifully escaped. He was but 18 years old at the time. He has purportedly identified Neil Acourt and Luke Knight, two of the accused at this court, as participators in the attack. He did this on 13 May 1993 and 3 June 1993 respectively.

It is necessary to look at these identifications that have been made in context: on the night of the attack the witness Brookes made a written statement to the police describing the man or young man we have referred to as "the stabber". I read his precise words":

> *"Of the group of six youths I can only really describe one of them. The one who had struck Stephen was white, about 5 feet 8 inches tall, medium build and about 18 to 22 years of age. I would describe his hair as being long, over his ears and it was frizzy and stuck out at the sides. Most of his hair was down at the sides and I could clearly see his forehead.*
>
> *He had an oval face. I can't really describe his facial features but I think I could recognise him again from his hair and general look.*
>
> *Of the others I can only say they were all white, about the same age and they were all wearing jeans."*

*The circumstances surrounding the offence of relevance to my duty in this case and the decided case of **Turnbull**, which is too well known to bear repetition are as follows: first, the sight that Duwayne Brookes had of the offence was at night, although he told me that the street was well lit;*

Secondly, the offence happened suddenly and was over in seconds. The attacking group, whom I have already described, ran across the road and struck Stephen Lawrence in the mouth of Dickson Road. That it was sudden and over in seconds cannot be doubted in the light of the evidence already given by Mademoiselle Marie, a bystander, and a witness called Westbrook;

Thirdly, this is a fleeting glimpse case, since no sooner than the attack had been made than the group responsible ran off up or along Dickson Road.

Mr Brookes, the witness, himself says that it was all over in three seconds. His view was over some 20 yards from along the street. His observation of the man responsible for striking Stephen was made whilst he, Brookes, was running off backwards at the relevant time.

On 1 May 1993 a policeman saw Mr Brookes again. Brookes told him he could not add anything new to his original statement, which I have already incorporated into this judgment. Brookes confirmed to the policeman that his first statement had been made when things were fresh in his mind.

On 6 May 1993 Brookes was visited at home by a policeman who is a member of the facial identify team, an expert in creating from the description of witnesses likenesses of persons suspected of crime. He painstakingly, over about an hour and a half, obtained a description from Brookes and took notes of what he told him.

Brookes told the policeman that the closest he got to the stabber was about 15 to 20 yards. He had a view of him for about three seconds and it was pretty good lighting.

He added that the only detail he could give was "hair mainly". "The hair", he said, "was fairly long, covered the ears, straight hair". Then he added: "It was very light brown in colour. After he had been running it was messed and fell to the sides of the man's face".

No facial description was given by Mr Brookes to the policeman, though he did describe the face as very full oval. He said he was not too sure that he could identify this man again. That resulted in the creation by the police facial identification officer, of our Exhibit 8, from which it is abundantly clear that there is no face at all, in all practical terms, just a hair style.

From that police officer the witness Mr Brookes was taken to another police officer who was charged with the duty of dealing with the clothing side of descriptions that were available to those enquiring into this case. This bears on the problem I have to resolve because the witness Brookes went through much the same procedures as I have already described, giving the officer the chance to compose a computer picture of the suspect. That has resulted in our Exhibit 9. What is of interest is that on this occasion the hair of the stabber is shown as blond. Mr Thwaites submits the proper description is peroxide blond and that certainly recommends itself to me. Once again, no face is shown.

Proceeding chronologically, there is no doubt on the evidence before me that at this time names were being bantered about in Eltham, including the names of the Acourt brothers, that is to say Neil, a current defendant, and his brother Jamie, as being responsible for Lawrence's death. That is Brookes' own evidence and also that of his solicitor Mr Khan, which is to the like general effect.

In the course of this trial Brookes has agreed that he had discussed with friends what has happened on the identification parade that took place, as I shall fully describe in a moment. He has agreed that from what the friends said he has been enabled to work out that the person he was to pick out on 13 May was an Acourt.

Let us look at the particulars: on 7 May Brookes went on an identification parade. Jamie Acourt, a brother of Neil Acourt and a suspect, was on the parade. Brookes did not identify him. The fact that this accused's Neil Acourt's brother was on the parade is of significance in view of what Brookes was later to say about the appearance of Lawrence's attacker.

On the 13th Brookes attended another identification parade. On the first he identified number 7 who was a volunteer and nothing to do with this case. On the third he identified nobody, although there was a suspect on the parade. On the second he identified Neil Acourt as in the group of attackers but not doing anything, that is to say not the stabber. On 3 June 1993 he attended a further parade and identified Luke Knight as involved, or as he said later, "one of the attacking youths", however he did not see him use any weapon.

Immediately following this parade the witness Brookes had a conversation with his liaison officer DS Crowley. That officer was an officer who knew nothing about the case and was chosen for his duty as liaison officer for just that reason. There is no dispute between Brookes and Crowley that the policeman told him, Brookes, that he did not wish to discuss the case. His duty was to take the witness to and from identification parades and in normal parlance to "mind" him.

I have seen and heard both these witnesses. Brookes has agreed with much of the substance of what Crowley has reported to the court. Also, in my judgment significant parts of what Crowley has reported is borne out by other evidence that I have heard, namely that Brookes was being fed with information, including the names of the two Acourts as responsible for the offence at the time material to this enquiry.

What I am concerned with is not the mechanics but whether the substance of what Brookes has said is true and, bearing in mind the proximity of the conversation to the events in question, whether it is reliable and, in particular, more reliable than what is being said much later on.

The main points of concern are Brookes' statement that he had been told it was the Acourt brothers and that this one, that is a reference to Neil, this accused, was the brother of the youth he had identified before. What matters is not that Brookes thought he had identified Jamie Acourt, which we know that he had not, but that Brookes had by inference seen the likeness of Neil Acourt to a member of the line-up on the earlier parade of 7 May 1993.

The second point was that he, Brookes, had been given by his friends promptings of the Acourts' physical features and hair.

Thirdly, that he did not see how the victim died.

From his recollection, and I quote his words, he can only remember, "their physical description and hair", and did not in any way see the face of the youths around Stephen Lawrence.

Brookes has agreed in evidence in this court that that last proposition is correct, though at one stage he did say he could not remember saying it but later he agreed that he did not indeed see the stabbing. This is in line with what he said to a policewoman called Bethel on the night of the murder.

It follows if the substance of these statements by Brookes to the police is true, first the witness Brookes was from the start in major difficulties in recognising the attackers and, in particular, the stabber; second he had gone on at least one and possibly two identification parades, it matters not which, with information he should not have had and made an identification on one parade which was not based on true recognition.

It is clear to me on the first issue that Detective Sergeant Crowley has correctly reported both at the time, and that is important, and later to this court, what Brookes told him about his limited ability to recognise the offenders.

On the second issue, as Brookes himself says he was given the Acourt brothers, amongst others, as responsible within days of the offence by friends. He could not or would not name those "friends".

From that and all the evidence I have seen and heard I conclude that Brookes did say that which Detective Sergeant Crowley has reported about the promptings to which I have referred under the second head of the issues.

I accept Mr Thwaites' submission that the conflict between Brookes and Crowley does not need to be fully resolved in the usual way since on Brookes own account his evidence as to the vital matter that I am concerned with, namely the identification of one of the attackers, in particular the stabber, is contaminated.

Matters do not stop there. As a matter of history, I record that in July 1993 the Director of Public Prosecutions decided not to continue the case. On 23 September 1993 there was a further development, the witness Brookes told the police in writing, he could now add that he was chased at or near the scene of the murder by a youth with an iron bar or something similar and who after chasing him returned to hit Stephen Lawrence on the head. It is to be observed that Stephen Lawrence sustained no head injury at all and that this account varies with the eye-witnesses' accounts and I refer to Westbrook and Mademoiselle Marie.

Importantly Brookes did not describe that youth. Importantly he did not alter his previous description of the stabber. It is important that he, Brookes, had not mentioned this matter before to anyone, including his solicitor Mr Khan who had been advising him. It is equally important to appreciate that on this account that person was the last of the group of attacking youths that Brookes saw before his departure from the scene.

It also now transpires, according to Brookes, that in September, the month when he had seen the police and reported the matter of the individual chasing him with the iron bar, and again on 6 November 1993 Brookes saw two young men in or near a Star Burger restaurant and at The Plough somewhere in the area of London that we are concerned with.

On 9 December 1993, so a considerable time later, he made a statement to the police that the two young men at the Star Burger were definitely there when the murder occurred and as between themselves they looked very similar, as if they were brothers or even twins.

After that committal proceedings took place at which the defendants currently at this court were, of course, present, but so was Jamie Acourt. For the record I observe that he was discharged by the Stipendiary magistrate.

On oath Brookes said to that court that one of these Star Burger men, as we have called them, with short black hair was the attacker and that he recognised him immediately he saw him as the brother of a youth he identified on an identification parade.

We then move to the trial at this court in front of me. Brookes gave evidence that the man that he had picked out on 3 June identification parade was the attacker. That was Luke Knight. Nobody has ever suggested that he was ever at the Star Burger or the Plough.

It will be remembered that originally Brookes had stated that the identified suspect of 3 June had no weapon and that he did not see him with one. That of itself might not matter very greatly but that piece of evidence flies in the face of his previous descriptions of the attacker, "the man with the fluffy hair", or what has been referred to as "curtains" and what he had said about the Star Burger man. In the circumstances no jury could possibly accept the validity of that piece of evidence that he gave to me.

I should also deal with Mr Thwaites' closely argued submission, which I can summarise by saying is to the effect that the solution to the problem of why Brookes identified Luke Knight on 3 June 1993 is that he, Brookes, was looking for a man who looked like the one he had seen on 13 May parade.

In my judgment that analysis is likely to be correct. However, if one appreciates first that there was no true recognition at the time of the offence from which this identification could be made and an identification of a kind I have described in this court with the contradictory events that have occurred subsequently, that in my judgment is fatal to the admission of this evidence.

Whatever may be the reasons and whether they are good, bad or in-between, the fact is that this court is having to adjudicate in April 1996 on alleged identification which took place in May and June 1993. I have heard Brookes evidence and seen him. As I have said, I am entirely satisfied that where recognition or identification is concerned he simply does not know in ordinary parlance whether he is on his head or his heels. This, I hasten to add, is understandable: he was undoubtedly shocked at the terrible events I shortly described at the beginning.

Second, he only had a snap look at one and no more of his friend's attackers.

Thirdly, since then many people and many times he has been asked about identification matters.

Next, nearly three years further on in effect he has identified three if not four people as the stabber: the man we have called Curtains, Jamie Acourt effectively, Luke Knight, and the Star Burger man making four.

When one remembers also that his identifications are unsupported by other evidence one could see why the submissions that are made to me not to allow the jury to hear this evidence are made.

What is the duty of the judge? However horrific the crime and however objectionable the motive for it may be, that does not enable any judge to remove or alter the legal safeguards already in place to prevent, so far as humanly possible, the convictions of anybody on a misidentification. The perils of misidentification are well known, and an Act of Parliament and the established cases require the trial judge to act as a screen to see that the material to go before the jury is material on which they can properly convict according to law.

It will be obvious to any intelligent listener that Mr Brookes' evidence of identification is impeachable not on just one but two grounds, that is to say no true identification recognition at the time and identification thereafter not by recognition but which is also tainted.

*In view of the Act of Parliament, which for those who are interested is s.78 of the Police and Criminal Evidence Act, and the **Turnbull** case and in my common law discretion as well, I shall direct that Brookes' identification of each of these defendants does not go before the jury, to do so would amount to an injustice.*

Adding one injustice to another does not cure the first injustice done to the Lawrence family.

I so rule for the reasons that I have given.

Other matters were urged on me about Mr Brookes' medical condition following the stabbing and a solicitor's note that has lead to a submission that Brookes had seen some statement which might be another witness's statement. I only mention it out of deference to the arguments of counsel to say that I have not overlooked those points but I do not need to pronounce on them in view of what I have already said.

Before I finish speaking I would remind those who have just joined us that I have banned any reporting of what counsel say to me in the absence of the jury and anything I may say in court, since the jury are in their room and are to hear presumably further evidence and because the third defendant is not affected by the matters we have been discussing. He too has been identified and remains to be tried on an identification issue as well. Consequently, until I have heard further argument from counsel and they have had a chance to assess the consequence of my ruling the ban remains in place without any alteration whatever."

41.17 **It should be said that Mr Justice Curtis was careful to focus on the most basic problem with Mr Brooks' evidence, namely the absolute confusion apparent from his own evidence and from the conflicting descriptions and evidence given by Mr Brooks from time to time. He relied upon DS Crowley's evidence only where it coincided with Mr Brooks' own evidence about their *"conversation"*. He did not need to rely upon the medical evidence about Mr Brooks or the suggestion that Mr Brooks had seen other witnesses' statements.**

41.18 **In our judgment anybody reading all the evidence put before Mr Justice Curtis could properly reach only one conclusion, namely (as Mr Justice Curtis put it), that *"where recognition or identification is concerned he simply does not know in ordinary parlance whether he is on his head or his heels. This I hasten to add, is understandable. He was undoubtedly shocked at the terrible events I shortly described at the beginning. Second, he only had a snap look at one or more of his friend's attackers. Thirdly, since then many people and many times he has been asked about identification matters. Next, nearly three years further on in effect he had identified three if not four people as the stabber ...."*.**

41.19 **However much we look at the case before Mr Justice Curtis we remain convinced that his proper assessment of the evidence in the light of the law inevitably led the Judge to reach the conclusion set out above. There simply was no satisfactory evidence available. Where this is the position the Courts cannot change the law or the rules out of sympathy or upon suspicion. The burden and standard of proof and the legal principles involved govern all cases, and there must never be differential rules or standards applied because of the horrendous nature of a case.**

41.20 That decision ended the case. On 25 April Mr Mansfield indicated that *"it would not be proper for the prosecution to place before the Court, without the Brooks' evidence, which your Lordship has ruled inadmissible, that* [other] *evidence as a reliable basis for any jury or court to infer the guilt of the three who remain in court."* He added later, in the presence of the jury, *"It is felt the fair and proper course is not to proceed further".* The three men were then formally acquitted upon the Judge's discretion. The prosecution costs were ordered to be paid from public funds.

CHAPTER FORTY-TWO

THE INQUEST

42.1 At the full hearing of the Inquest into the death of Stephen Lawrence (February 1997) the Coroner, Sir Montague Levine, explained to his jury the nature and purpose of the Inquest. He quoted a familiar 1982 dictum of the then Lord Chief Justice (Lord Lane) in this connection:-

> *"....... an inquest is a fact finding exercise and not a method of apportioning guilt. The procedure and rules of evidence which are suitable for one (namely a trial) are unsuitable for the other.*
>
> *........ It is an inquisitorial process, a process of investigation, quite unlike a trial .... The proceedings and evidence at an Inquest shall be directed solely to ascertaining the following matters, namely who the deceased was, how, when and where the deceased came by his death, and the particulars for the time being required by the legislative Acts to be registered concerning the death".*

42.2 The Inquest had been formally opened on 5 August 1993, by Sir Montague, and it continued on 21 December 1993. Various parties were represented in December 1993. A jury was sworn to consider the evidence. The Coroner opened the case, clearly and shortly, and introduced the lawyers to the jury. The jury then retired, and the Coroner raised some preliminary matters as to the screening of certain witnesses and the method of calling young witnesses.

42.3 Mr Mansfield, on behalf of the Lawrence family, then indicated that he was seeking an adjournment. He said that there was fresh evidence which had led to the identification of *"Three more individuals .... over and above the one that was originally identified"*. There was plainly some confusion about this, because (as the Coroner pointed out) two persons had been picked out in 1993 by Mr Brooks as being involved in the murder. But Mr Mansfield said in terms that *"there are another three people who .... are now identified ...."*. Mr Mansfield added that there was further information which might lead or *"point to named individuals .... who are the subject of the identification ...."*. He also said that there could be evidence available from *".... a potential witness who disappeared at the time but is known to be an associate of at least one or two of the alleged assailants."* Finally he said that there was *".... information, possibly, and I put it no higher, because it relates to a professional position, possibly available in relation to one of the statements made by one of the suspects about this whole incident."* There is much mystery about this allegedly potent evidence. Nothing later came of it.

42.4 Plainly, however, Mr Mansfield was acting upon instructions, and he indicated that since the *"prosecuting authorities are not going to take the matter further then the family is, and the family would intend given the further information which they did not have until today, that this matter may form a private prosecution ...."*.

42.5 Counsel for the MPS, Mr Wiggs, said that *"Most of what my friend has said to you just a moment ago is completely new to me ...."*, and he asked for time to consider the matter. He indicated, understandably, that the information given to the police as to fresh evidence was *"vague"*, and seemed to consist of (sic) *"... a name that has been given of two people who might be able to assist with the Inquiry"*.

42.6 The Coroner indicated his fear that a future hearing might be prejudiced if the Inquest went ahead with the use of restricted evidence. **Mr Mansfield returned to his reasons for seeking an adjournment, and although he did not say who the possible fresh witnesses were he said that his four categories of further evidence were "*.... not nebulous. The information we have is very specific and in one case dramatic,*" and he said that "*This information comes from a reputable source*".**

42.7 The Local Authority (Greenwich Council) indicated through Counsel, Miss Gearey, that it was involved in the reception or the passing on of some unidentified relevant information to the police.

42.8 The Coroner was understandably unhappy about what had happened. After a short adjournment he indicated that he proposed to put the matter over for a few weeks. In a wisely short ruling to the jury Sir Montague said that " *.... there is a suggestion that there is some new evidence which has just come to light - in the interests of fairness and justice, and being mindful of the possible prejudicing of a future hearing, possibly in another court, I am going to adjourn for a set period*". Sir Montague made an appeal to " *.... anyone with any information, no matter how tenuous, or possibly trivial, to come forward in the interests of justice and fairness to all concerned*". The jury were discharged, and no future date was fixed.

42.9 There was one further date for the Inquest scheduled later (10 October 1994). But as we know the private prosecution did go ahead, and the full Inquest hearing did not take place until February 1997.

42.10 **We have set these preliminary matters out in some detail because they illustrate yet again the strange and unsatisfactory nature of the progress of this case. The evidence referred to by Mr Mansfield certainly turned out to be unavailable. When the private prosecution went ahead it does not appear that there was new *"dramatic"* or *"specific"* evidence available to Mr & Mrs Lawrence's legal team other than that which had become available in the first months of the investigation.**

42.11 It was natural that Mr & Mrs Lawrence should wish to pursue any opportunity to obtain justice after their son's murder. However, as the events unfolded the adjournment of the first Inquest was achieved upon scant evidence and information. The root of their frustration and disappointment lay in the failure by the police to give any information about the first investigation; the failure to explain why the prosecution was as they saw it "*abandoned*"; and why there was a lack of viable evidence. They did not believe in the police's well publicised explanation namely that there was "a wall of silence".

42.12 The full Inquest was held in February 1997. Mr Mansfield again led for the Lawrence family. Mr Gompertz (wrongly named Gumplett throughout the transcript) represented the Commissioner of the MPS. Both the Acourts and David Norris and Luke Knight were represented by Mr Conway. Miss Hawley appeared for Mr Brooks. The jury were sworn, and the Coroner opened the case to them, after calling officers to prove maps and photographs of the area involved.

42.13 **The Coroner then called Mrs Lawrence. He dealt with her with conspicuous care and sympathy. Mrs Lawrence gave her evidence about her son and about the awful circumstances of his death clearly and fully. It would be unfair and unhelpful to summarise all that she said. The full transcript is available as a matter of record. At the end she said that she had "*written something down* [about] *Stephen, I'll just get*** *myself together"*. **The Coroner told her to take her time - and she then read the following prepared statement. It is necessary to set it out in full, since it vividly summarises Mrs Lawrence's own views at that time:-**

"My son was murdered nearly four years ago; his killers are still walking the streets, when my son was murdered the police saw my son as a criminal belonging to a gang. My son was stereotyped by the police, he was black then he must be a criminal and they set about investigating him and us. The investigation lasted two weeks, that allowed vital evidence to be lost, my son's crime is that he was walking down the road looking for a bus that would take him home. Our crime is living in a country where the justice system supports racists murders against innocent people. The value that this white racists country puts on black lives is evidence as seen since the killing of my son. In my opinion what had happened in the Crown Court last year was staged. It was decided long before we entered the court room what would happened but the judge would not allow the evidence to be presented to the jury. In my opinion what had happened was the way of the judicial system making a clear statement saying to the black community that their lives are worth nothing and the justice system will support any one, any white person who wishes to commit any crime or even murder against a black person, you will be protected, you will be supported by the British system. To the black community your lives are nothing you do not have feelings, you do not have any rights to the law in this country that is only here to protect the white man and his family and not you. Since my son's murder we as a family have not been able to grieve for the loss of Stephen, even though the system was against us we tried to re-address this injustice against us, we felt we have to and with the dedication of our legal team and supporters we mounted our own private prosecution to seek justice for our murdered son. I hope our family will be the last, even though there is no sign to the date, will be the last to put through this night mare which it has been for us. There needs to be changes for the future, the establishment needs to have in place a system that will allow all crimes to be treated in the same way and not to be investigated, and to be investigated in the same way regardless of who the victim, of who the perpetrators might be, not to have one rule for the white and another for the black people who just happened to be in the investigation into the murder of Stephen to that of a white boy who was killed in Kings Cross. We as a family felt because the early stages which would have given the evidence that would have ensure that those who killed my son would have paid for their crime, they wasted that time because as far as they were concerned for them to come across a young black man who had no criminal record who is studying that is something they seem to be unaware of. They were very patronising to me in the early stages and instead of them being a support to us they became to be an injury because they were not supporting us as a family every time we spoke to them it was like a banter that we had to go through we had to fight, on one occasion when I went, that was the first time that I ever went to a police station, my husband and a group of us, I felt that maybe they didn't get all the information, the names that were coming to us, I personally wrote the names down and I took it to the station, as

I walked in I presented it to one of the officers and while we were there talking I sat and watched him and he folded the paper and rolled it into a ball in his hand and at the end of our meeting I said to him you are going to put that in the bin now and he said to me no, no, we treat all the information we have but at the time they would not taking my son's case as they should have done."

42.14 There followed considerable discussion about the evidence to be called. In particular, the question of how much Mr Brooks might be asked (as to the names and identification of those involved) loomed large. Mr Mansfield accepted that he could not ask him *"about identification about the various people that were there"*. Everybody realised that the position was a tricky one, because Mr Brooks' identification evidence had effectively been eliminated at the Central Criminal Court.

42.15 **Miss Hawley stressed the state of Mr Brooks' health. The Coroner saw a consultant psychiatrist's report about Mr Brooks, but pointed out that Mr Brooks had said to the doctor that he did want to come to give evidence. Again the Coroner was most thoughtful and sympathetic in his approach to Mr Brooks as he started his testimony. The Coroner took him carefully through his evidence. Mr Brooks described the quick and terrible attack upon Stephen Lawrence, led (as he said then) by one man in front who had dark hair. *"He was tall, slim and dark"*, said Mr Brooks. *"He starts to draw something out of his trousers .... it was just long"*. This evidence again confirms the understandably confused state of Mr Brooks' memory of the event.**

42.16 **Then Mr Brooks described all that followed, when both he and then Stephen ran up the road to the point where Stephen collapsed. He told the jury about his telephone call for an ambulance, and about the arrival of the police, and about all that happened at the hospital. At the end of the Coroner's examination Mr Brooks described two more of the people involved - *"There was another one that was shorter, he had blonde hair. .... Another one that had short black hair .... he wasn't tall or short"*.**

42.17 Mr Mansfield asked Mr Brooks questions - primarily perhaps in order to elicit further descriptions of some of those involved. Other Counsel did not cross-examine.

42.18 There then followed a considerable body of familiar evidence. Royston Westbrook and Joseph Shepherd (both at the bus stop with Stephen Lawrence) gave their accounts of all that they had seen. Largely their evidence was "led" by the Coroner, using their early statements made to the Police. Neither witness had identified any person on any parade. Both gave descriptions, so far as they could, of some aspects of the men involved in the murder. Mr Shepherd told the Court of the unfortunate way in which he was *"named"* at the identification parade. He would not attend further parades although *"They did make several attempts to drag me along to 'em!"* Mademoiselle Marie's statement was read out.

42.19 Then the police officers who came to the scene were called (PC Geddis, PC Gleason, PC Bethel and Acting Inspector Little). Mr Mansfield, understandably, asked questions (particularly of Mr Little) about what had or had not been done at the scene. He was pursuing the lines which both we and the PCA have subsequently followed in this regard. Mr Conway interjected after a time, saying that *" .... we are getting miles away from the purpose of these proceedings"*.

42.20 In this respect we have some sympathy both for Mr Mansfield and the Coroner. Mr Mansfield was acting for the family who believed that much had gone wrong in connection with the policing of this crime, both as to "action" and as to family liaison. Here were witnesses who could deal with all of that. The Coroner rightly allowed latitude in the questioning of witnesses, but at the same time he was fully conscious (as his opening indicated) that the remit of the Inquest was limited to when, where, and by what means Stephen Lawrence met his death.

42.21 Negligence in policing after the death was not strictly within the province of the Inquest. Yet some flavour of the family's complaints or unhappiness was inevitably being voiced. Furthermore, as their own questions showed, members of the jury were themselves interested in the investigation that followed the death.

42.22 The pathologist and the Ambulance Service Controller gave evidence. And then the Coroner indicated that he was about to call *"the first of some boys I've called to this Court ...."*. These were, of course, the five suspects. Three had been acquitted at the Central Criminal Court. Two had not been committed for trial. Counsel (Mr Conway) acting for the two Acourts, Mr Knight and Mr Norris argued that they should not be called. The discussion was somewhat diffuse, but Counsel was questioning both the basis and the fairness of calling these witnesses. He indicated that they would refuse to answer questions and would in traditional terms make *"no comment"*. Mr Mansfield argued that the witnesses should be called, so that he could at least ask them (for example) whether *"they were there"* on the night of the murder.

42.23 **Eventually the Coroner gave his reasons why he intended to call the five young men. His aim was, he said, to try to establish the full facts. He said that he believed that "....** *particular persons may have knowledge of the facts of the death, and it would be expedient to call such persons; the factors which lead me to such a conclusion are, that it is widely suspected that the five men knew more about the death than hitherto appeared. Just knew more, I don't say commit, but the anxiety in the community amongst black and white members that all the facts should become known because of the evidence that the death was racially motivated".**

42.24 The Coroner was in a difficult position. He was rightly most sympathetic to Mr & Mrs Lawrence. He was also fully conscious of the boundaries of the Inquest. We fully understand why the Coroner decided as he did, if only in the hope that at least some of Mr & Mrs Lawrence's worries might be allayed.

42.25 **As it turned out nobody gained anything by calling these witnesses because they all simply refused to answer virtually all questions, in spite of Mr Mansfield's protestation that certainly the three who had been acquitted had no basis for arguing that their answers might incriminate them. Neil Acourt (and Mr Conway) simply put up the shutters. *"I'm claiming privilege, yes, full stop"*, was Neil Acourt's attitude and his assertion. Mr Mansfield pressed and pressed Neil Acourt to answer, but he would not do so.**

42.26 **Luke Knight adopted the same course. He did in fact answer one or two questions, including one which indicated a denial that he had been at or near the scene of the incident. But in effect he kept his silence, and claimed privilege.**

42.27 **David Norris refused to answer any questions. *"Are you called Mr Norris"*, asked Mr Mansfield, in some exasperation. *"I'm claiming privilege"*, said Mr Norris, to general ironic laughter.**

42.28   It was indicated that Jamie Acourt and Gary Dobson would also refuse to answer questions. Mr Mansfield argued that the conduct of the witnesses amounted to *"an abuse and it amounts to a contempt"*. A long and sometimes acrimonious discussion followed, and eventually Jamie Acourt was called. He claimed privilege, in parrot fashion, repeating the well rehearsed mantra, *"I claim privilege"* almost throughout. Gary Dobson behaved virtually in the same way. He did agree that murdering *"anyone for no other reason than the colour of their skin is particularly serious"*, but he would not deal with any of the other questions put to him about his jacket and other matters.

42.29   **This part of the Inquest must have been both frustrating and indeed almost farcical to the jury. We fully understand the Coroner's reasons for summoning the five suspects to Court and calling them. Although the fact is that calling them did, in fact, achieve nothing. Some may argue that the manner in which the "five" claimed privilege against self-incrimination, by putting the shutters up right from the start, earned themselves the description of "the five suspects" which is how they will always be regarded by the public. The Coroner is not to be criticised for the situation which developed. He must have been as much frustrated as the jury. It is doubtful whether these men were acting within their legal rights by their blanket refusal to answer. But no steps were taken to challenge their lawyers' advice which plainly led to their decision to remain arrogantly silent.**

42.30   A great deal more evidence was then called. How much of it was strictly necessary is again not truly for us to say. The Coroner hoped that he could, by calling such evidence, defuse Mr & Mrs Lawrence's unhappiness and produce some answers to the many questions in their minds about the case. In the end we doubt whether the volume of evidence achieved this or served much purpose. But again this is simply the fact, and we do not criticise the Coroner in any way for calling many witnesses and for allowing many questions to be asked which were in reality upon the fringe of the Inquest's remit, if not altogether outside it.

42.31   PC Gleason gave evidence. Witness B was called. His evidence has already been the subject of considerable comment. He was allowed to say that he had seen Jamie Acourt (or Neil Acourt) and David Norris at the scene, as he watched from the top of the bus. The same challenges were made to him as had been made at the Magistrates' Court, when his evidence as to identity of those two had largely been discredited.

42.32   Mr Groves' evidence was read to the jury. Mr Jeynes gave evidence. Mr Mansfield was understandably sceptical about the efficiency and methods of the police and, without much objection, he asked many questions which were critical of what had been done or left undone. The Coroner wondered whether *"we should go down too many channels and widen the scope because I think to no purpose"*. But sensibly he did allow Mr Mansfield considerable scope, on behalf of Mr & Mrs Lawrence.

42.33   Detective Chief Inspector John Carnt was the last witness. He had only joined the Plumstead ranks in 1996, but the Coroner asked him about the initial inquiries, and about the sequence of events of the police activity, gleaned from records and statements. Many of his, and later of Mr Mansfield's, questions were in truth asked because of the criticisms by Mr & Mrs Lawrence of the police. Whether this was relevant is somewhat doubtful. We do not criticise the Coroner, who plainly hoped that this investigation would give the jury a somewhat fuller picture and perhaps would help Mr & Mrs Lawrence to come to terms with what had happened. Thus he did not restrict this Inquest to the bare terms of *"How, when and where did Stephen Lawrence meet his death"*. Mr Gompertz eventually remonstrated mildly at the latitude of inquiry, but Mr Carnt's evidence went on in the same vein, and without much being achieved, apart from considerable ventilation and foreshadowing of the complaints justifiably made about the police methods and lack of activity.

42.34 Finally, the Coroner summed up to the jury. He dealt fairly and fully with the case. He was admirably sympathetic to Mr & Mrs Lawrence, and also to Mr Brooks. He summed up the factual evidence well and thoroughly. He also dealt with much of the evidence called as to the police and what they had done or not done. And he directed the jury very positively as to the questions to be answered by them. Furthermore, he rightly told the jury that there was really only one available verdict, namely that Stephen Lawrence was unlawfully killed. **When the jury returned from retirement that was the verdict given. They added the details required and indicated that they wished to say (as the Coroner recorded) that Stephen Lawrence was killed** *"in a completely unprovoked racist attack by five white youths"*.

42.35 The Coroner again sympathetically referred to that verdict and then he said this:-

> *"Now I say this with all the sincerity at my command. Society must increase its efforts to rid itself of the paranoia of racism and its intolerance. We must teach our young, both in the family and in our schools that each individual, regardless of their race, regardless of their colour, regardless of their religion has the right to live peacefully without any fear or intimidation. These levels must extend to all levels of our society. Stephen LAWRENCE's death should always be a focus of our determination to eradicate racial intolerance. Now I am sure I am echoing the sentiments of everyone in this court when I extend my deepest sympathy to Mr and Mrs LAWRENCE and their family in their tragic bereavement and I know that all the police I have been in contact with feel exactly the same way. I wish them well."*

He made suggestions about the need for *"a review of local intelligence computerised data banks in police stations"*. And he ended with a wish for racial harmony.

42.36 As we understand it this was the last Inquest held by this distinguished Coroner. He was appropriately thanked by Counsel.

42.37 After the Inquest a statement was read out publicly on behalf of Mrs Lawrence:-

> *"First of all I wish to express my gratitude to the Coroner, Sir Montague LEVINE, for giving me the opportunity to tell some of the experience of my family and I have been suffering in the last three and a half years since the murder of our son.*
>
> *There were times this week when I was not sure whether I was in a court room listening to evidence of how my son was killed, or at a circus watching a performance. The performance of someone who is a member of the Bar trying his best to keep the truth from coming out of who was involved in the murder of my son. The performance did not end there. It became a mockery of trying to get to the truth. What was coming across for me was that none of the officers saw it fit to go round to known suspects homes even just to eliminate them from the enquiry.*

The wall of silence was not only in the surrounding area where my son was killed but with the police officers who were supposed to be investigating the crime. What I have seen and heard in the last three days only confirms what I have been saying all along. Right from the start, the night our son was murdered, it seems that in minds of the police he was only a black boy, why bother. No-one can convince me otherwise the evidence is clear to see by the action they took or didn't take.

What had shocked me, then again I should not be shocked because black people in the past have talked about the treatment they have received at the hands of the police. Nevertheless what I was hearing was, none of the police officers attending the scene made any attempts to see if there was anything they could do. They just stood there while my son bleeds to death. None of them check to see where the blood was coming from. No-one checked to see how serious his injuries were, they just stood there waiting for the ambulance. Maybe there was nothing they could have done to save him. But the fact was they never even tried, that says it all. There are two questions I would like the police to answer, are all officers trained in basic first aid, or was it because they just did not want to get their hands dirty with a black mans blood. Before yesterday I was beginning to think there might be the odd few police officers who believed in justice for all. Whatever trust that I was beginning to build up again towards the police shattered yesterday. I suppose once a policeman always a policeman who protects their own and not the black community."

42.38 The measure and depth of the Lawrence family's feeling are only too evident from the two statements made by Mrs Lawrence.

42.39 **On 13 February 1997, (the day when the Inquest was completed), Mrs Lawrence made her formal complaint to the Commissioner of the MPS, through her solicitors, *"against those officers responsible for the investigation into Stephen Lawrence's murder on the night of 22 April 1993 and the period thereafter* [the first investigation]."**

42.40 **Before leaving the Inquest we should stress that Sir Montague handled a difficult and somewhat fraught hearing with sensitivity and common sense. He knew full well the boundaries which must be imposed upon an Inquest. He rightly saw that some elasticity must be allowed to those boundaries. No criticism has ever been made of his conduct of the case. He is to be applauded for his handling of a delicate situation.**

42.41 As to the lawyers' decision to advise the five men to remain silent we have little to add. It must be remembered that two of them were still able to be prosecuted. Persons who are discharged by a Magistrate, as they were, can legally be brought to trial as a result of a voluntary bill of indictment obtained from a High Court Judge, or by a fresh committal. Anything said on oath by them, or by the three who had been acquitted at trial, might be damaging to the fair trial of the two who were still liable to prosecution. Also an inquest is not a trial. So that once the method of Stephen Lawrence's killing (how the death came about) was proved, it was not necessary to establish the identity of the group of violent men who committed the murder, and the Coroner would not have allowed this to be done.

CHAPTER FORTY-THREE

IMRAN KHAN

43.1 The last two days of the evidence called before the Inquiry consisted of the testimony of Imran Khan. He is a solicitor of the Supreme Court, having been admitted in October 1991. Since then he has worked with the firm of J R Jones in which he is now a partner. He had had no previous contact with Mr & Mrs Lawrence before the murder of their son. Mr Khan's introduction to the case came as a result of a telephone call from Junior Counsel, Martin Soorjoo, who had apparently been instructed previously in other matters by Mr Khan.

43.2 That call was on Friday 23 April 1993, the day after Stephen's murder, and Mr Soorjoo indicated that Mr Khan could expect to receive a telephone call asking if he could assist the family of Stephen. Mr Khan apparently had some experience of helping victims or families in previous cases of racist attacks. His general experience was limited and he had only been a solicitor for about 18 months before his contact with Mr & Mrs Lawrence.

43.3 **There followed a telephone call from a Miss Palma Black who was a member of the Anti Racist Alliance, known throughout this Inquiry as ARA. She asked Mr Khan to attend at the family's home and she gave Mr Khan Mr & Mrs Lawrence's telephone number. Miss Black told Mr Khan to announce himself as the ARA lawyer. Mr Khan was not at all happy to do that, since he has no direct connection with the ARA and he was not in any sense their lawyer.**

43.4 He telephoned Mr & Mrs Lawrence's home on the Friday afternoon and he told the Inquiry that he arranged to go there on Sunday 25 April 1993. There is some documentary evidence which suggests that it was known that Mr Khan would be attending Mr & Mrs Lawrence on Saturday 24 April. But we accept that the first actual attendance at Mr & Mrs Lawrence's home by Mr Khan was on Sunday 25 April.

43.5 There Mr Khan first met Neville Lawrence, and a number of people who were also present at the house including members of the ARA. There was some discussion as to whether another lawyer, a Mr Reid, who had previously been in touch with the family might be the more appropriate solicitor to act since he worked in south-east London. Mr Lawrence however wished Mr Khan to act, and from then onwards Mr Khan was solicitor for Mr & Mrs Lawrence.

43.6 On the first occasion when Mr Khan attended at Mr & Mrs Lawrence's home DS Bevan and DC Holden were present. It is interesting to note that Mr Khan told the Inquiry that he observed that these two were *"nothing but supportive on that particular day"*. Other than that Mr Khan made little reference in his evidence to the state of the family liaison and the relationship between Mr & Mrs Lawrence and DS Bevan and DC Holden. But he appreciated early on that the family liaison was in difficulties, and he was present on 6 May at the meeting between Mr Ilsley, Mr Philpott and Mr & Mrs Lawrence.

43.7 There are those who express surprise that a solicitor acted at all for Mr & Mrs Lawrence in the early days after the murder. It is apparent that where there is a publicised racist attack many people may come quickly to the victim's home. The ARA were very early on the scene, and so was a representative of GACARA; and apparently other organisations sent representatives to Mr & Mrs Lawrence in the early days. There was a suggestion that a candle lit vigil should be held organised by GACARA. This in fact did not take place. It is plain that Mr & Mrs Lawrence felt that others were taking over the management of their affairs without proper consultation or instructions.

43.8 **It may well be that the presence of the various agencies and indeed of a solicitor in the early days was unfamiliar particularly to DS Bevan and DC Holden. We have dealt already with the problems which arose in connection with family liaison. The fact is that police officers who are involved in family liaison must accept a bereaved family as they find it. By that we mean that the way in which a black family reacts to a tragedy such as this may well be different from the reaction of a white family. It is the business of the police to ensure that they fit in with the customs and behaviour of those to whom they are attached for family liaison purposes. Otherwise the relationship is doomed from the start. The presence of a solicitor may well have been unfamiliar to DS Bevan and DC Holden in the circumstances. But the family is perfectly entitled to use a solicitor if they wish, and every step must be taken to fit in with the family's wishes and the family's arrangements.**

43.9 It is apparent that DS Bevan was reluctant to give information to Mr & Mrs Lawrence which they sought. We have already commented upon this in other chapters of this Report. The fact that DS Bevan was both an active member of the investigating team and the liaison officer to Mr & Mrs Lawrence, and incidentally to Mr Brooks as well, led to problems and difficulty. DS Bevan felt reluctant to give information as to the steps being taken in the investigation, and this created a problem for Mr & Mrs Lawrence who were most eager to obtain up to date information as to what was happening.

43.10 Mr Khan quickly became involved in the search for information. We know that he wrote letters dated 26, 27 and 28 April seeking information on behalf of Mr & Mrs Lawrence. Effectively Mr Khan sought details of the present state of the investigation. He wished to know whether there were suspects who had been identified, arrested or interviewed, or whether there was any likelihood of these steps being taken. He wished to know whether witnesses were being interviewed and traced and he also asked for details in relation to the post mortem examination. He also asked for confirmation that, as had been stated publicly, the police remained committed to the view that this was a racist murder.

43.11 Mr & Mrs Lawrence were perfectly entitled to be given this information or at least to be told why the information could not be made available to them. On the other hand the arrangements made for sending the letters to Mr Weeden and the AMIP team were not the best. Two of the letters, namely those dated 26 and 27 April were faxed to Mr Weeden on the morning of 27 April within a few hours of each other. And in the last letter Mr Khan threatened to make a report to the Commissioner of MPS if the answers were not made available.

43.12 It is not right to describe the correspondence as a *"bombardment"* of requests. At the same time we can understand why Mr Weeden was surprised by the correspondence. It should however have been the catalyst for him to seek personally to visit Mr Khan and the family in order to ensure that relations were satisfactory. Instead, and quite wrongly in our view, he decided that he must detach any relationship between Mr Khan and the police from the AMIP team. This was done on 30 April by the somewhat strange arrangement made through and by Mr Adams to which reference is made elsewhere (Chapter 31). Mr Adams' letter referred to the investigators being *"inundated with inquiries"*.

43.13 **Mr Khan described the correspondence as *"sniper fire"*. The fact is that the three letters did not lead to a happy relationship between the senior police officers and Mr Khan. Again however it does seem to us that it is the duty of the police to be tolerant**

and understanding in cases of this kind, and to conduct of this kind by a solicitor. It is unusual that requests should be made in somewhat peremptory fashion and in legal language so early in the investigation of a murder. But it is not for the police to tell a family and their lawyer how to behave.

43.14 There was also a lack of satisfactory communication between Mr Khan and the liaison officers during the first week after the murder. Names of suspects were reaching the family which Mr Khan passed on to DC Holden. DC Holden had a mobile telephone, and Mr Khan recalls that she was irritated by his late night call during the night of 29/30 April. Mr Khan said in evidence that it was his impression that DC Holden did not treat the names of the suspects as crucial information. The fact is that any information which came from Mr Khan was processed into the system. It is plain that the connection between Mr Khan and the liaison officers was not happy.

43.15 Later, on 11 May 1993, Mr Khan was instructed by the family to write to various organisations including GACARA indicating that their presence was not wanted at the family home. The family's instructions were that communications should be addressed to the Anti Racist Alliance who were still represented at Mr & Mrs Lawrence's home at that time.

43.16 A suggestion was made in the first week that Mr & Mrs Lawrence might attend the Incident Room. Mrs Lawrence was unenthusiastic about that proposal in any event, and the family was unhappy that the police decided that they would not invite their solicitor to attend with them. This was another irritation between Mr Khan and the family and the police, and another symptom of the failure of the liaison.

43.17 On 6 May 1993 there was the meeting between Mr & Mrs Lawrence and Nelson Mandela, of which Mr Khan was ignorant until after it had taken place. He was however present at the meeting on 6 May with Mr Ilsley and Mr Philpott. Mr Khan told us that although he had little specific recollection of the details of the meeting Mr & Mrs Lawrence did appear to have been reassured to some extent. On the other hand the incident involving the note with the names of suspects given by Mrs Lawrence to Mr Ilsley took place at that meeting, and Mr Khan remembers that as the meeting dispersed Mrs Lawrence said that she believed that the police would pay no attention to the information that she had given them.

43.18 **Mr Khan indicates that his general impression of the meetings between the family and Mr Ilsley after 6 May was that by and large they were cordial. He gave no details of what took place at those meetings, and indeed his evidence is in general terms somewhat vague as to what was said on specific occasions when he was present. Exactly what his role was after the very early requests for information had been made is uncertain. But he was there or thereabouts during the whole of the time up to and after the discontinuance of the proceedings which took place at the end of July 1993. Mr Khan was in fact telephoned by Mr Bullock who told him that the CPS had advised that there was insufficient evidence and that there would be a discontinuance, but that the police investigations would continue.**

43.19 That was the first intimation given to Mr Khan that the CPS were even considering discontinuance. Mr Khan had contact with Mr Medwynter and Mr Grant-Whyte, since he hoped to try to arrange some system whereby there could be liaison meetings between the CPS and the family. But he had not been told that discontinuance was contemplated. At that time Mr & Mrs Lawrence were in Jamaica, and it is most regrettable that the discontinuance took place in their absence and that no proper arrangements were made to warn them that this was to occur.

43.20 On 2 August Mr Khan met Mr Ilsley and Mr Philpott, and it was his impression that there was a measure of disagreement between the police and the CPS as to the sufficiency of the evidence available to take the matter further.

43.21 There is considerable dispute between Mr Barker and Mr Khan as to Mr Khan's availability during the period of Mr Barker's Review. Mr Barker says that he made numerous telephone calls and attempts to contact Mr Khan but that there was never any satisfactory response. Mr Khan says that the investigating team had all his telephone numbers, and that there should have been no difficulty in contacting him should Mr Barker have seriously wished to see him. As a result Mr Khan had no input into the Review and indeed he only heard that it had been completed from a member of the family. He knew from Mr & Mrs Lawrence that they had seen Mr Barker, but he really played no part in the connection between them and Mr Barker during the review period. Mr Khan said that he was not told what was the content of the Review, but he knew that the impression to be gained from reading the Review was that the investigation had been satisfactory and that there had been nothing amiss with the first investigation.

43.22 On 2 May 1993 Mr Khan saw Mr Brooks. He told us that he then and there became Mr Brooks' solicitor. There is no evidence showing that he was retained to act formally as Mr Brooks' solicitor. However, Mr Khan accepts that that was the case, and in his evidence he accepted that he should have provided greater support for Mr Brooks in the early days.

43.23 It seems to us strange that Mr Khan should have become involved with Mr Brooks who was a vital and most important potential prosecution witness. There is some criticism to be levelled against Mr Khan, who interviewed Mr Brooks without the police being told that this was to take place. He furthermore took a statement from Mr Brooks, and a detailed note was made by a solicitor called Ratip of the conversation which took place on 2 May. Mr Ratip's evidence was highly unsatisfactory, and little reliance can be placed upon anything said or recorded by him. The note of the conversation and of the meeting between Mr Brooks and Mr Ratip and Mr Khan did not surface until shortly before evidence was given by Mr Brooks and Mr Khan at the Central Criminal Court in 1996.

43.24 Mr Khan says that he believed that the documents concerning his meeting with Mr Brooks were protected by solicitor/client privilege. That note and the evidence of Mr Ratip and Mr Khan played its part in the destruction of the validity of the evidence of Mr Brooks at the Old Bailey. The note suggested that Mr Brooks might have been shown statements of other witnesses, so that his identification of Mr Acourt and Mr Knight was thereby flawed. We have not relied upon that note, having seen Mr Ratip in the witness box.

43.25 The last contact that Mr Khan had directly with Mr Brooks as a client was, according to Mr Khan in June 1993. Later, probably in November or December 1993, Miss Jane Deighton came to act for Mr Brooks, and she has continued to be his solicitor until the present day. Letters were written by Mr Brooks to Mr Khan indicating dissatisfaction, for example, in respect of the security of his home which Mr Khan had promised to undertake. It is apparent that for some reason which is unexplained Mr Brooks was plainly cool towards Mr Khan and felt he had let him down in various respects.

43.26 Criticism has been made of the police for their failure to ensure that Mr Brooks was looked after as a victim and was properly counselled and assisted. Some of that criticism must be deflected to Mr Khan, since he was Mr Brooks' solicitor and it was his duty to his client, as he accepts, to see that proper steps were taken to ensure that this vital witness who was also a victim of the murderers of Stephen Lawrence was properly looked after and properly protected and cared for.

43.27   When Mr Khan was cross examined it did appear that attendance notes and copies of letters written by him were missing. Simply for example the letter written to Mr Barrah of GACARA on 11 May 1993 to which reference has been made was not contained within Mr Khan's own files. Furthermore various attendance notes and other documents were missing from his files. What he said was that there had been a *"reshuffling of the files"* in 1993 or 1994. The Inquiry has been given unfettered access to Mr Khan's files. A number of documents are not there to assist the Inquiry.

43.28   Mr Khan was cross examined by Mr Gompertz on behalf of the Commissioner of the MPS. It is purposeless to try to rehearse the whole of that cross examination now. It is available for anyone who wishes to read it. The main suggestion was that Mr Khan should bear a measure of responsibility for the failure of the connection between the police and the family. It is a feature of the case that Mr & Mrs Lawrence were very upset by the questions which were asked of them in connection with a pair of gloves and a hat found at the scene of the murder. Mr & Mrs Lawrence's reaction to the questions asked of them and indeed to investigations which were being made about the background of Stephen Lawrence and of the family was understandable. They were suspicious of the police and they believed that the police were acting with insensitivity, and indeed were harassing young people who were known to Stephen Lawrence by suggesting that he might have been involved in some sort of gang. Furthermore they believed that the questions about the hat and the gloves implied that Stephen had been involved in some nefarious activity on the night of his murder.

43.29   **The police say correctly that these investigations and questions were routine. But it is obvious that Mr & Mrs Lawrence were very much upset by them, and there is no doubt but that the way in which these matters were approached was insensitive. The police should have realised that great sensitivity was required in these respects, and should have meticulously prepared the ground before such questions were raised either with the family themselves or with Mr Khan.**

43.30   We do not accept that it is established that Mr Khan could or should have intervened, or that he had any duty to explain police methods, or to salvage the situation on behalf of the police. No doubt the police did find it awkward to deal with Mr Khan, and the course of correspondence and telephone calls in the first two or three days did not help the relationship between himself and the police to get off on the right foot.

43.31   **It would be wrong to criticise Mr Khan, since he was doing what the family wished him to do and they had confidence in the methods which he was employing. Furthermore he believed once Mr Ilsley took over the family liaison that things were reasonably satisfactory.**

43.32   It can be said that Mr Khan may have allowed a somewhat cavalier attitude in connection with appointments to damage the relationship between himself and the police. Mr Ilsley prepared and set out a catalogue of cancellations and postponements of meetings which cannot have assisted the relationship. Mr Khan was ready to criticise, and to contact the media, more than might be expected. This also may not have assisted the relationship between him and the police. It is the duty of the police to ensure good relations both with a bereaved family and its representatives.

43.34 Mr Gompertz also questioned Mr Khan about a young man named Dean Simpson, who was known to both Stephen Lawrence and Mr Brooks. The police wished to see Mr Simpson, because a message on 28 April from another friend named Oduro suggested that Mr Simpson had pertinent information indicating that a man named Mutts might have been involved in the murder.

43.35 DC Holden spoke to Mrs Lawrence about this, and she said that she would try to get Mr Simpson's mother to contact the police.

43.36 Soon thereafter Mr Khan seems to have become involved. He says that he persuaded Mr Simpson to agree eventually to co-operate with the police.

43.37 The evidence on this topic may indicate that on occasions Mr Khan was difficult to contact. We see no solid basis for other criticism of him.

43.38 As to his connection with Mr Brooks it is of significance that there was contact between Mr Brooks and Mr Khan during at least one of the identification parades attended by Mr Brooks. Exactly why there was telephone communication between the two of them is uncertain. Apparently Mr Brooks indicated that he wished to speak to Mr Khan, and he was allowed to make his telephone call. Mr Westbrook reports that Mr Brooks seemed to be giving a running account of the identity parade to the person at the other end of the telephone, and when the call was finished Mr Brooks came back into the room and asked questions and wanted to know whether anyone else had identified persons on the parade, and he sought addresses from the witnesses. Mr Khan says that he does not recollect having any telephone conversation with Mr Brooks. We have no doubt that there was such a conversation. The connection between Mr Brooks and Mr Khan is a curious one.

43.39 After the discontinuance in July 1993 Mr Khan continued to act for Mr & Mrs Lawrence, and indeed he has been their solicitor ever since. Probably late in 1993 Mr Mansfield was briefed, and a team of junior counsel has also played its part since the end of 1993.

43.40 In particular the legal team took on the private prosecution, and worked closely with Mr Nove, Mr Mellish and Mr Carnt.

43.41 The CPS, particularly through Mr Youngerwood, had indicated that it would be unwise to go ahead with the private prosecution, because there simply was not satisfactory or sufficient evidence available to support it. Chapter 39 deals with this advice.

43.42 The attitude of the police was that the decision to go ahead was not for them to make. Assistant Commissioner Johnston realised that the case was weak, and so did Mr Nove and Mr Mellish. But their decision was that they would do all that they could to support the prosecution, should Mr & Mrs Lawrence's legal team decide to go ahead. This was a proper attitude for the police to adopt, and it is certain that they did provide every assistance in connection with the production of witnesses and documents.

43.43 We fully appreciate the feelings of Mr & Mrs Lawrence, who wanted to take every step which might lead to the conviction of Stephen's murderers. We are not privy to the terms of the advice which was given.

43.44 As Mr Youngerwood forecast the evidence of Mr Brooks was effectively destroyed by fair and logical cross-examination. There was nothing left to put before the Court. Rightly the prosecution was abandoned. The trial is fully discussed in Chapter 41 of our Report.

43.45 **Different rules and standards cannot be applied to crimes which are particularly horrific or spurred on by particularly evil motive unless statute so provides. Unless there is evidence available which establishes guilt beyond reasonable doubt there can be no conviction.**

43.46 **Furthermore the Judge has the absolute duty to stop any case in which he concludes that there is no evidence to go to the jury, or that the evidence is of such a quality that it should not be put before the jury. There is no place for alternative rules in hard or terrible cases.**

43.47 **The result of the unsuccessful prosecution was that the three men who were acquitted can never be tried again, even if final appeals for fresh witnesses were to bear fruit, or if the three men were to admit their guilt. Any change in the law in this respect would be solely a matter for Parliament. A suggestion made to us is that the Court of Appeal might be given jurisdiction to consider whether a second prosecution could be brought, particularly if fresh evidence supported such a course. The suggestion deserves examination.**

43.48 **Overall there is no doubt but that Mr Khan has supported Mr & Mrs Lawrence with determination and with vigour. Both he and they have been proved right as to many of the criticisms of the failure of the police investigation. It is a bitter disappointment to all that nobody has been successfully prosecuted for this terrible murder.**

CHAPTER FORTY-FOUR

THE POLICE COMPLAINTS AUTHORITY

44.1 After the Inquest Mr & Mrs Lawrence made a formal complaint against the MPS. Mr Khan says that he wrote to the Commissioner on 13 February 1997 a letter which ended, *"Please accept this letter as registration of the formal complaint."* An unsigned copy of the letter appears in Mr Khan's file. That letter may not have been posted at once, but the Kent Police Report indicates that their inquiry on behalf of the PCA began on 20 March 1997.

44.2 For some months there was no direct input from Mr & Mrs Lawrence or Mr Khan. The PCA agreed terms of reference for its inquiry relying upon comments made publicly by Mr & Mrs Lawrence, and upon Mrs Lawrence's statements made at the Inquest. Transcripts of the Inquest proceedings were available which to some extent foreshadowed the complaints about the MPS investigation of the murder.

44.3 On 29 September 1997 Mr & Mrs Lawrence and Mr Khan did give positive support to the Kent inquiry. On 9 October 1997 Mr Lawrence made a statement to Kent, setting out in short form the nature of his complaints. Much of that statement dealt with the *"insensitivity"* of the MPS in their dealings with the family. Later Mr Lawrence voiced the opinion that there must have been *"collusion"* from outside with police officers which led to deliberate slowing down of the investigation in order to favour one or more of the suspects.

44.4 The terms of reference of the PCA were:-

> *"To investigate the MPS' handling of the murder of Stephen Lawrence on 22 April 1993 and any related matters but with specific regard to:-*
>
> > i.   *The initial response.*
> > ii.   *Family liaison.*
> > iii.   *The conduct of the murder investigation up to and including the review carried out by the MPS."*

44.5 **A team of Kent officers led by Deputy Chief Constable Robert Ayling investigated the case for some nine months. Many police officers and other witnesses were seen afresh. Long interviews were conducted with 17 officers. Statements were taken from many more officers. We are grateful to the PCA for full co-operation and for full access to all their documents, including the Kent Investigating Officer's Report. Public interest immunity from production can be claimed for such reports. The PCA made no such claim, and for the purposes of our Inquiry the full text of the Report, other than the chapters setting out conclusions and recommendations, was made available to all parties. The short form of the PCA's own Report was placed before Parliament in December 1997: it is reproduced in full in the Appendices to this Report. The Investigating Officer's full report was made available in January 1998 to this Inquiry.**

44.6   We say at once that in many respects we agree with the content of the Kent Report, particularly where the text shows plain criticism of decisions made by senior officers, and of the family liaison, and of the conduct of the first investigation of the murder, including the Barker Review.

44.7   **We do not agree with the Kent/PCA conclusions as to the actions taken or not taken during the first night, the initial response of the MPS at the scene. Our reasons for our conclusions are set out in full in Chapter 11.**

44.8   The PCA inquiry was geared towards an assessment of the work done in professional terms. It investigated the *"endeavours and judgment of those responsible for leading the investigation"*. Perhaps disturbingly the Kent Report in its Preface said this:-

> *"The depth of detailed scrutiny applied in the complaints investigation could have found fault in most police criminal investigations. The reader of this report should bear in mind that the benefit of hindsight and the luxury of having time to assess all of the information that was available to the MPS is bound to reveal errors, omissions and flawed judgement."*

We have been conscious throughout of the dangers of hindsight. But we hope that such errors and flawed judgment as have been detected by the PCA and by this Inquiry are in fact rare.

44.9   **As to racism we must indicate that in our view the approach of the PCA/Kent investigation was incomplete. Many officers were asked directly whether racism had an impact upon their activities in the case. Predictably they replied in strong terms denying such impact. The result was the finding by Kent that,**

> *"Kent Police have found no evidence to support the allegation of racist conduct by any MPS officer involved in the investigation of the murder of Stephen Lawrence."*

44.10   **This conclusion was preceded by two paragraphs which should be quoted:-**

> *14.25.   The inquiry by Kent Police was an investigation into complaints against specific officers and as such could not cover the broader issue of racism and whether or not it existed within the MPS.*
>
> *14.27   The inquiry nevertheless gave careful consideration to this allegation throughout. Despite what appeared to be genuine personal denials from officers concerned, the inquiry proceeded on the basis that this did not preclude the possibility that the conduct and actions of individual officers may have been unintentionally influenced by inappropriate assumptions or beliefs.*

44.11 **These paragraphs appear to be inconsistent. But insofar as Paragraph 14.27 suggests that regard was paid to the allegation that institutional racism may have influenced officers in the case, we cannot accept the conclusion set out in Paragraph 9 above that there was** *"no evidence to support the allegation of racist conduct".* **No overt racism, other than perhaps the use of inappropriate language, was evident. But the conclusion that there was a "collective failure" to provide an appropriate and professional service to the Lawrence family because of their colour, culture and ethnic origin is in our view inescapable.**

44.12 Otherwise we do not propose to comment upon the content of the PCA Report. The report itself and the statements and interviews recorded have been most useful to us. We are grateful to the PCA for its full co-operation in the conduct of our Inquiry.

44.13 **There are two further areas of concern. First it must be noted that in the case of at least five officers criticism was made by PCA/Kent which would have led to disciplinary charges, but such charges could not be pursued because the officers had retired. Most of the officers concerned had reached retirement age. This raises the important question as to whether or not the terms of employment or service of officers should allow disciplinary proceedings to be brought after retirement. This matter is dealt with in our Recommendations.**

44.14 **Secondly we have heard regularly during our Part 2 meetings of disquiet as to the perceived lack of independence of PCA inquiries and procedures. This does not in any way mean that the members of the PCA are personally subject to criticism. But since PCA inquiries, certainly in major cases, are conducted with or through other police forces, the perception is that such investigations of police by police may not be seen to result in independent and fair scrutiny and that justice is not seen to be done by such investigation.**

44.15 This matter will be referred to in our Recommendations. We stress however that this general criticism or perception is not aimed at the present Kent inquiry in itself. The investigation was thorough and painstaking and fair. The question is one of principle, and the perception must in any event be addressed.

44.16 We do depart from the PCA/Kent in important respects referred to above. Furthermore if racism was not within the PCA terms of reference it might have been better for Kent not to have addressed the issue. As this Inquiry has abundantly shown the issues involved are subtle, and vitally important to all who wish to live in a decent society.

44.17 One important result of the complaint by Mr & Mrs Lawrence was the uncovering of 11 identified "Lines of Enquiry" which Kent put forward to be followed up by MPS in order to try to advance the Stephen Lawrence murder case. These lines have formed the basis for further MPS activity, but we know of no truly productive results so far. The case is still active, and DAC John Grieve is now in charge of ongoing investigations.

CHAPTER FORTY-FIVE

PART TWO OF THE INQUIRY

45.1   Part 2 of the Inquiry was aimed at the second part of our Terms of Reference. We sought to gather information and opinions in order to help us to make recommendations as to the *"investigation and prosecution of racially motivated crimes"*.

45.2   The first step taken was the collection of written material and suggestions from a large number of individuals and organisations. During the summer and autumn of 1998 we received many carefully prepared and helpful documents. The names and particulars of all those who co-operated in this exercise are set out in the Appendices to this Report. It would be truly impossible to try to summarise the large volume of material which has been before us, and which we have digested during the past months. We are most grateful to all who contributed to this part of the Inquiry. Literally thousands of suggestions reached us. Every contribution has been considered.

45.3   Between 24 September and 7 October 1998 we conducted public hearings at Hannibal House. Again many individuals and organisations provided evidence for us, and they are listed in the Appendices. We were able to question the teams taking part, and we obtained much valuable information and assistance. All that was said has been transcribed, and is available both to the public and to those who will carry forward the impetus provided by this Inquiry.

45.4   The hearings in London were followed by public hearings between 8 October and 13 November at:-

> Ealing/Southall
> Manchester
> Tower Hamlets
> Bradford
> Bristol
> Birmingham.

Again all the evidence received was transcribed. The names of the witnesses and the organisations which they represented are set out in the Appendices to this Report.

45.5   At each hearing the Chairman indicated at the outset that the objective was to gather information and opinions from a broad cross-section of people to inform the recommendations which we would ultimately make, and to "take the temperature" of the community and of the Police and other agencies.

45.6   **It soon became apparent that a narrow interpretation of our terms of reference would have been pointless and counterproductive. Wherever we went we were met with inescapable evidence which highlighted the lack of trust which exists between the police and the minority ethnic communities. At every location there was a striking difference between the positive descriptions of policy initiatives by senior police officers, and the negative expressions of the minority communities, who clearly felt themselves to be discriminated against by the police and others. We were left in no doubt that the contrast between these views and expressions reflected a central problem which needs to be addressed.**

45.7 **We are most conscious that the Inquiry is not a commission into race relations generally. Nor could we, as many would have wished, contemplate the full investigation of other individual cases. However, the atmosphere in which racist incidents and crimes are investigated must be considered since that will condition the actions and responses which may follow. That atmosphere was strongly voiced in the attitude of those who came to our hearings. In the words of David Muir, representing senior Black Church Leaders** *"the experience of black people over the last 30 years has been that we have been over policed and to a large extent under protected"*. **That theme was heard wherever we went. It was also echoed by a simple but eloquent and clearly heartfelt plea which occurred and reoccurred with frequency and force at every location:** *"Please treat us with respect".*

STOP AND SEARCH

45.8 If there was one area of complaint which was universal it was the issue of "stop and search". Nobody in the minority ethnic communities believes that the complex arguments which are sometimes used to explain the figures as to stop and search are valid. In addition their experience goes beyond the formal stop and search figures recorded under the provisions of the Police and Criminal Evidence Act, and is conditioned by their experiences of being stopped under traffic legislation, drugs legislation and so called 'voluntary' stops. It is not within our terms of reference to resolve the whole complex argument on this topic. Whilst there are other factors at play we are clear that the perception and experience of the minority communities that discrimination is a major element in the stop and search problem is correct.

45.9 In the 1998 statistics on race and the criminal justice system, commended both by the Home Secretary and Lord Justice Rose, the figures for 1997/98 show that *"black people were, on average, five times more likely to be stopped and searched by the police than white people. The use of these powers for Asians and other ethnic groups varied widely."* Black people are also *"more likely to be arrested than white or other ethnic groups"*. There is no doubt that for the minority communities the formal statistics are the tip of an iceberg. If all the other stops under additional legislation were recorded it is clearly felt that discrimination would be even more evident.

45.10 **It is pointless for the police service to try to justify the disparity in these figures purely or mainly in terms of the other factors which are identified. The majority of police officers who testified before us accepted that an element of the disparity was the result of discrimination. This must be the focus of their efforts for the future. Attempts to justify the disparities through the identification of other factors, whilst not being seen vigorously to address the discrimination which is evident, simply exacerbates the climate of distrust.**

RACIST INCIDENTS

45.11 According to the same statistics referred to above the number of racist incidents rose 6% in 1997/98 to 13,880. This may reflect better recording and reporting of such incidents, since some services have clearly identified the need to increase confidence to achieve this and have addressed it as a priority. The fact remains that the number of incidents is undoubtedly in excess of these figures. The information repeatedly given to us at our public hearings was of distrust and dissatisfaction with the police and other agencies in the investigation of such incidents leading to a disinclination to report. The allegation is that the Police Service and other agencies regularly ignore and belittle such incidents. Over and over again we were told that black victims reporting such incidents were "turned into" perpetrators, and that the "white" version of such incidents was all too readily accepted by police officers and others.

45.12 **The consistent message given to us was that the police and other agencies did not or would not realise the impact of less serious, non-crime incidents upon the minority ethnic communities. Their collective experience was of senior officers adopting fine policies and using fine words, but of indifference on the ground at junior officer level. The actions or inactions of officers in relation to racist incidents were clearly a most potent factor in damaging public confidence in the Police Service.**

HOUSING AND EDUCATION

45.13 The same message was consistent and clear in relation to the complaints of minority ethnic communities in the field of housing and education. There were some examples of developing good practice. In the housing field we heard of the use and development of up-to-date tenancy conditions, and the prompt application of legislation designed to deal with racist tenants. In the field of education we heard of some enlightened development of anti-racist policies. But too often housing departments were seen to be slow and bureaucratic in their response to racist behaviour.

45.14 The evidence we had earlier heard about the racist attitudes of very young children was often confirmed during our public hearings. The consistent concern was that, as in the Police Service, there was a divide between policy and practice, rhetoric and reality. Local Education Authorities had anti-racist policies. But these policies were often not implemented. Even at Governor level schools were not inclined to "advertise" or make public racist problems which might adversely reflect upon the image of the schools.

45.15 **There was a weight of opinion and concern in relation to two specific aspects of education. First the failure of the National Curriculum to reflect adequately the needs of a diverse multi-cultural and multi-ethnic society. Secondly the number of exclusions from schools which were apparently disproportionate to the ethnic mix of the pupils.**

RACIST INCIDENT DEFINITION

45.16 **Another topic regularly addressed both in many written submissions and at public meetings was the definition of the term "racial incident". The current definition used by the Association of Chief Police Officers (ACPO) is:-**

> *"A racial incident is any incident in which it appears to the reporting or investigating officer that the complaint involves an element of racial motivation, or any incident which includes an allegation of racial motivation made by any person."*

This definition has been adopted by agencies other than the police, and it is right to say that it is widely used. There is positive support for its retention. On the other hand strong arguments indicated that the emphasis upon motivation was potentially confusing. Furthermore the apparent priority of the views of investigating or reporting officers was unhelpful. A significant view was that the definition should be crisper and that it should plainly be more victim oriented. Mr Crompton, Her Majesty's Inspector

of Constabulary, confirmed the impression which we had formed in both parts of our Inquiry, namely that the definition was poorly understood by many officers.

45.17 We believe that the use of the words "racial" or "racially motivated" are in themselves inaccurate and confusing, because we all belong to one human race, regardless of our colour, culture or ethnic origin. When referring to crime or incidents involving racism we believe "racist" to be the appropriate adjective. Our Recommendation (12) is that the universally used definition should be:

> *"A racist incident is any incident which is perceived to be racist by the victim or any other person".*

MULTI-AGENCY PARTNERSHIP

45.18 Another much canvassed topic during our meetings was the importance of and the need for genuine multi-agency partnership and co-operation to combat racism, and to bring together all sections of the community with this aim. Such partnership between the police, local Government, Housing and Education officers, Probation Officers and many others is a vital part of the necessary co-operation which is required. Again there is evidence of promising good practice. We heard of encouraging advance in Lambeth, Collyhurst (Manchester), Bristol, and elsewhere. But there is plainly a need for much more co-operation, both in directly combating racism and in the vital arrangements which must be made for the collection, recording and exchange of information between agencies. Racist incidents in schools or between tenants may provide most useful intelligence for the police, and vice versa.

45.19 When multi-agency partnership was discussed at our meetings there was much reference to the provisions of the Crime & Disorder Act 1998, and in particular those which set out the new crime prevention strategies (Sections 5-7). We share the frequently expressed view that the Act provides a timely and fresh opportunity for genuine co-operation in developing anti-racist strategy within the framework of that legislation.

45.20 A significant concern voiced to us was the harm caused by short term funding and the withdrawal of funding and support for community initiatives such as Youth Projects and local Monitoring Groups. This could reflect understandable limitation of available funding. But it may also represent a tendency of funding agencies to withdraw support from groups perceived to be confrontational. The Crime & Disorder Act strategies will provide an opportunity for agencies to agree priorities, and in so doing to ensure that available funding and support are focused so they give such local initiatives the opportunity to be effective through longer term and consistent support. Only by full co-operation will the problems of racism and racist crime be combated. There must be a "multi-stakeholder" approach involving all parts of the community (Recommendation 70).

DEATHS IN CUSTODY

45.21 Next we refer to two themes much heard at our meetings. The first can loosely be termed "Deaths in Custody". We are clear that this issue is outside our terms of reference. But we cannot fail to record the depth of the feelings expressed. There is a need to address the perceptions and concerns of the minority ethnic communities in this regard. Such an issue if not addressed helps only to damage the relationship between police and public, and in its wake there is an atmosphere which hinders the investigation of racist incidents and crimes.

THE COMPLAINTS SYSTEM

45.22 **The second strong theme concerns what may generally be termed the complaints system. It will be no surprise that almost universally we were told that there is little confidence amongst minority ethnic communities in the present system. It may seem to some that this issue is hardly within our terms of reference. But again there is no doubt but that this lack of confidence affects adversely the atmosphere in which racist incidents and crimes have to be addressed. Some believe that more direct investigation of complaints by the Police Complaints Authority is desirable. The majority view was that the whole system needs as a matter of principle to be independent. In particular there is much unease at the regularity of investigations, particularly in serious cases, of one police service by another. We fully appreciate the cost and other implications involved, but the matter requires urgent further consideration. The importance of this public disquiet must not be underestimated. The criticism is not in any way of the Members of the PCA. It is a criticism of the method of investigation imposed upon them. Lord Scarman (The Scarman Report, 4.28) said:**

> **"I conclude that any system for considering complaints against the police which is subject to the range and weight of criticism I have heard ..... must be unsatisfactory and ineffective. Unless and until there is a system for judging complaints against the police, which commands the support of the public, there will be no way in which the atmosphere of distrust and suspicion between the police and the community can be dispelled".**

We echo his words in our Recommendations (55-59).

THE METROPOLITAN POLICE SERVICE

45.23 We also detected a greater degree of distrust between the police and the minority ethnic communities in the MPS area than elsewhere. We are concerned that there appears to be a different measure of accountability in connection with the MPS, in comparison with other Police Services. This may be reflected in evidence heard by us which showed for example that policy was disregarded in some areas, that there was a lack of clarity in lines of command, and that AMIP teams acted as a force within a force. Furthermore presentation to us by National Police Training suggested that different standards of training pertained within the MPS compared with other Police Services. As Deputy Assistant Commissioner Osland said to us in Part 1:- *"You probably know the Metropolitan Police does consider itself to be apart from most other police forces in some respects and the way we are structured encourages that sort of view ...."*. We believe that there is a need to bring the MPS into line with the national pattern of accountability.

OVERALL

45.24   The message is uncompromising. A new atmosphere of mutual confidence and trust must be created. The onus to begin the process which will create that new atmosphere lies firmly and clearly with the police. The Police Services must examine every aspect of their policies and practices to assess whether the outcome of their actions creates or sustains patterns of discrimination. The provision of policing services to a diverse public must be appropriate and professional in every case. Every individual must be treated with respect. "Colour-blind" policing must be outlawed. The police must deliver a service which recognises the different experiences, perceptions and needs of a diverse society.

45.25   We must at the same time warn some of those who are most vociferous in their condemnation of police officers that they should guard against their own racism. Not only during our Inquiry but in general there is readiness without justification to assume and to say that because police officers are white they must be acting to the disadvantage of minority ethnic communities. Racist prejudice and stereotyping can work and be evident both ways. In the search for justice, and in the quest for better relationship between the Police Services and minority ethnic communities this must be firmly borne in mind. Racism either way must be treated with zero tolerance.

45.26   Furthermore blanket condemnation of the Police Services is both unfair and unproductive. Every day police officers all over this country show courage and dedication in what are often dangerous and challenging circumstances. We saw and heard senior and junior police officers at all our meetings who plainly wish to correct the imbalance which is apparent. Chief Officers who appeared before us acknowledge that action is necessary. Too many of those who decry the Police Services allow themselves to go beyond fair criticism. We simply say that there must be full co-operation on all sides to combat racism. Surely there must be optimism and hope that this will be achieved.

CHAPTER FORTY-SIX

CONCLUSION AND SUMMARY

46.1 **The conclusions to be drawn from all the evidence in connection with the investigation of Stephen Lawrence's racist murder are clear. There is no doubt but that there were fundamental errors. The investigation was marred by a combination of professional incompetence, institutional racism and a failure of leadership by senior officers. A flawed MPS review failed to expose these inadequacies. The second investigation could not salvage the faults of the first investigation.**

46.2 At least now many of the failures and flaws are accepted. For too long the family and the public were led to think that the investigation had been satisfactorily carried out. The belated apologies offered at this Inquiry acknowledge the truth, but there is no remedy for the grief which the unsuccessful investigation piled upon the grief caused by the murder itself.

46.3 We were not presented with evidence to persuade us that collusion and corruption infected the investigation of the murder (Chapter 8).

46.4 There are dangers in summarising, but it is necessary to set out here the main thrust of our criticisms. Only a reading of the Report will fully convey its message. The impact of the evidence itself is hard to convey. Those who heard all the evidence found the experience depressing. The following paragraphs simply attempt to refer to the heart of the deficiencies which marred the investigation.

FIRST AID

46.5 No police officer did anything by way of First Aid, apart from the small amount of testing to see whether Stephen Lawrence was still breathing and whether his pulse was beating. We strongly criticise the training and retraining of police officers in First Aid. A senior officer (Inspector Groves) signally failed properly to assess the situation and to ensure that proper steps were being taken to recognise and deal with Stephen Lawrence's gross injuries (Chapter 10).

INITIAL RESPONSE

46.6 We were astonished at the lack of direction and organisation during the vital first hours after the murder. Almost total lack of proper documentation makes reconstruction of what happened during those hours difficult. But lack of imagination and properly co-ordinated action and planning which might have led to the discovery and arrest of suspects was conspicuous by its absence. No officers early on the scene took any proper steps at once to pursue the suspects. There were large numbers of police officers available, but inadequate measures were taken to use them actively and properly. This was due to failure of direction by senior officers, many of whom attended the scene, who seem simply to have accepted that everything was being done satisfactorily by somebody else (Chapters 11 & 12).

FAMILY LIAISON AND VICTIM SUPPORT

46.7   From the first contact with police officers at the hospital, and thereafter, Mr & Mrs Lawrence were treated with insensitivity and lack of sympathy. One of the saddest and most deplorable aspects of the case concerns the failure of the family liaison. Mr & Mrs Lawrence were not dealt with or treated as they should have been. They were patronised. They were never given information about the investigation to which they were entitled. Family liaison failed, despite the good intentions of the officers allocated to this task. Senior officers never intervened to rectify the failure. Both Mr & Mrs Lawrence as the murder victim's parents, and Duwayne Brooks who was himself a victim of the attack, were inadequately, inappropriately and unprofessionally treated and were not treated according to their needs. (Chapters 4, 5 and 26).

THE SENIOR INVESTIGATING OFFICERS

46.8   Detective Superintendent CRAMPTON - Mr Crampton was SIO until Monday 26 April. Revealing and detailed information reached the investigating team from 23 April onwards. There was no wall of silence. A vital and fundamental mistake was made in failing to arrest the suspects named in that information by the morning of 26 April. Enough information was available to make the arrests by the evening of 24 April, at about the time when Mr Crampton says that he made a *"strategical"* decision not to arrest. This decision is nowhere recorded. By Monday 26 April evidence, in a statement signed by Stacey Benefield, reinforced the information available about two of the suspects. That evidence would in itself have justified the arrest of David Norris and Neil Acourt and would have entitled the team to search their premises in connection with the murder of Stephen Lawrence. This flawed decision as to arrest is fundamental. Its consequences are plain to see (Chapter 13).

46.9   Detective Superintendent WEEDEN - When the investigation was handed over to Mr Weeden he perpetuated the wrong decisions made in the vital early days. He did not exercise his own critical faculties in order to test whether the right decisions had been made. He was confused as to his power of arrest. His fundamental misjudgment delayed arrests until 7 May, at which time the arrests were made because of outside pressures. His decisions and actions show lack of imagination and a tendency simply to allow things to drift. He failed to address with sensitivity the problems of family liaison (Chapter 14).

46.10   Detective Inspector BULLOCK - As Deputy Investigating Officer Mr Bullock must be associated with the decisions and actions of the SIOs. He failed to process properly vital information given to the team by James Grant. He was often passive, and not up to his job. The major responsibility for the team's failures lie with those who supervised Mr Bullock, but as DIO he bears his share of responsibility for the team's failures (Chapter 15).

46.11   Detective Chief Superintendent ILSLEY - Mr Ilsley allowed himself to go along with the weak and unenterprising decisions made by his SIOs, in which he had been himself directly involved. He tended to disconnect from responsibility for the investigation when faced with justifiable criticisms. He failed to supervise and to manage effectively this highly sensitive murder investigation. He acted insensitively and unwisely when arranging to take over the family liaison on 6 May 1993 (Chapter 27).

FAILURE TO ARREST CLIFFORD NORRIS

46.12 The failure of the team to do all that was possible to arrest Clifford Norris and to remove him from the scene is unexplained and incomprehensible, particularly in the light of the Stacey Benefield case and the belief that Clifford Norris' influence was inhibiting young potential witnesses (Chapter 9).

SURVEILLANCE

46.13 The surveillance operation was ill-planned, badly carried out, and inadequately documented. If this surveillance was part of the SIOs' strategy in substitution for arrests the decision-making in this regard was flawed and incompetent. The indications are that the team was simply going through the motions in order to establish association. There was inadequate direction and lack of urgency in this operation (Chapter 18).

THE INCIDENT ROOM

46.14 The HOLMES system was inadequately staffed. The Incident Room was not supervised by responsible and trained officers. This may account for many delays apparent in the processing of information reaching the investigation team (Chapter 16).

THE RED ASTRA AND ELIMINATION OF SUSPECTS

46.15 It is a cause of concern and criticism that there was serious delay and failure to take necessary action in connection with the occupants of the red Astra car seen twice on the night of the murder. Furthermore there were serious omissions and failures in the steps taken properly to investigate and eliminate from the investigation associates of the five suspects who were reported also to be suspected of involvement in the murder (Chapter 20).

IDENTITY PARADES

46.16 The identification parades were poorly planned. There were clear breaches of the Codes of Practice governing identity parades. In particular witnesses were allowed to be together before parades took place. Witnesses were not properly supervised. Successful identification might well have been compromised by these breaches (Chapter 21).

THE FAIR HAIRED ATTACKER

46.17 Witnesses, including Duwayne Brooks, indicated that one of the offenders was fair haired. Further information supported this evidence. We agree with Kent's conclusion that the failure to deal logically and thoroughly with this line of inquiry is a clear source of criticism of the first investigation (Chapter 20).

SEARCHES

46.18 When the arrests were made on 7 May it is plain that the searches of all the suspects' premises were inadequate. Information expressly suggested that knives might be concealed under floorboards. There is no evidence that a single floorboard was removed during any of the searches (Chapter 23).

"JAMES GRANT"

46.19 The handling of James Grant by Detective Sergeant Davidson and Detective Constable Budgen, and the failure to register him as an informant is the subject of criticism. Senior officers failed to ensure that this man, and other hesitant witnesses, were properly followed up and sensitively handled (Chapter 19).

POLICY AND RECORDS

46.20 Policy decisions were ill considered and unrecorded. Records and notes were not made or retained.

THE BARKER REVIEW

46.21 Detective Chief Superintendent BARKER - The Review was factually incorrect, and inadequate. Mr Barker allowed himself to impose shackles upon his consideration of the investigation which resulted in the production of a flawed and indefensible report. There is concern about the reception of the Barker Review by all senior officers. That part of his Review which dealt with Mr & Mrs Lawrence is inaccurate, insensitive and thoughtless (Chapter 28).

46.22 Deputy Assistant Commissioner OSLAND - Mr Osland accepted that he was responsible for all operational and administrative activities on 3 Area. Yet the evidence shows that he was much too ready to accept that things were going satisfactorily during the course of the investigation. Having established the Barker Review he uncritically accepted what had been reported, and allowed the Review to go to senior officers including the Commissioner without critical appraisal. No senior officer at any level tested or analysed the Review. Mr Osland's attitude to Mr & Mrs Lawrence and their solicitor is reprehensible (Chapter 29).

46.23 **There can be no excuses for such a series of errors, failures, and lack of direction and control. Each failure was compounded. Failure to acknowledge and to detect errors resulted in them being effectively concealed. Only now at this Inquiry have they been laid bare.**

THE SECOND INVESTIGATION

46.24 The second investigation attempted to salvage the situation. Forthright steps were taken. Clifford Norris was arrested. Sophisticated surveillance of the suspects took place. By 1994 however the case was becoming stale. No satisfactory fresh witnesses have ever come forward. We have no criticism of this investigation by Mr Mellish. Indeed it was managed with imagination and skill. The trust of Mr & Mrs Lawrence was regained by the sensitive approach of Mr Nove (Chapter 33).

RACISM

46.25 We do not attempt to summarise Chapter 6 which deals with this central and vital issue. Save to repeat two of its paragraphs, which we apply to the evidence and facts of the Stephen Lawrence case:

> **6.4** **"Racism" in general terms consists of conduct or words or practices which advantage or disadvantage people because of their colour, culture or ethnic origin. In its more subtle form it is as damaging as in its overt form.**

> **6.34** **"Institutional Racism" consists of the collective failure of an organisation to provide an appropriate and professional service to people because of their colour, culture or ethnic origin. It can be seen or detected in processes, attitudes and behaviour which amount to discrimination through unwitting prejudice, ignorance, thoughtlessness, and racist stereotyping which disadvantage minority ethnic people.**

46.26 At its most stark the case against the police was that racism infected the MPS and that the catalogue of errors could only be accounted for by something more than incompetence. If corruption and collusion did not play its part then, say the critics, the case must have been thrown or at least slowed down because officers approached the murder of a black man less energetically than if the victim had been white and the murderers black. An example of this approach was that posed by Mr Panton, the barrister acting for Greenwich Council, who argued that if the colour of the victim and the attackers was reversed the police would have acted differently:

> *"In my submission history suggests that the police would have probably swamped the estate that night and they would remain there, probably for the next however long it took, to ensure that if the culprits were on that estate something would be done about the situation".*

46.27 **We understand why this view is held. We have examined with anxiety and care all the evidence and have heeded all the arguments both ways. We do believe, (paragraph 6.48) that institutional racism is apparent in those areas described. But we do not accept that it was universally the cause of the failure of this investigation, any more than we accept that a finding of institutional racism within the police service means that all officers are racist. We all agree that institutional racism affects the MPS, and Police Services elsewhere. Furthermore our conclusions as to Police Services should not lead to complacency in other institutions and organisations. Collective failure is apparent in many of them, including the Criminal Justice system. It is incumbent upon every institution to examine their policies and the outcome of their policies and practices to guard against disadvantaging any section of our communities.**

46.28 Next we identify those areas which were affected by racism remembering always that that emotive word covers the whole range of such conduct. In this case we do not believe that discrimination or disadvantage was overt. There was unwitting racism in the following fields:

(i) Inspector Groves' insensitive and racist stereotypical behaviour at the scene. He assumed that there had been a fight. He wholly failed to assess Duwayne Brooks as a primary victim. He failed thus to take advantage of the help which Mr Brooks could have given. His conduct in going to the Welcome Inn and failing to direct proper searches was conditioned by his wrong and insensitive appreciation and conclusions.

(ii) Family Liaison. Inspector Little's conduct at the hospital, and the whole history of later liaison was marred by the patronising and thoughtless approach of the officers involved. The treatment of Mr & Mrs Lawrence was collective, in the sense that officers from the team and those controlling or supervising them together failed to ensure that Mr & Mrs Lawrence were dealt with and looked after according to their needs. The officers detailed to be family liaison officers, Detective Sergeant Bevan and Detective Constable Holden, had (as Mrs Lawrence accepted) good intentions, yet they offended Mr & Mrs Lawrence by questioning those present in their house as to their identity, and by failing to realise how their approach to Mr & Mrs Lawrence might be both upsetting and thoughtless.

This sad failure was never appreciated and corrected by senior officers, in particular Mr Weeden, who in his turn tended to blame Mr & Mrs Lawrence and their solicitor for the failure of family liaison. The failure was compounded by Mr Barker in his Review.

(iii) Mr Brooks was by some officers side-lined and ignored, because of racist stereotyping particularly at the scene and the hospital. He was never properly treated as a victim (Chapter 5).

(iv) At least five officers, DS Davidson, DC Budgen, DC Chase, DS Bevan and DC Holden simply refused to accept that this was purely a racist murder. This (as we point out in the text) must have skewed their approach to their work (Chapter 19).

(v) DS Flook allowed untrue statements about Mr & Mrs Lawrence and Mr Khan to appear in his statement to Kent. Such hostility resulted from unquestioning acceptance and repetition of negative views as to demands for information which Mr & Mrs Lawrence were fully entitled to make. DS Flook's attitude influenced the work which he did (Chapter 16).

(vi) The use of inappropriate and offensive language. Racism awareness training was almost non-existent at every level.

COMMUNITY CONCERNS

46.29 Wider issues than those closely connected to the investigation of the murder of Stephen Lawrence dominated Part Two of our Inquiry. It may be thought that in this respect we have strayed outside our terms of reference. We are convinced that the atmosphere in which racist crime is investigated is bound to influence the outcome of such investigation. We believe that Mr & Mrs Lawrence and all who have been involved in this Inquiry would agree that this is so.

46.30 First and foremost amongst our conclusions flowing from Part 2 is that there is a striking and inescapable need to demonstrate fairness, not just by Police Services, but across the criminal justice system as a whole, in order to generate trust and confidence within minority ethnic communities, who undoubtedly perceive themselves to be discriminated against by *"the system"*. Just as justice needs to be *"seen to be done"* so fairness must be *"seen to be demonstrated"* in order to generate trust. An essential first step in creating that trust is to ensure that it is a priority for all Police Services. The existing system of Ministerial Priority is the obvious route by which this may be achieved (Recommendation 1).

46.31 The need to re-establish trust between minority ethnic communities and the police is paramount. Such distrust and loss of confidence is particularly evident in the widely held view that junior officers discriminate in practice at operational level, and that they support each other in such discrimination. We have referred (Para 45.8) to the primary problem of "stop and search", including those stops which are unrecorded within the present statistics. The minority communities' views and perceptions are formed by their experience of all "stops" by the police. They do not perceive any difference between a "stop" under the Police and Criminal Evidence Act from one under the Road Traffic Act whilst driving a vehicle. It is essential to obtain a true picture of the interactions between the police and minority ethnic communities in this context. All "stops" need to be recorded, and related self-defined "ethnic data" compiled. We have considered whether such a requirement would create too great a bureaucracy for operational officers, and we are persuaded that this is not the case. The great weight of extra recording would undoubtedly relate to "traffic stops" many of which are already recorded via the HORTI (production of driving documents) procedure. In this context we have also specifically considered whether police powers to "stop and search" should be removed or further limited. We specifically reject this option. We fully accept the need for such powers to continue, and their genuine usefulness in the prevention and detection of crime (Recommendations 60-63).

46.32 Seeking to achieve trust and confidence through the demonstration of fairness will not in itself be sufficient. It must be accompanied by a vigorous pursuit of openness and accountability across Police Services. Essentially we consider that the principle which should govern the Police Services, and indeed the criminal justice system, is that they should be accountable under all relevant legislative provisions unless a clear and specific case can be demonstrated that such accountability would be harmful to the public interest. In this context we see no justification for exemption of the Police Service from the full provisions of the Race Relations Act. Chief Officers should be vicariously liable for the actions of their officers. Similarly we consider it an important matter of principle that the Police Services should be open to the full provisions of a Freedom of Information Act. We see no logical grounds for a class exemption for the police in any area (Recommendations 9-11).

46.33 The depth of the failure of the investigation into the murder of Stephen Lawrence is such that there is a particular need for the MPS to be given a current *"clean bill of health"* by a process of vigorous independent inspection. The MPS must also be shown to be as open and accountable as possible by ensuring that the levels of their accountability mirror those of other services. We therefore welcome the forthcoming introduction of a Police Authority for London. However we see neither logic nor justification for limiting its powers in comparison with those existing in other Police Services in England and Wales. In particular we suggest that openness and accountability require that all the MPS Chief Officers should be appointed by the Police Authority and be fully accountable to them (Recommendations 3, 4 and 6).

46.34 If racism is to be eliminated from our society there must be a co-ordinated effort to prevent its growth. This need goes well beyond the Police Services. The need for training of police officers in addressing racism and valuing cultural diversity is plain. Improved understanding and attitudes will certainly help to prevent racism in the future, as will improved procedures in terms of recording and investigating racist incidents. Just as important, and perhaps more so, will be similar efforts needed from other agencies, particularly in the field of education. As we have indicated, the issue of education may not at first sight sit clearly within our terms of reference. Yet we cannot but conclude that to seek to address the well founded concerns of minority communities simply by addressing the racism current and visible in the Police Services without addressing the educational system would be futile. The evidence we heard and read forces us to the conclusion that our education system must face up to the problems, real and potential, which exist. We therefore make a number of Recommendations aimed at encouraging schools to address the identified problems (Recommendations 67-69).

46.35 We have referred (paras 45.22 and 45.33) to the minority communities' doubts and concerns about "deaths in custody" and the existing complaints system. Distrust is generated by what is perceived to be a lack of openness and accountability in both areas. Particularly in the complaints system our conclusion is that a strong element of independent investigation must be considered. A significant benefit of such independence would be that it would also address the distrust which currently surrounds the question of "deaths in custody" and their investigation as a result of complaint by those concerned. Furthermore in the context of complaints we have given specific consideration to the issue of whether Investigating Officers' reports produced during the investigation of complaints should continue to attract class exemption under public interest immunity rules and procedures. Having seen and used the Kent IO's Report in the course of our Inquiry we are sceptical of the need for class exemption. There appears to us to be little, if anything, in the Report which could not and should not be made available to the complainants. We consider that to make such reports available to complainants would be a helpful short-term step in building public confidence in the complaints system, and would be in accord with the principle of ensuring the greatest degree of openness and accountability (Recommendation 10).

46.36 Furthermore there is, as this case shows, a need to ensure that nobody obscures the approach to incidents involving racism because of lack of appreciation or willingness to accept that racism is involved. A clear and uncompromising definition of such incidents is needed to ensure that there is no shelter for such views (Recommendation 12).

46.37 Systems of inspection and the existence of objective external appraisal are part and parcel of the process of accountability and reconciliation. They need to be strong and independent. In this context we are attracted by the "standards based" approach adopted by OFSTED which in a transparent way shows the standards against which schools, colleges and other educational establishments will be judged. A similar approach in inspection of Police

Services could have advantages and should be more broadly adopted. Furthermore in the future work may profitably be done by "cross-cutting" inspection work across the criminal justice system as a whole, with appropriate and fair treatment as the aim. Perhaps a change of approach would help to produce a criminal justice <u>service</u> which is accessible and acceptable throughout to all those who experience it (Recommendation 5).

46.38 **The public and the Police Services of the United Kingdom are justifiably proud of the tradition of an unarmed police service which polices with the consent of the public. The recent perceptive HMIC thematic report *"Winning the Race"* reinforces our view that at present the confidence and trust of the minority ethnic communities is at a low ebb. Such lack of confidence threatens the ability of the Police Services to police by consent in all areas of their work, not simply in the policing of racist incidents and crimes.**

46.39 Our Recommendations which follow are intended to reflect our main conclusions and findings, and to address issues encompassed by this Report. It will be noticed that we make few specific Recommendations as to police disciplinary hearings. We do however record that following our examination of a number of discipline and related files in the course of our Inquiry we all felt concern that there may be insufficient vigour in the area of discipline, supposed sickness and retirement. The need for change is already highlighted by the strong Report of the Home Affairs Committee into *"Police Disciplinary and Complaints Procedures"* which led to the Home Secretary announcing in 1998 changes which would be made, to take effect on 1 April 1999. The key changes were:

- Procedures to deal with unsatisfactory performance - as distinct from misconduct - will be introduced. These are modelled on normal employment provisions although there are some differences of detail;

- The standard of proof at discipline hearings will be the civil rather than the criminal standard;

- Hearings will be able to go ahead in the absence of the accused officer if necessary. This is designed to prevent the misuse of claimed sickness to delay matters;

- Fast track procedures will be available for the most serious criminal allegations where the evidence is overwhelming and does not rely on witness testimony. This will mean that some officers will be able to be dismissed before criminal charges against them are heard. Officers will retain their right to legal representation in these cases and will have full rights of appeal;

- Normal discipline procedures will be speeded up; and

- Because of the change in the standard of proof the double jeopardy rule falls and officers who are acquitted at court may still be disciplined upon the same facts.

No doubt the operation and efficacy of these changes will be carefully monitored. We believe that the changes are apt and important. They have our full support.

46.40 **First and foremost and fundamentally we believe that there must be a change so that there is genuine partnership between the police and all sections of the community. This cannot be achieved by the police alone. The onus is upon them to start the process. All other agencies, particularly those in the field of education and housing must be involved. Co-operation must be genuine and vigorous. Strategies to be delivered under the new Crime & Disorder Act will provide an opportunity in this respect. Training will play its part. The active involvement of people from diverse ethnic groups is essential. Otherwise there will be no acceptance of change, and policing by consent may be the victim.**

46.41 The Commissioner himself, in the context of his own suggestion that an appropriate Ministerial Priority would be welcome, said to us:

> *"I believe that the way the police meet the needs of minority ethnic communities in terms of their experience of crime and harassment is of such importance that a Priority is needed in order to achieve lasting change. It has become increasingly clear that nothing short of a major overhaul is required".*

46.42 We hope and expect that implementation of our Recommendations will ensure that the opportunity for radical thinking and root and branch action is seized. Nothing less will satisfy us and all those who so passionately spoke to us during our hearings in and out of London during the long months of the Stephen Lawrence Inquiry. We also hope that as Police Services reach out to local communities their approach will not be rejected. The gap between Police Services and local communities may seem to be great, but early steps welcomed and encouraged by both sides will surely lead to confidence and co-operation. This may then be the start of the beginning of change.

CHAPTER FORTY-SEVEN

RECOMMENDATIONS

We recommend:

OPENNESS, ACCOUNTABILITY AND THE RESTORATION OF CONFIDENCE

1. That a Ministerial Priority be established for all Police Services:

    "To increase trust and confidence in policing amongst minority ethnic communities".

2. The process of implementing, monitoring and assessing the Ministerial Priority should include Performance Indicators in relation to:

    (i)   the existence and application of strategies for the prevention, recording, investigation and prosecution of racist incidents;

    (ii)   measures to encourage reporting of racist incidents;

    (iii)   the number of recorded racist incidents and related detection levels;

    (iv)   the degree of multi-agency co-operation and information exchange;

    (v)   achieving equal satisfaction levels across all ethnic groups in public satisfaction surveys;

    (vi)   the adequacy of provision and training of family and witness/victim liaison officers;

    (vii)   the nature, extent and achievement of racism awareness training;

    (viii) the policy directives governing stop and search procedures and their outcomes;

    (ix)   levels of recruitment, retention and progression of minority ethnic recruits; and

    (x)   levels of complaint of racist behaviour or attitude and their outcomes.

    The overall aim being the elimination of racist prejudice and disadvantage and the demonstration of fairness in all aspects of policing.

3. That Her Majesty's Inspectors of Constabulary (HMIC) be granted full and unfettered powers and duties to inspect all parts of Police Services including the Metropolitan Police Service.

4. That in order to restore public confidence an inspection by HMIC of the Metropolitan Police Service be conducted forthwith. The inspection to include examination of current undetected HOLMES based murders and Reviews into such cases.

5. That principles and standards similar to those of the Office for Standards in Education (OFSTED) be applied to inspections of Police Services, in order to improve standards of achievement and quality of policing through regular inspection, public reporting, and informed independent advice.

6. That proposals as to the formation of the Metropolitan Police Authority be reconsidered, with a view to bringing its functions and powers fully into line with those which apply to other Police Services, including the power to appoint all Chief Officers of the Metropolitan Police Service.

7. That the Home Secretary and Police Authorities should seek to ensure that the membership of police authorities reflects so far as possible the cultural and ethnic mix of the communities which those authorities serve.

8. That HMIC shall be empowered to recruit and to use lay inspectors in order to conduct examination and inspection of Police Services particularly in connection with performance in the area of investigation of racist crime.

9. That a Freedom of Information Act should apply to all areas of policing, both operational and administrative, subject only to the "substantial harm" test for withholding disclosure.

10. That Investigating Officers' reports resulting from public complaints should not attract Public Interest Immunity as a class. They should be disclosed to complainants, subject only to the "substantial harm" test for withholding disclosure.

11. That the full force of the Race Relations legislation should apply to all police officers, and that Chief Officers of Police should be made vicariously liable for the acts and omissions of their officers relevant to that legislation.

DEFINITION OF RACIST INCIDENT

12. That the definition should be:

> "A racist incident is any incident which is perceived to be racist by the victim or any other person".

13. That the term "racist incident" must be understood to include crimes and non-crimes in policing terms. Both must be reported, recorded and investigated with equal commitment.

14. That this definition should be universally adopted by the Police, local Government and other relevant agencies.

REPORTING AND RECORDING OF RACIST INCIDENTS AND CRIMES

15. That Codes of Practice be established by the Home Office, in consultation with Police Services, local Government and relevant agencies, to create a comprehensive system of reporting and recording of all racist incidents and crimes.

16. That all possible steps should be taken by Police Services at local level in consultation with local Government and other agencies and local communities to encourage the reporting of racist incidents and crimes. This should include:

    - the ability to report at locations other than police stations; and
    - the ability to report 24 hours a day.

17. That there should be close co-operation between Police Services and local Government and other agencies, including in particular Housing and Education Departments, to ensure that all information as to racist incidents and crimes is shared and is readily available to all agencies.

POLICE PRACTICE AND THE INVESTIGATION OF RACIST CRIME

18. That ACPO, in consultation with local Government and other relevant agencies, should review its *Good Practice Guide for Police Response to Racial Incidents* in the light of this Report and our Recommendations. Consideration should be given to the production by ACPO of a manual or model for such investigation, to complement their current *Manual of Murder Investigation*.

19. That ACPO devise Codes of Practice to govern Reviews of investigations of crime, in order to ensure that such Reviews are open and thorough. Such codes should be consistently used by all Police Services. Consideration should be given to such practice providing for Reviews to be carried out by an external Police Service.

20. That MPS procedures at the scene of incidents be reviewed in order to ensure co-ordination between uniformed and CID officers and to ensure that senior officers are aware of and fulfil the command responsibilities which their role demands.

21. That the MPS review their procedures for the recording and retention of information in relation to incidents and crimes, to ensure that adequate records are made by individual officers and specialist units in relation to their functions, and that strict rules require the retention of all such records as long as an investigation remains open.

22. That MPS review their internal inspection and accountability processes to ensure that policy directives are observed.

FAMILY LIAISON

23. That Police Services should ensure that at local level there are readily available designated and trained Family Liaison Officers.

24. That training of Family Liaison Officers must include training in racism awareness and cultural diversity, so that families are treated appropriately, professionally, with respect and according to their needs.

25. That Family Liaison Officers shall, where appointed, be dedicated primarily if not exclusively to that task.

26. That Senior Investigating Officers and Family Liaison Officers be made aware that good practice and their positive duty shall be the satisfactory management of family liaison, together with the provision to a victim's family of all possible information about the crime and its investigation.

27. That good practice shall provide that any request made by the family of a victim which is not acceded to, and any complaint by any member of the family, shall be formally recorded by the SIO and shall be reported to the immediate superior officer.

28. That Police Services and Victim Support Services ensure that their systems provide for the pro-active use of local contacts within minority ethnic communities to assist with family liaison where appropriate.

VICTIMS AND WITNESSES

29. That Police Services should together with the Home Office develop guidelines as to the handling of victims and witnesses, particularly in the field of racist incidents and crimes. The Victim's Charter to be reviewed in this context.

30. That Police Services and Victim Support Services ensure that their systems provide for the pro-active use of local contacts within minority ethnic communities to assist with victim support and with the handling and interviewing of sensitive witnesses.

31.   That Police Services ensure the provision of training and the availability of victim/witness liaison officers, and ensure their use in appropriate areas particularly in the field of racist incidents and crimes, where the need for a sensitive approach to young and vulnerable victims and witnesses is paramount.

PROSECUTION OF RACIST CRIMES

32.   That the standard of proof of such crimes should remain unchanged.

33.   That the CPS should consider that, in deciding whether a criminal prosecution should proceed, once the CPS evidential test is satisfied there should be a rebuttable presumption that the public interest test should be in favour of prosecution.

34.   That Police Services and the CPS should ensure that particular care is taken at all stages of prosecution to recognise and to include reference to any evidence of racist motivation. In particular it should be the duty of the CPS to ensure that such evidence is referred to both at trial and in the sentencing process (including Newton hearings). The CPS and Counsel to ensure that no "plea bargaining" should ever be allowed to exclude such evidence.

35.   That the CPS ensure that a victim or victim's family shall be consulted and kept informed as to any proposal to discontinue proceedings.

36.   That the CPS should have the positive duty always to notify a victim and victim's family personally of a decision to discontinue, particularly in cases of racist crime, with speed and sensitivity.

37.   That the CPS ensure that all decisions to discontinue any prosecution should be carefully and fully recorded in writing, and that save in exceptional circumstances, such written decisions should be disclosable to a victim or a victim's family.

38.   That consideration should be given to the Court of Appeal being given power to permit prosecution after acquittal where fresh and viable evidence is presented.

39.   That consideration should be given to amendment of the law to allow prosecution of offences involving racist language or behaviour, and of offences involving the possession of offensive weapons, where such conduct can be proved to have taken place otherwise than in a public place.

40.   That the ability to initiate a private prosecution should remain unchanged.

41.   That consideration should be given to the proposition that victims or victims' families should be allowed to become "civil parties" to criminal proceedings, to facilitate and to ensure the provision of all relevant information to victims or their families.

42.   That there should be advance disclosure of evidence and documents as of right to parties who have leave from a Coroner to appear at an Inquest.

43. That consideration be given to the provision of Legal Aid to victims or the families of victims to cover representation at an Inquest in appropriate cases.

44. That Police Services and the Courts seek to prevent the intimidation of victims and witnesses by imposing appropriate bail conditions.

TRAINING

FIRST AID

45. That First Aid training for all "public contact" police officers (including senior officers) should at once be reviewed and revised to ensure that they have basic skills to apply First Aid. Officers must be taught to "think first aid", and first and foremost "A (Airways), B (Breathing) and C (Circulation)".

46. That training in First Aid including refresher training should include testing to recognised and published standards in every Police Service.

47. That Police Services should annually review First Aid training, and ensure that "public contact" officers are trained and tested to recognised and published standards.

TRAINING

RACISM AWARENESS AND VALUING CULTURAL DIVERSITY

48. That there should be an immediate review and revision of racism awareness training within Police Services to ensure:-

    (a) that there exists a consistent strategy to deliver appropriate training within all Police Services, based upon the value of our cultural diversity;

    (b) that training courses are designed and delivered in order to develop the full understanding that good community relations are essential to good policing and that a racist officer is an incompetent officer.

49. That all police officers, including CID and civilian staff, should be trained in racism awareness and valuing cultural diversity.

50. That police training and practical experience in the field of racism awareness and valuing cultural diversity should regularly be conducted at local level. And that it should be recognised that local minority ethnic communities should be involved in such training and experience.

51.   That consideration be given by Police Services to promoting joint training with members of other organisations or professions otherwise than on police premises.

52.   That the Home Office together with Police Services should publish recognised standards of training aims and objectives in the field of racism awareness and valuing cultural diversity.

53.   That there should be independent and regular monitoring of training within all Police Services to test both implementation and achievement of such training.

54.   That consideration be given to a review of the provision of training in racism awareness and valuing cultural diversity in local Government and other agencies including other sections of the Criminal Justice system.

EMPLOYMENT, DISCIPLINE AND COMPLAINTS

55.   That the changes to Police Disciplinary and Complaints procedures proposed by the Home Secretary should be fully implemented and closely and publicly monitored as to their effectiveness.

56.   That in order to eliminate the present provision which prevents disciplinary action after retirement, disciplinary action should be available for at least five years after an officer's retirement.

57.   That the Police Services should through the implementation of a Code of Conduct or otherwise ensure that racist words or acts proved to have been spoken or done by police officers should lead to disciplinary proceedings, and that it should be understood that such conduct should usually merit dismissal.

58.   That the Home Secretary, taking into account the strong expression of public perception in this regard, consider what steps can and should be taken to ensure that serious complaints against police officers are independently investigated. Investigation of police officers by their own or another Police Service is widely regarded as unjust, and does not inspire public confidence.

59.   That the Home Office review and monitor the system and standards of Police Services applied to the selection and promotion of officers of the rank of Inspector and above. Such procedures for selection and promotion to be monitored and assessed regularly.

STOP AND SEARCH

60.   That the powers of the police under current legislation are required for the prevention and detection of crime and should remain unchanged.

61.   That the Home Secretary, in consultation with Police Services, should ensure that a record is made by police officers of all "stops" and "stops and searches" made under any legislative provision (not just the Police and Criminal Evidence Act). Non-statutory or so called "voluntary" stops must also be recorded. The record to include the reason for the stop, the outcome, and the self-defined ethnic identity of the person stopped. A copy of the record shall be given to the person stopped.

62.   That these records should be monitored and analysed by Police Services and Police Authorities, and reviewed by HMIC on inspections. The information and analysis should be published.

63.   That Police Authorities be given the duty to undertake publicity campaigns to ensure that the public is aware of "stop and search" provisions and the right to receive a record in all circumstances.

RECRUITMENT AND RETENTION

64.   That the Home Secretary and Police Authorities' policing plans should include targets for recruitment, progression and retention of minority ethnic staff. Police Authorities to report progress to the Home Secretary annually. Such reports to be published.

65.   That the Home Office and Police Services should facilitate the development of initiatives to increase the number of qualified minority ethnic recruits.

66.   That HMIC include in any regular inspection or in a thematic inspection a report on the progress made by Police Services in recruitment, progression and retention of minority ethnic staff.

PREVENTION AND THE ROLE OF EDUCATION

67.   That consideration be given to amendment of the National Curriculum aimed at valuing cultural diversity and preventing racism, in order better to reflect the needs of a diverse society.

68.   That Local Education Authorities and school Governors have the duty to create and implement strategies in their schools to prevent and address racism. Such strategies to include:

-   that schools record all racist incidents;

-   that all recorded incidents are reported to the pupils' parents/guardians, school Governors and LEAs;

-     that the numbers of racist incidents are published annually, on a school by school basis; and

-     that the numbers and self defined ethnic identity of "excluded" pupils are published annually on a school by school basis.

69.   That OFSTED inspections include examination of the implementation of such strategies.

70.   That in creating strategies under the provisions of the Crime & Disorder Act or otherwise Police Services, local Government and relevant agencies should specifically consider implementing community and local initiatives aimed at promoting cultural diversity and addressing racism and the need for focused, consistent support for such initiatives.

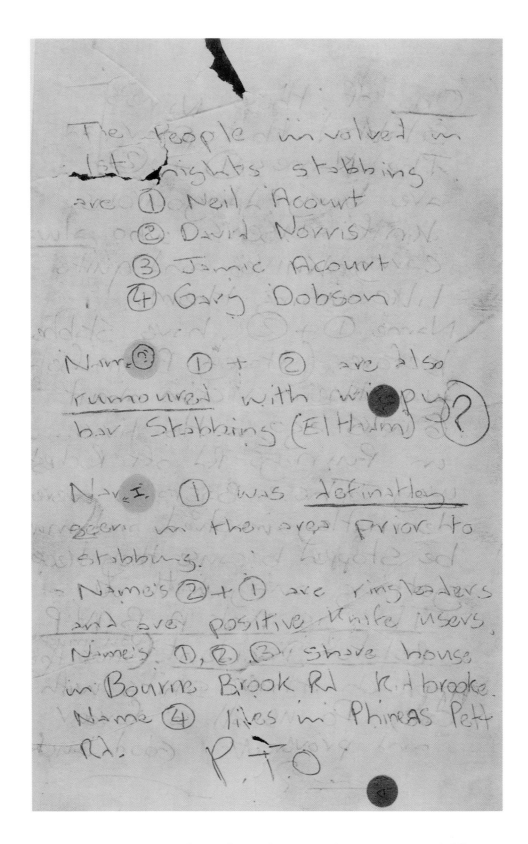

Anonymous letter found in a telephone kiosk (see para 13.29)

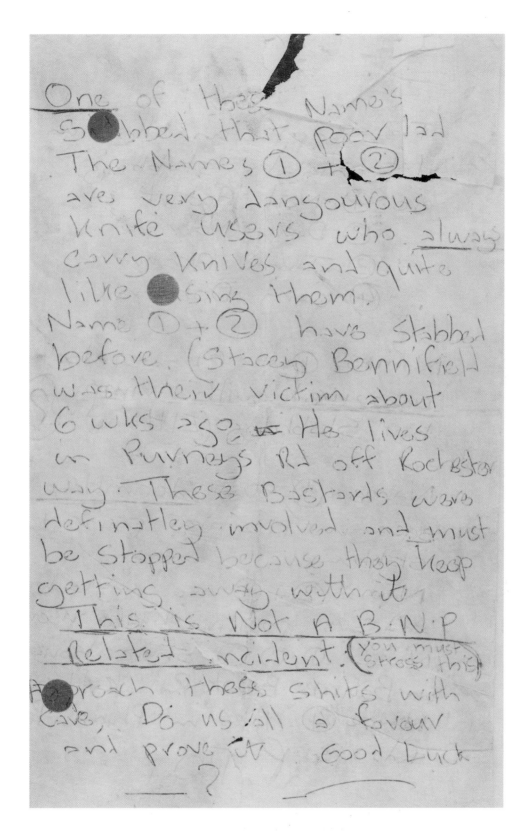

Anonymous letter found in a telephone kiosk (see para 13.29)

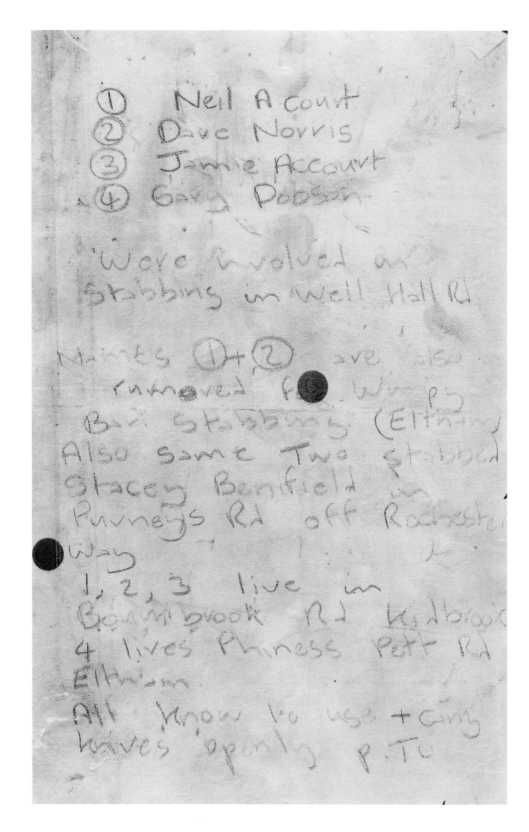

Anonymous letter left on car (see para 13.29)

Anonymous letter left on car (see para 13.29)

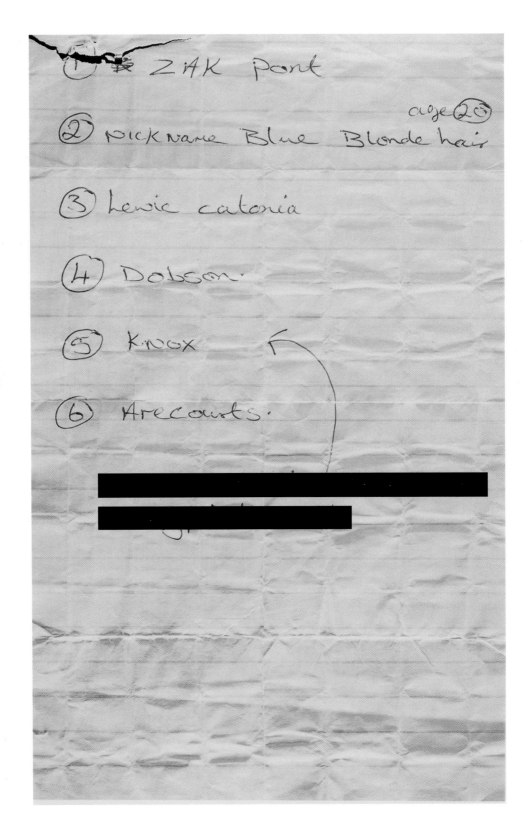

Note handed to Mr Ilsley on 6 May 1993 by Mrs Lawrence (see para 27.16)

Aerial photograph, looking north. Well Hall Road running from bottom right to upper right; junction with Dickson Road bottom centre

Aerial photograph, looking south west. Well Hall Road roundabout at left, with Well Hall Road running to bottom right; junction with Dickson Road at centre of photograph.

Printed in the UK for the Controller of Her Majesty's Stationery Office
by The Stationery Office Limited
Dd 5069054   8/99   19585   Job No. J0089636
Reprinted 1999